3606299837

D1422374

JESUS ACCORDING TO S. JOHN

Works by the Same Author

THE GOODNESS AND THE SEVERITY OF GOD
(Hulsean Lectures, 1917–18)

DU BOSE AS A PROPHET OF UNITY

THE EPISTLE TO THE EPHESIANS
(Cambridge Greek Testament)

THE REVELATION OF THE LAMB

THE COURAGE OF HOPE

ASKING GOD

THE CHRISTIAN ARMOUR

STUDIES IN THE TEMPTATION OF THE SON OF GOD

THE TEXT-BOOK FOR SCHOOLS OF PRAYER

THE MAGNET OF THE CROSS

THE OBEDIENCE OF THE CROSS
(To be published in 1937)

JESUS ACCORDING TO S. JOHN

by

J. O. F. MURRAY, D.D.
Hon. Canon of Ely Cathedral and late Master
of Selwyn College, Cambridge

LONGMANS, GREEN AND CO.
LONDON NEW YORK TORONTO

FOREWORD

THIS book contains a series of studies in the Gospel according to S. John. Its object is to enable a student to see what help the Evangelist can give us in forming a coherent picture of the public ministry of Jesus, including on the one hand the efforts that He made to explain to the political and religious leaders of the Jews the nature of the office with which He had been entrusted, and on the other the inner life of communion with His Father in heaven by which He had been guided and sustained throughout that ministry.

There is strong internal evidence that it comes to us from one who must have belonged to the inmost circle of the personal disciples of Jesus, and that in it the Evangelist records memories which lived on and became luminous as he reflected on them in the light of the experience of a long life.

There is strong external evidence that the Church in fixing its canon of the Gospels in the middle of the second century accepted this Gospel, in spite of its divergences from the others which were already in possession, because they believed that it was the work of the son of Zebedee. It is at least worth while to see what the book has to tell us on the hypothesis that it comes, as it professes to come, straight from him.

It may not be out of place to recall here the fundamental principle of intelligent criticism on which S. T. Coleridge justified his suspension of judgement in face of what seemed to him at first sight puerilities in Plato's *Timæus*. The principle is that "Until you understand an author's ignorance, presume yourself ignorant of his understanding". He illustrates this from his experience in re-reading the treatise.

"Whatever I comprehend impresses me with a reverential sense of the author's genius: but there is a considerable portion of the work to which I can attach no consistent meaning. In other treatises of the same philosopher, intended for the average comprehension of men, I have been delighted with the masterly good sense, with the perspicacity of the language, and the aptness of the inductions. I recollect likewise that numerous passages in this author, which I thoroughly comprehend, were formerly no less unintelligible to me, than the passages now in question. It would, I am aware, be quite fashionable to dismiss them at once as Platonic jargon. But this I cannot do with satisfaction to my own mind, because I have sought in vain for causes adequate to the solution of the assumed inconsistency. I have no insight into the possibility of a man so eminently wise, using words with such half-meanings to himself, as must perforce pass into no meaning to his readers. When in addition to the motive thus suggested by my own reason, I bring into distinct remembrance the number and the series of great men, who after long and zealous study of these words have joined in honouring the name of Plato with epithets that almost transcend humanity, I feel that a contemptuous verdict on my part might argue want of modesty, and would hardly be received by the judicious as evidence of superior penetration. Therefore, utterly baffled in all my attempts to understand the ignorance of Plato, I conclude myself ignorant of his understanding."

I need not labour the application of this illustration.

I cannot help feeling that S. John has at least as much claim as Plato to be taken seriously. There can be no surer way to shut the door against any lesson that he may have to teach me than to assume that all he has to tell me must fit into my preconceptions of what, apart from the revelation of God in Christ, I should have held to be true with regard to the capacities of human nature and to inner relations in the Being of God.

These studies of mine have been worked out in connexion with many different classes of pupils in the course of the last fifty years. They have taken shape during the last twenty-five in "Bible Studies" written for the *Lay Reader Magazine*. They retain obvious traces of their origin. I have been at no pains to remove them. I am deeply grateful to Dr. Hort for teaching me that "critics of the Bible, if they are taught by the Bible, are unable to forget that the duty of guileless workmanship is never superseded by any other." But he taught me also that Christ is the Truth for men, because He is first the Life. I make no apology, therefore, for the efforts that I make from time to time to go over ground already covered a second time to help my readers to think out the practical bearing of different elements in the teaching. I have found it a great help towards understanding S. John's Gospel to try to expound it to men who are actively engaged in preaching.

I have not, of course, been able to confine myself in my exposition to the material directly provided by S. John, though that has throughout been my main objective. When S. John wrote, the Synoptic Gospels were, I believe, already in circulation. I have no doubt that the circle to whom he is addressing himself in the first instance were already well-grounded at least in the substance of the Synoptic tradition. I have endeavoured, therefore, to set his record against the background which this grounding presupposes in the minds of his readers in every age.

I have made no attempt to compile an index, but I have supplied in the Table of Contents a full summary of the contents of the separate chapters. This will, I hope, help my readers to trace the sequence of thought between the scenes, which S. John places side by side, trusting his readers to supply the links of connexion between them.

I am not writing primarily for scholars, so I have not felt it necessary to provide a complete Bibliography. Those who want guidance through the maze of recent literature on the subject can find it in "The additional note on the authorship of the Gospel" written by Charles Harris for the article on S. John in the *New Commentary on Holy Scripture* published by S.P.C.K. in 1928. Fuller information is available in a book published in 1931 on *The Fourth Gospel in Recent Criticism and Interpretation* by W. F. Howard. I have found this most valuable.

Even this, however, is not quite up to date. Within the last year we have had a fresh treatment of the subject from Central Africa in *John, Peter and Fourth Gospel* by G. W. Broomfield; *The Gospel of Fulfilment* by R. A. Henderson; and an able review of the external evidence in *The Authorship of S. John's Gospel* by J. Donovan, S.J.; besides *The Christ of Experience* by Beatrice Ferguson, which expresses our relation to the Incarnate Word with singular fidelity in the terms of our reaction to the master-personality of Jesus.

I have, however, a special debt of gratitude to earlier workers in the same field for the help that they have given me towards the understanding of S. John. I am the more anxious to record their names, because in the excitement of pursuing the trail of the latest hypothesis, it is fatally easy to take as read the masterpieces of an earlier generation.

I must put first the great teachers of my own student days at Cambridge, Lightfoot, Westcott and Hort. Lightfoot's main work was devoted to S. Paul, and his work on S. John was in comparison of secondary importance. It was published after his death in *Biblical Essays*. He was second to none as a judge of historical evidence, and he was especially at home in the sub-apostolic period. I cannot think that his work on "The Historical Character and Genuineness of the Fourth Gospel" has received the attention that it deserves.

In the case of Dr. Westcott, his work on S. John was central. His introduction to the Gospel in his commentary is a closely knit structure, which none who dissents from his conclusion has ever, so far as I know, set himself to answer in detail.

Dr. Hort's contribution, apart from his work on the Greek Text, is limited to his Hulsean Lectures, *The Way, the Truth, and the Life*. But in that he not only gives masterly surveys of the place of the Johannine writings in the development of thought in the apostolic period, he also gives us an object lesson showing us the depths of meaning that are hidden in a single verse for any one who is prepared to study it patiently, and to give full value to every word in it.

Dr. Hort called my attention to the lessons of a very different kind to be learnt from his master, F. D. Maurice. Such grasp as I have been able to get of the Gospel as a revelation of the Word Incarnate I owe to Maurice's *Sermons on the Gospel of S. John*. Fresh ground on the problem of Christology was broken in America by Dr. W. P. Du Bose, the value of whose work is strangely overlooked in Europe.

Professor Sanday's early work on *The Authorship and Historical Character of the Fourth Gospel* helped me to appreciate the substantial harmony between S. John and the Synoptists in their record of our Lord's teaching.

I desire also to record my debt to *The Central Teaching of Jesus Christ* (a devotional study of S. John 13–17) by T. D. Bernard, Canon of Wells; and to a volume of studies in the reiterated Amens of the Son of God by Andrew Jukes, called *The New Man*.

Among the Germans I have owed most to Keim's *Life of Jesus of Nazara*, Bernhard Weiss's *Life of Christ* and Theodor Zahn's *Introduction to the New Testament*. Godet's commentary on S. John is instinct with spiritual insight. M. Lepin in *L'Origine du Quatrième Evangile* helps us, as I think only a Frenchman can, to answer Renan and Loisy.

Among more recent books Lord Charnwood's *According to John* brings a refreshing breeze from the great world into an atmosphere that is always in danger of becoming narrowly academic.

Dr. Abbott's monumental works on *The Son of Man*, on *Johannine Vocabulary*, and on *Johannine Grammar* are mines in which one can always dig with profit.

I wish I could have had access earlier to Dr. J. H. Bernard's International Critical Commentary, and to the fragments, all too few, of Scott Holland's lecture notes.

The text of the Gospel is that of the Revised Version, by courtesy of the Delegates of the Clarendon Press, Oxford, and the Syndics of the University Press, Cambridge, to whom my thanks are due.

PAGE

III. THE RELATION OF HISTORY TO THEOLOGY - 24

It is contended that it is impossible that anyone writing with a dogmatic purpose can write true history. This is based on the assumption that it is impossible that God should reveal Himself in history. S. John writes his Gospel in the belief that that assumption was in direct contradiction to the facts of Christian experience.

IV. THE PROLOGUE 1 : 1–18 - - - - 28

The background of S. John's doctrine of the *Logos* is to be found, not in Greek philosophy, but in Palestinian theology. The new element contributed by S. John to the doctrine is that the communion between God and His Word expressed in creation implies (1) such a living dependence on the created universe, and of man, its divinely appointed head, on the Word, and (2) such an interdependence of Personalities in the unity of the Divine Being as to make it possible for God to reveal Himself to men in the course of human history by the appearance of the Word in human flesh to live before men under human conditions the life of communion with the Father which was His as Son from all eternity.

V. THE FIRST WEEK OF THE MINISTRY 1 : 19–2 : 12 47

The Gospel opens with an account of the decisive moment in the life of S. John the Baptist. In answer to the challenge of an official deputation he disclaimed any function but that of a herald; and testified to his sense of the over-mastering personality of his Successor. The next day he pointed out Jesus as the Lamb of God who bears the sin of the world, testifying that he had seen the Spirit descending and abiding on Him at His baptism, and that He was the Son of God. On the third day he pointed Him out to two of his own followers. This was the beginning of the Christian Church. The first disciples found in Jesus the fulfilment of the promises made by

PAGE

God to the Fathers. The hold of their Master over them was rooted in His power to read the thoughts of their hearts. He accepted their homage: but tacitly substituted the title "Son of Man" for the more specifically Messianic titles in which their faith had at first found expression.

The Son of Man. This title was not in common use. It had its roots in the Old Testament. Jesus connects it directly with the vision of Daniel 7. The human race was created by God to reign as His representative over creation. In this vision it is conceived as a living organic unity, as "a man," or rather as "Man". Christ as "Son of Man" claimed to be the reality foreshadowed here. He is the true centre of the life of the race, the Master Personality in subjection to whom each individual finds his true self, the Son of God and King of men in whom the race will attain the end of God in creating it. This function of the Church and the consequent present relation of each of its members to Him as the true life of the whole was revealed by Jesus under the similitude of the Vine. It was expressed by S. Paul in his vision of the Church as the Body of Christ. In S. John the Word is the Light that lighteth every man. He keeps every man in conscious relation to the will of the Father. He in His humanity is the Mediator between God and Man. What the Father is to Him, He is to us. What He is to the Father, we are to Him.

The Beginning of Signs. The action of Jesus in turning water into wine at the wedding-feast is the first in a series of significant acts by which Jesus built up the faith of His disciples. The story shows Jesus, in strong contrast to the Baptist, as entering fully into human interests and pleasures. The sign itself involves a manifestation of creative energy, and as such recalls the teaching of the Prologue on the work of the Word in creation. But it was worked silently, and attracted no attention outside the circle of disciples.

PAGE

VI. THE FIRST PUBLIC ACT OF JESUS AS THE LORD'S ANOINTED. 2 : 13–22 - - - - - 67

After a brief visit to Capernaum Jesus goes up to Jerusalem for the Passover. He proceeds at once to exercise the authority which His Father had given Him, and to which the Baptist had borne public testimony, by cleansing the Temple. His zeal for His Father's house recalls to the minds of the disciples a marked feature in the portrait of the Messiah. The Jews ask for a sign in support of His claim. They are told, in language which only the event could interpret, that they were powerless to destroy the outward symbol of God's presence among men.

VII. NICODEMUS. 2 : 23–3 : 36 - - - - - 75

Jesus made no attempt to enforce His authority. But the powers of the age to come began to show themselves in a ministry of healing to which the people would have responded with enthusiasm if Jesus had encouraged them. The grounds of His reserve are revealed in the conversation with Nicodemus, who was prepared to accept Him as a teacher sent from God. Jesus begins with the new birth which all must experience before they can perceive the presence of the Kingdom of God. They must enter it, as Jesus had done, by a birth of water and Spirit. The Spirit, like the flesh, has power to create life after its kind. Jesus claims to be bearing witness to the presence of the Kingdom from within. Since His baptism He had been living on earth in conscious communion with the Father as Son of Man. Confirmation of this claim must, however, wait till the truth foreshadowed by the lifting up of the serpent in the wilderness had been consummated in Him, and death, which is the instrument of God's judgement on sin, had become on the Cross a fountain of eternal life. This utterance bears witness to foreknowledge of His coming doom, the fruit of direct intuition, confirmed by the witness of the Scriptures as He understood them.—The Evangelist then

PAGE

passes on to consider the reactions of men to the appeal of the Cross. That appeal is rooted in love and its goal is salvation; but its immediate issue is judgement. It separates those who love the light from those that love the darkness. But even this judgement can only be an incident on the way to the goal.—The first appeal to the Jews in Jerusalem is followed by a brief ministry of baptism by the disciples of Jesus in Judæa. This leads to a final statement by the Baptist of his position as "the friend of the Bridegroom". It is followed by a declaration, which may be due either to the Baptist or to the Evangelist, relating to the source and character of the teaching of the Son of God, and of the consequence of disobeying Him.

VIII. THE WOMAN OF SAMARIA. 4: 1–54 - - 103

Retiring from Judæa to Galilee, Jesus rests by Jacob's well in Sychar. In conversation with a Samaritan woman He claims the power of bestowing on man a gift of living water, of which the water in the well was only a partial antitype. Then after making her conscious of His prophetic power by His knowledge of her past life, He declares the advent of an age in which the worship of God as Father in Spirit and truth will render obsolete the sanctuaries both at Gerizim and at Jersualem. The Messiah for which she was looking was primarily a Prophet, so Jesus can accept the name without protest.—While the woman goes home to her people, Jesus explains to His disciples the sustaining power of obedience to the Father's will, and the law of the spiritual harvest-field. The woman's report brings out her townsfolk to hear for themselves and confess their faith in Jesus as "the Saviour of the world".—Jesus then establishes Himself in Galilee abandoning the prospect of a permanent sphere of work in Judæa. His return to Cana is marked by a second sign, which revealed His power over disease even from a

PAGE

distance, and evoked and crowned a faith that was independent of sight.

IX. JESUS AND THE PHARISEES. 5: 1–47 - - 124

Jesus declares to the Pharisees the personal relation in which He stood to God, and to the Law of Moses. In S. Mark they keep a constant and suspicious watch over all that He did, and are roused to murderous hate by His attitude to the Sabbath. S. Matthew defines the difference between the righteousness required by Jesus and by the Pharisees. He gives a scathing indictment of their shortcomings in the Seven Woes of Ch. 23. S. Luke strikes a note of more personal appeal in some of the parables peculiar to him. In S. John Jesus deliberately throws down a challenge by healing an impotent man, and telling him to carry his bed home on the Sabbath. This challenge was deliberately made at Jerusalem, and explains the constant suspicion with which the Pharisees watched His work in Galilee. Jesus in conscious sympathy with His Father singled out this sufferer. He quickened hope by His challenge, and healing followed the sick man's obedience to His command to take up his bed and walk. His obedience called attention to what Jesus had done, and Jesus is arraigned for breaking the Sabbath. He meets the charge by pleading His Father's example. The claim to divine Sonship involved in this plea was an even more serious offence. Jesus in His defence explained that He held His power in strict subordination to His Father. At the same time He expanded His claim to include the power of raising the dead and of judgement, declaring that His voice had a quickening power for those who listened in to it, and that His judgement, based on His obedience, was just. He then summarizes the evidence in support of His claim: the witness of the Baptist to the commission given Him by His Father: the witness of the works given Him to do by His Father: and the witness of the

PAGE

Scriptures. He then analyses the causes which prevented them from accepting this witness. Jesus in S. John appeals directly to His mighty works affording strong corroboration to His claim. In the Synoptists greater stress is laid on His persistent refusal to work a sign to order. But each portrait contains both elements.

X. THE FEEDING OF THE FIVE THOUSAND. 6: 1–71 141
The next scene brings us back to Galilee and contains two signs (1) the Feeding of the Five Thousand, a sign of the power of Jesus to sustain the life of men, and (2) the Walking on the Water, a sign of His power to help His disciples in distress, even when He seemed separated from them. The first sign led to an outburst of popular excitement, and then to a long public discussion. The second was kept secret from the multitude. Jesus begins the discussion of the first sign with an appeal to men to come to Him for the satisfaction of their deepest needs. To attain this, they must surrender themselves in faith to Him. Such surrender requires evidence in support of His claim. This is supplied by the nature of the gift that God had given to the world in Him. He was the true manna, the Bread of Life. It required also an action of their own will. They must come to Him. This also is the Father's gift to Him and to them.—The discussion is renewed in the Synagogue at Capernaum. Murmuring against His claim, based on local prejudice, is met by a further exposition of the Father's working in the hearts of men; and of the flesh that He would give for the life of the world. Cavils against the possibility of such a gift are met by a statement of the necessity, and of the consequences of participating in it. He adds an illuminating reference to the fact that He is subject to the same law of spiritual feeding. His own spirit feeds on His Father, as theirs must feed on Him.—This teaching causes a fresh murmuring, and a secession even of

PAGE

disciples, in spite of further teaching on the source of faith.—An express challenge to the Twelve leads to a memorable confession by Simon Peter, and to the Lord's declaration of the presence of a devil even among His closest friends. There are interesting parallels between the accounts of S. John and S. Luke of preachings in the Synagogue at Capernaum. The confession of Simon Peter at Cæsarea Philippi, while closely akin to the confession here, is different both in occasion and in substance.

XI. THE SELF REVELATION OF JESUS IN JERUSALEM. 7: 1–8: 59 - - - - - - - 160

Jesus refuses the challenge of His brethren to go up openly to the feast. The time for that would not come till Palm Sunday. He goes up, however, unofficially, and teaches publicly in the Temple. He declares that only those whose wills were set to do the will of God could recognize the divine source of His teaching. The murderous designs that they were cherishing showed that this was not yet so with them. He reminds them of their reaction to His healing of the Impotent Man on the Sabbath. The townsfolk declare that He cannot be the Christ, because they know too much about Him. He answers that they know only too well that He had come from God.—A party is sent to arrest Him. He warns them that He would before long be out of their reach. On the last day of the feast He promises to bestow on believers spiritual refreshment, and the power to refresh others. This teaching rekindles controversy about Him in the crowd and in the Sanhedrim.—His next claim is to be the true Shekinah, "the light of the world". He justifies His claim on the ground that He alone knows His true origin, and has His Father with Him in the judgement that His coming brought to men, and in His witness to Himself. He warns them again that only by faith in Him could they find deliverance from their sins, but their rejection of Him would in the end open their

PAGE

eyes. Meanwhile He is refreshed by His consciousness of His Father's approval.—He turns then to make one more appeal to those who were prepared to take His claim seriously. He promised them that abiding in His word would bring a freedom from sin, which none but the Son could give them: and which in spite of their protest they sorely needed, for, as the murderous designs which they cherished against Him show, they were true sons neither of Abraham nor of God, but of the devil. This teaching seemed like the the raving of a demoniac, but it is reasserted. He is the Son and knows His Father, and His word has promise of immortality, for He knows the Father, and "was" before Abraham was born. The issue proved the truth of the charge that He had brought against them. They take up stones to stone Him.

XII. THE MAN BORN BLIND. 9: 1–41, 10: 19–21 - 184

Jesus then works another sign. He heals a man born blind. He teaches His disciples incidentally to spend their time in helping, not in passing judgements on their brothers when they were in need. The sign, wrought once more on a Sabbath, attracts the attention of the Pharisees. The fact being undeniable, they try to browbeat the man who had been cured into an admission that the author of his cure was a sinner. When he refused and rebuked them for their blindness, they excommunicated him. Jesus seeks him out and reveals Himself to him as "the Son of Man". He then passes sentence on the spiritual condition of the Jewish leaders, as revealed by their treatment of the man. The issue once more is a division of opinion among the people and revives the charge of possession.

XIII. THE GOOD SHEPHERD. 10: 1–42 - - - 191

At the Feast of the Dedication Jesus is once more pressed to declare Himself. He replies that He has already done so in word and by

PAGE

His works, but that only His sheep understand Him. He shows that the true Shepherd enters by the door of the sheepfold, and is recognized by His sheep. In contrast with thieves and robbers He claims to be "the Door" through which the sheep pass to find rest and food. In contrast with hirelings He claims to be the Good Shepherd who knows His sheep, and will lay down His life for them that He may make one flock of them, and prove worthy of His Father's love. Here the self-consecration to death for His sheep in obedience to His Father's will comes into clear expression. It is linked directly with His claim to be one in heart and will with His Father. This claim is regarded as blasphemous, and once more the Jews prepare to stone Him. This time Jesus reasons with them. He defends the truth of the intimate fellowship between human nature and the divine which His claim implies by reference to the title "Gods" conferred on the Judges of Israel by Lawgiver and Psalmist. The title "Son of God" had been given to Him at His baptism, and the works which the Father wrought through Him implied nothing short of a mutual indwelling of the Father and the Son. He then retires beyond Jordan where the associations of the place revive the memories of the preaching of the Baptist. And men realize that his witness to Jesus was evidence that he was a true prophet, even though he had brought with him no other credentials.

XIV. Jesus face to face with Death. 11: 1–57 - 201

Jesus evinced in the whole of His life and teaching a supreme sense of absolute mastery over the power of death. In working out the purpose for which He had come into the world He paid no consideration, and would allow His followers to pay no consideration, to the possibility or even to the certainty that any particular course of action would involve the sacrifice of earthly life. There is nothing incredible in the fact that one who lived and

PAGE

taught in this spirit should claim to be Himself the "Resurrection and the Life", and manifest His sovereignty over quick and dead by such a sign as that which S. John says that he saw worked at Bethany.—The death of a friend calls Jesus out of His retirement at the risk of His life in spite of the protest of His disciples. He reveals Himself to Martha as "the Resurrection and the Life", and then goes with her, and with her sister, weeping to the tomb. Standing by the tomb while the Jews wonder why He had not exerted His power to save His friend's life, and while Martha's expostulation shows how low her hopes had sunk, He gives thanks to the Father in acknowledgement of answered prayer, and then calls Lazarus back to life on earth. This is the last recorded sign before His own resurrection. It brings the conflict with the Jewish authorities to a head. The High Priest prophesies that Jesus must die to save the whole nation from destruction. Jesus meanwhile waits at Ephraim until it is time to go up to the Passover.

XV. THE CLIMAX AT JERUSALEM. 12: 1–50 - - 216

Six days before the feast Jesus returns to Bethany, and is anointed by Mary the sister of Lazarus. The act involved a considerable sacrifice. The other Gospels suggest that it was meant to indicate her sense of the approaching end. Judas protests against the waste. Our Lord's words in her defence, as recorded by S. John, seem to suggest that before long the ointment could be used to prepare His body for burial. The authorities began to plot against the life that Jesus had so recently restored.—The next day He enters Jerusalem in triumph surrounded by crowds, not only of Galileans but of townsfolk attracted by the raising of Lazarus, deliberately fulfilling prophecy.—The request of certain Greeks to see Jesus leads to His last public teaching on sacrifice, based on a law of nature. The shadows of His coming Passion gather round

PAGE

His soul, and He prays for the glory of His Father's name. A voice from heaven answers Him, and then He declares that the judgement of the world is at hand and the casting out of its prince. He promises that after He has been lifted up "out of" the earth, He would draw all men to Himself. These words suggest a difficulty to those who were listening and wishing to learn. His words though full of triumph spoke of death. The Messiah whom they were expecting was "to abide for ever", but He kept calling Himself "Son of Man", so once more the question bursts out "Who is this Son of Man?" In the accepted text this question is left without an answer. The transposition of a small section restores coherence into the passage. The question could not be answered by a definition. Our personality is defined by our relationships. "The Son" is only intelligible by His utter subordination to His Father. The evidence for the truth of His claim is in the light and life that it brings, even though the coming of the light brought judgement. He therefore closes with a last appeal to His hearers to follow the light and surrender themselves to its transforming influence. In these words He takes His leave of them.—The Evangelist points the moral of the failure of his people by the help of the written word. The tragedy is taken up into the eternal purpose of God.

XVI. INTRODUCTION TO THE PASSION. 13: 1–30 - 229

S. John begins by setting the scene for the Last Supper. Later reflection had shown him that Jesus had come to the table with a clear vision of all that was to follow, and had chosen to make it the occasion of a supreme manifestation of His love for His chosen.—Jesus uses the occasion to give them all a final lesson in the sovereignty of service by washing the feet of each and all. In doing so He overruled a vehement protest on the part of Simon Peter, while dropping a hint that He was aware of

PAGE

deep inner defilement in one of them. S. John's account of our Lord's last appeal to Judas before He sent him forth into the night to consummate his treachery clearly comes to us at firsthand.

XVII. INTRODUCTION TO THE DISCOURSES. 13: 31–38 - 237
Jesus regards the departure of the traitor as the first act in the Passion. He begins therefore by describing the whole action in the light of its goal. Now at last the veil is withdrawn. God and the Son of Man can be seen by men in their true light. He then gives His little children the new commandment to bind them into one, both with one another and with Him in face of the unconverted world.—Simon Peter resents the thought of the possibility of any barrier between him and His Master which it would be beyond the power of his loyalty to transcend. He has to be warned that he was weaker than he knew.

XVIII. CONDITIONS OF LIFE IN THE NEW ORDER. 14: 1–31 - - - - - - - 245
Jesus then begins to help them all to face the coming separation. He was only moving from one room to another in His Father's house; and before long full communion with Him would be restored under new conditions. Thomas is puzzled. How can we know the way, when as yet we do not know the goal. Jesus answers that His disciples at least know Him. In communion with Him they would find the Light and the Life that they needed to follow Him to His goal with His Father. Philip gives expression to the need of a revelation of God to give the thought of Him distinctness. Jesus in reply claims that the life He had lived in human flesh supplied the need. He had revealed the Father by surrendering Himself into His Father's hands, so that the Father could work through Him. The Father would in like manner work through them when they realized their responsibility as bearing their

PAGE

Master's name in the world. The thought of the responsibility of bearing the name of Jesus Christ before men brings out the inner meaning of life for disciples in the new order; and the directness of their continued dependence on Him for power to do what was required of them. On the one side they must learn to approach Him confidently for power to act "in His name", and on the other to trust the other Comforter whom the Father would send in answer to His prayer on their behalf. They would not be bereft of His presence, though He was out of sight. The world could no longer see Him but His presence would be a reality to those whose love for Him found expression in keeping His commandments. The love for Himself which inspired this obedience was the fruit of their years of discipleship. This fruit the Comforter would enable them to garner for the use of all succeeding generations when He came. He begins to take a formal farewell. He challenges them to rejoice with Him in His return to the Father in whose will His own peace had been rooted. Then He braces Himself to go forward to His final encounter with the prince of this world, that the world might know that His life of obedience to His Father had been rooted from first to last in love.

XIX. THE CHURCH AND ITS HEAD. 15: 1–17 - - 263

At this point the company leaves the Upper Room and visits the Temple Courts. There, under the figure of a Vine, He expounds the mystery of His personal union with all His disciples, and their union with one another in Him. S. Paul describes the same mystery under the figure of a body. The union is vital and organic. The Father is watching over it all the time. Each believer is a branch. Jesus Himself is the indwelling life and law of the whole tree, depending for His fruitfulness in the world on the faithfulness of each and all of His branches. His life would flow into them

PAGE

as they lived listening in to Him. To do this would give glory to the Father and keep them in the love of the Father and of the Son. It would also fill their lives with joy, as they lived in the spirit of the new commandment, laying down their lives after His example for their friends. He underlines His use of this term. He was deliberately making them members of His Privy Council, and sharing His secret thoughts with them. The duty of the branch is simply to abide in the Vine. In keeping His commandment they would enter into His joy, and find themselves sharing His inmost secrets.

XX. THE CHURCH AND THE WORLD. 15: 18–16: 15 271

He passes on to their reception by the world. They would be met with hatred and persecution. Men wilfully reject a fully attested revelation. The Comforter would all the time support the witness of the disciples. The companionship of the Comforter would not bring immunity from suffering. The shock of His departure would be terribly hard to bear, but they would find that it had been worth while. He must die on the Cross before He could send the promised Comforter.—The work of the Comforter was not limited to His effect on the Church. As the Church lived the new life of the Spirit, the sight would in the end convince the world that they were missing the true end of life unless they believed in Christ. It would help them to attain to the new life of peace and power with God in communion with the risen and ascended Lord, and in victory over all the power of the enemy.—The mission of the Comforter is not exhausted even by this. The Church started on its work with everything to learn. She had, however, the promised help of the Comforter to guide her in the end into all the truth.

XXI. THE SORROW AND THE JOY OF THE DISCIPLES. 16: 16–33 - - - - - - - 280

Jesus has to bring them back to the fact of the

PAGE

coming separation. The disciples are perplexed and alarmed, but dared not ask Him. He could only assure them that the agony through which they had to pass would be a travail pang. New life would be born into the world as the fruit of it. They would know that they would from henceforth have His eye upon them. Their new relationship to Him would open for them a door of direct access to the Father in the name of His Son. This condition did not imply any reluctance on the part of the Father, which could only be removed by the intercession of the Son. He has already admitted them of His own choice into the circle of His friends. The fact that they had loved the Son and believed in His mission was in itself a link with the Father. Something in this last utterance came home to the hearts of the disciples, and they declared their faith in the fact that He had indeed come from God. There was still self-confidence in this faith which the experience of that evening would help to crush. In His closing words He brings them back to His parting legacy of peace.

XXII. THE HIGH PRIESTLY PRAYER. 17: 1–26 - - 287

This is the counterpart in S. John of the Agony in the Garden in the Synoptists. Face to face with the cross of shame He commits His honour into His Father's keeping, knowing that His Father's honour depended on it. The eternal life that He had come to bring can only be found in communion with the Father as revealed by His Son. His life on earth had provided for men a flawless mirror in which they can see God. So He puts Himself entirely in His Father's hands to vindicate His honour in the sight of men by restoring Him to the throne and the communion which He had left. He then prays for His disciples. He begins by thinking of His Father and His disciples together. They were bound by the Father's gift into a wonderful unity both with

PAGE

Himself and His Father. Their response to His teaching had made it possible for Him to manifest Himself.—The ground is now prepared for specific intercession. He outlines the the situation. He then prays the Father to keep them in the power of the name which He had been commissioned to reveal to men. This "keeping" is to be manifested especially in their unity as a body, reflecting the inner life of the Divine Being. This petition is reinforced by recording the work He had already done on earth to this end. The fact that they had heard Him pray in these terms would bring them joy.—He next faces the dangers to which they would be exposed in the world. He will not pray that they may not be tempted, but that they may be brought safely out of the power of the evil one. The deliverance from the spirit of error can only come by "sanctification in the Truth", that is "in the Word", which Jesus had given them from the Father, and which they had received and kept. The prayer is not simply for their individual perfecting. They are called to share their Lord's commission to preach the Gospel to the whole world. He must therefore "sanctify Himself" if He is to pray for their sanctification. So He deliberately takes up His Cross, for the last time before Gethsemane. In so doing He reveals the open secret of the power of the surrender of His own will on the Cross to bring the rebellious wills of men back into submission to the will of God.—The horizon expands to include the whole Church to the end of time, and to declare the effect of the witness of their unity on all the world. The prayer is still for the unity into which the Church enters. This however is not the end. He is not praying for the world, but the sight of the unity of the Church has power to convert the world. This thought is repeated and expanded in the words that follow in regard to the glory that He would share with the Church. The recognition of the divine mission of the Son will include the

PAGE

recognition of the mission of the Church. The final stage of the prayer is for a perfect restoration of communion for Himself with His disciples within the veil. It closes with a concise summary of the deliverance that He had come to bring by the revelation of the Father in the terms of love. (A short summary of the self-revelation of Jesus follows.)

XXIII. GETHSEMANE IN S. JOHN. 18: 1–40 - 321

After the High Priestly prayer Jesus and His party go to Gethsemane. Judas knew where to look for Jesus if he found that He had left the Upper Chamber. He came with a strong force, not only of the Temple police, but also of Roman soldiers. S. John does not repeat the story of the Agony in the Garden. He concentrates on the fact that Jesus remained all the time master of the situation. He could have escaped from His enemies had He chosen. Instead He surrenders Himself into their hands only taking steps to secure the safety of His disciples. The impetuosity of Simon Peter might have wrecked His plan. But He rebuked Peter in words that recall the agony through which He had just passed. It is only from S. John that we learn that it was Peter that struck the blow and that the servant's name was Malchus. S. John was familiar with the High Priest's household. The only stage in the proceedings against Jesus before the Jewish authorities recorded by S. John is a preliminary trial before Annas. The Evangelist must be "the other disciple" who was himself present in the courtyard of the High Priest's house that cold night.—The trial before Pilate took place, according to S. John, in the Roman courthouse, the Jews staying outside for fear of defilement. They failed to secure a condemnation offhand. Jesus had been condemned for blasphemy, but Roman Law could not take cognizance of that. So they substituted a political charge. When Pilate confronts Jesus with it He naturally asks where it came from.

PAGE

Jesus makes it clear that the Kingdom He claimed was not of this world. It was a Kingdom which those who "were of the Truth" would acknowledge. The ideal wise man of the Stoic philosophers was a King. So the answer might have suggested to Pilate the existence of a spiritual kingdom. But he was not "of the Truth". He was prepared to condemn a man whom he believed to be innocent. So his question evoked no answer. Still he did at least formally acquit the Prisoner, and made an appeal to the people to use the privilege of the feast to deliver Jesus from their rulers.

XXIV. THE CRUCIFIXION. 19: 1–42 - - - - 332

After this attempt had failed Pilate tried to satisfy the Jewish leaders by scourging Jesus and presenting Him in public mockingly arrayed in a general's cloak with a chaplet of thorns. This was answered by a demand for His crucifixion. When Pilate reasserts the innocence of the Prisoner, he is confronted with the claim that Jesus had made to be the Son of God. This leads to a fresh interview in which Jesus reminds Pilate that he was responsible to God for the exercise of the authority committed to him. The rulers counter the impression that this made by reference to the jealousy of Tiberius. Pilate in answer seats Jesus on the judgement seat saying "Behold your King", exacting as the price of his acquiescence a public acknowledgement that it was a capital offence for a Jew to make such a claim.—The sentence is dated by S. John at 6 a.m. on Nisan 14, the day on which the paschal lambs were sacrificed. They were eaten after nightfall. He also tells us that Pilate was himself responsible for the superscription on the Cross, and refused to alter it. He calls special attention to the fulfilment of Ps. 22: 18 in the division of the raiment of Jesus among the soldiers who were guarding Him. He describes a group of four women gathered round the Cross. He tells how Jesus bade His Mother

PAGE

find in the beloved disciple a son whom she could care for in His stead, and bade the beloved disciple take His own place in caring for His Mother. S. John passes over the three hours' darkness, and the cry which marked its passing in S. Matthew and S. Mark. He records instead the one cry from the Cross which expresses physical suffering. "Thirst" was part of the experience of the divine Sufferer as foreshadowed in the Psalms. S. John believed that Jesus in saying "I thirst" was consciously claiming to be entering into that experience. The cry moved one of the bystanders to do what was possible to relieve the suffering. S. John records one more word expressing our Lord's confidence that His work had attained its appointed goal before He laid His head to rest on the bosom of His Father. —Before he comes to the account of the entombment S. John records an incident to which he clearly attached great importance. It was the occasion for the fulfilment of two more elements in the divine foreshadowing. In order to expedite the death of the victims soldiers were sent to break their legs. Jesus was already dead when the soldiers came, so His bones remained unbroken. But one of the soldiers pierced His side and there came out a stream of blood and water. S. John appeals to His Lord to confirm the truth of this testimony. He then points to the two passages in the Scriptures which the soldiers were unconscious instruments in fulfilling.—The Old Testament Scriptures were for the Jew not only authoritative but also predictive. Jesus expressly claimed to be the direct subject of Old Testament prophecy. The thought of the fulfilment of Scriptures seems at times to go beyond simple prediction and to credit the written word with a strange power to control the course of history.—S. John's account of the entombment associates Nicodemus with Joseph of Arimathæa. Henry Latham's *The Risen Master* called attention to

PAGE

the importance of the reference to the grave clothes in S. John. The recent discoveries with regard to the Holy Shroud at Turin, if they can be substantiated, are even more important.

XXV. THE FIRST EASTER DAY. 20: 1–31 - - 358

Roused by Mary Magdalene, Peter and John run to the tomb. John gets there first, but Peter is the first to enter. John following sees the condition of the grave clothes and is convinced by the sight that Jesus is risen. He is a little ashamed that he should have needed the evidence of sight to convince him. Mary Magdalene returns to the tomb, and, after the apostles have gone, looks in. She sees the angels who greet her. Then she looks round and sees Jesus, but does not recognize Him till He calls her by name. He tells her to relax her grasp on Him and bear a message from Him to His brethren.—In the evening Jesus appears through closed doors and assures them of His identity. S. Luke shows that others besides the apostles were present. Their first reaction is joy. He commissioned them to carry on the work that the Father had given Him. Then after breathing on them He defined the work that they were to do for Him. They were to go into the world to set men free from the bondage of sin. They must learn to look at all men in the light of their redemption. This is the characteristic activity of the whole Church.—Thomas refuses to believe at second-hand. He demands the evidence of touch as well as of sight and sound. He does not however forsake the company of believers. A week later Jesus appeared again, and offers Thomas the confirmation he had demanded. The evidence that Jesus could read his thoughts must have done for him what it had done for Nathanael. He says, "My Lord and my God". Jesus accepts the confession, but He pronounces a special benediction on those who had been able to dispense with sensible confirmation. The Gospel closes with a simple

PAGE

statement of the creed which it had been written to establish.

XXVI. THE APPEARANCE BY THE LAKE. 21 : 1–25 - 370

The closing chapter is clearly a postscript, added after the Gospel had reached a formal conclusion, to correct a popular misunderstanding with regard to a word of the Lord relating to the Evangelist. He brings us back once more to Galilee. Simon Peter goes fishing with six companions. They toil all night to no purpose. At dawn Jesus appears. The beloved disciple recognizes Him. Peter leaps into the water to get to Him. They breakfast with Him on the shore.—Jesus takes Peter apart and after a thrice repeated challenge to his love and a threefold commission to a pastoral office, Jesus warns him that he must learn to surrender all initiative into the hands of God.—The lesson for the beloved disciple is strangely different. Curiosity with regard to the future is sternly checked. The only point that is revealed is that he must look forward to a protracted discipline of waiting and watching. This saying had given rise to the impression that the beloved disciple should live on till the final advent. It was important to recall the exact terms.—Nothing remains but that the body of witnesses, in whose name the Evangelist has been writing, should add their attestation. It may be that the amanuensis added the last verse on his own responsibility.

EPILOGUE - - - - - - - - 381

CHAPTER I

THE ORIGIN OF THE GOSPELS

IT is well in studying the origin of the Gospels to begin by reminding ourselves of certain fundamental facts with regard to the documents that we are to consider.

Let us begin with what is, I believe, a demonstrable element in the life of Him of whom they treat. As Dr. P. Carnegie Simpson points out in *The Fact of Christ*, Jesus, unlike all other religious and philosophical leaders, deliberately and without reserve made Himself the centre and sum of all His teaching. Discipleship, as He taught it, was a direct personal relationship. The success of His mission on earth was to be measured by the extent to which He could reveal Himself to men according to the inmost truth of His being, and win their love, their faith, and their obedience.

I do not think that anyone will challenge the accuracy of this description of the ministry as recorded in each of the four Gospels, with differences of emphasis, but with remarkable harmony in general impression. In view of the uniqueness of the phenomenon, this is no doubt, as Dr. Carnegie Simpson claims, a strong guarantee of the faithfulness of the narrators to historical fact: all the more, because they do nothing to call attention to this feature in the life they are relating, and may well have been unaware of it.

Notice next what also is surely an undeniable fact. The personality of Jesus is to-day a vital and growingly important power in the life of the world. Mankind at large, and not only believers in Christ, have a clear grasp of the fundamental characteristics of His character and teaching. The Hindu is capable of convicting Christian believers of their failure in various ways to embody His likeness.

The fact that he can do this, and that we can check for ourselves the extent of our failure, is due to the fact that "the Gospel" has been embodied for us in the four small volumes which are practically the sole source of information with regard to the life that Jesus lived in Palestine 1,900 years ago.

This does not mean that we must regard the Gospels as immune from criticism, or be anything but grateful for the immense labour that has been bestowed in the course of the last century on the question of how they came to be what they are. But it should make us review very carefully any argument which would require us to believe that the authors were fundamentally mistaken, and that the Jesus whom they described was not the true historical Jesus.

We must pass from this general statement of the claim of the Gospels on respectful attention, to consider what we can discover with regard to the forces that brought them into existence.

It is surely a noteworthy fact that, when so much depended on the truth of the impression that He left behind Him, Jesus should not have done what the prophets of old time did, and committed at least some part of His teaching to writing.

We cannot doubt that He deliberately chose to concentrate on the training of a small band of disciples, and to trust entirely to their memory of things that they had seen and heard, for the influence that the story of His life and teaching was to have in the world to the end of time.

The wonder of that confidence grows on us the more we dwell upon it. The disciples on whose witness He relied were what the professional theologians of the day called unlearned and ignorant. They had no professional training either in letters or religion. They were deeply conscious, as they looked back, of their moral imperfections and their lack of spiritual apprehension. The inner meaning of what He did and of what He taught had inevitably been hidden from them at the time. It could not but be, as a Victorian critic noted, that Jesus had always been "ahead of His reporters". And yet here the Gospels are, producing from the memories of these imperfect witnesses (surely not without the help of the promised Comforter [Jn. 14: 26]) the result that we behold.

How, then, we cannot but ask, has this come about? The latest development of Gospel criticism essays, by the application of the method that scholars are content to describe under its German title as *Formgeschichte*, to get behind S. Mark, and back to the material out of which he composed his Gospel. It claims to be able to identify a certain number of sections, some of them relating a characteristic incident, and some of them a distinctive utterance of the Lord, which may have formed the text of a discourse which had as its object the conversion of the Gentiles. This is not in itself a probable suggestion. Detached incidents in our Lord's life and specimens of His teaching can hardly have had much appeal to the unconverted. It is well no doubt to be reminded that such traditions, in certain circumstances, might have an apologetic or controversial value, and that a preacher might be tempted to modify them in detail to sharpen their point to suit his purpose. But that does not throw any light on the source of the original store of reminiscences. And so far as the preacher yielded to the temptation he would falsify the deposit which he had inherited.

The attraction of the method to its inventor would seem to be that it affords an opportunity of eliminating from the Gospels elements that are too aggressively supernatural, and so to reduce the shock to the critical consciousness caused by the fact that even S. Mark, the earliest of our Gospels, cannot, as it stands, fit such a picture of Jesus as it is prepared to recognize as historical. In the end, however, I cannot but believe we shall have to acquiesce in the fact that all our traditional story of the life of Jesus comes to us from those who believed Him to be the Christ, the Son of God, who had died and risen again from the dead. Neither they nor their disciples would have cared to revive the memories of His life had they not believed that.

We shall recognize that where we can test the operation of the bias of early reporters by the minutest comparison of the divergences between the first three Evangelists, the utmost that can be said is that the later writers shew a tendency to avoid using language that might suggest any limitation in the power of Jesus to heal or in the success of His ministrations. They also now and then seem to seek to save the credit of the apostles by passing over some instances of their failure. But it is clearly impossible on the strength of this evidence to credit their predecessors with the complete transformation of the original picture which the critical position demands. It is indeed possible to hope that the day may come when the features in the narratives, to which Dr. Carnegie Simpson points as evidence of their fundamental veracity, will be allowed their due weight. The appearance of such a book as *The Original Jesus*, by Otto Borchert, should remind us that there is in Truth a self-evidencing quality which must in the end carry conviction.

I do not, therefore, as I have shewn, anticipate much permanent assistance from the *Formgeschichte* hypothesis in the understanding either of the origin or of the content of the Evangelic tradition.

The Bishop of Bradford at the Church Congress at Bournemouth in 1935 found in the hypothesis a timely reminder of the fact "that the Gospels were not only written *for* the Church by members of the Church," but also "were in a sense written *by* the Church, in that the Church corporately sponsored the traditions which the Gospels have compiled".

I cannot myself see how the hypothesis supports this conclusion. Surely the growth of the Gospel Canon, and the abundant evidence that the second century provides of the watchful criticism of which that growth is the outcome, is the real justification of our confidence in the resultant supremacy of "the Four".

At the same time it is well to be challenged to think out again the process by which the Gospels were in fact written not only *for* the Church, but also *by* the Church.

In regard to the matter immediately in front of us, I feel that we are not likely to make much progress as long as we give free reign to our imaginations without any reference to the masterly analysis of the conditions under which the oral Gospel took shape in Jerusalem in the first twenty years after Pentecost, given by Dr. Westcott in his *Introduction to the Study of the Gospels*, Chapter III, "On the Oral Gospel". It is true that later study seems to have shewn that the oral hypothesis does not provide an adequate solution of all the facts. But at the same time Dr. Westcott's account of the conditions under which the Gospel tradition passed while it was still in its oral stage does throw light on that which we have seen to be the true riddle of the Gospels. I mean the way in which results of such surpassing value came through men who to all appearance were hopelessly inadequate for the task committed to them.

The apostles must have found themselves from the day of Pentecost onwards confronted with the task of training others in the discipleship of Jesus, into which they had themselves been admitted.

When we put ourselves into their position and realize how far they must have been from any adequate intellectual apprehension of the person and work of their Master, or of the principles which had regulated the development of His ministry, we see how impossible the task committed to them would have been (1) without the assurance of His triumph over death, which came from their intercourse with Him after His resurrection; (2) without the gift of the Spirit in token of His present power over their hearts and lives; and (3) without the hope of His return and of the final consummation. His death, so far from marking the close of their discipleship, had only intensified their sense of personal dependence. Their primary duty, therefore, was to call men to enter with them into a present experience.

In the fulfilment of their task they had, we must remember, from the first, as we still have, the help of the two sacraments of the Gospel: Baptism and the Breaking of Bread, outward and visible signs of the inner and spiritual bonds by which each disciple is bound in a direct and personal relationship to his invisible Lord.

At the same time we have what the converts on the day of Pentecost had not, the help of the written Gospels to give definite content to our thoughts about Him, and to enable us to enter intelligently into His mind and heart and will. We have the inestimable advantage of being able to turn to them (to use the language of S. Ignatius) "as to the flesh of Christ." They help us, as Erasmus said, to form a clearer picture of Him in our minds than we could have acquired by the sight of our eyes. The earliest disciples could not have this help. They had to depend instead on the personal witness of the apostles. Our Gospels are the outcome of the efforts of the apostles to deliver this part of their witness faithfully. It will be worth while to try to trace the steps by which this result was brought about.

The teaching of the apostles rested, of course, from the first on a basis of historic fact. That basis, however, was strictly limited. It consisted, to start with, simply of the death and the resurrection of Jesus. S. Paul summarizes it concisely in 1 Cor. 15: 3 f: "For I delivered unto you first of all that which I also received, how that Christ died for our sins according to the Scriptures; and that He was buried and that He hath been raised on the third day according to the Scriptures".

In the earliest days the memory of Jesus was still fresh in Jerusalem and in Palestine generally, so that the apostles could pass from the notorious fact of the Cross to the evidence of the Resurrection, and to the Scripture proofs that suffering was the divinely appointed gate of entrance into glory for the Messiah.

At the same time, at an early stage in the training of their newly enrolled fellow-disciples, the apostles must have found themselves drawing on their memories of "the things that they had seen and heard." The meaning of discipleship for them was closely bound up with these memories, which supplied a natural and ready way to help men who had not known their Master to understand the traditions of the school of which they had become members. It would, however, be a mistake to suppose that the motive which led the apostles in the first instance to draw on their reminiscences was strictly biographical. The significance of the personality of Jesus in the educational system of the Church would not have been apparent at the outset. Pupils in a Jewish school would expect primarily to be given a rule of life; and the commission of the risen Lord expressly charges the apostles (Mt. 28:20) to teach men to observe all that He had commanded them. Interest would, therefore, be concentrated at first on the words of the Lord, especially those which had a direct bearing on character and conduct. If so, reports of our Lord's teaching, such as those that are collected by S. Matthew in the Sermon on the Mount, the instructions to the Twelve, the parables, and the eschatological discourse, would constitute the oldest stratum in the oral Gospel, and form the basis of the catechetical instruction of which S. Luke speaks in the preface to his Gospel.

It is in harmony with this that we find from the Acts that the Church was early known in Jewish circles as "The Way." S. Paul was clearly acquainted—and expected other disciples to be acquainted—with "the words of the Lord Jesus." The first step towards the formation of a New Testament was taken as soon as Christian writers began to quote the words of the Lord as authoritative side by side with "Moses and the Prophets." From the first, therefore, when they began to expound the law of the Spirit of Life in Christ Jesus for the guidance of the infant Church in Jerusalem, the apostles must have drawn on their memories of the instruction that they had themselves received. Pupils in Jewish schools were trained to trust to their memories. To put anything in writing might encroach on the prerogatives of the Scriptures. So teaching would lack a text-book, and the teachers would quote and apply to the need of the moment any relevant saying of the Lord that occurred to them. And so little by little the experience of life would sift out the sayings that had the most universal and abiding significance.

Special incidents associated with memorable sayings

would, in course of time, establish their place in the tradition. These would include examples of "the mighty works, and wonders, and signs which God had done" through Jesus. But no effort would be made to stress the element of wonder. Jesus being what the Resurrection declared Him to be, there was nothing surprising in their occurrence. It was a matter of common knowledge that such signs had been wrought in the course of His ministry, and they had their lesson for disciples. But the faith of the Church did not spring from or rest upon them. There was nothing evidential about them, except their agreement with the prophetic portrait of the Servant of the Lord. Still there they were, and little by little the oral Gospel grew till it contained material, if not for a life of Jesus, at least for a vivid picture of His manifold activities, when at last the need for a written record became urgent, with the lapse of time, and the spread of the Church beyond Palestine.

S. Luke in his preface (1 : 1-4) comes to our assistance just at this point, and enables us to picture to ourselves the steps by which the oral teaching of the apostles passed into the shape with which we are familiar in the first three of our Gospels. The chief points, as Dr. Westcott draws them out in his *Introduction to the Study of the Gospels* (pp. 185 f.), are these: "The common basis of the Evangelic narratives is said to be the oral '*tradition of those who from the beginning* (Ac. 1 : 21 f.) *were eye-witnesses and ministers of the word*'. The two elements in the apostolic character which have been already pointed out, personal knowledge and practical experience, are recognized by S. Luke as present in those who originally *handed down* the history, which many attempted to draw up and arrange afresh in a connected shape. The work of these unknown first evangelists was new only in form, and not in substance. The tradition which they incorporated in a narrative was not peculiar to themselves, but was common to all; for the common belief was independent of these written records. . . . Theophilus was already *instructed in the words* of the exact truth of which S. Luke wished to assure him; and his instruction was derived from that oral teaching which is described by the same term from the first foundation of the Church (Ac. 18: 25; 1 Cor. 14: 19; Gal. 6: 6)".

It is on some such presuppositions as these that the Synoptic criticism of the last seventy years has been built. We used to think that one assured result of that criticism was that a document substantially identical with our Mark was in the hands of Matthew and Luke. The arrangement of incidents in Mark seems presupposed in S. Matthew 14-28, and in the relevant sections in Luke. And, furthermore, Dr. E. A. Abbott[1] gave strong grounds for believing that "at all events in some passages Mark contains the whole of a tradition from which Matthew and Luke borrowed parts". It is, therefore, not easy to see how a comparison of the sections that Matthew and Luke have in common with Mark can throw light on the form in which they came to Mark, except possibly in the rare cases where Matthew and Luke agree in a variation from his text.

We must, therefore, wait for some more solid evidence than has as yet been produced on behalf of the hypothesis of *Formgeschichte*, before we throw away the evidence of Papias that connects the origin of Mark with the preaching of Peter. That evidence comes, if not from the elder John himself, at least from one who belonged, as Papias did not, to the generation that was contemporary with the apostles, and who therefore cannot be supposed to have invented the connexion in order to bolster up the authority of a document which he was in a position to criticize.

1 *Common Tradition of the Synoptic Gospels*, p. vi f.

CHAPTER II

THE ORIGIN OF THE FOURTH GOSPEL

WHEN we pass from the consideration of the materials out of which our Gospels were composed to consider the origin of particular Gospels, it is natural to begin with S. Mark, because as we have already seen, there is a general consensus of opinion that it was in the hands both of S. Luke and of S. Matthew before their Gospels assumed their present shape.

That Gospel, according to a tradition which Papias records as coming from John the Elder (who may well have been the apostle S. John himself), had its origin in S. Peter's preaching. The Elder explains the defects of the Gospel, especially its lack of systematic arrangement, from the circumstances of its origin, while he commends its accuracy. The Gospel is in fact open to the criticism which S. Luke makes on his predecessors. It is no doubt possible, if you read S. Mark carefully, to trace lines of historical development in it. This would follow naturally if S. Peter's reminiscences followed in the main a true chronological sequence. But there is no evidence that S. Mark was conscious of the development. He seems to have had no vision of his subject as a whole. The individual scenes that he pictures so vividly do not constitute a history even of the public ministry of Jesus, though they provide admirable material for a Greek with a literary sense like S. Luke, when he came to write a systematic account of things that Jesus began to do and to teach before His ascension; or for a Jew, like S. Matthew, when he set to work to compile a book of the generations of Jesus Christ after the precedent of "the book of the generations of Adam" (Gen. 5: 1) which is incorporated in the book of Genesis.

S. Luke's aim, as we see from his preface, was strictly scientific. He felt the importance of a written record to safeguard the accuracy of a tradition from the dangers to which it is exposed in the process of oral transmission.

History in the Old Testament is a department of prophecy. The historical books are called the books of the earlier Prophets. Their object is to help the Chosen People to trace the hand of God in the experiences through which He had led them. It is not surprising, therefore, to find a distinct dogmatic purpose in S. Matthew's Gospel. He groups his material in a precise and formal way. He lays stress on the fulfilment of prophecy at each stage in his narrative. He emphasizes the importance of Simon Peter's confession at Caesarea Philippi, making it the turning-point in the public ministry. His gospel sums up the case of the Church in controversy with the Jews. It has been finely described as "Jehovah's ultimatum to His People".

When we come to S. John the same dogmatic purpose is openly avowed and clearly expressed. "These signs are written that ye may believe that Jesus is the Christ, the Son of God". We have, however, passed out of the region of Jewish apologetic. The thought of the Christ has shed its association with Jewish nationalist aspirations. If we read the Gospel, as we ought, in close connexion with the first Epistle of S. John, we see that the public addressed were Christians of the second generation. They had been brought up on the Synoptic tradition. They needed to be reminded of the moral claims of the Gospel, and to have their eyes opened to the full riches of their spiritual inheritance. But chiefly they were in danger from a subtle form of heresy, which distinguished the Christ from the historic Jesus, and denied that He was Himself the Christ who had come and is still coming "in the flesh".

There is evidence in Irenaeus[1] to shew that the false teacher whom S. John has especially in view was Cerinthus,

[1] *Irenaeus*, Book III: xi: 1, Stieren's Edition. See Brooke I.C.C., *The Johannine Epistles*, p. xlv.

who identified the Christ with the Spirit that descended on Jesus at His baptism, but left Him (so he held) before His passion, coming in fact "in water only, not in the water and in the blood". Irenaeus thus gives definiteness to the polemical reference of the Gospel and the Epistle. He adds that S. John published his Gospel during his stay at Ephesus.

There are besides two early traditions with regard to the publication of the Gospel. One is quoted in an abbreviated form by Eusebius from Clement of Alexandria. "Last of all (the Evangelists), John perceiving that the material facts had been made plain in the gospels, being urged by his friends and inspired by the Spirit, composed a spiritual gospel".[1] Clement (about A.D. 190) is here reporting "the tradition of the earliest Elders". Notice the suggestion that S. John wrote the Gospel under pressure from his friends.

The other tradition is found in a curious fragment known as the Muratorian Canon (A.D. 170–200). It contains an interesting account of the pressure. It says that when John's fellow-disciples and bishops were urging him to write, he said: "Fast with me for three days from to-day, and let us tell each other any revelations that are made to any of us". That same night it was revealed to Andrew, one of the apostles, that John should write everything in his own name, while the rest should revise.

The document itself is anonymous. It is generally supposed to have been written in Rome not later than A.D. 200. Bishop Lightfoot ascribed it to S. Hippolytus. He also points out that the account of the Gospels contained in it shows signs of dependence on Papias, who was bishop of Hierapolis, a friend of Polycarp, and a pupil of S. John. If that dependence extended to the account of the Fourth Gospel, we could not have a better authority.

In itself it does in a remarkable way throw light on some peculiar features in the Gospel.

The author in the Prologue (1 : 14) and in the opening words of his first Epistle (1 Jn. 1 : 1-4), uses the first person plural, as if he were speaking in the name of a body of

[1] Eusebius, H.E. VI. 14.

witnesses. Now this tradition calls special attention to the part played by Andrew in persuading John to write. If it is accurate John was not, as we are commonly told, the only surviving apostle at the time of the composition of the Gospel.

Again, in Jn. 21 : 24, "This is the disciple, which beareth witness of these things, and wrote these things: and we know that his witness is true", we have evidence that the work after it was completed was countersigned by a body of people who claim power to authenticate the document.

It is true that the whole chapter is an appendix to the Gospel, which seems to have worked up to a climax in 20:31. At the same time it is difficult to believe that any one but the author of Chapters 1-20 can have written it; or that the beloved disciple can have been dead when it was first published. In the attestation "the disciple which beareth witness of these things" is spoken of as alive. And "who wrote these things" clearly refers to the whole Gospel.

According to the Muratorian fragment this attestation was part of the original plan. It is true that no names are attached. There is no reason, however, to suppose that the witnesses, any more than the writer of the Gospel and the First Epistle, desired to remain anonymous. A man does not write to strangers, and call them his "little children". The circle for whom the Evangelist was immediately writing could have had no doubt as to his identity. Nor, we may add, as to the identity of the attesting body.

It is interesting to notice that S. Jerome[1], who either knew our fragment, or the authority on which it is based, says that the bishops who came to S. John comprised "almost all the bishops of the Roman province of Asia, accompanied by deputations from many churches". If so, the book would naturally circulate in the first instance in the churches to which letters are expressly addressed in the Apocalypse. There is no evidence that the author or his associates were consciously addressing a wider public.

This tradition with regard to its origin supplies at the same time a natural explanation of another feature in the

[1] See *Catal. Ser. Eccl.* eq, and *Com. in Mat. Proem.*

Gospel, I mean its conversational character, to which Lightfoot called attention (*Biblical Essays*, p. 197 f). The passage is worth quoting at length.

"The Fourth Gospel was addressed to an immediate circle of hearers. In this respect it differs from the other three, S. Luke's Gospel approaching most nearly to it. But Theophilus, if a real person, and not a *nom de guerre*, the type of a God-loving or God-beloved Christian, soon disappears out of sight. On the other hand, the Fourth Evangelist keeps his disciples before his mind. He has to correct misapprehensions, to answer questions, to guide and instruct a definite class of persons, his immediate circle of acquaintance. Hence he assumes a knowledge of himself in the case of those for whom he writes. He does not give his own name, because his hearers already know his personal history.

"For the most part, however, the reference to these disciples is indirect. They are before the Evangelist, but he does not address them in the second person. Instances of allusions to misapprehensions, or to questionings rife in those about him are 1: 41, 'He was the first to find', etc.; 2: 11, '*This* was the beginning of his miracles'; 3: 24, 'John was *not yet* cast into prison'; 4: 54, 'This again was the second miracle which Jesus did'; 18: 13, 'He (Annas) was father-in-law to Caiaphas, who was high-priest of that year'; 19: 34 f, 'There came out water and blood.' Great stress is laid upon this last point, doubtless in allusion to some symbolism which is not explained, because they would understand it. So 21: 14, 'This was now the third time that Jesus manifested Himself'; 21: 23, 'The saying therefore went abroad among the brethren that that disciple should not die. Yet Jesus said not unto him, he shall not die', etc. Thus we find the Evangelist clearing up matters which the current tradition left doubtful, or on which the popular mind wished to be further informed. Through the main part of the narrative we see these parenthetical additions, these conversational comments. At length (19: 35, 20: 31) there is a direct appeal to these disciples, for whom the whole has been written. 'He knoweth that he saith true, that *ye* might believe.' 'These things are written that *ye* may believe that Jesus is the Christ, the Son of God, and that believing ye might have life through His name.' "

There is in fact evidence of a tradition that the Gospel was written by dictation. Indeed Papias himself is said in one of the Prologues to the Gospel to have acted as S. John's amanuensis.

Early Church tradition, then, as recorded by writers who on general grounds are, to say the least, worthy of respectful attention, informs us, as we have seen, that the Fourth Gospel was written by S. John in Ephesus, at the request of his friends and neighbours, to counteract the errors of Cerinthus.

It is true that after the rise of Montanism, some champions of orthodoxy, apparently in Rome, sought to cut the ground from under their opponents by ascribing both the Apocalypse and the Gospel to Cerinthus. They can have known nothing of Cerinthus beyond his name, or they could not have made so stupid an attribution. At the same time, they deserve all credit as pioneers in the comparative study of the Gospels. The account of their criticisms, as reported by Epiphanius, gives us good reason for thinking that the defence of the fourfold canon of the Gospels which we find both in the Muratorian Fragment and in Irenaeus owes its shape, especially in the stress laid by both of them on the different starting-points of the Gospels, to the objections brought by these men, whom Epiphanius nicknames Alogi.

The incident is interesting as shewing that the Churches which had been brought up on the Synoptic tradition were jealous of their inheritance, and inquired carefully into the credentials of the Fourth Gospel before they allowed it co-ordinate authority with the first three. The traditional account of its authorship has stood the fire of criticism.

This evidence is, of course, external. It needs to be confronted and checked at every point by the internal evidence supplied by the contents of the book. But even if it did no more, it would suggest fruitful lines of inquiry.

Dr. Rawlinson, indeed, in his important and illuminating Bampton lectures on *The New Testament Doctrine of the Christ*, maintains that "the Evangelist seeks to set forth the Lord Jesus to cosmopolitan Hellenists as the Saviour of the world, and his narrative is governed by this purpose". There are, no doubt, elements in the Gospel which would give it an apologetic value for this class of inquirers. I cannot, however, help feeling that the traditional account is nearer to the truth when it tells us that the primary object of the Evangelist was, not to attract and convert outsiders, but to instruct and quicken the faith of his fellow-Christians.

If we read the Gospel in close connexion with the first Epistle of S. John, we see that the minds of Christians were already being exercised by the fundamental problem of Christology, the relation of the divine to the human elements in the personality of Jesus. The problem is sure to rise as soon as men begin to reflect seriously on the Synoptic tradition. And, as the experience of the last century shews, the Synoptic tradition by itself does not give us light enough to solve it. It is surely not incredible that if, when the problem was first raised, one of the original witnesses was still alive, the leaders of the Church should have turned to him to give them an account, on the ground of his own experience, of the faith which they had learned from him, and which they felt was being subtly undermined by these new and plausible speculations. The object of the writer, as defined by himself, was, we must remember, "that ye may believe that Jesus (the historic Jesus) is the Christ, the Son of God, and that by believing ye may have life in His name, i.e. by an intelligent apprehension of His person".

When we pass from the internal evidence of the document as to the occasion and object of its production to consider what it has to tell directly and indirectly with regard to its author, we find that it is strictly speaking, anonymous.

The author is addressing a definite circle of readers, but he has no occasion to mention his own name. In the last chapter a verse is added by a revising committee identifying the author with an unnamed "disciple whom Jesus loved", to whom reference is made in Chapters 13, 19 and 20, as well as in the immediate context in Chapter 21: "This is the disciple who testifieth concerning these things, and we know that his witness is true".

It is worth while collecting these references. The first occurs in an account of the seating of the apostles at the last supper.

"One of his disciples", we read (13: 23), "whom Jesus loved, was reclining on the bosom of Jesus". This was not the position of honour, about which there had been unseemly disputing (Lk. 22: 24). But it was a position of affectionate intimacy, and the disciple was no doubt occupying it by special invitation. It comes into the narrative because it enabled him to receive a special hint of the coming treachery of Judas.

The second reference is in 19: 26. "Jesus therefore seeing His mother and the disciple whom He loved standing by, saith to His mother: 'Woman, behold thy son'. Then He saith to the disciple: 'Behold thy mother'."

Here we shall, I think, feel that the special designation helps to prepare us for the revelation of tender and thoughtful love for His mother and His dearest disciple, which is enshrined in the wonderful commission whereby He bound them each to each and to Himself by the link of His love for them and their common love for Him.

The third reference is in 20: 2. Mary Magdalene runs from the empty tomb to Simon Peter and the other disciple who was Jesus's friend. Here we find him in a relation of close intimacy with Peter, strictly analogous to that in which the apostle John stands in the Synoptic Gospels and in the Acts (Lk. 22: 8, Ac. 3: 1, etc.).

The story that follows is told throughout from the Evangelist's point of view. He is ashamed that he should have needed the sign of the deserted grave-cloths to convince him of the Resurrection. If it is true, and not a dramatic fiction, it must come directly from him.

The last reference is that in chapter 21 : 7, 20-24. In it we find the same close connexion with Simon Peter, the same quickness of spiritual apprehension, the same longing to keep as near as possible to the manifested presence of his Lord that characterize him throughout. The object of the narrative seems to be to correct a popular misunderstanding of the word of the Lord to Simon Peter, uttered with regard to S. John on this occasion.

Dr. Rawlinson contends that the author was not John, the son of Zebedee, but another John, the Presbyter, who "remembered and idealized S. John as the apostle with whom he had had personal associations" (though not lengthy or exceptionally intimate). "It appears to have been his habitual practice, for example, to think and to speak of S. John, not by name, but as 'the disciple whom Jesus loved'. He is always so described in the Gospel, and the name 'John' in the usage of the writer, denotes always the Baptist. It is not altogether surprising that posterity identified the Evangelist himself with the beloved disciple. But, on the other hand, such a description is not really natural, and would hardly have been in good taste as a self-designation".

To arrive at this result he is bound to regard Jn. 21 : 24 as a later addition to the text of the Gospel, embodying an erroneous assumption with regard to the authorship. This is a peculiarly difficult position in view of the emphatic assertion of first-hand knowledge contained in the verse.

Dr. Rawlinson is also mistaken in his assertion that the Evangelist always uses this title in describing the apostle S. John. It is, for instance, very difficult to dissociate "the other disciple (18: 15), who was known to the High Priest", who follows Jesus with Simon Peter to the court of the High Priest, and who speaks on his behalf to the maid who kept the door, from the beloved disciple. And there is another unnamed disciple in 1 : 37, 40, 41, who must surely be one of the sons of Zebedee.

The real sting of the objection to identifying the Evangelist with "the disciple whom Jesus loved" lies in the feeling in which Dr. Rawlinson does not stand alone, that the title is "in bad taste as a self-designation". In a matter of taste it is proverbially difficult to dogmatize. Still, I have sufficient confidence in "the disciple whom Jesus loved" to believe that his action, if we could see it in its true light, would stand the closest scrutiny. Suppose, for instance, that the description itself is true—and if it is not, the use of it violates even more sacred canons than those of taste—suppose, that is, that in fact Jesus not only picked out three of the Twelve for special intimacy, but that His heart went out with peculiar tenderness towards one, very possibly the youngest—certainly the most affectionate and responsive of the three. Suppose that that tenderness found expression in the arrangement of couches at table on an occasion when feeling would be strained to the uttermost by His last appeal to the traitor. Suppose that He set a public seal to the memory of His affection by leaving the care of His Mother as a dying legacy to this son of His love. Is it incredible that Andrew and Philip and others of the early disciples who gathered in Ephesus and its neighbourhood after the fall of Jerusalem should have been in the habit of thinking and speaking of him, in the light of the days that were gone, as the beloved of Jesus, and that he may have felt constrained in no spirit of boasting, but in utter self-abasement, in the interests of historic truth, and for a complete revelation of the perfect humanity of his Master, to adopt the designation from them on some of the rare occasions when he had to bring himself into the picture?

Dr. Brooke, in Peake's *Commentary on the Bible*, sums up in favour of the same solution as Dr. Rawlinson's as follows: "Many details, probable in themselves, which are not easily explained as due to invention, or even modification, in the interest of the author's views, point to such sources resting finally on the testimony of an eye-witness. At the same time the later elements of this gospel, its silence as to much of the best authenticated gospel history, its scant record of ministry in Galilee, its transformation of the style and contents of the Lord's teaching in the light of later reflection and experience, the imperceptible transition from speech to comment till the original speakers disappear, the extent to which all speakers use the language and reflect the ideas of the Evangelist, are now more fully recognized. The difficulty of attributing the Gospel as it stands to an eye-witness of the ministry or an intimate friend and disciple of the Lord is clearly seen. The theory which comes nearest to satisfying all the conditions is that which attributes the Gospel in its present form to the disciple of an eye-witness. To find an eye-witness in the beloved disciple, who is probably the younger son of Zebedee, and the actual author of the Gospel in a disciple of his, who carried on his master's work at Ephesus, and perhaps, in consequence of identity of name, was in tradition confused with his master, is the best answer we can at present give to a question on which the evidence does not enable us to speak with authority."

Dr. Brooke's opinion deservedly carries great weight. At the same time, when we come to look into "the later elements of this gospel", which he enumerates, we find that they have really no bearing on the question whether the Gospel, as it stands, is the work of an eye-witness or of a disciple of his. Granted that the Gospel was written when the other Gospels were already in circulation, its silence as to much of the best authenticated gospel history, "and its scant record of ministry in Galilee" have really no bearing on the question whether the writer was himself an eye-witness of the events that he selects for record. Nor, again, is there anything in the "transformation of the style and contents of the Lord's teaching in the light of later reflection and experience" to exclude the possibility that the transformation was due to the eye-witness himself. The seed sown in him by the words he had heard was even more likely to take root and grow in his own mind than in the mind of a disciple of his.

On the other hand, look at passages like: "When, therefore, He was raised from the dead, His disciples remembered that He said this, and they believed the Scripture and the word which Jesus had spoken" (2: 22); and "Now this He spake of the Spirit, which they that believed on Him should receive. For as yet 'spirit' was not, for Jesus was not yet glorified" (7: 39); and again, "These things His disciples knew not at the first, but when Jesus was glorified, then they remembered that these things had been written of Him, and that they had done these things to Him" (12: 16). Do not these show that the narrator was able to distinguish at first-hand between the original impression received by the disciples and the fulness of meaning in word or act, which he had only discovered in the light of later experience?

"The imperceptible transition from speech to comment till the original speaker disappeared" is not a likely feature in a narrative in which a disciple is composing with considerable freedom an account of the teaching of his master for the use of a third generation. In the case of a studied literary composition it would have been comparatively easy and natural for a third person to make an effort to distinguish if not between the words of the Lord and the comments of the eye-witness, at least between the tradition that he had received and his own expansion of it. On the other hand, if the basis of the Gospel is in the oral teaching of the beloved disciple, nothing would be more natural than that he should now and then illustrate and expand an utterance of Lord in such a way that text and comment became inextricably blended.

Once more, the strong family likeness in vocabulary and style between the different speakers whose utterances are reported in the Gospel, would result naturally from the fact that they all spoke Aramaic, and that the Evangelist translated them into his own remarkably individual variety of Greek.

The fact is that the real difficulty that is felt in attributing the Gospel as it stands to an eye-witness does not lie in any of these things, but in the difficulty that is found in accepting as historical, facts like the raising of Lazarus, and the empty tomb, which are recorded with such extraordinary verisimilitude. Of course, if we feel justified in asserting *a priori* that these phenomena, together with the intimacy of communion between the Father and the Son to which the recorded words of Jesus testify, are evidently incredible, we are bound to postulate some intermediate link between the original eye-witness and the narrative in our hands. Only it is as well that we should recognize where the source of the difficulty really lies. From a strictly literary point of view, the internal evidence for the authorship of the son of Zebedee, as Lightfoot and Scott Holland present it, is overwhelming.

There remains, indeed, one verse (19: 35), which has been claimed as decisive on the other side: "He that hath seen hath borne witness, and his witness is true, and he knoweth that he saith truth, that you in your turn may believe." This is a characteristic form of expression in S. John. It recurs in 21: 24: "This is the disciple which beareth witness of these things and that wrote these things, and we know that his witness is true"; and again in 3 Jn. 12: "And we also bear witness, and thou knowest that our witness is true". In each case there is a reference first to a specific witness, and then an appeal to an outside authority for corroboration. It seems, therefore, impossible to assume, what is otherwise linguistically barely possible, that in 19: 35 "he", to whom appeal is made as "knowing that he saith true" is the same as "he who hath seen and borne witness '. It has been maintained, therefore, that in this verse the writer expressly distinguishes himself from the beloved disciple "who hath seen and borne witness". This is in itself, on other grounds, an extremely improbable hypothesis. A far simpler solution has been proposed by Dr. Zahn, and I am glad to see commends itself to Dr. Rawlinson though not, I am sorry to say, to Canon Scott Holland. It is based on the very characteristic use of the pronoun "He" by S. John in his First Epistle. He uses it again and again without any definition from the context, assuming that his readers would understand that he meant the Lord.

Here, in view of the importance which S. John—as we see from 1 Jn. 5 : 6—attached to the twofold stream of blood and water, we understand why he pauses to call special attention to the significant phenomenon (not necessarily a miraculous phenomenon) which he had seen with his own eyes. Then, having done this, he makes a solemn appeal in corroboration to the Lord Himself. On this view, the verse instead of suggesting a distinction between the author of the Gospel, and the eye-witness, supplies a strong confirmation of their identity.

CHAPTER III

THE RELATION OF HISTORY TO THEOLOGY

THE Gospel according to S. John was meant to be, and is, a touch of hearts. "These things", says the Evangelist, "are written that ye may believe that Jesus is the Christ, the Son of God, and that by believing ye may have life in His name". In other words, he confesses openly that he has written his history with a purpose. His years of discipleship had borne fruit for him in a new quality of life. He hopes that the record of what he has seen and heard will help others to share his experience.

He says the same thing even more clearly in the opening words of his First Epistle: "That which was from the beginning, that which we have heard, that which we have seen with our eyes, that which we beheld, and our hands handled, concerning the Word of life (and the life was manifested, and we have seen, and bear witness, and declare unto you the life, the eternal life, which was with the Father, and was manifested unto us); that which we have seen and heard declare we unto you also, that ye also may have fellowship with us: yea, and our fellowship is with the Father, and with His Son Jesus Christ: and these things we write, that our joy may be fulfilled" (1 Jn. 1 : 1-4).

The substance of his message, the story based on intimate personal experience, is not recorded in the letter. It had no doubt for long been the substance of his witness to his flock. But there were conditions which they on their part had to fulfil, if they were to share the fellowship with the Father and the Son which is the Eternal Life. So he has to take up his pen again after he had in the Gospel given them the materials from which the Creed in which they had been brought up could derive continuous inspiration, to warn them, on the one hand, against the lying spirits that would undermine their faith in the Incarnation, and on the other hand, against moral insensibility to the claims which their creed made on their surrender to the service of their fellows in righteousness and love.

It is very easy to be content with possessing the "form of godliness" in the Gospel, while in our lives we deny its power. It will be well, therefore, in all our study of S. John to keep clear before our minds his avowed object in writing. It is not easy for us to believe that such power can radiate from what looks like a merely formal confession of faith in a fact of history, or rather in a historical Person. But at least we may be sure that the Evangelist's purpose is to get us into and to keep us in touch with historical fact.

Robert Browning in *A Death in the Desert* pictures S. John facing the prospect of the world after his death:

> How will it be when none more saith 'I saw'?
>
> . . . . . .
>
> My book speaks on, because it cannot pass;
> One listens quietly, nor scoffs but pleads
> 'Here is a tale of things done ages since;
> What truth was ever told the second day?
> Wonders, that would prove doctrine, go for naught'.

In these words he sums up the difficulty with which we are all confronted when we try to recreate for ourselves the story of the past. All human tradition is fallible. There is in all of us a very strong tendency to mould our account of an incident or a series of incidents to provide evidence in support of a conclusion which, on other grounds, we wish to establish.

We have no reason, therefore, to be surprised at the prevalence in certain circles to-day of a conviction that a man who writes as a theologian by that very fact forfeits all credit as a writer of history. Indeed, it is put forward as self-evident, with no attempt at closer analysis or justification.

And yet the very fact that we continue to write history shews that we still believe that it is possible to recreate at least a reasonably reliable account of the facts of the past. So that we do not believe ourselves condemned to sheer agnosticism because all tradition must be misleading. And at the same time we are bound to recognize, if we are fair-minded, that while no doubt every observer has his own personal equation, bias is not always in one direction. The prejudices of a rationalist have to be allowed for with no less scrupulous care than the prejudices of a traditionalist. The axiom that would rule out the evidence of a theologian to a fact of history is only valid for those who assume either that there is no God, or that if in any sense He can be supposed to exist, it is incredible that He should make His presence felt objectively in the universe of our experience. All that we can, in fairness, ask of any witness is that he should let us know his position on the points at issue, that we may make the necessary allowances.

On this point S. John is, as we have seen, perfectly frank. Of course, if you assume that no human experience can have any theological implications, you cannot regard a book produced under these conditions as historical. You must either reject the theological implication, or maintain that the intuition created for itself an imaginative embodiment, which has been misread as an actual experience. In this case, however, you have to remember that the book itself was written to maintain the exact opposite of your fundamental assumption. It is written in the conviction that all human experience is full of theological implications, and to put into our hands the means of verifying the truth of that conviction for ourselves. S. John was convinced, on the strength of his own experience, that vitalizing power can radiate into human life from a fact in history, and from a historical person. His appeal is from experience to experience, and the appeal cannot be foreclosed by *a priori* considerations.

If man was really, as the Bible says, made in the image of God to shew forth His likeness, is it not natural to believe that all nature is sacramental? and that in the fulness of time a man should have appeared who could say with truth: "He that hath seen me hath seen the Father"?

That, at least, is what S. John believed. And his whole Gospel is his answer to the suggestion that this phenomenon could be sufficiently accounted for as the result of a superficial and temporary alliance between the human and the divine.

As he had reason to believe that the union between God and Man in Christ had not been destroyed by death, so he found reason to believe that that union had not first begun when the child Jesus was born at Bethlehem.

God had, no doubt, in time past, spoken again and again to His people through the prophets, as the Epistle to the Hebrews says "in divers portions and in divers manners". But Jesus was, somehow, in a different class from them. They were the servants of the Lord of the Vineyard. He was His Son, His well beloved. The Word of the Lord had come to them. With this presupposition we can pass to the study of the Prologue in which S. John defines what he means when he says that in Him the Word became flesh.

CHAPTER IV

THE PROLOGUE

1 *In the beginning was the Word, and the Word was with God, and*
2 *the Word was God. The same was in the beginning with God.*

WE come now to consider the opening verses of the Gospel that S. John wrote "in order", as he says, "that he might establish his fellow-Christians in the faith that Jesus was the Christ, the Son of God, and that by believing they might have life in His name" (20: 31).

In the beginning was the Word. And the Word was in communion with God. And the Word was, in His inmost being, one with God.

In order that we may understand the story that he has to tell, John finds it necessary to go back, as the Book of Genesis does in its account of creation, to the very beginning, and indeed beyond it. For he tells of a communion between God and One whom he calls the *Logos* (or the Word), who was already in communion with God before the world was made.

Unfortunately for us the Greek term *Logos* cannot be precisely rendered in English, because it has in Greek two distinct meanings. It can connote either the faculty of reason, by which we apprehend truth, or the language with which we clothe our vision of the truth in the effort to clear our own thinking and to communicate what we think we have seen to one another.

The term *Logos* had a recognized place in Greek philosophy in the first of these two senses. And the Christian thinkers in the earliest times, who came to the study of S. John's Gospel after a training in Greek philosophy, took it for granted that S. John used the word in its philosophical sense.

And modern scholars have for the most part followed their example. In consequence they assume that the Gospel must have been written primarily to commend the Christian faith to Greek seekers after truth.

This, however, is not really in harmony either with the content of the Gospel or with the earliest traditions with regard to its origin. And though no doubt an Alexandrian Jew, Philo, in the first half of the first century, used the term freely in his effort to commend the religion of the Jews to Greek thinkers, it is generally admitted that he would have repudiated the suggestion that the *Logos* that he had in mind could ever have been made flesh.

The *Logos* as Reason does not lead us to look for an incarnation.

We must also remember that S. John was, like S. Paul, a Hebrew of Hebrews. But he had been born and bred in Palestine. His outlook was not metaphysical. He had no more interest in abstract speculation than any of the prophets of the Old Testament. His concern is with the problems of human life and duty; and primarily with the relations between man and God and the conditions of intercourse between them. He wrote, indeed, in Greek, but it seems to be becoming increasingly clear that he thought, as no doubt Jesus had for the most part spoken, in Aramaic.

Now the Jews in Palestine had developed a doctrine of a relation between God and the world on lines of their own. They shrank, indeed, from supposing that God could come directly into contact with the world or with men. But they believed that one whom they called His Word was His intermediary. This "Word", or *Memra*, they found revealed expressly in many Old Testament passages, and even when He was not mentioned by name they introduced references to Him freely in their vernacular paraphrases of the Hebrew Scriptures.[1]

For a Palestinian like S. John, therefore, the thoughts connected with "the Word", which he had to call *Logos* when he wrote in Greek, would not be those which corres-

[1] See Burney, *The Aramaic Origin of the Fourth Gospel*, p. 38.

pond to Reason. It would suggest the thought of language as the means by which communion is made possible between a man and his fellows. Language is essentially utterance or outward expression. And however it may be with the thought of the *Logos* regarded as the divine Reason, the thought of the *Logos* as the faculty of self-expression in language clearly has a close affinity with the thought of the Incarnation.

S. John, we know, believed that all the partial and preparatory revelations that God had given His people in time past through the prophets, when, as they themselves said, "The Word of the Lord" had come to them, had come to a focus in a perfect and final manifestation of Himself in One who stood to Him in the relation not of a servant, but of a Son. A most natural way of expressing this fact would clearly be to say that "the Word" had Himself appeared on earth as Man. S. Paul had made bold to say that God had been in Christ reconciling the world to Himself. S. John had become conscious that the inmost secret that his discipleship to Jesus Christ had revealed to him went deeper even than this mighty interposition in human history for our redemption. In the life of unbroken communion between the Father and the Son, which had been lived out before his eyes, he had not only been in touch with One in union with whom men could pass out of death into life: God had through Him, been revealing the true nature of His own Eternal Being. So he can make bold to say that the Word had taken flesh in Jesus Christ to reveal the inmost secrets of the life of God to man.

The vision of life that Jesus had brought to S. John was in strange contrast to the life of aweful, if splendid isolation which men are accustomed to regard it as a mark of piety to attribute to "Him that sitteth on the throne of the universe", without a suspicion that in so doing they are worshipping an image of the essential selfishness that is the enemy of us all.

Life is no true life in isolation. There can be no life but in communion. And this remains true in the highest region of all. That is why nothing short of the communion of the

Father and the Son lived out before the eyes of men under our conditions could suffice for a revelation of the divine rooting of all life in love. And the point in which I think S. John adds the crowning touch to the teaching which he had inherited, lies in his declaration that there existed from all eternity within the Divine Being a provision which in the fulness of time would make that final revelation possible. For this revelation depended on the fact that the relation between God and His Word implied, even in the Godhead, an interpenetration of personalities in the unity of a perfect communion.

Let us listen once more to the words which he puts in the forefront as embodying the conviction which was at once the postulate and the fruit of his experience.

In the beginning was the Word. And the Word was in communion with God, and the Word was, in His inmost being, one with God.

THE WORD AS LIFE AND LIGHT

S. John passes on to describe the relation in which the creation, of which we are part, stands to that same Word.

3 *All things were made by him; and without him was not anything*
4 *made. That which hath been made was life in him; and the life was*
5 *the light of men. And the light shineth in the darkness; and the darkness overcame it not.*

Every part of that creation, he declares, came into being in obedience to the will of God, through the operation of the Word, and no single thing came into being that was not in living touch with Him.

This view of creation underlies the religious thinking of Israel: "By the word of the Lord", the Psalmist declared, "were the heavens made". "The heavens declare the glory of God, and the firmament showeth His handiwork". It was in the power of this sacramental view of nature that the prophet of the exile poured scorn on the idol-makers and the idol-worshippers in Babylon. Jesus Himself would have us trace the beauty of the flowers of the field to its source in the immediate operation of God.

From this point of view, we may note in passing, that if the source and constant strength and stay of the universe is to be sought in the living God, we cannot be content to regard that universe as a mere machine. The fact, that owing to its constant submission to law it seems to be dead, can only be due, as James Hinton taught years ago in a remarkable book called *Man and His Dwelling Place*, to a defect in us. The deadness which we impute to nature is really in ourselves. "I can see", he wrote, "in all nature nothing but the loving acts of spiritual beings".

This may seem fanciful, but I cannot think that it is alien to the profound thought of S. John. For he goes on, according to what seems to be the oldest text and punctuation: *That which hath come into being in Him was Life, and the Life was the Light of men.*

These words have been interpreted in very different ways. "That which hath come into being" is generally taken to refer to particular elements in the creation. The creation as a whole is regarded as having been represented in the preceding verse as "all one act at once": and then as progressively brought into being bit by bit—each element as it appears, being traced back to its source in a fountain of Life that pre-existed in the Word. This view is expressed with singular force and freshness by Dr. Hort, who, we must remember, had been trained in natural science as well as in theology (*Hulsean Lectures*, p. 144): "Of the Word, who was in the beginning with GOD and was God, S. John says, with reference to the initial and perpetual coming of all things into being through him, that in Him was Life, and the Life was the Light of men. What He specially was as the Light to men, as beings endowed with the power of knowing truth, had its source, so to speak, in what He was as the Life, not of them only, but of all finite things. That which gave to all things whatever they had of form and order and unity and motion and function was their life, and that life was but the multitudinous efflux of Him, the Life. This designation best expressed the most comprehensive relation in which He stood to the universe who is the Word of GOD, the eternal fundamental utterance of HIM whose diffracted and remoter utterance is the universe".

This is certainly an illuminating exposition of one side of S. John's thought. But the paraphrase is clearly based on what I cannot help regarding as the less probable punctuation. I cannot get away from the conviction that a strong contrast is intended between that which came into being *through* the Word, and that which hath come into being *in* Him. Nor do I see that the difference in tense between that which *came* into being and that which *has come* into being strictly justifies the contrast between the initial and the perpetual coming of things into being. The first thought is that creation as a whole came into being through the Word acting upon it as it were from without. Then S. John, I think after a pause, proceeds to call attention to something which has come into being, and has from the beginning been an abiding reality, "in Him". It is this which he calls life and declares to have been the light of men.

One side of the thought is, no doubt, as Dr. Hort suggests, that the Word was not an impersonal instrument in the work of creation, but took His share in it, by virtue of the life that was in Him. S. John's words, as I understand them, imply further that this capacity for taking a share of His own in the work of creation was itself generated within the Word, "came into being in Him" as the result of His own inner response to the will of the Creator.

We are expressly told in the Gospel (5: 26) that the possession of "life in Himself" was a special gift from the Father to the Son. The condition for the reception of that gift is no doubt to be found in the perfect surrender on the part of the Son of His own will to the will of the Father. And the share that He was called to take in the work of creation may well have been a no less searching test of the reality of that surrender than the share that He was called to take in the work of redemption.[1]

[1] cf. George Macdonald *Unspoken Sermons*, Series III, Ch. 1.

THE LIFE AS THE LIGHT OF MEN

In the opening words of his First Epistle, S. John tells us that the eternal life of which the Christian finds himself a partaker through the Gospel had its roots in the hidden depths from the beginning. There is nothing, therefore, surprising in the fact that he should go on here to point out that the Word, as the source and spring of that life, was the light which has enabled men in every age and in all parts of the world to see the path marked out for them by the will of God. But the reference to the light brings us directly into contact with its dread opposite. In the next verse he strikes a tragic note, breaking into the harmony of the provision so made for communion between God and man. He goes on:

The Light shineth in the darkness and the darkness overcame it not (or *failed to understand it*).

It is strange that the first result of the presence of the Light should be to make us conscious of the reality and the extent of the dominion of darkness. But after all there is comfort in the thought. Darkness is in the last resort only the shadow cast by light. It is only by virtue of the presence of the light that we can become conscious of the existence of darkness. The darkness again and again threatens us with forces that seem irresistible. But the light goes on shining. The issue was tried out on Calvary—and the darkness could not overwhelm it.

We may even take comfort from the fact that matter ceases to cast a shadow when it becomes a translucent gem. The walls of the new Jerusalem are built of jewels, and there is no night there. When our nature has been "recreated out of distraction into the unity of a perfect crystal", we shall see God.

THE WITNESS OF THE BAPTIST TO THE LIGHT

6 *There came a man, sent from God, whose name was John. The*
7 *same came for witness, that he might bear witness of the light, that*
8 *all might believe through him. He was not the light, but* came *that he might bear witness of the light.*

Up to the end of verse 5 S. John's thoughts have been expatiating over an unlimited field alike in space and time. It was only the tense of the last verb that suggested that the darkness had on one specific occasion failed in an effort to overwhelm the Light. It is, therefore, not a little startling to find ourselves in the next verses brought down to earth, with our attention fixed on a single definite historic personality.

There came into being a man sent with a commission from God (his name was John); he came for witness, that he might bear witness concerning the Light, that all men might believe through him. He was not himself the Light, but came to bear witness concerning the Light.

This reference has been regarded, quite unnecessarily, as an interpolation. The avowed object of the Gospel is to give Christians the evidence, based on personal experience, that had led the apostles to believe that Jesus was the Christ, the Son of God, and to find in that faith a spring of eternal life. The object of the Prologue is to shew what S. John, after years of meditation on that experience, had learnt with regard to the eternal invisible background out of which the revelation had come. But his whole story is based on the interaction of the eternal *and the temporal*. And he has to choose a point in time from which to start his reminiscences of the founding of the new order. It was natural for him to begin at the moment of his own first introduction to it. But there is more than the affectionate loyalty of an old disciple involved in the special office that he assigns to the Baptist.

The apostolic teaching had from an early date marked the preaching of the Baptist as the beginning of the Gospel of Jesus Christ (Mk. 1: 1, cf. Ac. 10: 37; 13: 24). The opening words of *Ecce Homo* call our attention to a fact, which we are very apt to overlook: "The Christian Church sprang from a movement, which was not begun by Christ".

Profoundly significant and vital in its appeal as is the story of the manger-cradle at Bethlehem, we shall do well to remember that in the providence of God a veil was deliberately drawn over that incident in the life of Jesus when the time came for Him to make His public appeal to the allegiance of His people. A little reflexion will enable us to realize the necessity for that reticence. It ought at the same time to set us to work thinking out the significance of the method that God did ordain for His shewing to Israel.

The work of the Baptist, as defined by the angel (Lk. 1 : 17) was "to make ready for the Lord a people prepared for Him". But this was only one side of the task that was committed to him. When the call came to him to preach his baptism of repentance, it was, as he himself tells us (Jn. 1 : 33), made known to him that that same baptism would be the means of manifesting the "Mightier than he" who would perfect the work that he had begun, by baptizing with the Holy Spirit. His own baptism would have its part to play, not only in preparing the hearts of the people, but also in providing a searching test of the fitness of the Messiah for the task which He was being called to undertake, and an occasion when He could be publicly and officially commissioned by God to undertake it.

We must not spend time on considering the way in which the call to be baptized tested the fitness of Jesus for the work assigned to Him. Our immediate interest is with the part that the Baptist had to play. There was a widespread conviction that the Messiah, when He came, would remain unknown until Elijah had appeared to declare Him; and though, when challenged, the Baptist refused to take the title of Elijah to himself, Jesus expressly gave it to him, declaring that in him the old-world order of prophets had reached its culmination.

It was of the greatest importance that the claim that Jesus had to put forward to divine appointment should not rest on His own unsupported assertion. But when the fact to be attested was an act or word of God, the witness must himself be spiritually qualified. S. John throughout his Gospel lays special stress on the witness and the qualifications of the Baptist. There is nothing, therefore, surprising in the fact that he should regard the commission given to John as the starting-point of the new order. It is possible that there may have been in certain quarters a tendency to lay too much stress on the work of the Baptist, which S. John has to counteract, and he therefore distinctly subordinates him. But there can be no doubt that the main interest of the Evangelist here is to stress the importance of his testimony as an indispensable element in the foundation of our faith.

THE TRUE LIGHT

9 *There was the true light*, even the light *which lighteth every* 10 *man, coming into the world. He was in the world, and the world* 11 *was made by him, and the world knew him not. He came unto his* 12 *own, and they that were his own received him not. But as many as received him, to them gave he the right to become the children of* 13 *God*, even *to them that believe on his name: which were born, not of blood, nor of the will of the flesh, nor of the will of man, but of God.*

After this interlude S. John brings us back from the witness to the Light to consider the Light itself in its relation to the world and to individual men. The Light itself is called "the true Light" in contrast to the light, which was in comparison contingent and transitory, that shone out in John, who is described in 5: 35 as a lamp that had to be kindled before it could give light. We as men are all directly in touch with this true Light. It has from the beginning been increasingly making its influence felt in the world, the human society of which we are parts.

The Word as Light was all the while present in the society, the inner secret of its coherence and capacity for order, and yet public opinion, the corporate consciousness, failed to acknowledge Him. He had made His home in a specially chosen race. He came into their midst, and they who were His own rejected Him. This rejection was indeed not complete. There were some "who received Him". To all of them He gave power to live as children of God. They were those who were prepared to take the revelation that He brings as the law of their life, and who in the power of it "are begotten, not of blood nor of the will of the flesh, nor of the will of a man, but of God".

The fundamental thought here is of a vital, organic connexion between the Word as Light and every man by virtue of his humanity. The Light has power to recreate all who surrender themselves to its guidance. This thought came home to the heart of George Fox, and was the basis of his doctrine of the inner light. The most illuminating account of that doctrine that I know is contained in the first volume of F. D. Maurice's *Letters to a Quaker*, p. 13 ff.[1] He writes in answer to those who would try to explain away Fox's discovery by saying that he only means the natural conscience:

"Would it not be far more correct to say that the conscience means this, and that the facts of conscience can be explained on no other principle? Would it not be far more right to say, that precisely that which does awaken all thoughts, and reflections, and remorse in men whatever, and has its seat in what he rightly calls his conscience, does arise from the presence of this divine Word, and is the consciousness of that presence and of His right to command us?"

He goes on to point out that: "It is this feeling of a twofold life in man—of a struggle upwards and a tendency downwards, a stretching after a yet unseen and unmanifested friend of man, who seemed to be upholding him against the enemies who were continually striving to overwhelm him, against his own nature, against the world around him, which has in every age given an interest to the philosophy, and even to the mythology of the old world".

And again, speaking of the prophets of Israel: "To what end was the training of these holy men, by so many secret processes, and by such sore discipline; but to know Him as the secret Lord of their hearts,—to hold fellowship with Him by day and by night,—to recognize Him as the King of their nation, who directed all its plans according to justice and truth; to declare Him to their countrymen, as the Lord to whom they must submit their hearts, if they would not sink into slavery to their evil natures, and to the world around them;—the Lord, who by judgements and invitations was

[1] The book was afterwards recast and expanded, and is accessible as *The Kingdom of Christ* in the Everyman Library. The reference is to the original edition.

leading them away from the idols of sense, to seek Him and to find Him".

This revelation was made no doubt to members of the chosen race—but that is not inconsistent with the belief that this Word is in touch with all men, because, as Maurice points out, the promise to Abraham was "that in him and in his seed should all the nations of the earth be blessed". And it was not till the unseen Word began to reveal himself to his servants the prophets that the hope of the fulfilment of this promise began to dawn upon the Jew. But "then, when they began to feel their own real connexion with this Being, they did feel the possibility of all nations being brought into the covenant; then they were able, though dimly, to anticipate the manifestation of this great Lord of their nation, as the King who should reign over the Gentiles, and in whom the Gentiles should trust. They felt that their Lord was the Lord of man; and that, as such, He would be revealed".

This truth is not indeed to be regarded with George Fox as the characteristic message of Christianity. But the recognition of it is essential, if we are to win to the heart of our creed. S. John, as we see, here lays it down as a foundation on which to build up faith in the Incarnation. If he is right, it is clear that deeper mysteries are involved in the possession of a conscience than we generally recognize. It may help us, when we try to think them out, to remember that there are always two factors involved in every act of hearing. The conscience is on the one side the voice of God. But on the other it is a spiritual ear. And what message gets across depends on our spiritual sensitiveness and on our power of interpretation. Our experience of broadcasting should help us to understand how important for true reception is the condition of our instrument and the accuracy of our tuning in.

Life cannot be quite the same again for any one of us when once we realize that the voice, which we each hear in our own hearts, bearing witness to the will of God for us, and the claims of all our brothers and sisters upon us, is none other than the voice of the Word who was with God and was

God. It opens up the prospect of a new quality of life for us.

At the same time we must not shut our eyes to the fact that in order to enter fully on His office as mediator between God and man, the Word who was God had to reveal Himself as being at the same time truly Man. We cannot, therefore, evade the question: If in the case of all other men, the Word is the witness of the will of God, what are we to say of the Word that witnessed to the will of God in the human consciousness of the Word made flesh?

It is difficult to inquire wisely concerning this. There is a strange and apparently inevitable duality in the phenomena of self-consciousness—as evidenced, for instance, in S. Paul's declaration: "I know nothing against myself" in 1 Cor. 4: 4. And yet it seems as if the Word made flesh must have stood in an unique relation to the will of God. He must in some sense have known directly that which all the other members of the race, of which He is the Head, know through Him.

This should at least prepare us for utterances like 5: 30 "as I hear I judge", 8: 26 "What I heard from Him I speak to the world", and 8: 55 "I keep His word". If this be true we can see why He should teach us to see in His relation to the Father a perfect mirror of our relation to Himself (10: 14 f.).

There are two points in the interpretation of the section (verses 9–13), and one various reading, on which something should be said before we pass on.

In verse 9 the words "coming into the world" may qualify either, as I have supposed, the main subject of the sentence, *the Light*, or the man on whom the Light shines. It is difficult to see why the action of the Light on the man should be connected with the fact, and indeed the moment, of his coming into the world. It seems very much in place as suggesting a gradual dawning of the "dayspring from on high".

In verse 11 Dr. Hort was anxious to limit the reference to

the pre-incarnate activity of the Word. But as I understand S. John, he has already in verse 5 referred to the defeat of the darkness on the Cross, and it is difficult to see in what sense "faith in His name" was possible before Jesus had appeared in flesh.

It is also just worth notice that some very early authorities read the singular, "He who was begotten", instead of the plural in verse 13. If this reading is accepted, it would of course be a very explicit assertion of our Lord's birth from a virgin. But the phrase as a whole seems to be much better understood as an echo of the teaching on the second birth given to Nicodemus.

THE INCARNATION AND ITS EFFECT

14 *And the Word became flesh, and dwelt among us (and we beheld his glory, glory as of the only begotten from the Father), full of* 15 *grace and truth. John beareth witness of him, and crieth, saying, This was he of whom I said, He that cometh after me is become* 16 *before me: for he was before me. For of his fulness we all received* 17 *and grace for grace. For the law was given by Moses; grace and* 18 *truth came by Jesus Christ. No man hath seen God at any time; the only begotten Son, which is in the bosom of the Father, he hath declared* him.

The time has now come for the stupendous declaration in which the whole content of the Gospel is summed up:

The Word became flesh, and tabernacled among us, and we beheld His glory, glory as of an only begotten from a father, full of grace and truth.

In these words S. John asserts that the coming of the Light into the world came to a focus in a special incarnation: not merely in a physical body, but in human nature. That coming had been under the direct observation of witnesses (cf. 1 Jn. 1: 1–3). The first person plural does not recur till 21: 24 where the company confirms the testimony of the beloved disciple.

S. John's language is carefully chosen to remind us of the experience through which the people of God had been led when they came out of Egypt. S. Paul in 1 Cor. 10: 1–15 lays great stress on the typical character of that experience. Jesus, we may see, not only took the lessons that that experience had been meant to teach home to Himself when He met the tempter in the wilderness, but also claimed to be the reality of the gifts of God to men foreshadowed by the manna, the brazen serpent, and the pillar of cloud and fire (Jn. 3, 6, 8). This should help us to understand why S. John speaks of His life on earth as a tabernacling. The tabernacle was for Israel a visible token that God was dwelling in the midst of His people, and had set apart a special tent in which they could come to hold communion with Him. That is exactly the function that the body of our Lord, both before and after His crucifixion, is meant to fulfil. Jesus said expressly of His personal presence "greater than the Temple is here".

When on the Feast of Tabernacles (Jn. 8: 12) He claimed to be the Light of the world, He took to Himself the other symbol of God's presence with His people, the pillar of cloud and fire by which He had guided them in their wanderings. This is spoken of also as "the glory of the Lord". S. John's language here, therefore, when he says not only that the Word tabernacled among us, but that we beheld His glory, suggests not only that He had spread His tent among them, but that a radiance had gone forth from Him that suggested the presence of the symbol of divine guidance. He speaks of it as the glory of an only begotten from a father, full of grace and truth.

We must look more closely into the meaning of this vision of glory. When the Jews were speaking of that which constituted the inner being of God, they called it holiness. When they were speaking of the outer manifestation of His presence among them, or of His mind and character, they called it glory. So the seraphim in Isaiah's vision sang, "Holy, holy, holy is the Lord of Hosts—the fulness of the whole earth is His glory". And the Psalmist sang, "The heavens declare the glory of God, the firmament showeth His handiwork".

In close connexion with this is the word of our Lord in the Upper Chamber after Judas had gone out (13: 31), "Now is the Son of Man glorified and God is glorified in Him". The Cross here comes full in view, and Jesus declared that in and through it a manifestation would be given by which all the world for all time would be able to know what was in the inmost heart both of the Father and the Son in their relations to man.

Of this glory S. John says that it suggested the relation of an only begotten Son to his Father. It had nothing in it of self-seeking or display. It was the glory that came from complete subordination and subjection. He revealed the Father by the perfection of His obedience and at the same time helped men to realize the essential divinity of a life of Sonship.

In this relation the qualities of deepest significance for the life of man that found expression in His humanity were grace and truth. These are the counterparts in the highest region of human experience to the two qualities of life and light, which, as we have seen, characterized the Word in His relation to creation. In its simplest form grace is simply favour or loving-kindness. And in this connexion it connotes the power from God that comes into a man to overcome the deadness to which he has condemned himself by his sin, and to restore him to communion with God, when once he grasps the fact that God is on his side and not against him in his fight with sin. Truth is the ultimate reality and substance of the revelation of God, which otherwise we can only receive in type and symbol and shadow.

Before saying more about this grace and truth, S. John interjects another reference to the Baptist. This time he recalls the specific witness that the Baptist gave to the surpassing greatness of his successor, in answer to a challenge from an official deputation from Jerusalem: *John testifies of Him and has cried aloud saying—this is He that used the words—* (or *This is He whom I meant when I said*), *He that cometh after me has taken His place ahead of me because He was eternally my Chief.*

We must not spend time now on this testimony. It must be enough to notice that "He that cometh after me" cannot refer simply to relative priority in time. Jesus by accepting baptism at John's hands enrolled Himself as a disciple. "My First" may refer to an absolute priority in time, but it is possible to take it as "my Chief" (cf. Ac. 13: 50, Jn. 15: 18, Abbott's *Johannine Grammar*, 1900). But the protest on the part of the Baptist recorded in S. Matthew seems to suggest that he felt, even before the sign that followed the baptism, that there was a certain incongruity in the relation that Jesus was assuming towards him. And it is important to remember that the Baptist was, in the prophetic picture, expressly "the Forerunner". So that in his case "He that cometh after me" must connote "Him who is to be the object of my testimony" (cf. 1: 33).

After this parenthesis, S. John resumes the record of his own experience and that of the rest of the witnessing body. He had just, on the strength of the glory they had beheld, borne witness that Jesus was "full of grace and truth". He goes on: "For of His fulness did we all receive and grace for grace"—meaning either "a grace in us to match a grace in Him", or, I think more probably, "grace in exchange for grace": every gift that we receive at His hands becoming the ground and occasion of a fresh gift, the result being an inexhaustible stream of grace.

The Rabbis had a saying, "The reward of a proverb is a proverb". They taught in proverbs, and when a pupil had mastered one, it was a sign that he was ready to be challenged with another.

This experience calls attention to a fundamental distinction between the old dispensation and the new. The pride of the Jew centred in the Law which had been given him on tables of stone through Moses. It gave him an opportunity of acquiring merit by conforming to external regulations. But all its ordinances were only "shadows of the true". With the new order a new relation of free favour with God came flooding in. It implied an entry into the region of direct communion with the ultimate reality: grace and truth became part of the Christian inheritance, as the natural outflow of the life and light of the Word that were manifested in Jesus Christ.

The condition of this communion is to be found in the knowledge of God. So S. John sums up the teaching of his whole Prologue in this crowning declaration:

God as God no one has ever seen. One who is at once an only begotten Son and Himself one in nature with God, even He whose eternal home is in the bosom of the Father, hath declared Him.

It is important, as Archbishop Gregg has recently pointed out in a sermon before the University of Cambridge, to give full weight to this climax to which the Prologue leads us up. We are apt to regard the Prologue, and the Gospel story to which it forms the introduction, as primarily concerned with establishing faith in the Godhead of the Son. That is, no doubt, included in its purpose. But the dominant interest in the life that it portrays is the revelation of God the Father. Jesus Himself warns us expressly against supposing that He had come in His own name and not in His Father's. The eternal life which He came to bring is rooted in the knowledge of God. At the end of His ministry He resigns His work into His Father's hands in the words—"I glorified thee on the earth having accomplished the task which thou gavest me to do".

This then is the situation in which we find ourselves when the Gospel comes to us, and opens our eyes. On the one side we see that we have been living in darkness, blind and deaf to the spiritual world to which we belong, shut out from the vision of God and from communion with God, yet retaining in our conscience a rudimentary sensitiveness to spiritual influence, which may be the germ in every man for the development of an infinite capacity for knowing God.

On the other side there is the inexhaustible tenderness and faithfulness of God coming forth to help us into life and light, and striving to find a way to open our eyes and ears and create a means of communication by which He can speak to us and we can answer Him.

He does it by Himself entering into our nature, and living our life right through under our conditions, even the most testing, and so getting into direct touch with our hidden capacity for spiritual response: Himself showing at once what human life may be, if it is turned from self to God; and at the same time the infinite longing in the heart of God to draw us back to Himself.

CHAPTER V

THE FIRST WEEK OF THE MINISTRY

19 *And this is the witness of John, when the Jews sent unto him*
20 *from Jerusalem priests and Levites to ask him, Who art thou? And he confessed, and denied not; and he confessed, I am not the Christ.*
21 *And they asked him, What then? Art thou Elijah? And he saith,*
22 *I am not. Art thou the prophet? And he answered, No. They said therefore unto him, Who art thou? that we may give an*
23 *answer to them that sent us. What sayest thou of thyself? He said, I am the voice of one crying in the wilderness, Make straight*
24 *the way of the Lord, as said Isaiah the prophet. And they had*
25 *been sent from the Pharisees. And they asked him, and said unto him, Why then baptizest thou, if thou art not the Christ, neither*
26 *Elijah, neither the prophet? John answered them, saying, I baptize with water: in the midst of you standeth one whom ye know not,*
27 even *he that cometh after me, the latchet of whose shoe I am not*
28 *worthy to unloose. These things were done in Bethany, where John was baptizing.*

29 *On the morrow he seeth Jesus coming unto him, and saith, Behold, the Lamb of God, which taketh away the sin of the world!*
30 *This is he of whom I said, After me cometh a man which is become*
31 *before me: for he was before me. And I knew him not; but that he should be made manifest to Israel, for this cause came I baptizing*
32 *with water. And John bare witness, saying, I have beheld the Spirit descending as a dove out of heaven; and it abode upon him.*
33 *And I knew him not: but he that sent me to baptize with water, he said unto me, Upon whomsoever thou shalt see the Spirit descending, and abiding upon him, the same is he that baptizeth with the Holy*
34 *Spirit. And I have seen, and have borne witness that this is the Son of God.*

AT this point S. John begins his account of the witness of the Baptist. He takes for granted a general acquaintance with the current traditions of the birth and childhood of Jesus, and of the ministry of the Baptist up to and including the Baptism of our Lord. For a full understanding of the story we shall do well to think out what we can still recover from the material in our hands with regard to the waiting time at Nazareth, and to the causes which led Him to insist in spite of the reluctance of the Baptist on submitting Himself to the rite. We must not, however, embark on these studies here. Our immediate business is with the story as S. John tells it.

His narrative begins simply and directly with a diary, day by day, of a week that was of vital significance in the spiritual history both of the Evangelist and of the world. It is, I believe, a diary of the events of the first week of our Lord's public ministry. And it owes its preservation, under God, to the fact that it was also the first week of the Evangelist's discipleship.

It begins with an account of an official deputation from Jerusalem to the Baptist. In answer to their challenge John disclaimed any pretensions to be himself any of the messengers from God, for whom the religious leaders of the people were looking in accordance with the Messianic anticipations of the time. He was not the Christ. He was not the Prophet. He was not Elijah. The only account he could give of himself, which was not liable to fatal misconception, was that he was the "Voice" foretold in Is. 40 : 3. His function was to point inquirers away from himself to his transcendently mightier Successor, who was already in the midst of them.

These are the events of the first day. It is clear that the witness to Jesus contained in it implies that the deputation did not come till after the baptism. The appearance of Jesus Himself on the scene next day shows that the temptation in the wilderness was also over. We are not told whether the appearance of Jesus on this second day marked His arrival from the wilderness, or whether he had already had an opportunity of conferring with the Baptist over the events of the baptism and of the forty days.

In any case the second day is marked by a direct and specific witness of the Baptist to Jesus, pointing Him out to the nation as "The Lamb of God who takes away the sin of the world", and identifying Him with the Successor of whom he had spoken the day before. It seems reasonable, therefore, to suppose that some at least of the deputation from Jerusalem were present and heard this testimony. It was accompanied by a statement of the evidence of the sign from Heaven, the descent and the abiding of the Spirit upon Jesus, which was the ground of the Baptist's witness; by a declaration of the work that Jesus was to do, completing and substantiating the preparatory baptism with water by baptism with the Holy Spirit; and by the ascription to Him of the title "Son of God", which had been ascribed to Jesus by the Voice from Heaven, and already, as we learn from the other Gospels, had been the occasion of temptations which He had just overcome.

This public witness of the Baptist to Jesus is the outstanding event of the second day. We are not told of any impression produced by it on the official deputation. They seem to have shown no inclination to inquire further into a matter not expressly included in their commission. At the same time Jesus expressly alludes in Jn. 5: 32 to a witness from John, of which the authorities in Jerusalem had official cognisance: and, as we shall see, His whole relation to them and to the people is determined by the fact that they had received and disregarded a witness to the truth of His claim, given by a messenger whom in their hearts they knew to have been sent to them by God (6:27, 10:36). The important fact is that it was borne, and that among the disciples of the Baptist there was at least one who heard and was able in after times to bear record of his master's witness.

THE WITNESS OF THE DISCIPLES

35 *Again on the morrow John was standing, and two of his disciples:*
36 *and he looked upon Jesus as he walked, and saith, Behold the Lamb*
37 *of God! And the two disciples heard him speak, and they followed*
38 *Jesus. And Jesus turned, and beheld them following, and saith unto them, What seek ye? And they said unto him, Rabbi (which is*
39 *to say, being interpreted, Master), where abidest thou? He saith unto them, Come, and ye shall see. They came therefore and saw*

where he abode; and they abode with him that day: it was about
40 *the tenth hour. One of the two that heard John* speak, *and followed*
41 *him, was Andrew, Simon Peter's brother. He findeth first his own brother Simon, and saith unto him, We have found the Messiah*
42 *(which is, being interpreted, Christ). He brought him unto Jesus. Jesus looked upon him, and said, Thou art Simon the son of John: thou shalt be called Cephas (which is, by interpretation, Peter).*

43 *On the morrow he was minded to go forth into Galilee, and he*
44 *findeth Philip: and Jesus saith unto him, Follow me. Now Philip*
45 *was from Bethsaida, of the city of Andrew and Peter. Philip findeth Nathanael, and saith unto him, We have found him, of whom Moses in the law, and the prophets, did write, Jesus of*
46 *Nazareth, the son of Joseph. And Nathanael said unto him, Can any good thing come out of Nazareth? Philip saith unto him,*
47 *Come and see. Jesus saw Nathanael coming to him, and saith of*
48 *him, Behold an Israelite indeed, in whom is no guile! Nathanael saith unto him, Whence knowest thou me? Jesus answered and said unto him, Before Philip called thee, when thou wast under the fig tree,*
49 *I saw thee. Nathanael answered him, Rabbi, thou art the Son of*
50 *God; thou art King of Israel. Jesus answered and said unto him, Because I said unto thee, I saw thee underneath the fig tree, believest*
51 *thou? thou shalt see greater things than these. And he saith unto him, Verily, verily, I say unto you, Ye shall see the heaven opened, and the angels of God ascending and descending upon the Son of man.*

The witness on the third day is confined to the disciples of the Baptist. Once more Jesus appears on the scene, and once more John calls attention to Him as "The Lamb of God". He says nothing to explain the meaning of this strange title. If we assume that our Lord, like the other candidates for John's baptism, made a preliminary confession, it would, in His case, express His relation to the sin of the world; and to this relation the title evidently refers.

Its significance for a disciple of the Baptist would lie in the fact that it was closely connected with the consciousness of the burden of sin, which it was the object of the Baptist's preaching to awaken, and which, as he and his disciples knew, his baptism in water had of itself no power to remove. The title had this further advantage, that it stood remote from current Messianic anticipations, and, therefore, though no doubt obscure, was free from the danger of serious misconception.

The two disciples interpret this witness as a hint from their old master that the time had come for them to attach themselves to his Successor. At any rate they follow Jesus, and when He turns and, after fixing His eyes on them, challenges them to put into words the thought of their heart, they reply giving Him, perhaps half-mechanically, the title by which they were accustomed to address the Baptist (Jn. 3: 26) "Rabbi where dwellest thou?" He had been pointed out to them as "The Lamb of God". They had, no doubt, heard their master speak of Him the day before in terms of the deepest veneration. But there was nothing in their master's words to show what form His public activity would take. In calling Him "Rabbi"[1] they were simply transferring to Him the title they had been used to give to the Baptist, shewing that they expected Him in some undefined, but no doubt wonderful way, to complete the work which their first master had begun. They took it for granted that Jesus would, at least to this extent, work on the lines already familiar to them. He would have truths to communicate to those who were willing to associate themselves with Him. They were seeking admission to His school.

And they were right. He accepts the title and the relationship it implied, and offers them at once an opportunity of closer and more personal intercourse, the longing for which lay at the heart of their request. *Come*, He said, *and ye shall see. They came, therefore, and saw where He abides, and they abode with Him that day. It was about the tenth hour.*[2] So the third day has an importance in history, which it is difficult to overestimate. It marks the first step in the foundation of the Christian Church.

[1] "Rabbi" was not at that time, we may remember, an official title. If it had been, neither our Lord nor the Baptist would have a right to it. Neither of them had received a professional training. (Jn. 7: 15.)

[2] It is uncertain whether this means 10 a.m. or 4 p.m. I believe that Dr. Westcott is right in contending for the morning hour. If it was already afternoon, and the Jewish day had only two more hours to run, the Evangelist would hardly have used language which implies that the visit lasted a full day. See on 19: 14.

The first step was followed at once, on the same day or on the next, by a second. Each of the first pair of disciples had a brother. "One of the two, named Andrew, finds first his own brother Simon, and brings him to Jesus." The turn of the phrase "findeth first his own brother", suggests that Andrew found next the brother of his unnamed companion.

On the next day, the fourth or fifth of this opening week, Jesus takes the initiative and Himself calls Philip, a fellow-townsman of Andrew and Peter, to follow Him. Philip brings in Nathanael. And two days after Jesus and the little band of those who are now expressly called "His disciples", are present at a marriage-feast in Cana of Galilee.

Such is the introduction to the public ministry as it is sketched for us by the beloved disciple. Could anything be simpler or more natural, though in fact it is quite unlike anything that we should have anticipated? The old order passes into the new with the minimum of disturbance in the normal course of the national life. A man comes sent from God, and draws the people to his baptism; and trains disciples and bears his witness. The Mightier than he has nothing to mark Him out before the eyes of men beyond the testimony of the Baptist. He has a mighty rôle to fill. The fulfilment of age-long hopes was entrusted to Him, a task all the more difficult, because the form in which the hopes were current was confused and mistaken. He could not claim at first the name which was His by right for fear of encouraging fatal misconception. So He has first of all to develop the prophetic side of His office. In so doing it was natural that He should follow the example of John, and of Old Testament Prophets like Isaiah, and surround Himself with an inner circle of personal disciples.

The ground had been already prepared. Those who were looking for the redemption of Jerusalem had been called together by the Baptist, and had been studying afresh the sacred pages of Moses and the Prophets for light on the counsels of God. The preaching of repentance had awakened a sense of need and expectancy. There were men ready at a hint from the Baptist to gather round the new Teacher. The nature of their hopes is indicated in the words which sum up their first impressions. "We have found the Messiah". "We have found Him of whom Moses in the Law and the Prophets did write". "Rabbi, Thou art the Son of God, Thou art the King of Israel." They were far as yet from understanding the full meaning of their words. The confession had not the significance of Simon Peter's confession at Cæsarea Philippi (Mt. 16: 16). The important point was that they were prepared to go to school with "The Messiah", "The Son of God", and "King of Israel".

Jesus Himself at this stage makes no comment on their use of these titles. Only in His answer to Nathanael He substitutes for all of them the title "Son of Man", which was, till the end of His ministry, what we may call His own official designation of Himself. His self-revelation was to be in act and life rather than in a generally accepted name, and in revealing Himself He was revealing the Kingdom.

From the point of view of self-revelation the outstanding features of this narrative are two, one inherent in the method adopted, the other brought into manifestation by His words to Simon and Nathanael.

Let us take first the revelation inherent in the method adopted. He is willing to be recognized at first simply as a Teacher. He is determined to work on men, heart on heart, from within. The faith that He is seeking for cannot result from any form of external compulsion. No one, indeed, as He knows, can come to Him without the drawing of the Father (Jn. 6: 44). So He is content to wait the Father's time for fuller revelation. Meanwhile, it is His business to welcome all that come to Him: and to accept and guard and train them as a trust from His Father (Jn. 17: 6).

Let us pass on now to the more purely personal revelation involved in the words addressed to Simon and Nathanael. In the first case I believe that the new name which Jesus gave to Simon was a pledge and a prophecy of what he would become, standing out in somewhat startling contrast to his natural disposition. Simon, when he first came to

Jesus, and for long after, must have been known by his friends as impulsive and enthusiastic, anything rather than a man of rock-like consistency.

The treatment of Nathanael strikes me as different. He was at the time rising superior to the cramping force of local prejudice. The man from Cana (21: 2), brought up to despise the neighbouring village of Nazareth, was prepared at least to come and test for himself the claim put forward by Philip on behalf of Jesus. His designation as an "Israelite indeed in whom is no guile" (Israel with the Jacob in him purged out) strikes home. He would not have dared to regard it as a true description of himself at the moment: but it so directly expressed the inmost longing of his heart, (a longing, we may well believe, which had just been awakened as the result of a spiritual wrestling in prayer under the fig-tree), that he was startled. He knows he is in the presence of one who can read his thoughts. He is bound to ask: "Whence knowest thou me?" And he gets his answer in a form which at once removes all hesitation. One who knew what the solitary crisis under the fig-tree had meant for him, could be none other than "The Son of God, the King of Israel".

In each of these cases the power which Jesus displays is a power to read the heart similar in kind to that recorded of Elisha in regard to Gehazi (cf. Lk. 7: 39). It is a revelation, I imagine, of the highest power of spiritual insight of which human nature is capable when fully possessed by the Spirit of God. There are more wonderful revelations to follow: "Thou shalt see greater things than these". "Ye shall see the heavens opened and the angels of God ascending and descending on the Son of Man".

Jacob at Bethel had had a vision of a ladder set up on earth which reached to heaven, and of angels ascending and descending on it ministering to the intercourse between man below and God above. Jesus Himself had seen the heavens opened at His baptism, and was living in the conscious communion with His Father, which that vision symbolized. The time would come, after His ascension, when the same communion might become an abiding reality to all His disciples. To open the kingdom of heaven to all believers was a greater thing even than the power to read their hearts.

THE SON OF MAN

We saw above that Jesus in answer to Nathanael's confession of faith in Him as "Son of God" and "King of Israel", substitutes the title "Son of Man" for these titles. On Nathanael's lips they were no doubt connected with his hope that Jesus had come to fulfil the promises of God given through Moses and the Prophets, and that He was the Christ whom His people were expecting to set them free from their enemies and to bring all their rivals into subjection.

There was an element of truth in Nathanael's confession. And he was clearly prepared to leave his Master free to choose His own way of asserting His divine Sonship and His sovereignty. Jesus was able, therefore, to develop the truth in it from within, without directly challenging any misconceptions that may have been mixed up with it.

It sprang from the conviction that he was in the presence of One whose sovereignty over him was based, not on anything outward or adventitious, but on His power to read the inmost secrets of the heart. Experience alone could shew what the promised visions of angels ascending and descending might mean: but they clearly must belong to the same spiritual sphere as Nathanael's original conviction. If we remember this, we shall not be surprised that our Lord's first allusion to Himself as Son of Man should remind us of Jacob's ladder, with its foot based on the solid earth, but with the top of it reaching to heaven.

This title, Son of Man, that Jesus chose for Himself calls for very careful examination. It clearly was not one in popular use at the time, and was no doubt in part chosen for that reason. It was free from disturbing associations. Etymologically it is singularly colourless, and especially when we retranslate it into its original Aramaic form, it need not mean more than "a man" pure and simple. On the lips of Jesus, however, it clearly had a specific meaning, which is intimately bound up with His whole conception of His Person and work. What that meaning was can only be determined by examining the Old Testament background of the expression, and the different connexions in which Jesus uses it.

The culminating example comes in His trial before the Sanhedrim. There, in answer to the specific challenge of the High Priest, "Art Thou the Christ, the Son of the Blessed?" He says, "I am, and ye shall see the Son of Man sitting at the right hand of the Power and coming with the clouds of heaven" (Mk. 14: 62). There can be no doubt that this confession was meant to recall the vision recorded in Dan. 7.

Of the other instances in which S. Mark records the use of the phrase, one (13: 26) is certainly based on Daniel, and so probably is 8: 38. On eight other occasions it occurs in prophecies of His approaching death and resurrection, including (10: 45) the declaration of the atoning character of His death. In Mk. 2: 10 Jesus declares that "the Son of Man has authority on earth to forgive sins," and in 2: 28 that "the Son of Man is Lord even of the Sabbath" because the Sabbath was made for man.

The title is found in a few passages in S. Matthew and S. Luke which have no parallels in S. Mark: but we need not call attention to any of these, except perhaps to the passage in which Jesus says that "the Son of Man has not where to lay His head", and the passage in which the Son of Man is criticized by the common people as "a gluttonous man and a wine-bibber", because He came eating and drinking like other men.

In these passages the main stress is no doubt laid on the regal and judicial authority with which the Son of Man would be invested by His triumph over death. But there is strong insistence on the suffering and humiliation through which He had to pass on the way. It is, I think, only in connexion with the power to forgive sins on earth, and with His lordship even over the Sabbath, that stress is laid in S. Mark on the fact of His humanity as a qualification for the office that He is called to fulfil.

When we come to S. John, it will be worth while to review the whole series. After its use in the answer to Nathanael, it occurs first in the conversation with Nicodemus (3: 13), "No one hath ascended into heaven, but He that descended out of heaven, the Son of Man".

Then in 3: 14, "As Moses lifted up the serpent in the wilderness, even so must the Son of Man be lifted up, that every one who believeth may in Him have eternal life".

With this we may take 8: 28, "When ye have lifted up the Son of Man, then shall ye know that I am he". And 12: 32, "I, if I be lifted up out of the earth will draw all men unto myself", which leads on to 12: 34, "How sayest thou the Son of Man must be lifted up? Who is this Son of Man?"

In connexion with this (for in each case the reference is to the fruit of the approaching Passion), we may take 12: 23, "The hour is come that the Son of Man should be glorified", and 13; 31, "Now is the Son of Man glorified and God is glorified in Him".

We have besides the one passage in which Jesus directly challenges a confession of faith in Himself as "the Son of Man", 9: 35, "Dost thou believe on the Son of Man?" and meets the question "And who is he, Lord, that I may believe on Him?" by saying, "Thou hast both seen him, and he it is that speaketh with thee".

There remain three instances in Chapter 6:

"Work not for the meat that perisheth, but for the meat which abideth unto eternal life, which the Son of Man shall give unto you; for Him hath the Father, *even* God, sealed" (6: 27);

"Except ye eat the flesh of the Son of Man and drink His blood, ye have not life in yourselves" (6: 53);

"What then if ye should behold the Son of Man ascending where He was before?" (6: 62).

In S. John, as in the Synoptists, the use of the title is only found in words attributed to the Lord Himself.

There is indeed no direct mention of shame or suffering, but that is only because for S. John the shame of the Cross has been swallowed up by its glory.

Without using the title he connects the function of judgement with the Son because He is a son of man (5 : 22).

In Chapter 6 His capacity for supplying men with the food of eternal life comes from the fact that His humanity is clothed as ours is in flesh and blood. It is remarkable that on three different occasions (1 : 51; 3 : 13; 6 : 62) stress is laid on the fact that His true home as Son of Man is all the time in heaven.

It is clear that if we would understand our Lord's use of the title, we must look closely into the significance of the vision as it is recorded for us in Daniel. The subject of the vision is a succession of kingdoms on earth rising out of the sea, represented in animal forms, leading up to a kingdom in human form which is revealed from heaven. It does not contain the title "Son of Man". It describes a figure "like a son of man". It is a prophecy of the coming Messianic Kingdom rather than of a personal Messiah.

At an early period, however, in the *Similitudes of Enoch*, the title "The Son of Man", which is clearly derived from Daniel, is ascribed to the Messiah who is regarded as already existent in heaven waiting the time of His manifestation.

Jesus in Jn. 15 identifies Himself, under the similitude of the True Vine, with the people of God as a living whole, of which each of His disciples is a branch. He is Himself the source and spring and the ultimately determining factor in the development of the whole organism, over which His Father is watching.

The same thought appears in S. Paul under the similitude of a human body. We are all "one man in Christ Jesus" (Gal. 3 : 28).

"As the body is one, and hath many members, but all the members of the body, many as they are, constitute but a single body, so also is the Christ" (1 Cor. 12 : 12).

And with a natural variation (Eph. 1 : 22) "He gave Him to be Head over all things to the Church, which is His body".

And S. Paul regards all Christians as having in some sense

been chosen in Him before the foundation of the world (Eph. 1 : 4).

It will be worth while to put by the side of this intuition of the solidarity of the human race the exposition of Ps. 8 in Heb. 2. For that Psalm also has its place in the Old Testament background of the thought of the Son of Man. The author of the Epistle calls attention to the completeness of the sovereignty with which man is endowed by divine appointment. And while he has to admit that mankind has not yet entered into the fulness of its inheritance, he calls attention to the beginning that has already been made towards its complete attainment by the triumph of Jesus through the suffering of death.

If we may trust the vision that these hints open out to us, we must regard mankind as, from the foundation of the world, designed in Christ to be the goal and crown of this creation, at once the perfect image and the vice-gerent of God. If so, we can see how the Christ when He came in our flesh could manifest the Image after which we were one and all created, and lay the foundation of the Kingdom which in the end must cover the whole world. It may also give much needed help in approaching those fundamental problems which are presented for our consideration by the Person of Jesus Christ, and which each generation seems to have to face afresh for itself.

One result of more than a century of intensive study of the Gospels has been the recovery of faith in the true humanity of Jesus, and though there are welcome signs of a revival of faith in His true divinity, which has for a time been under a cloud—or rather because of that revival—we find that there are depths in that humanity which we have still to explore before we can apprehend even dimly what S. John meant when he said that "the Word became flesh". For indeed we have been far too ready to take for granted that while the being of God was of course inscrutable, at least we knew all about the personality of man, and must rigidly confine our thought of Jesus within what we assume to be the limits of our own nature.

It is clearly not enough to say that Jesus was a man in all points exactly like ourselves, even if we grant the one exception of His sinlessness. No two of us are exactly alike. So we must go on to ask what was distinctive in His individuality? In what respect is our relation to Him different from our relation to any other member of our race?

For an answer to that question, we shall do well to see what S. Paul found his relation to Jesus to be in his own experience. "I live", he writes (Gal. 2: 20) "yet no longer I, Christ lives in me". He had found in union with Christ, the risen Jesus, the secret of an unified personality. He maintained that what was true for him, would be found to be true for every man.

The same experience was no doubt at the back of his declaration that Christ was the Head of His body the Church. He taught that every member of that body has his place and function defined by its relation to Him. And that—because the Church is designed in the end to include all mankind—must mean that Christ is in this sense the true Head of the whole human race.

It is clear, therefore, that one whom S. Paul in another place (1 Tim. 2: 5) describes as the Mediator between God and man, because He was Himself Man, cannot have been an ordinary individual. He must at least have been in more intimate relation to God than the rest of His brethren.

It has, of course, been suggested that in these speculations S. Paul was corrupting the simplicity of the original Gospel. But there is no evidence that in this respect his teaching roused any protest from those who were in Christ before him. And after nineteen centuries men of every race still find in Jesus Christ the highest embodiment of the human ideal, and find for themselves the secret of an unified personality in devotion to His service.

It is strange that S. Paul should make no allusion to the title "Son of Man" in this or in any connexion. Indeed neither he nor any of the writers of the New Testament, except the author of the Apocalypse, refer to the vision of Dan. 7. At the same time, S. Paul's vision of the Church in its corporate unity as "the Christ" (1 Cor. 12: 12), and of all its members as united to one another by their common allegiance to their Head, who bears the name Christ *par excellence*, shews how naturally the title "the Son of Man" might be ascribed *par excellence* to the Head of a body that can represent and realize the divine sovereignty in the world, because it expressed the divine ideal for man, and embodies the divine likeness.

There is a deep mystery, and, as the state of Europe to-day shews, infinite danger underlying the power exercised over men by a dominant personality, unless that power is consciously rooted in a loyalty to something beyond itself. The situation with which we are confronted here, and which is implied in our Lord's teaching under the similitude of the vine, is something which can only be very partially illustrated by the phenomena of group-consciousness, at least if this consciousness is psychologically identified with the mere instinct of a herd. While we cannot really doubt that we are meant to dwell together in unity, this is only possible at the cost of a willing submission to an authority recognized, both by the governors and the governed, as in itself dependent on divine appointment. One who is to be a true king of men must be first and foremost Himself a loyal and obedient Son of God.

If the Gospel story is true, He, who was and is eternally Son of God and King of men, came from His Father to claim His Kingdom, and so to bring in righteousness and peace.

THE BEGINNING OF SIGNS

1 *And the third day there was a marriage in Cana of Galilee;*
2 *and the mother of Jesus was there: and Jesus also was bidden,*
3 *and his disciples, to the marriage. And when the wine failed,*
4 *the mother of Jesus saith unto him, They have no wine. And Jesus saith unto her, Woman, what have I to do with thee? Mine hour*
5 *is not yet come. His mother saith unto the servants, Whatsoever*
6 *he saith unto you, do it. Now there were six waterpots of stone set there after the Jews' manner of purifying, containing two or three*
7 *firkins apiece. Jesus saith unto them, Fill the waterpots with*

8 *water. And they filled them up to the brim. And he saith unto them, Draw out now, and bear unto the ruler of the feast. And they* 9 *bare it. And when the ruler of the feast tasted the water now become wine, and knew not whence it was (but the servants which had drawn the water knew), the ruler of the feast calleth the bride-* 10 *groom, and saith unto him, Every man setteth on first the good wine; and when* men *have drunk freely,* then *that which is worse: thou* 11 *hast kept the good wine until now. This beginning of his signs did Jesus in Cana of Galilee, and manifested his glory; and his disciples believed on him.*

12 *After this he went down to Capernaum, he, and his mother, and* his *brethren, and his disciples: and there they abode not many days.*

On the third day, the seventh or eighth after the opening of S. John's narrative, two days after leaving the Jordan, Jesus and His disciples are present with His mother at a wedding feast at Cana, the home of Nathanael, a village probably four or five miles from Nazareth. It is natural to assume that He had already been home, and that He had communed with His mother in regard to the momentous events of the last fifty days. But on this point the Evangelist is silent.

His account of the feast itself brings before us a typical scene of homely merry-making under a jovial master of ceremonies. The presence of Jesus at such a scene brings into the sharpest relief the contrast between His whole relation to life and that of His forerunner. The preparation for the Kingdom must be made by the stern ascetic in the wilderness. The Kingdom itself must be manifested in the closest contact with the regular occupations, the business and pleasures of ordinary men, by One who has to take His chance of being called "a gluttonous man and a winebibber". Testing moments, in which He might find an occasion of putting forth the characteristic powers of the Kingdom, might arise at any time, out of any conditions. For the Kingdom is related to every part of the life of man: and men in all ages have noted with delight that "the beginning of signs" not only consecrated the most vital of human relationships, but also revealed the Kingdom as concerned no less with filling the cup of human joy than with the relief of suffering.

The occasion seems to have arisen without premeditation. It is likely that the accession of an unexpected number of guests was the cause of the deficiency in the supply of wine. If so, the mother of Jesus may well have felt that she was at least indirectly responsible, and had a special claim to call on her Son for help in the emergency. Her words indeed, "They have no wine", only call His attention to the need. They may only be the outcome of her past experience of His helpfulness. But His answer shows that He found in them an appeal for active intervention on His part—an appeal, I cannot help thinking, for the putting forth of His Messianic power in such a way as to attract public attention.

His words, indeed, are ambiguous. Literally translated they stand: "What is that to me and thee?" They need not mean more than "That is no business of ours". Yet it is on the whole more likely that they are a tender warning against a natural wish to have a word in a department of His life in which He feels that He must from henceforward depend for guidance only and directly on His Father in heaven.

The words "Mine hour is not yet come" have clearly to do with His public manifestation as Messiah (cf. Jn. 7: 4, 13: 1, etc.), and correct a misapprehension on His mother's part in regard to that manifestation. They cannot be taken as referring merely to the supply of the need of wine. For the time for that, as the issue shews, had come. And His mother's words to the servants, "Whatsoever He saith unto you, do it", shew that she realized that He had that matter in hand.

The details of what follows have been variously interpreted. I follow Dr. Westcott. The waterpots, containing one hundred and twenty gallons or more, are wanted for the ceremonial washing of the guests' hands between the different courses of the feast. They are first filled, that there may be no deficiency of water, and that the ordinary routine may go on without interruption. The servants are then told to go back to the well and draw from it when they wanted wine.

This was in itself a severe test of their obedience, and of their readiness to trust Him not to put them to shame before the assembled guests. And they have their reward. They know a secret hidden from the master of ceremonies. They know where the wine came from. We are not told whether that knowledge had any further results in their case. The Evangelist simply notes that the incident was the first of the signs that Jesus wrought, and that the effect of it was seen in the deepening of the faith of those who were already His disciples. There is nothing to show that the other guests were conscious that anything extraordinary had taken place.

Such was "the beginning of His signs" that Jesus did. The words suggest that the Evangelist felt that it had a peculiar appropriateness as the first in the series. He describes it, we must notice, as a "sign". He does not call it a "miracle". He never uses that word. What he wishes us to notice about the incident is not its strangeness, its capacity to arouse astonishment or wonder, but the fact that it had a meaning. It manifested the glory of Jesus. It was the expression, that is, of His nature. It helps us to recognize who He is, and what powers are committed to Him.

We have already seen something of the significance of the occasion that called forth the sign, and of the fact that its immediate object was to minister to simple human enjoyment. What are we to say of the sign itself? Was "a change wrought i' the shows of the world", or did "the change come from our minds, which see of shows o' the world so much as and no more than God wills for His purpose?"

There will, no doubt, always be some to welcome the suggestion that in this case the change was not in the element itself but in the minds of the guests, that they were in fact persuaded by some sort of group hypnotism to believe that they were drinking wine, when, in fact, they were drinking nothing but pure water. But this suggestion, while it removes the physical difficulty, raises a moral one which is in reality far more serious. It is morally incredible that "the beginning of signs" can have been a conjuring trick.

Accepting, then, the narrative as a record of an actual experience (I cannot help feeling that the statement of the effect of the sign on the faith of the disciples comes straight from the personal experience of one of them), we are face to face with a miracle of creation, the method of which it is beyond our power to comprehend. Is it, therefore, incredible? Surely not.

We are driven to believe that the world in which we live is itself not self-existent, but created. Indeed, we are being taught by men of science to believe that it is even now in process of creation, even though the nature of the vital force at work in evolution remains a mystery.

This narrative, then, if we accept it as it stands, only brings us, through the faith and word of the Son, into direct touch with the Father, the eternal Creator of heaven and earth. It helps us to realize the truth of the statement in the opening verses of the Gospel that it was the same Word through whom all things were made, who took flesh and dwelt among us (Jn. 1: 3–14). And it may help us to remember that this narrative does not stand alone. The first temptation, to turn stones into bread, implies a consciousness of the possession of just this power. And the feeding of the multitude on two separate occasions is an example of its exercise under conditions which exclude the possibility of a merely subjective change. (Cf. Jn. 6.)

It does not, however, follow that the disciples of Jesus saw all that was implied in it from the first. The stories of Elijah and Elisha would be enough to show that the creative power of God could go forth at the word of a man "of like passions with us". The sign, therefore, would be enough to assure them from the first that their Master was indeed a prophet. How much more He was, they had to learn by the experience of a life-long discipleship.

The "beginning of signs" at Cana was followed by a short visit to Capernaum. The members of the party were, besides Jesus Himself, His mother and His brethren, and His disciples. It is natural to assume that the disciples were the six of whom we heard in the first chapter. If so, four of them were fishermen whose homes were in Capernaum. When the Galilean ministry began, Jesus made His headquarters there (Mt. 4: 13), and local jealousy was one of the causes of His rejection by Nazareth (Lk. 4: 23). This visit may have led to that change.

CHAPTER VI

THE FIRST PUBLIC ACT OF JESUS AS THE LORD'S ANOINTED

13 *And the passover of the Jews was at hand, and Jesus went up to*
14 *Jerusalem. And he found in the temple those that sold oxen and*
15 *sheep and doves, and the changers of money sitting: and he made a scourge of cords, and cast all out of the temple, both the sheep and the oxen; and he poured out the changers' money, and overthrew*
16 *their tables; and to them that sold the doves he said, Take these things hence; make not my Father's house a house of merchandise.*
17 *His disciples remembered that it was written, The zeal of thine*
18 *house shall eat me up. The Jews therefore answered and said unto him, What sign shewest thou unto us, seeing that thou doest these*
19 *things? Jesus answered and said unto them, Destroy this temple,*
20 *and in three days I will raise it up. The Jews therefore said, Forty and six years was this temple in building, and wilt thou*
21 *raise it up in three days? But he spake of the temple of his body.*
22 *When therefore he was raised from the dead, his disciples remembered that he spake this; and they believed the scripture, and the word which Jesus had said.*

THE next scene is the first public act of Jesus as the Lord's anointed. He had gone up to Jerusalem for the Passover, and finding a busy market in sacrificial victims going on as usual in the outer court of the temple, the court of the Gentiles, He proceeded at once and single-handed to cleanse it. He drove out the sheep and oxen with a scourge of small cords. He overthrew the tables of the money-changers. He forced the sellers of doves to remove their cages, saying: "Take these things hence. Make not My Father's house a house of merchandise."

The situation, I gather, was something like this. The days had long passed when each worshipper had flocks and herds of his own, from which to bring his offering to the Lord. It was inevitable, therefore, that a market should be established at Jerusalem to provide what was necessary. As no victim with a blemish could be accepted for sacrifice, and as the inspection of the victims was in the hands of the priests, the High Priest had no difficulty in securing a highly lucrative monopoly. At the same time convenient scruples against the use of Gentile coins, stamped with idolatrous emblems, in the purchase of the sacred offerings gave profitable occupation to the money-changers. In the circumstances, what could be more natural or convenient than to hold the market as close to the Temple as possible? Why not actually in the outer court? So the abuse arose, as far as we know without protest, and was strongly entrenched behind ramparts of vested interest, custom, and popular convenience, when Jesus came and shewed what spirit He was of by forcibly sweeping it all away. He could not be in authority in His Father's house and tolerate the scandal for a single hour.

It was a startling act, certain to rouse bitter opposition on the part of the interests affected. It was only too likely to deprive His appeal to the nation of any chance of success by alienating their leaders. Nor could the effect of His purge be more than temporary without the co-operation of the Temple police.

How then, we cannot help asking, did it come about that Jesus chose this way of declaring the presence of the Kingdom of God, and of claiming for Himself the allegiance of priests and people?

There was nothing wrong in the trade itself. The phrase which our Lord used on the occasion of the second cleansing[1]

[1] It must suffice to note that if there were only one Cleansing of the Temple, it is admirably in place where S. John puts it. The difficulty in establishing the charge brought against Jesus at His trial before Caiaphas, as recorded by S. Mark, which is clearly based on a reminiscence of the utterance recorded by S. John, would be intelligible, if three years had elapsed. It would be strange, if the utterance itself was not a week old. There is further a striking difference in the words of our Lord's protest, as recorded in the two authorities, which certainly fits in best with the hypothesis that our Lord deliberately repeated the act on the occasion of His last visit to Jerusalem. On the first occasion He says: "Make not my Father's house a house of merchandise". He is claiming authority, no doubt, in His Father's Name, but it is to remove

"Ye have made it 'a brigands' cave'" does not refer to any dishonesty on the part of the traders, but to the fact that the Temple authorities, knowing by that time that they were in the presence of "the Heir" had made up their minds to kill Him that they might seize His inheritance.

But if there was nothing inherently wrong in the trading, why should it matter so much where it was carried on? Is it not strange to find Jesus setting so much store by the sanctity of a particular place? Does He not teach the Samaritan woman that the special virtue attaching to Jerusalem and to Gerizim would soon be things of the past?

Deeper reflection however will show us that, whatever was to happen after His resurrection, no other attitude on His part was really possible at that time. The Temple was still, in fact, the one place where the presence of the Lord was pledged to His people. That was the ground on which the Jew felt justified in despising the Gentile, and in threatening death to anyone uncircumcized who should profane His Sanctuary. Clearly, therefore, to hold the market even in the Outer Court meant that those in authority put motives of personal convenience and private gain before the honour due to God. Would any less drastic method have sufficed to reveal the gulf of atheism into which the leaders of Israel were sinking? Are we really surprised at the noble scorn of consequence with which Jesus allowed His zeal for His Father's House to blaze forth, even though He should Himself be consumed in the conflagration?

The cleansing was, obviously, admirably fitted to try the hearts of men. It needed no justification. If it had carried conviction of sin with it, it might have prepared the

---

an open abuse. On the second occasion His words were: "My house shall be a house of prayer for all nations; but ye have made it a brigand's cave".

From this point of view Jesus began His public ministry by a direct challenge to the civil and ecclesiastical authorities in the nation to take the first step in a movement of national repentance.

It is fruitless to speculate on what might have happened had they been ready to follow His lead. As the Servant of the Lord He knew that He must not take any steps to compel them to acknowledge Him. He has made His protest, and for the time being He must leave it at that. What He had done was so obviously righteous that they could not call Him to account for it. He is left, for the present, undisturbed, to make His appeal to the rest of the people.

way for a truly national turning to God. But it could only do this, if the religious leaders were prepared to admit that they had been in the wrong, and to recognize that Jesus had indeed a commission from God to bear rule over them.

Now the High Priestly party, who were Sadducees, had, as we have seen, a vested interest in the market. The trial, therefore, was in their case most direct and searching. They had to show, once for all, whether they were prepared, at personal cost to themselves, to transfer the market to some other site, or whether they held the honour of God of less account than their private gain.

The Pharisees were not personally implicated in the traffic. Their sympathy would naturally have been on the side of the Cleanser of the Temple. With them the question seems to have been simply whether they could be content to follow instead of to lead.

Neither party was prepared to make the sacrifice the situation required of them. They seem to have tried to avoid an immediate decision by raising the previous question: Who was Jesus, that He should claim authority in the Temple courts? What proof could He give that He had indeed been sent by God? So they challenge Him to justify His claim by a sign from heaven.

It is certainly remarkable that Jesus does not on this occasion refer them to the witness of the Baptist, as He does, at least indirectly, after the second cleansing (See Mk. 11: 27–33). I cannot help feeling, however, that the incident as a whole remains unintelligible, unless we presuppose that the report of the official commission which had been sent to S. John from Jerusalem was already in the hands of the Jewish authorities. The fact that they made a report, and that it included a reference to the testimony of John to Jesus, is implied in Jn. 5: 33. And there is no reason to doubt that the commission reported immediately on its return. If so, the fact of the Baptist's witness must have been common ground between Jesus and the Jewish authorities, and the question at issue was simply whether that witness was sufficient by itself to justify His claim to authority in His Father's house, or whether that claim needed to be substantiated by some further sign from heaven.

In this form the problem raised by their demand was precisely the same as that raised in the temptation on the pinnacle of the Temple. Jesus had then refused to put His Sonship to a self-imposed test on the ground that the evidence He had already received was sufficient, and that to ask for a fresh sign would be to tempt the Lord, as the children of Israel had tempted Him in Massah.

This did not, indeed, mean that the witness of the Baptist to the sign vouchsafed to him, and through him to the people, did not need, and could not receive, confirmation. All through the Gospel of S. John, Jesus is represented as appealing to the works that the Father gave Him to do, and the words that He gave Him to speak, as supplying such confirmation. But on the present occasion, men whose wills were set to do the will of God (Jn. 7: 17) would have needed no further witness than the act of righteous heroism that Jesus had just performed before their eyes to convince them that the witness of the Baptist was true. So the mere fact that the Jewish authorities made it the ground for asking for further credentials was a clear sign that they had in heart revolted from the Father, and would pay no heed to any witness coming from Him to His Son.

We can see, therefore, in some measure how it came about that Jesus saw in this seemingly innocent challenge to produce fresh credentials the germ of a national apostasy, which would issue first in His own crucifixion, and then in the destruction of Jerusalem. For that, and nothing less than that, is contained in the startling reply that He made to their challenge: "Destroy this Temple"—Consummate your rebellion until it finds its appointed goal; until the judgement of God descends upon you, and wipes away from the face of the earth the visible pledges of His presence which He has entrusted to your keeping—"Destroy this Temple".

Yet even so, His covenant with mankind in the person of

His Son will stand inviolate, despite all that man can do to render it ineffective. "Destroy this Temple, and in three days I will raise it again," or, as the words lived on in popular memory, to come up again against Jesus both at His trial and on the Cross, "I will destroy this Temple made with hands, and in three days I will build another made without hands" (Mk. 14: 58). In either form, they mean that the new building would be in spiritual reality what the material building had been in divinely appointed type and shadow—a true home for the Father among the sons of man.

It was an amazing utterance surely, the mystery of which grows as we ponder upon it. It is not surprising that the rebellious-hearted Jews could make nothing of it at the time. They could think of nothing but the physical impossibility of re-building in three days a structure that had already been forty-six years in building, and was even then, as we are told, not yet finally complete. They refuse, therefore, to take the answer seriously, or to inquire further into His meaning or His claim; content, apparently, to overlook the inconvenience that His action had caused, rather than raise any public inquiry into the legality or seemliness of the traffic against which He had entered His protest, and glad that He showed no desire to take any further steps to assert His authority, whatever it might be.

The Evangelist, however, is not interested in analysing the state of mind of men who loved the darkness rather than the light. He is eager to help his fellow-disciples to apprehend the meaning of the utterance of the Lord. So He adds a note to the comment of the Jews, to the effect that the new Temple, which was to take the place of the old, was "the temple of His body", meaning by this, no doubt, first of all His natural body, which even in the days of His flesh was an habitation of God by the descent and abiding of the Spirit, and was raised in three days according to the promise; but meaning also His mystical body (whatever be the precise relation in which that stands to the body of His glory) even the Church, which, as S. Paul teaches us in Eph. 2: 22, is now growing into a holy temple in the Lord, being built together into an habitation of God in the Spirit.

The saying was not indeed intelligible even to the disciples when they first heard it, and they did not yet know their Master well enough to ask Him to interpret it to them. But in the light of the resurrection, the words came back with a new clue to the interpretation of the passage from Ps. 69: 9, which had haunted them as they had watched the outburst of His zeal for the house of the Lord. And they recognized the truth (note again the significant touch of personal autobiography) both of the Scripture and of the word which Jesus had spoken.

THE EFFECT OF THE CLEANSING ON THE MINISTRY

The cleansing of the Temple seems at first sight to have produced far less effect on the development of our Lord's work than we might have expected from its intrinsic importance. The rulers of the people seem to have come to the conclusion that, as Jesus had as yet no force of public opinion behind Him, and refused to put forth supernatural power in support of His claim, they might safely ignore His pretensions, and allow His outburst of righteous indignation to pass quietly into oblivion. This policy was adopted all the more easily because the act itself was one which they could not openly condemn; and further, because Jesus Himself shewed no signs of any desire to assert any permanent authority over the Temple Courts, or to take any active steps to assert His authority.

It would be a mistake, however, to imagine that the issues of the act were as insignificant as they seem. The record of our Lord's trial before the High Priest three years later shows how the memory of the words spoken on this occasion lived on in the minds of the people; though no doubt the people were no less at a loss than their rulers to understand why Jesus took no steps to follow up the policy of national reformation to which the cleansing of the Temple would have formed a natural introduction.

But it is just there that the act and its reception by the

leaders of the people really determined the whole course of subsequent events.

As S. Matthew helps us to see at a later crisis (Mt. 12: 15–21), it was a fundamental principle in our Lord's plan to use no force to secure His ends. His people must be willing in the day of His power (Ps. 110: 3). He will not strive nor cry aloud (Is. 42: 2). His appeal to the conscience of the nation was made clearly and unmistakably. But the response was left to those to whom the appeal was made.

If the rulers had been prepared to accept His authority and follow His lead, He could have gone forward, step by step, with the work of national repentance. But since they refused to follow Him, as they had refused to follow John, His ministry must develop along other lines. He must turn to the people and call out, from among them, those who could constitute the New Israel when the time came for the sweeping away of the old. He must lay the foundations of the new Temple which was to take the place of that which the Jews were destroying by their rebellion.

His reply to the challenge for a sign from heaven, shewed that this alternative was present to His mind from the first. It is not surprising, therefore, that He should have begun at once to work for that end, sifting the wheat from the chaff, by "the winnowing fan" of His call. It is, of course, the method of the whole ministry, as portrayed in the first three Gospels. But it is only from S. John that we learn how it came to be adopted.

CHAPTER VII

NICODEMUS

23 *Now when he was in Jerusalem at the passover, during the feast,*
24 *many believed on his name, beholding his signs which he did. But Jesus did not trust himself unto them, for that he knew all men, and*
25 *because he needed not that any one should bear witness concerning man: for he himself knew what was in man.*

THE ministry at Jerusalem, in the days that followed the cleansing of the Temple, was marked by signs which are not further described, though the effect of them is noted both on the inhabitants of Jerusalem (2: 23–25) and on the Galilaeans who had come up for the feast (4: 45). In each case the first impression produced by the signs seemed to augur well for the future. In Jerusalem many "believed on His name". Many, that is, were ready to acknowledge Him as entrusted with a mission from God. On the strength of the signs the Galilaeans welcomed Him on His return to the north. There was, however, a subtle danger lurking in this proffered loyalty. Many a leader fails because he is unable to retain control of the enthusiasm that he has evoked. And in this case everything turned on the readiness of the would-be disciples to put on one side their preconceived notions of the meaning of Messiahship, in order that Jesus might choose His own time and His own way of revealing the true nature of His office and fulfilling its obligations. It would have been fatally easy (it must have been a temptation not unlike that encountered on the mountain-top) to grasp at immediate popularity by a seemingly innocent accommodation to current anticipations. S. John must have been struck at the time by his Master's reserve. It was not until he came to reflect on the course of events in the light of the issue that he appreciated the insight into human nature which had dictated that reserve.

1 *Now there was a man of the Pharisees, named Nicodemus, a ruler*
2 *of the Jews: the same came unto him by night, and said unto him, Rabbi, we know that thou art a teacher come from God: for no man*
3 *can do these signs that thou doest, except God be with him. Jesus answered and said unto him, Verily, verily, I say unto thee, Except*
4 *a man be born anew, he cannot see the Kingdom of God. Nicodemus saith unto him, How can a man be born when he is old? can he*
5 *enter a second time into his mother's womb, and be born? Jesus answered, Verily, verily, I say unto thee, Except a man be born of the water and of the Spirit, he cannot enter into the kingdom of*
6 *God. That which is born of the flesh is flesh; and that which is*
7 *born of the Spirit is spirit. Marvel not that I said unto thee, ye*
8 *must be born anew. The wind bloweth*[1] *where it listeth, and thou hearest the voice thereof, but knowest not whence it cometh, and whither it goeth: so is every one that is born of the Spirit.*

[1] *The Spirit breatheth.*

S. John proceeds to give at once the report of an interview with an inquirer of high rank in the religious world of the time, which illustrates in a remarkable way our Lord's attitude towards this class of applicants for discipleship.

Nicodemus was a member of the Sanhedrim. His attention, and that of his friends, must have been called to Jesus by the cleansing of the Temple, and they must have been following with close attention the next stage in His career. For "the signs" made so much impression on them that they were convinced that Jesus must have a divine commission of some kind. They were prepared to see in Him, as Nicodemus says, "A Teacher come from God". The signs were, they felt sure, a proof that God was with Him.

The designation of His office as that of a teacher must have been due partly to the absence of any express claim on His part to royal dignity or political authority, and partly to the place which teaching must have occupied from the first in His public ministration.

It must have been difficult for a man in the position of

Nicodemus to avoid adopting something of a patronizing tone in approaching a Man much younger than himself, who had had no scientific training in the Law. This being so, the reception that his advance met with must have been not a little startling.

It would, of course, be perfectly possible to suppose that Nicodemus himself gave S. John an account of what passed between Him and the Lord on that memorable night. But Jesus speaks, we cannot but notice, from time to time in the first person plural, implying that there were others who in some sense had already shared His experience, and who could corroborate His testimony. And I cannot help feeling that these words gain in power if we regard them as uttered in the presence of His disciples. I find it at the same time easier to believe that this report records the impression made by the conversation on a third person, than that it comes to us from either of those who took part in it. The point is of course, quite a subordinate one, and nothing in the interpretation of the various utterances depends upon it.

His visit was paid, as S. John notes twice over with obvious intention (3: 2, 19: 39) "by night". A man in the position of Nicodemus must make sure of his ground before committing himself openly. So this confession of an embryo faith was virtually, if not expressly, a request for further information with regard to Jesus Himself, and to the message He had come to bring. It was met, therefore, quite naturally by instruction in regard to the Kingdom of God.

It is strange that this should be the only place in S. John's Gospel where the Kingdom of God is mentioned. But it must have been in everybody's mind just then. The advent of the Kingdom had been heralded by the Baptist (Mt. 3: 2) and it was the subject, as we learn from the other Gospels, of our Lord's earliest preaching in the synagogues of Galilee (Mk. 1: 15; cf. Lk. 4: 18 f). The point on which everything turned was the form that this long-expected manifestation of the sovereignty of God would take.

Everyone was agreed that it would include two elements.

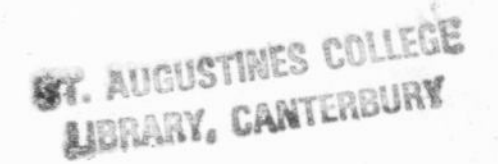

It would be, on the one hand, a manifestation of the wrath of God against His enemies, coming out in a terrible judgement: it would, on the other hand, be a manifestation of His loving care for His people, coming out in a signal act of salvation (Lk. 1: 71) or redemption (Lk. 2: 38), which would deliver them from their enemies, and establish them in their predestined position as sovereign over the nations of the world. The Pharisees, many of whose predecessors had in the past laid down their lives for their faith (Heb. 11: 35ff.), believed further that this deliverance would involve the breaking of the bonds of death.

The Baptist had not said anything inconsistent with this view of the Kingdom. Only, like all true prophets, he had warned those who were inclined to trust to outward signs of membership in God's people that these would not of themselves provide any shelter from "the wrath to come". The seed of Abraham after the flesh were not essential to the triumph of God's purpose. God could "from these stones" raise up inheritors of the promises made to the Fathers.

The point from which Jesus begins in His teaching of Nicodemus is the spiritual qualification for "seeing", that is, for perceiving the presence of, "the Kingdom" (3: 3) and then of "entering", that is of becoming a living and active member of it (3: 5).

Jesus is speaking throughout, we must remember, in the light of the experience through which He himself had recently passed at His baptism. His teaching has two aspects. On the one side it is a warning of the impotence of man as he is, even of a cultivated and devout teacher of Israel, to apprehend spiritual realities. On the other side it points the way by which the requisite faculties can be imparted and acquired.

The opening words can be translated (see R.V.mg.) in two ways. The word translated "again" recurs in verse 31, and is then translated "from above". The ambiguity need not trouble us. In any case a new birth is implied, as the difficulty felt by Nicodemus shows; and our Lord's answer shows that it must be a birth "from above".

There is a further ambiguity in the word "born". It may

be translated (see R.V.mg. Jn. 1: 13) "begotten". In that case it would describe the relation of the new life to its source under the figure of the relation of a child to its father. Nicodemus, however, seems to understand the word as referring to the deliverance of the babe from its own mother's womb. F. D. Maurice in his volume of expository sermons on *The Gospel of S. John* shows how full of meaning the thought of the new birth is from that point of view. Birth is for the babe a deliverance from darkness into light, from a close prison into the freedom and air of a new world, which has a close analogy with the liberty of the glory of the children of God.

So interpreted the figure describes a crisis in the development of an already existing life, and is free from a serious difficulty which attaches to the words on the other interpretation. To say that we must "be begotten again" seems to imply that we must look to a new father for the source of the new life which we need. And it is not easy to see how that can be without not merely a transformation but an absolute change of personality.

We must not, of course, forget that we are dealing with a material figure which cannot be safely pressed in all its details in the spiritual sphere. God mothers (Jas. 1: 18) as well as fathers us. And S. Paul not only begets (1 Cor. 4: 15), but also is "in travail" with his spiritual children (Gal. 4: 19).

And yet there can be no doubt, I think, that the context here is in favour of the translation "begotten". The emphasis is primarily on a source of new life, and not on a change in conditions and environment, closely related as the life is and must always be to its environment. And the difficulty to which attention has been called, must be met in the light of the thought that the new life that we need springs from the same source as the old. We are raised on to a higher plane and endowed with fresh capacities by an act of the same God, to whom we owe our original being. His voice calls us to the conscious recognition of the relationship of accredited and responsible sonship, which was His purpose for us from the beginning.

This result is in close agreement with what may well have been the significance of His baptism for the development of our Lord's humanity. His sonship seems at that time to have entered on a new phase. His human nature was in a true sense raised to a higher plane, and endowed with "the powers of the age to come" when He heard the voice of the Father saying to Him "Thou art my beloved Son, in thee I am well pleased". He is, I believe, teaching Nicodemus that we must each in our measure share that experience before we can hope to "see the Kingdom of God".

Nicodemus was certainly a humble-minded, teachable man. Instead of cavilling at the declaration of his incompetence, or attempting to excuse it, he starts at once considering how he can fulfil the required condition. He has been often blamed for the crass literalism which involved him in difficulty at the outset of his thinking. It is pointed out that Pharisees were in the habit of speaking of proselytes as "born again", when they entered the privileged circle of the Chosen People. But even if this form of speaking was current in his circle, and so might have supplied Nicodemus with a key to our Lord's meaning, it is only too easy to use such words metaphorically without being conscious of any substantial reality behind them. It is at least to the credit of Nicodemus that he was sure that Jesus was speaking of a real birth, not a metaphorical one, and that he saw quite truly that such a birth could not be in any sense a repetiton of the old.

A grown man cannot enter a second time into his mother's womb and be born. So he puts his difficulty frankly and boldly before "the Teacher come from God", and he is met, not with scorn for his stupidity, but with a re-statement of the original requirement, with such modifications as contain in themselves a hint of the solution he was looking for.

Verily, verily, I say unto you, except a man be born of water and spirit he cannot enter into the Kingdom of God.

If this sentence is carefully compared with that which preceded it, it will be seen that two new phrases are introduced into it. Birth "of water and Spirit" takes the place of "being born again" or "from above". "Entering into" is substituted for "seeing" the Kingdom.

The second change presents the Kingdom as something within reach. A man may seek to enter into it even though the faculties for perceiving its presence are as yet undeveloped in him.

The other change from the new birth to the birth of water and of Spirit picks up two key words in the Baptist's witness. John had told the deputation that his own work was to baptize with water, but that Jesus had been baptized not with water only but with the Holy Spirit, and would in due course baptize others with the Spirit that He had received.

So when Nicodemus heard that the new birth was a birth of water and Spirit, his thoughts must have been carried back once more to the Baptist. He must have begun to wonder whether, if he was really in earnest in his desire for regeneration, it might not be his duty to become a candidate for the Baptism of Repentance in preparation for the coming of the Kingdom.

This must have been at least in part what Jesus meant him to infer. It is clear from Mt. 21 : 32, that Jesus felt that the Pharisees ought to have submitted to the baptism of John as the publicans and harlots did, and as He Himself had done. And, as we shall see later in this chapter (3: 26f.), Jesus Himself at this stage in His ministry baptized through His disciples (4: 2) with a baptism, which, as the Spirit was not yet given, must have been a continuation of the baptism of John, just as His early preaching in Galilee was a repetition of the preaching of the Baptist (Mt. 3 : 2 ; 4 : 17) with, according to S. Mark, a significant expansion (Mk. 1 : 15), showing that the Kingdom was really within reach.

His instruction, however, did not stop there. Further help could be given by light on the nature of the new life to which the new birth was the introduction. If Nicodemus could catch a glimpse of it even from afar, it would deepen his desire for it, and at the same time help him to understand the conditions laid down for attaining it. So Jesus proceeds: "That which is born of the flesh is flesh, and that which is born of the Spirit is spirit."

By these words He calls the attention of Nicodemus to the fact that all life corresponds in its nature to the source from which it springs. Seeds bear fruit after their kind. Our physical life belongs to the region of the visible. The sign of the presence of physical life is the growth of a material body from a material germ. "That which is born of the flesh is flesh". That the Spirit should have power to quicken into newness of life a man who opens his heart to receive Him is not as surprising, though not so familiar, as the power of generation implanted in the flesh. There is, therefore, nothing to be amazed at in the declaration "You must be born from above". There is in the universe a power capable of imparting the kind of life we need. But the new birth that the Spirit gives belongs to another order than the physical, and the tokens of its presence must be sought within.

The words in which these tokens are described once more admit of two quite different renderings into English. The sentence as a whole is a condensed parable drawn from the wind or breath, which is an universal emblem of the Spirit. It is generally translated as if the opening clauses described the action of the wind. "The wind bloweth where it listeth, and thou hearest the sound thereof, but thou knowest not whence it cometh or whither it goeth". And only the last clause, where the translation "wind" is no longer possible, refers directly to the action of the Spirit, "So is everyone that is born of the Spirit".

It should, however, be noticed that, even in the opening clauses, the words used are strangely personal. The wind has a "will", and its "sound" is strictly a "voice", an utterance with a meaning (cf. 1 Cor. 14: 8f.). So the words may quite well run: "The Spirit breatheth where He wills, and thou hearest His voice, but thou knowest not whence He cometh and whither He goeth, so is everyone that is born of the

Spirit". This translation has a further advantage in the light that it throws on the real point of the last clause.

As ordinarily understood the thought illustrated by the comparison is simply that, as we infer the presence of the wind in spite of the fact that we cannot see it, or give any account of its action, from the noise that it makes, so we can tell when a man has been born again by the new power that has come into his life, however little we can understand how the change has been brought about.

The whole sentence, however, surely grows in force and coherence, both in itself and in its relation to the context, if we take it to be a description of the new life, the life of a son of the Kingdom, as a man may know it from within. The life of the Spirit is no doubt incomprehensible, alike in its motives and in its goal, to the outsider. As our Lord told the Jews on a later occasion (Jn. 8: 14), "Ye know not whence I came and whither I go". But to him who shares it, its chief characteristic is the new consciousness of freedom which it brings. The new life is of water and of Spirit. It springs from the surrender of the flesh, the offering of the whole man to God, with that deliberate devotion to destruction of all selfish impulses which is implied in baptism. It issues in the glorious liberty of the children of God, free as the wind, from moment to moment obedient to law, but with no consciousness of restraint.

WITNESS FROM WITHIN THE KINGDOM

9 *Nicodemus answered and said unto him, How can these things be?*
10 *Jesus answered and said unto him, Art thou the teacher of Israel,*
11 *and understandest not these things? Verily, verily, I say unto thee, We speak that we know, and bear witness of that we have seen;*
12 *and ye receive not our witness. If I told you earthly things, and ye believe not, how shall ye believe, if I tell you heavenly things?*
13 *And no man hath ascended into heaven, but he that descended out of of heaven, even the Son of man.*

We have now reached the stage in our Lord's conversation with Nicodemus in which He began to comment on the situation created by the failure of Nicodemus and his friends to accept the witness which had been given them by Himself and by the Baptist. The witness was the witness of experts, based on first-hand experience, relating to matters within the reach of ordinary human powers. If such witness failed to carry conviction, it is not easy to see what way was open for bringing home to men the transcendent revelation of heavenly things, the mind and heart of the Father, which Jesus had come to bring. Still, the work had to be done. As the next two verses (14f.) shew, the way to its accomplishment led through the Cross. But before Jesus comes to that, He lays stress on His personal qualification for speaking of "the heavenly things":

And no one hath ascended into heaven, save He that came down from heaven, that is, the Son of Man.

These are strange words on the lips of a man still clothed in a mortal body. On the other hand, they describe simply and accurately the present condition of the Revealer of the mysteries of heaven. It is not surprising, therefore, that some have thought that the Evangelist breaks off his report of the conversation with Nicodemus at verse 12, and introduces in verse 13 a reflection of his own on the words he has just recorded.

We cannot rule out this explanation as impossible. Something of the kind must, it would seem, have taken place in any case before verse 16. Unfortunately inverted commas had not been invented, so authors and scribes had no convenient way of making such transitions obvious to the eye when they occurred.

I cannot, however, regard this as a satisfactory solution of the difficulty. If verse 13 is a comment of the Evangelist, the connexion of thought would be something like this: "The failure of men to believe in the heavenly things taught by Jesus is serious because we have no other means of acquiring the knowledge of them. No man has ascended into heaven but the Son of Man, who first descended, and was therefore able while He was upon earth to reveal the secrets of His eternal home." Now this is not a natural interpretation of the words. If that had been the thought in S. John's mind, it could have been expressed directly by saying: "No man hath descended out of heaven." For it makes the capacity to give the evidence depend on the descent which preceded the earthly ministry, and not on the Ascension, which came at the end of it, whereas in the sentence, as we have it, the stress is laid on an Ascension. The thought of descent is subordinate. It is only referred to as explaining the Ascension (cf. 6: 62), not as being itself the qualification for witness.

Again, this interpretation fails to supply any tolerable connexion with the verses (14f.) that follow, when our Lord is once more the speaker. For verse 14 speaks of the Crucifixion as an event still in the future.

It is a minor, but still real, objection, that the title "Son of Man" does not occur elsewhere in the Gospels except in words of the Lord.

We come back, then, to see what meaning the words bear regarded as uttered by Jesus Himself in His conversation with Nicodemus. Regarded in that setting, the first point that strikes us is that Jesus is claiming to be already living an ascended life. Other people have not, but He has already, ascended into heaven. That is His qualification for speaking while still upon earth of heavenly things.

If so, it is clear that the words do not refer to the Ascension of which we speak in the Creed, when He passed out of human sight, taking His risen body to the right hand of the Majesty on high, but to an ascension which He enjoyed while yet on earth, an ascension in heart and mind similar in kind, however higher in degree, to that for which we pray in our Collect for Ascension Day. Is this incredible? The heavens, we remember, were opened at His baptism. What reason is there for supposing that they were ever thereafter closed to Him? These words are quite natural, if we assume that He entered on the banks of the Jordan into the kingdom of heaven, and thenceforth saw its wonders from within. We, whose faith is as yet too weak and dim to enable us to make our own the inheritance which He has won for us, and whose birth from on high in consequence still lingers, find it no doubt impossible to conceive such an experience. But the

Gospels are at least consistent in their description of the life that resulted from it. The Transfiguration, recorded by the first three Evangelists, is a scene in this new communion of earth and heaven, which was enacted in the presence of chosen witnesses to give us an assurance of its reality. And S. John has preserved utterances which are intelligible only on the hypothesis that that communion was not intermittent only, but abiding. Sentences, for instance, such as "My meat is to do the will of Him that sent Me, and to finish His work," "I live because of the Father", "The Son can do nothing but what He sees the Father doing", "As I hear I judge", "I am in the Father and the Father in Me", "The Father abiding in Me doeth His works", express simply and directly the experience of one who lived on earth as a citizen of heaven, and whose life was continually and consciously "hid in God". Even the word to Nathanael: "Ye shall see the heavens opened and the angels of God ascending and descending on the Son of Man", may have begun to receive its fulfilment before the Lord was taken up out of our sight.

Jesus, then, we must suppose, is Himself in these words explaining to Nicodemus His unique qualification for speaking of the heavenly things. He had made Himself one with us, and then in our nature a door had been opened for Him into heaven. And as He had learnt our language, He could testify of the things that He saw and heard.

The reference to the descent out of heaven, which preceded the ascent, is noteworthy. It is the first hint of our Lord's consciousness of pre-existence. Signs of this consciousness recur later in the Gospel, and culminate in 16: 28 and 17: 5, 24. We need not assume that He brought with Him into this world clear memories of the home that He had left. That would be inconsistent, it would seem, with the perfect humanity of His experience. The reference can be sufficiently accounted for as the result of reflection on the message of the angel to His mother, and on the word of His Father at His baptism, understood in the light both of the anticipations of the prophets and of the experience to which it formed the introduction.

The title "Son of Man" is here clearly personal, and in a sense official. It is capable of a singularly wide range of interpretation. For instance, its use here emphasizes the fact that the experience to which our Lord lays claim was not one which separated Him from His brethren. It came to Him in virtue of the perfection of His humanity.

At the same time, as we have seen, our Lord's use of the title in His answer to the High Priest shows that a reference to the vision of Daniel (Dan. 7) was implied in the title. If Nicodemus was familiar with the Book of Enoch, our Lord's use of the title, coupled with a claim to pre-existence might have started a fruitful series of questionings, on the same lines as the challenge with regard to David's Lord at the end of the ministry.

The last clause in the common text "who is in heaven" is omitted in the best authorities. It is probably a later addition. The thought in it is implied in the perfect tense used in the reference to the Ascension—because that describes an action the results of which continue into the present.

Jesus claims to live, even while on earth, continually in the realized presence of His Father, and so to be able to give to all, who were willing to receive it, a revelation of the mind and heart of the Father, which would mean eternal life to them. At the same time, and this is the point of the verse which follows, the way in which this revelation could be given to men was conditioned by their unbelief. The refusal of the leaders of God's people to accept the witness of the Baptist made the Crucifixion inevitable. "The Son of Man *must* be lifted up".

THE SYMBOL OF THE SERPENT

14 *And as Moses lifted up the serpent in the wilderness, even so*
15 *must the Son of Man be lifted up: that whosoever believeth may in him have eternal life.*

Let us consider first the nature of the foreknowledge implied in this prediction. The words used have a singular fulness of meaning. When our Lord uses the phrase on a later occasion (Jn. 12: 32), He says: "I, if I be lifted up *out of* (not simply on the surface of) the earth, will draw all men unto myself". Here it is clear that the "lifting up" of which He is speaking will not be complete before the Ascension. At the same time S. John's comment in 18: 32 shows that the physical elevation on the Cross was from the first included in the thought, and the same is implied in this passage by the reference to the brazen serpent. Some will, I know, find it hard to believe that our Lord can really have given such teaching so early in His ministry. We are familiar, of course, with the fact that after Simon Peter's confession (Mt. 16: 16) at Cæsarea Philippi, Jesus began to prepare His disciples for the sufferings that were in store for Him, and that, as the time drew nearer, the prediction was repeated with ever-growing clearness of definition (Mt. 16: 21, 17: 22f., 20: 17ff., 26: 1f.). When we reach the Last Supper, the scope of the prophecy widens and includes the future ahead of the disciples. Jesus points out the traitor, and predicts Peter's denials and the scattering of the Apostolic band.

Peter's remonstrance (Mt. 16: 22) shows that the teaching was as unfamiliar as it was unwelcome. And we are inclined to assume that a thought which did not find expression in His teaching must have been absent from the mind of the Master. This is, however, a baseless assumption. If Jesus knew what was coming six months or six hours before it came to pass, it is clearly possible that He was Himself familiar with the thought from the first, and was only waiting to communicate it to His disciples till their faith was strong enough to bear the revelation. And, in fact, occasional phrases, which belong apparently to the earlier days of the ministry, show that our Lord dropped hints from time to time, the full meaning of which would only become clear in the light of His later teaching. Such phrases occur in Mt. 9: 15, "The days will come, when the bridegroom shall be taken away from them, and then will they fast", and in Mt. 10: 38 "He that doth not take his cross and follow after Me, is not worthy of Me."

There is, therefore, nothing to preclude the possibility of a real but veiled allusion to the Cross, even as early as this first conversation with Nicodemus. It only states as a fact what the challenge "to destroy this temple" in 2 : 19 had contemplated as a possibility. And in all the Gospels the refusal to accept the evidence that God had given, unless it were supported by some fresh sign from heaven, is met by a prophecy of the Resurrection, such as that which we have already seen to be implied in the "lifting up", which we find here. It remains, however, a difficult task to read the whole life in the light of this foreknowledge.

We can feel, of course, the heroism to which S. Luke calls attention, when he prefaces his account of the last journeyings after the Transfiguration with the words "when the days were well-nigh come that he should be received up *he steadfastly set his face* to go up to Jerusalem". And this in itself can cause no trouble. It is a perfectly human feature. Men can and do face certain death in answer to the clear call of duty. It makes comparatively little difference whether this feature was characteristic of the whole ministry, or whether it only began when the disciples first became conscious of it, six months before the end. We can well believe that Jesus, knowing what the end must be, in a true sense took up His Cross day by day from the beginning. What is strange is the clearness and accuracy of the prevision. An insight capable of seeing from the beginning that the way He had chosen must rouse the murderous hate of the leaders of the people, and that in consequence His ministry must come to a violent end would be sufficiently striking, but it would not transcend the limits of normal human capacity. But how did it come to pass that He foresaw not only the fact but the exact form of the death that He must die? And how did the possession of this foreknowledge affect His normal human consciousness and react on the daily life of the ministry?

We must set ourselves first to examine the source of the knowledge of events yet in the future which Jesus shews in the course of His ministry. The first, and it may be the final answer to our question, is that Jesus was Prophet as well as Priest and King. S. Peter quotes as fulfilled in Him the promise given through Moses, "A prophet shall the Lord your God raise up unto you like unto me" (Dt. 18: 15, Ac. 3: 22). But we cannot accept this answer without examination. It is precisely the nature and content of a prophetic consciousness that we are seeking to understand.

There was a time when, in the light of the application of isolated utterances in the Old Testament to particular facts in the life of our Lord, men were accustomed to regard a prophecy as simply history written in advance. They assumed that the prophet's eyes were opened by the Holy Ghost to see exactly what was going to happen, and that he wrote down what he saw.

This view of prophecy is no longer possible. Close study has shewn that the main work of the prophets was in direct relation to their own age. Their characteristic endowment was their power to see the hand of God in the events that were going on around them, and in virtue of that insight to declare His will to their own contemporaries. They saw indeed the goal for which God was working, and some of the steps on the way that led to it. But we are more struck by the strength of their faith, and the glory of their hope, than by the clearness of their vision, and the precise accuracy of the details of their description of events that lay in the future.

To take a particular example. Isaiah was strong in the assurance that the Lord would deliver Jerusalem from the hand of the Assyrian. It was a wonderful faith, and the whole of his foreign policy was moulded by it; and the deliverance came. But it does not appear that any invading army ever followed the course so vividly pictured in the prophetic vision recorded in Isaiah 10: 28-34.

So we are coming to see that the chief use of the prophet's writings is to reveal eternal laws of God's working in the world by helping us to understand the principles on which He has acted in the past, rather than by a straightforward description of particular events that are still waiting in the womb of time.

We are bound, however, to admit that prophets, both in the Old Testament (e.g., 1 Kgs. 14: 5; 22: 17; 2 Kgs. 4: 27) and in the New Testament (Ac. 11: 28; 27: 24), had particular future events revealed to them. And we must also take into account the fact that the recorded words of the prophets were found to correspond in a wonderful way with particular incidents in the life of Jesus. We have, therefore, to take two factors into account when we try to understand the knowledge that Jesus shows of "the exodus that He was to accomplish at Jerusalem" (Lk. 9: 31), including as it did both the exact form the sufferings would take, and the date of the deliverance that would follow. We have to allow for the possibility of a direct revelation. We have to allow also for the light that might have come from the written word.

Let us take the second point first. We know from His own words how large a part the Scriptures played in opening His eyes to see what was coming upon Him especially in the hour of His Passion. He yielded Himself up into the hands of those who had come to arrest Him with the words, "How then shall the Scriptures be fulfilled that thus it must be?" (Mt. 26: 54). He had already earlier in the same evening quoted Ps. 41: 9 (Jn. 13: 18), "He that eateth my bread lifted up his heel against me," and Is. 53: 12 (Lk. 22: 37) "This that is written must be accomplished in Me, and He was numbered with the transgressors"; and Zech. 13 : 7 (Mt. 26: 31) "Ye all shall be offended in Me this night for it is written 'I will smite the shepherd and the sheep of the flock shall be scattered' ".

We know also that He regarded even the murder of the Baptist as implied in the Scripture (Mk. 9: 13), and after the Resurrection He upbraided the dull wits and sluggish hearts that failed to see that the prophets had foretold the sufferings of the Christ on the way to His glory. (Lk. 24: 25 f., 44 f.

In spite of this it is difficult to believe that all the light came from the Scriptures. It is difficult for us, even after the event, to find in them a clear prophecy either of the Cross, or of the Resurrection on the third day. It seems, therefore, that we must fall back on the other possibility of which I spoke. We must assume that Jesus knew what lay before Him by direct revelation, and came to the Scriptures to confirm and perhaps to define His interpretation of the vision that had been vouchsafed to Him.

The reference in the passage before us to the brazen serpent is a case in point. I do not see how the type, taken by itself, could have suggested a death by crucifixion. As soon, however, as the mind has been filled with the idea of the Cross, the elevation of the serpent on its pole might well attract attention. Then further meditation on the type would suggest visions of hope, that cast gleams of light into the deepest mysteries that surround the event that it prefigured. A dead body on a tree was an embodied curse (Dt. 21 : 23), an outward symbol of the sentence of God upon sin. It must have been hard for the Sinless One to contemplate the prospect of being publicly set forth before the eyes of men under that aspect. But this type suggested that a purpose of love underlay that display. It set forth, in a striking figure, sin made to minister to its own defeat, the instrument of divine judgement transformed by divine appointment into a source and spring of salvation to all who will lift their eyes to it that they may live.

We must not, of course, exaggerate the extent of the foreknowledge to which the evidence points. As far as the evidence goes, it was limited to the death and the incidents directly connected with it. And here there is no indication that the day or the hour were revealed long in advance; though He knew that the place must be Jerusalem (Lk. 13: 33), and may well have been sure that the time would coincide with the Feast of the Passover. And He knew, at least negatively, when the time was not ripe (Jn. 2:4, 7:6).

There is nothing to suggest that He knew in advance what to expect on any ordinary day in His ministry. So what we have to consider is simply the effect of living, as it were, continually under a sentence of death in the company of one whose treachery He foresaw from the beginning (Jn. 6: 64).

The first point that stands out is that the sentence of

death, foreseen and accepted, so far from inspiring a fatalistic spirit of dull, lifeless resignation, becomes a spirit of free, spontaneous, indomitable energy. The fact that He is acting in obedience to His Father's commandment does not make the laying down of His life one whit less His own act (Jn. 10: 18). It does not even prevent Him from praying to the Father in His agony that the cup might pass from Him.

It is natural, of course, that it should inspire courage. He has counted the cost. He is not afraid of them that kill the body and after that have nothing that they can do. Death itself has no terrors for Him. He is in His Father's hand. And in His Father's house are many abiding places. So to leave the world is simply to go to the Father. He never sees death, as we shall have other occasions to notice, except against a background of life. Whenever He speaks of His own death it is always as a gateway into fuller life, either for Himself, or for His brethren.

At the same time the consciousness that His days were numbered, instead of paralysing His will, only increased His sense of the value of time. No one ever numbered His days with such scrupulous care. "We must work the works of Him that sent me while it is day. Night cometh when no man can work" (Jn. 9: 4).

And again "Are there not twelve hours in the day? If a man walk in the day he stumbleth not, because he seeth the light of this world. But if a man walk in the night, he stumbleth, because the light is not in him." So He goes forward unfalteringly to follow the guidance of His Father's will, and to bring life to Lazarus and deeper faith to the sorrowing sisters in Bethany, in spite of the danger to Himself that the journey and the mighty work must bring. "We are all of us immortal till our work is done".

The result is a wonderful evenness of spirit. He lives ever looking to His Father. He is not troubled by the thought of what lies in store for Him: for in the true sense of the words He never thought of Himself at all. His meat is to do the will of Him that sent Him and to finish His work. His one care is to secure His Father's approval, to do what is well-pleasing in His sight. The result is a perfect freedom from worry and fret. He can let the morrow take thought for itself; while He bears the burden of each day in its day, supported by the bread for the daily need which He has taught us all to ask from our Father, casting all our anxiety upon Him, for He is in charge of us.

It is not surprising, therefore, that He is in no sense at the mercy of moods. It is not, of course, to be imagined that His life was passionless after the Stoic ideal. At least on one occasion we are told of a rapture of holy exultation (Lk. 10: 21). And we know from a single significant utterance, "I have a baptism to be baptized with, and how am I straitened till it be accomplished!" (Lk. 12: 50) that the agony in the garden did not stand altogether alone in His experience. He had to fight, as we have at times to fight, against fits of depression. Yet the abiding habit of His life, the characteristic fruit of the Spirit whose guidance He had followed all His days, was joy and peace: a joy and peace which were never so radiant as in the Upper Chamber, when the shadows of death were closing in, and He was imparting to those who were to carry on His work in the world the treasures that He had gathered in the course of His earthly experience. (See Jn. 14:27, 15:11, 16:33, 17:13.)

REFLECTIONS OF THE EVANGELIST

16 *For God so loved the world, that he gave his only begotten Son, that whosoever believeth on him should not perish, but have eternal* 17 *life. For God sent not the Son into the world to judge the world;* 18 *but that the world should be saved through him. He that believeth on him is not judged: he that believeth not hath been judged already, because he hath not believed on the name of the only begotten Son* 19 *of God. And this is the judgement, that the light is come into the world, and men loved the darkness rather than the light; for their* 20 *works were evil. For every one that doeth ill hateth the light, and* 21 *cometh not to the light, lest his works should be reproved. But he that doeth the truth cometh to the light, that his works may be made manifest, that they have been wrought in God.*

S. John's report of the conversation with Nicodemus ends,

I believe, with the reference to the brazen serpent. We are left to infer the effect it produced by the references to Nicodemus in 7: 50 and in 19: 39. S. John's interest is centred in the vision of the Cross called up by the words of the Lord which he has just recorded, and in the sad spectacle of the rejection by men of the offer of life which the Cross brings to them from God.

The issue of this rejection is judgement. The Baptist, we may remember, had represented the Messiah as coming with a winnowing fan in His hand to sift the chaff from the wheat on His threshing floor. The same message that declared that the Kingdom of Heaven was at hand declared also that an axe was being laid at the root of every unfruitful tree. For salvation and judgement are not two separate acts of God, but two strangely contrasted results of one and the same act. As Professor Seeley pointed out in a very striking chapter of *Ecce Homo*, Christ's call was His winnowing fan. It sifted out, as we should say automatically, the sound elements in the nation. It made each man judge himself. A man shewed in what direction his heart was set by his response, or by his refusal to respond, to Christ's invitation to all men to follow Him.

It is not surprising, therefore, that the end of the conversation with Nicodemus, and the thought of the wrestling of the light with the darkness in the heart of that earnest seeker after truth, and especially the reference to the Cross at its close, should have started in S. John's mind this train of reflection on the self-executing judgement of God.

He is anxious, however, from the first to guard against a natural misconception. The thought of God's judgement has, rightly or wrongly, such terrors for sinful men, that they forget that judgement is not and can never be the end, but only the means to the end, for which God created and sustains the world. S. John starts, therefore, from the Cross as the supreme evidence of the love of God for all that He has made. As S. Paul puts the thought (Rom. 8: 32), He spared not, He did not withhold the sacrifice, even of His own Son, but freely gave Him up for us all.

The giving began, to use human language of the timeless act of God, in the Incarnation; but all that the giving meant in absolute surrender to the service of man, on the part both of the Father and of the Son, was only revealed before the eyes of men in all its length and breadth and depth and height on the Cross. The Cross, therefore, as the inscription over the reredos in S. Paul's Cathedral testifies, is the measure of the immeasurable love of God. In the beautiful words of the prayer in which the Church of England continually shews forth the Lord's death till He come, the eternal Father, of His tender love to all mankind, did give his only Son that He might offer "a full, perfect and sufficient sacrifice, oblation and satisfaction for the sins of the whole world". Whatever, therefore, may be the immediate effect of the appeal of the Cross on those who reject it, no one can maintain that its object was to increase the guilt, and so to bring about the destruction of those who reject that appeal. Its object was to reveal the infinite love of the Father and the Son for sinful man, and so to open the one and only way to eternal life by quickening faith in the Crucified. The final goal of the Incarnation is the salvation of the world, though the Son could not help judging if He came. "God sent not His Son into the world to judge the world, but that the world should be saved through Him" (cf. Jn. 12: 47).

The judgement of the world, therefore, terrible as are its immediate consequences, cannot be inconsistent with the ultimate triumph of the real purpose of God.

We must be careful not to think of judgement and salvation as mutually exclusive opposites. Those who accept Christ do not come into judgement. They enter directly into life eternal. For the rest, unless the purpose of God is to fail, judgement must be a step on the road to salvation.

It is, indeed, difficult to see how this can be, as regards individuals, unless we can believe that a resurrection is possible from the second death. But the history of Israel, as recorded in the Old Testament, is enough to show that successive judgements have power to purge the life of a nation. And, though the discipline of a thousand years was not enough to prepare the Chosen People as a whole to accept Christ at His first coming, S. Paul assures us that God's purpose for Israel still holds good, and in the long last all Israel shall be saved (Rom. 11 : 25).

Whether, however, it be easy, or whether it be hard, to see how God can bring the world to the goal which He has purposed, it is of great importance that we should keep firm hold of the revelation that He has given us of what that purpose is. Living, as we do, in a world which is being continually called to give an account of itself before God, and in a dispensation the first word of which is a call to repentance in view of the all-embracing judgement which is to mark its close, it is peculiarly difficult for us to remember that this judgement, which looms so large and threateningly before us, is only the end of the present order, and not, as we sometimes allow ourselves carelessly to speak and think of it, the end of all things. Like every end that we can conceive of, it is at the same time a beginning. And so we forget what is surely obvious, as soon as we begin to think, that judgement was made for the world, and not the world for judgement. And we fail on the one hand to bear an adequate witness to the infinite depths of the wisdom and the love and the power of God, and on the other we miss the purifying and stimulating power which a clear vision of the revealed purpose of God is calculated to inspire.

For, as long as our horizon is limited by the last judgement, the members of the Church cannot help regarding themselves as elect to salvation out of a lost and perishing world, with the result that they are themselves in danger of being shut up in the prison-house of an exclusive Pharisaism, and are apt to give to the outsider the impression that the chief characteristic of the God in whom they believe is that "He drowned the world one day, and is going to burn it all up on another".

Of course neither of these consequences is inevitable, even with the narrower horizon; but they would both become impossible if we always kept before our eyes the vision of the true end of creation. The cure for a spirit of exclusiveness is to realize that our own personal hope of salvation is built on the rock of a world-wide redemption. And no one whom we have taught to believe that God sent not His Son into the world to condemn the world but that the world through Him might be saved, can confuse the relation between wrath and love in the character of God.

The concluding verses of this section, 3: 18–21, give us S. John's first analysis of the causes at work in the rejection of Jesus by the Jews. Sometimes, as in 5: 44; 6: 44; 8: 24, 43, he gives words of Jesus Himself throwing light on it. His own final summary is in 12: 39–43.

In these verses (3: 18–21) the Light that has come into the world is identified with the name of the only-begotten Son of God, i.e. with the perfect revelation of God as Father, which He brought to men. The man who turns his back on that revelation, shows by so doing that his mind is set on pleasing himself, and not on pleasing God. And so he finds himself excluded from His presence. He shrinks from the inexorable verdict of his conscience. On the other hand the Light has an irresistible attraction for the man who is set on being true to the truth, so far as he has hitherto been able to apprehend it. It opens to him a door into an assurance that he lives and moves and has his being in God. As Jesus Himself tells us in Mk. 3: 35, "He that doeth the will of God is my brother, and sister and mother". He has been born from above.

THE CROWNING WITNESS OF THE BAPTIST

22 *After these things came Jesus and his disciples into the land of*
23 *Judaea; and there he tarried with them, and baptized. And John also was baptizing in Ænon near to Salim, because there was much*
24 *water there: and they came, and were baptized. For John was not*
25 *yet cast into prison. There arose therefore a questioning on the part*
26 *of John's disciples with a Jew about purifying. And they came unto John, and said to him, Rabbi, he that was with thee beyond Jordan, to whom thou hast borne witness, behold, the same baptizeth, and*
27 *all men come to him. John answered and said, A man can receive*

28 *nothing, except it have been given him from heaven. Ye yourselves bear me witness, that I said, I am not the Christ, but, that I am*
29 *sent before him. He that hath the bride is the bridegroom: but the friend of the bridegroom, which standeth and heareth him, rejoiceth greatly because of the bridegroom's voice: this my joy therefore is*
30 *fulfilled. He must increase, but I must decrease.*
31 *He that cometh from above is above all: he that is of the earth is of the earth, and of the earth he speaketh: he that cometh from*
32 *heaven is above all. What he hath seen and heard, of that he*
33 *beareth witness; and no man receiveth his witness. He that hath*
34 *received his witness hath set his seal to* this, *that God is true. For he whom God hath sent speaketh the words of God: for he giveth*
35 *not the Spirit by measure. The Father loveth the Son, and hath*
36 *given all things into his hand. He that believeth on the Son hath eternal life; but he that obeyeth not the Son shall not see life, but the wrath of God abideth on him.*

The scene shifts from Jerusalem to the country districts of Judæa, in the neighbourhood of the Jordan. The memory of this interlude had entirely faded out of the common tradition. S. Mark, we may remember, passes straight from the baptism and the temptation to the ministry in Galilee (Mk. 1: 13–14) "after John had been delivered up". It is not surprising, therefore, that S. John's narrative shews signs that he had at this time to correct a popular misapprehension. "For John", he says (verse 24) "was not yet cast into prison". The work of the Baptist was not yet completed. There were others of the people, besides the Pharisees, who had not yet come forward to prepare themselves for the coming of the Kingdom by accepting baptism at his hands.

It is interesting to notice that though the time had not yet come for the full baptism with the Spirit, Jesus felt that there was still room for the preliminary baptism as a token of repentance, and, if not with His own hands (4: 2) at least by the hands of His disciples, He baptized those who wished to join His company. We are not told how long this custom continued. There seems no trace of it "after John had been cast into prison".

The main significance of the episode lies in the fact that it gave the Baptist an occasion to give a crowning expression to his great humility. It was called out by what looks like a misguided effort on the part of over-loyal disciples to provoke him to jealousy. The story is introduced by a reference to a discussion between some of John's disciples and a Jew (or Jews) concerning purification, which is generally assumed to be connected with the significance of the rite of baptism, as administered on the one side by the Baptist, and on the other by the disciples of Jesus. "They came to John and said to him, 'Rabbi, he who was with thee beyond Jordan, to whom thou hast borne witness, is baptizing and all men are coming to him'." To this John makes a memorable response. "No man can receive anything but what has been given him from heaven. Ye yourselves bear me witness that I said, 'I am not the Christ', but I have been sent before Him. He that hath the bride is the bridegroom. The friend of the bridegroom, who stands and listens to him, rejoiceth with joy for the voice of the bridegroom. This my joy, therefore, has been consummated. He must increase, but I must decrease".

This is surely an illuminating utterance. It rings true. The most loyal of disciples could not, we feel instinctively, have dared to create an expression of such utter self-effacement. Though if he had heard it, or heard of it, he might well cherish it as intimately characteristic.

There is indeed in a sense nothing new in it. The same spirit speaks in it that we hear in Mk. 1 : 7. "He that is mightier than I cometh, whose shoes' latchet I am not worthy to stoop down to unloose". This is he, who, as our Evangelist himself told us, said, "He that cometh after me has taken His place ahead of me, because He was eternally my Chief". Only the thought finds more poignant expression when it is brought up sharp against the temptation to gratify a natural desire to satisfy the expectation of enthusiastic disciples.

They were jealous for the honour of their master. They found it hard to think of his being superseded. And yet his true greatness, as the Evangelist, who had himself been a disciple, clearly feels, never came out so clearly as when he showed that he accepted wholeheartedly the subordinate position for which God had created him. We feel that we can share with fuller assurance his conviction that he had indeed a mission from God, because he expressly disclaims the highest place.

It is important also to notice the hidden implications of the position that he claims for his Chief, in asserting his subordination to Him. The bridegroom and the bride bring to our minds a beautiful and homely picture full of human interest. But to a student of the prophets, especially of Hosea, that picture has a heavenly meaning. It expressed the ultimate reality of the relation in which the God of Israel stood to His Chosen People. The Lord Himself was the bridegroom. The rebellious, apparently incurably unfaithful, people was His bride. In some real sense the Baptist testified that God Himself was in Christ betrothing His bride to Himself afresh. And by a natural extension of the same figure, the Baptist claims for himself a distinctive place as "the friend of the bridegroom", whose function, as Godet points out, was to conduct all the business connected with betrothal, including presiding at the marriage feast. It must be more than a coincidence that Jesus Himself uses the same figure, in His answer to a question on fasting, based on the agreement of the Baptist's disciples and the Pharisees against His own practice. "Can the wedding guests fast while the bridegroom is with them?"

The concluding verses of the chapter (31–36) are commonly regarded as a reflection by the Evangelist. Some are inclined to believe that it is really a continuation of the comment on the conversation with Nicodemus which began, as we saw, at verse 16. They think that there has been a dislocation in the text, here as at other points in the Gospel. They think that verses 31–36 should follow directly after verse 21.

No doubt the Evangelist is entirely responsible for the form of the report, and it not unnaturally echoes some of the phrases which he has just used in his account of the conversation with Nicodemus. But Godet is right in suggesting that the personal disclaimer of the forerunner in verse 30 requires as a complement a more positive witness to the true character of his Successor. So the section is really in place where it is. And in substance it may well be derived from the Baptist himself. We cannot imagine that the Baptist had not been informed of the result of our Lord's first appeal to the authorities at Jerusalem.

There is, in fact, fresh point in the words, if we regard them as the Baptist's comment on the rejection of his own testimony to Jesus by the Sadducean hierarchy. He had, we may remember, publicly declared (1: 34) that Jesus was "the Son of God", and that he had seen "the Spirit descending as a dove from heaven and abiding on Him". This was the ground of his conviction that Jesus was eternally His Chief (1: 33). He may well have had bright memories of their talks together before and after the baptism which he had tried to prevent. It is not incredible, therefore, that he may have taken this opportunity to restate his own conviction. "He that cometh from above is absolutely supreme". His whole teaching comes from a region to which we common men have no access. "He that is from the earth is from the earth and draws his inspiration from the earth: He that cometh from heaven testifies of what He has seen and heard, and no one receives His testimony" (Cf. Jn. 3: 11.).

This, however, is not a complete account of the matter. The Baptist himself was an instance to the contrary. So he can go on: "He that hath received His testimony has set his seal to this, that God is true". For he can recognize the voice of God speaking through His Chosen. God has by the gift of the Spirit fully equipped Him for that work. "He whom God sent speaks the words of God", for His gift of the Spirit is without reserve. The Son, as the object of His Father's love, has all authority committed to Him.

In some dim way the Baptist may even have been conscious that faith in the Son would open the way into the life of communion with God: while those who disobeyed Him must abide in the death of His displeasure.

CHAPTER VIII

THE WOMAN OF SAMARIA

1 *When therefore the Lord knew how that the Pharisees had heard that Jesus was making and baptizing more disciples than John* 2 *(although Jesus himself baptized not, but his disciples),* 3 *he left* 4 *Judæa, and departed again into Galilee. And he must needs pass* 5 *through Samaria. So he cometh to a city of Samaria, called Sychar,* 6 *near to the parcel of ground that Jacob gave to his son Joseph: and Jacob's well was there. Jesus therefore, being wearied with his* 7 *journey, sat thus by the well. It was about the sixth hour. There cometh a woman of Samaria to draw water: Jesus saith unto her* 8 *Give me to drink. For his disciples were gone away into the city* 9 *to buy food. The Samaritan woman therefore saith unto him, How is it that thou, being a Jew, askest drink of me, which am a Samaritan woman? (For Jews have no dealings with Samaritans.)* 10 *Jesus answered and said unto her, If thou knewest the gift of God, and who it is that saith to thee, Give me to drink; thou wouldest have asked of him, and he would have given thee living water.* 11 *The woman saith unto him, Sir, thou hast nothing to draw with, and the well is deep: from whence then hast thou that living water?* 12 *Art thou greater than our Father Jacob, which gave us the well,* 13 *and drank thereof himself, and his sons, and his cattle? Jesus answered and said unto her, Everyone that drinketh of this water* 14 *shall thirst again: but whosoever drinketh of the water that I shall give him shall never thirst; but the water that I shall give him shall become in him a well of water springing up unto eternal* 15 *life. The woman saith unto him, Sir, give me this water, that I* 16 *thirst not, neither come all the way hither to draw. Jesus saith* 17 *unto her, Go, call thy husband and come hither. The woman answered and said unto him, I have no husband. Jesus saith unto* 18 *her. Thou saidst well, I have no husband: for thou hast had five husbands; and he whom thou now hast is not thy husband: this* 19 *hast thou said truly. The woman saith unto him, Sir, I perceive* 20 *that thou art a prophet. Our fathers worshipped in this mountain; and ye say, that in Jerusalem is the place where men ought to worship.*

21 *Jesus saith unto her, Woman, believe me, the hour cometh, when neither in this mountain, nor in Jerusalem, shall ye worship the*
22 *Father. Ye worship that which ye know not: we worship that*
23 *which we know: for salvation is from the Jews. But the hour cometh, and now is, when the true worshippers shall worship the Father in spirit and truth: for such doth the Father seek to be his*
24 *worshippers. God is a Spirit: and they that worship him must*
25 *worship in spirit and truth. The woman saith unto him, I know that Messiah cometh (which is called Christ): when he is come,*
26 *he will declare unto us all things. Jesus saith unto her, I that speak unto thee am* he.

WHEN the Baptist, with the connivance, if not at the instigation, of the Jewish authorities (Mk. 1: 14), had been arrested by Herod Antipas, Jesus transferred the scene of His activity to Galilee, in order to secure greater freedom of action (Jn. 4: 3). On His way north He passed through Samaria, and was resting outside Sychar when the conversation with the Samaritan woman, which S. John has recorded for us, took place. The story is told from the point of view of someone standing by our Lord's side (verses 7, 27). It is not, I think, a necessary inference from verse 8 that Jesus was left quite alone; and though, of course, S. John might have learnt what had passed between them from either of the interlocutors, it seems easier to suppose that he is reproducing (as in the case of Nicodemus) the salient features of a conversation at which he had himself been present.

The contrast between the two conversations is complete. Nicodemus was a strict Pharisee, a member of the Sanhedrim, and eminently respectable. The woman was a Samaritan, living openly in a condition which her own conscience told her was sinful. Nicodemus came of his own accord to make overtures with a view to ultimate discipleship, and left without making the great surrender. The woman had no choice in the matter. Before she knew where she was, she found herself talking to a stranger who had something to say to her. But she only left Him to bring the whole city out to test the validity of a new-born hope.

They meet by the side of the well under the shadow of Mount Gerizim, near Sychar, one of the few sites in the Gospel story which seems still capable of precise identification. It is the sixth hour, i.e. either midday, or, as seems more probable, 6 p.m. The woman would hardly have come out to draw water in the heat of the day. Jesus has been walking all day, and is resting by the well, while His disciples go into the town to buy food. Jesus did not, during His earthly ministry, regard Samaria as coming within His province. He expressly forbad the apostles, when He sent them on their mission (Mt. 10: 5), to enter into any Samaritan town, and He may well have observed the same rule Himself in the opening months of His ministry. The refusal of hospitality recorded in Lk. 9: 52 may have been due to the fact that the Samaritans knew that He would not stay to preach to them.

At the same time, an individual Samaritan whom He could help had a claim on Him, and He forgot His fatigue in the effort to use the opportunity which His Father (verse 34) put in His way.

His method of approach is worth careful study by all who wish to become "fishers of men" in His spirit and after His example. It would be difficult to imagine a harder problem than this woman presented. There was, to start with, a barrier of convention between them. Even His disciples, when they returned, were startled to find their Master conversing with a woman (verse 27). But harder still to cross was the racial and religious animosity that separated the Samaritan from the Jew. They had nothing in common but their common humanity, and a common faith in the God of Jacob. Even deeper was the moral gulf between the sinner, who, as yet, had no desire to be set free from her sin, and the All Holy.

Jesus begins in the simplest and most natural way—a way so natural, that it is impossible to say whether it was of set purpose or by what we call accident that it opened the way for talk on the deepest things. All we know for certain is that

He was on the alert, and ready to use the opportunity that this opening gave Him. He asked her, as Eliezer asked Rebecca, to give Him to drink. His thirst was a link with her, and gave her an opportunity of service.

She is, however, in no hurry to avail herself of the opportunity. She is in a position of fancied superiority, and will humble the pride of the Jew before she will satisfy His need. "So the Jew, in His necessity, is not above craving help of the Samaritan?"

Centuries of cruel wrong and bitter hatred find a voice in the ungracious word. Jesus passes it by without comment. He is conscious only of His own longing to help, and the thick cloud of misconception that shuts her off from seeing Him. So He excites her curiosity, and at the same time helps her to a truer estimate of the relation in which He stands to her. He says: "If thou hadst known the free gift of God, and who it is that speaketh to thee, thou wouldest have asked Him, and He would have given thee living water".

There is here no touch of resentment, only, it may be, a touch of regret at the churlishness involved in the refusal to share the good gift of God for the quenching of physical thirst. The whole thought is of the spiritual thirst, which He had come to slake, a thirst none the less real that she could not, as yet, put it into words.

She is puzzled and interested. She was, of course, quite unable to fathom the meaning of the utterance. But she knew enough to know that she did not know. The only sense she could attach to the words "living water" was the water of a running stream. The well she had come to was, we are told, fed by a fresh spring. But that gave no satisfactory sense to the words. The water of the well was out of the stranger's reach, and it would take a greater than Jacob to give a greater boon.

She was right so far, and right also in laying bare her perplexity to Him who had caused it. He at once comes to her help by repeating His parable, with fresh illustrations of the blessings included in the boon that He offered. "The living water that I offer you is unlike the water of this well, cool and refreshing though it be. My living water satisfies. It becomes a part of those who drink it, springing up in them in a perpetual stream."

The woman has not, as yet, any clear conception of the nature of the gift. But it sounds attractive, has obvious advantages, and is to be had for the asking. So she asks for it, expressly as a deliverance from the daily drudgery of coming to fetch the means of quenching her thirst.

Samaritan as she is, she is humbled now to asking promised help of one who is a Jew. And Jesus at once takes steps to fulfil the promise according to His own meaning in it. She cannot, however, receive the gift without a clearer knowledge of the giver, and, we may well believe, without giving up her sin.

So He lays on her the seemingly simple condition that she should bring her husband with her to share the boon.

Startled and ashamed, she will not confess the whole truth, but she will not act a lie. She says, "I have no husband".

The way is now opened for a flash of piercing judgement. Characteristically laying stress on the fragment of truth which found expression in her answer, the admission of the illicit character of the state in which she was living, He says: "Thou saidst well, 'I have no *husband*', for thou hast had five husbands, and he whom thou now hast is not thine husband. In this thou hast spoken a true thing". The word is a sharp sword, piercing to the dividing asunder of joints and marrow, quick to discern the thoughts and intents of the heart. She recognizes, as Nathanael had done (1 : 48), that she is in the presence of one who, in some strange but most real way, knows her through and through. When she gets home, the point on which she lays stress is just this. "Come, see a man who told me all that I did" (verse 29).

At this point the woman, as I read the scene, stands for a time awed and irresolute. Did Jesus mean her to go and fetch the man, knowing the relation between them? If not, what was she to do? Silence at last becomes intolerable, and she breaks it with a confession of the faith which His power to read her heart had awakened in her, "Lord, I see that thou art a prophet." But she cannot stop there. The fact that she recognizes a spiritual power in Him only intensifies her consciousness of the gulf between them caused by the Samaritan schism. Does she fear that He has come to rebuke her people for apostasy, and to call them to submit to their haughty and hated rivals? Or does she believe that the arbiter has come for whom they have been waiting so long—the Prophet like unto Moses, who should solve all the questions that had been left in dispute pending His arrival? In any case, she seems to have felt instinctively that perfect confidence is impossible between people who cannot worship side by side, even though they look up to the same God. So she goes on to state the point at issue: "Our fathers worshipped in this mountain; but ye say that in Jerusalem is the place where men ought to worship".

The Samaritans, we must remember, were a mixed race. The worship of Jehovah, the God of the land, who could save them from the lions, was at first, for many of them, merely an adjunct to the worship of the gods they had brought with them from their own lands (2 Kgs. 17: 33). They had, at a later period, received the Book of the Law, and had built a Temple on Mount Gerizim, but their Bible contained neither the later historical books nor the writings of the Prophets. We gather from the account of the visit of Philip (Ac. 8) and from the history of the first two centuries A.D. that they were a superstitious, excitable people.

The dangers to which worship would be exposed among them must have been in marked contrast to the dangers which beset worship among the Jews. Jewish worship was, before all things, correct. It was liable at any time to become formal and mechanical. Samaritan worship was sure to be emotional, at the mercy of any strong influence, whether that of Simon Magus or any other who came their way. So, while the Jews were in danger of worshipping "in letter", not "in spirit", the Samaritans were in danger of having a false idea of God before them when they prayed, and therefore of failing to offer the true worship, which can only come forth from a man's heart in response to the revelation of the true God.

Jesus, "in the days of His flesh", had no commission to heal the Samaritan schism. That healing would come in due course as the result of the breaking down of all partition walls that came with His death, and was consummated by the destruction of the Temple at Jerusalem—that which, instead of opening its gates to become a house of prayer for all nations, had become the home of the most rigid and exclusive privilege.

Meanwhile He could prepare His listener for the good time coming by opening her eyes to the lessons which the value that she set on worship, and I think we may say on corporate worship, showed that she was capable of appreciating. Days were coming when both the rival shrines would be abolished. But worship would not thereby become impossible. Worship is determined by the character of Him to whom, and not by the place in which, it is offered. God was revealing Himself in His new name as Father through His Son, and the revelation of the Father will resolve all the differences between Jew and Samaritan.

The hour cometh when neither in this mountain nor yet in Jerusalem shall ye do homage to the Father.

This new name, "Father", appearing in the very sentence of doom on the sanctuaries, had in it the promise of a new mode of access to God's presence, and of full and perfect communion between men everywhere and their Maker. Jesus speaks of God here as Father absolutely (that is, not as My Father or your Father) for the first time in this Gospel. And He goes on to help the woman to understand that the thing that really matters in worship is not the place where, but the Person to whom, it is offered.

He points out, in passing, a fundamental difference between Jewish and Samaritan worship, to which this thought gives the key. In neither case did worship rise to the height of personal communion. In both clauses we find the neuter *that which* instead of the masculine *Him whom* of the object of worship. But the Samaritans were worshipping in the dark "that which they knew not". The Jews, on whose faithfulness to their trust the hope of the world depended, had received the oracles of God. God had revealed and was revealing Himself to men in and through them. They knew that which they worshipped, "for salvation is to spring forth from the Jews".

He then goes on at once to work out the characteristics of true worship from the point of view of the kingdom, the day for which had already begun to dawn. He does this in terms which are no doubt of universal significance. *The hour cometh and now is when the true worshippers*—those who offer living worship to the true God—*shall worship the Father in spirit and truth. For indeed the Father seeketh such to be His worshippers. God is Spirit—or a Spirit—and they that worship must worship in spirit and truth.*

These words, we feel instinctively, are very deep. But the teaching, we must not allow ourselves to forget, was given in the first instance to an ordinary Samaritan woman, below, it might seem, rather than above, the average in education and in the power of spiritual apprehension.

The words which remain on our minds as we read them again and again are the words "in spirit and in truth", so repeated as to form the climax in each of the two divisions into which the teaching falls. Under the old covenant the attention of worshippers had been directed upon the particular place for worship, which the Samaritan woman had been taught to suppose to be of the first importance, and upon its outward form. But the importance attached to these matters under the old dispensation only meant that God's people were being trained in acts of worship before its inner meaning was revealed to them. The goal of worship, indeed, under the old dispensation, "to appear before the presence of God", or "to see the face of God", was one with the goal in the new. But the secret of attaining what was implied in that goal was not yet fully opened. And in leading men into worship in the new order, our Lord makes it stand forth with new distinctness that the vitally important thing is the spirit in which the worship is offered. Reality and truth in this respect is the condition of worship attaining its end and bringing the worshipper into touch with God.

Jesus also uses the name "Father", we must not fail to notice, in His teaching of the Samaritan woman with emphatic reiteration. But nothing is said to develop the fulness of the meaning contained in it. It is a word of universal significance, common to all races of men, and is plainer than any explanation can make it. Jesus does, however, connect one most significant fact with it, which is not expressed with the same definiteness in the Sermon on the Mount, though the whole conception of prayer is there transfigured in the light of the revelation of the Fatherhood of God, and the Lord's Prayer is in every clause a revelation of the blessings that the Father has in store for His children, as soon as they have learnt to ask for them in spirit and in truth.

This fact is one which has an important bearing on all our thoughts about prayer. We are apt to regard prayer as having its spring and source in ourselves, in our own sense of need, and so as a movement from below upwards. But this is a mistake. The fountain and spring of all prayer, the spirit of grace and intercession, is in the heavens. "The Father seeketh such to be His worshippers." The very impulse to pray and to turn to God comes from Him. It is a sign that He is in touch with us, and is already at work through His Holy Spirit drawing us to Himself.

So the answer to the Samaritan woman unsealed (in its revelation of the same Spirit) the fountain of living water, by which alone the thirst of the human soul for God can be quenched. For her perplexity with regard to the place of worship raised at once the question of the use and meaning of worship in the life of the Kingdom, and of the power by which alone that worship could be offered acceptably.

On the surface the answer looks as if it were nothing more than a concise summary of the divine requirements, just as the answer to Nicodemus reads at first more like an iron law than a gospel. For the requirements are, no doubt, ideally perfect. The worship must be the response of the inmost being of a man to the surpassing glory of the vision of the true God. It must be "in spirit", that is, on man's side it must be a free, spontaneous, personal act, neither formal nor mechanical. It must be "in truth" or "reality", that is, it must be intelligent and sincere, free at once from the dangers of ignorance and superstition, and from any taint of hypocrisy. But nothing seems to be said to show us how we can satisfy the requirements. Yet even so it cannot be meant as a counsel of despair. And indeed the revelation of God as Father is, as we have seen, made the occasion here of the declaration of His longing for communion with His children. The Father Himself is seeking for men to fulfil the conditions of perfect worship. And it is suggested that there is a close connexion between these conditions and the revelation of God Himself as Spirit.

What then, we cannot but ask, is meant by saying that "God is Spirit"? If we try to define the spiritual to ourselves, we are apt to think of it simply as the opposite to the material. But on this definition the utterance does not carry us very far; for we are not, any more than the Jews or the Samaritans, inclined to bow down to wood or stone. And considering the person to whom our Lord is talking, is it likely that the revelation is couched in terms meant to be abstract and philosophical? Local conditions suggest another view. Samaria, we must remember, was the home of Simon Magus (Ac. 8). And the Samaritans seem to have been peculiarly susceptible to influences in some sense spiritual. It would seem, therefore, that the thought that the words would have conveyed to the mind to which they were first addressed would have been simply that God was a living force, active and personal.

Let us, then, start from that. Do the words so understood seem trite and common-place, singularly uninspiring? Put beside them the vision of a blind, soulless, mechanical universe, which has somehow blundered into the production of sentient beings. Then beside this, again, put the vision of a living God, whose will is a real power in the development of life and in the ordering of events, whether we are to conceive it as acting from without or from within. In the spirit of this latter vision, let us think of ourselves as creatures not existing by accident and without meaning, but called into being by a God who, as a living God, may conceivably love and care for what He has made to live. Then we may see something of the value of this assurance from our Lord that the Father of our spirits is, to say the least, not less alive than we.

It is a deep saying of Dr. Hort's: "If God sinks into the world, man sinks into it too". Our own sense of personality must be a delusion unless there is a true personality also in God.

But if there is, then a door is opened at once for the possibility of communion between man and God. "Spirit with Spirit can meet." What can be more natural than that the spirit of man, born again of the Spirit of God, should enter into conscious relation with its Source? And when we look closely into the phrase, this is what worship "in spirit" really means.

Competent interpreters are divided on the question whether these words, "in spirit", refer to the human spirit or to the divine. It is strange, but it is true, that there is an inveterate ambiguity in the phrase "in spirit" in the New Testament, and I cannot myself help feeling that the reference is characteristically to both. The life of the human spirit and the life of the divine Spirit are not by any means mutually exclusive. And when a man is "in spirit" his personality is not absorbed or destroyed. His human spirit is possessed, fulfilled, uplifted by the divine. At last he knows what it is to be truly man, and at the same time finds himself by his response raised into conscious communion with God (cf. Eph. 2: 18, 22; 6: 18; Rev. 1: 10; 4: 2).

And if the spirit of man is thus dependent on the Spirit of God for its own true life, it follows that the requirement that worship should be "in spirit" is not primarily a call to man to stir himself to action, it is the declaration of power coming from God to supply all his need. And, we may add, the further requirement, truth, must be interpreted on the same lines. It is the revelation of a provision made by God, not a condition which the man, as his part of the bargain, is bound to fulfil. The true worshipper is kept real and sincere because his worship is the response of his whole being to the vision of the truth.

If this be the nature of worship in the Kingdom, we see at once, that it is no longer a thing which can be limited to definite acts performed in particular places at specified times. The conditions are the conditions in which the whole life of the member of the Kingdom is being lived. His whole life, on its Godward side, must be worship. He must, as S. Paul exhorts him, continually present his body as a living sacrifice to God (Rom. 12: 1), and this requires the renewal of the mind. The community of believers is a spiritual house, in which the simplest acts of service are spiritual sacrifices acceptable to God through Jesus Christ (1 Pet. 2: 5).

This does not, of course, mean that there is no necessity for definite acts of worship, both private and public. The Gospel records of our Lord's prayers are in themselves sufficient proof to the contrary. And public worship must be performed in a particular place at a specified time. But these definite acts must conform to the conditions laid down for all worship. They are only in place in the context of a whole life lived "in spirit and truth".

The teaching on worship had soared to heights and sounded depths which were, for the time at least, beyond the reach of the Samaritan woman. Her answer, however, showed that she had been listening not unsympathetically. The words that she had heard raised living hopes in her heart, and her thoughts turned at once to the ultimate Solver of the difficulties she had raised,[1] whose advent both Jews

[1] It is worth noting that a doubtful point concerning the stones of the profaned altar in the Temple at Jerusalem was expressly reserved by Judas Maccabæus "until a prophet should come to give an answer concerning them" (1 Macc. 4: 46), and in *The Testament of Benjamin* (9: 2) the visitation of an only begotten (or belovèd) Prophet is expected to glorify the second Temple.

and Samaritans were expecting, in accordance with the promise in Dt. 18: 18.

She speaks of him as "Messiah". But her Christ was to to be a Prophet, not a King; a reader of the hearts of men (verse 29), not a ruler over them. Jesus could therefore reveal Himself to her in that capacity without reserve. "I that am speaking to you am He." So she leaves her waterpot, and goes to summon, not her husband only, but all the town, to share her discovery.

THE RETURN OF THE DISCIPLES

27 *And upon this came his disciples; and they marvelled that he was speaking with a woman; yet no man said, What seekest thou? or,* 28 *Why speakest thou with her? So the woman left her waterpot, and* 29 *went away into the city, and saith to the men, Come see a man, which told me all things that* ever *I did: can this be the Christ?* 30 *They went out of the city, and were coming to him.* 31 *In the mean-* 32 *while the disciples prayed him, saying, Rabbi, eat. But he said* 33 *unto them, I have meat to eat that ye know not. The disciples therefore said one to another, Hath any man brought him* aught 34 *to eat? Jesus saith unto them, My meat is to do the will of him* 35 *that sent me, and to accomplish his work. Say not ye, There are yet four months, and* then *cometh the harvest? behold, I say unto you, Lift up your eyes, and look on the fields, that they are white* 36 *already unto harvest. He that reapeth receiveth wages, and gathereth fruit unto life eternal; that he that soweth and he that reapeth may* 37 *rejoice together. For herein is the saying true, One soweth and* 38 *another reapeth. I sent you to reap that whereon ye have not laboured: others have laboured, and ye are entered into their labour.*

Meanwhile, the disciples returned with the provisions they had bought. The Evangelist notes their surprise at the freedom of their Master's intercourse with a woman. It was, we are told, contrary to Rabbinic etiquette. But they asked for no explanation. They simply asked Him to partake of the food they had provided.

It is natural to suppose that the physical weariness from which He had been suffering when they left Him had passed away in the absorbing interest of His conversation with the woman, and that the invitation of His disciples, recalling attention to the claims of His body, made Him conscious of the fact. And their words became the text of an instruction on spiritual feeding, just as His own request for water had formed the starting-point for a conversation on the thirst of the spirit.

His own opening words, "I have meat to eat that ye know not", were, not unnaturally, misunderstood by the disciples. Much later on in the ministry, they found it difficult to tell when He was speaking figuratively (Mk. 8: 21). It is not surprising, therefore, that they should have supposed that their Master was referring to friends unknown to them, rather than to a spiritual source of refreshment. Jesus, therefore, has to speak more plainly. "My food is to do the will of Him that sent Me, and to accomplish His work."

There is an old Greek legend which supplies a curiously illustrative antithesis to the thought conveyed by these words. One of the labours of Hercules was to overcome the earth-giant Antaeus. The difficulty of the task consisted in the fact that after any knock-down blow, the giant rose to renew the fight restored to fresh vigour by contact with his native element.

Our Lord's words suggest that He found new life and strength for spirit, soul and body through relations constantly maintained with a loftier native element—a heavenly one. He found these in His contact, while He was here on earth, with His heavenly Father's mind and will, a contact involved in every act of obedience, and in every effort to work out His plan. Work under these conditions could be in itself invigorating, not exhausting. He verified, in His own experience, the principle to which He had appealed in foiling the tempter in the wilderness. "Man does not live by bread alone, but by every word that proceedeth out of the mouth of God." And again, another Scripture (Is. 40: 31) says, "They that wait on the Lord shall renew their strength. They shall mount up on wings like eagles. They shall run and not be weary. They shall walk and not faint".

When we come to Jn. 6 we shall have to consider the same

law of spiritual feeding in its relation to ourselves. For us, as for Him, it remains true that "the Spirit feeds upon a Person". Meanwhile, the word surely is a wonderful revelation of the communion of the Father and the Son, which is the deep under-current of all the outward incidents, the words and deeds, of His earthly ministry.

Meanwhile the people of the city were on their way to the well, and the sight of the approaching crowds gave rise to a further lesson on the nature and effects of working for God. This teaching is given in the form of a condensed parable, and a great part of the difficulty of interpreting it springs from the fact that there is nothing to mark the point at which language descriptive of the earthly figure passes into language appropriate only to the heavenly reality. The opening words, it is natural to suppose, correspond to the physical fact at the moment. The fields, we must suppose, were covered with the young green shoots of the growing corn. Men spoke in confident anticipation—"There are yet four months, and then cometh harvest". Similarly the gathering multitude might have seemed, to ordinary spiritual apprehension, but the pledge and foretaste of a distant spiritual ingathering. But the eye that can see the promise of summer in the first sign of the rising sap in the branches of a fig-tree (Mk. 13: 28) can see, in the response of the Samaritans to the appeal of the woman, the vision of a spiritual harvest field already ripe (it may even be, as a farmer once suggested to me "dead-ripe") for the sickle. This response was in itself the fruit of long preparation, and the first task that fell to the lot of the workers for the Kingdom was to gather in the fruit of the labourers who had preceded them. And then they, too, are to work in the harvest field of God. To take a share in working out His plan, not only brings man into vivifying contact with God in the present, it links each workman with all who have gone before, and with all who shall follow after, in a wonderful unity. This unity will in the end be manifested in the common joy of all at the great harvest home of the universe, when God's purpose is at last fulfilled.

It may be observed that the proverb which our Lord proceeds to quote, "One soweth and another reapeth", does not describe the normal experience of a farmer. Through the picture of what occasionally happens on the harvest field it familiarly describes an experience which recurs again and again on the broad fields of human life, and to which we find it hard to reconcile ourselves. Ezekiel expresses the experience in another form when he says: "The fathers have eaten sour grapes, and the children's teeth are set on edge". Only it is characteristic of our Lord that He helps us to look at the bright side of this fundamental law of our human interdependence. Rightly understood, it is not "the evil that men do" that "lives after them". In the long last it is only the good that endures. Meantime God's workmen are continually reaping the fruit that has sprung from seed sown by their predecessors, and at the same time sowing seed which, in due course, it will be the work of others to reap.

And the work of the reaper brings both an immediate and an everlasting return. "Already he that reapeth receiveth wages;" but the harvest of souls which he gathers, and for which he sows the seed, is not consumed like an earthly harvest. It has in it the secret of eternal life. And in the eternal world, all who have contributed to the blessed result shall one day see it and exult in it together.

Life must remain an insoluble enigma so long as we look at it as if we were isolated units, and so long as we limit our horizon to the visible and temporal. Is it not a great thing for us to learn from Him who alone among men has been able to see life steadily and to see it whole, that so seen life becomes intelligible, something to thank God for, something on which we can base an assurance that "Joy is the last in every song"?

It is to another consequence of the law, however, that Jesus Himself directly calls attention. He proceeds, "I sent you to reap that which ye have not wrought by your own labour. Others have laboured, and ye have entered into their labours." While He has just been lifting the veil that His disciples may be cheered by the vision of the coming joy,

His immediate object is to stimulate gratitude in their hearts towards those who have laid the foundations for the success that had already attended their efforts (cf. 3 : 22 ; 4 : 2). And at the same time He would, no doubt, inspire them with a spirit of patient self-consecration to the task of preparing in their turn a harvest for others to reap.

THE ARRIVAL OF THE SAMARITANS

39 *And from that city many of the Samaritans believed on him because of the word of the woman, who testified, He told me all things that* 40 *ever I did. So when the Samaritans came unto him, they besought* 41 *him to abide with them: and he abode there two days. And many* 42 *more believed because of his word; and they said to the woman, Now we believe, not because of thy speaking: for we have heard for ourselves, and know that this is indeed the Saviour of the world.*

The prophecy of the harvest at hand finds an immediate verification. The men whom the woman had invited besought Him to tarry with them. And after two days the faith which had at first accepted the woman's testimony strikes a deeper root in personal experience, and finds expression in a very remarkable confession. "We know that He is of a truth the Saviour of the World."

Dr. Bernard is sure that this cannot be historical, because the Messiah is not called Saviour in the Old Testament, or in pre-Christian Jewish literature. No doubt the title on their lips could not have had the fullness of meaning that it has in 1 Jn. 4: 14, when the Gospel message of redemption was understood and appropriated. But the thought that His work was in a special sense connected with salvation would have been suggested by His name, Jesus. And the teaching that He had given on worship shewed that His work included the whole world in its scope.

SEEING AND BELIEVING

43 *And after the two days he went forth from thence into Galilee.* 44 *For Jesus himself testified, that a prophet hath no honour in his* 45 *own country. So when he came into Galilee, the Galilæans received*

him, having seen all the things that he did in Jerusalem at the feast; for they also went unto the feast.

46 *He came therefore again unto Cana of Galilee, where he made the water wine. And there was a certain nobleman, whose son was sick* 47 *at Capernaum. When he heard that Jesus was come out of Judæa into Galilee, he went unto him, and besought* him *that he would come down, and heal his son; for he was at the point of death.* 48 *Jesus therefore said unto him, Except ye see signs and wonders,* 49 *ye will in no wise believe. The nobleman saith unto him, Sir,* 50 *come down ere my child die. Jesus saith unto him, Go thy way; thy son liveth. The man believed the word that Jesus spake unto* 51 *him, and he went his way. And as he was now going down, his* 52 *servants met him, saying, that his son lived. So he inquired of them the hour when he began to amend. They said therefore unto* 53 *him, Yesterday at the seventh hour the fever left him. So the father knew that* it was *at that hour in which Jesus said unto him, Thy* 54 *son liveth: and himself believed, and his whole house. This is again the second sign that Jesus did, having come out of Judæa into Galilee.*

After the return through Samaria, Galilee became the chief centre of our Lord's activity until the end of His earthly ministry. He had made His appeal to Jerusalem and Judæa, the true home of the Messiah, and His own people, through their official leaders, had failed to respond. Indeed, their attitude towards the arrest of the Baptist made it clear that uninterrupted work was no longer possible in that quarter. So Jesus was compelled—in obedience to the strange law, to which He called His disciples' attention perhaps on more than one occasion, the law that "A prophet is not without honour, save in his own country and his own household" (Mt. 13: 57, Lk. 4: 24, Jn. 4: 44)—to devote Himself to work in what was outwardly the less respectable part of the Holy Land. We have all our lives been familiar with the fact, so we fail to understand the scandal of it to the strict Jew. But both S. Matthew and S. John feel it necessary to offer an apology for it (Mt. 4: 14, Jn. 4: 44; cf. 7: 52).

The opening incident under the new conditions, according to S. John (who for the most part confines his narrative to incidents in the occasional visits to Jerusalem, which had dropped out of the popular tradition), is the healing of the nobleman's son at Capernaum.

The story is sketched in the fewest possible strokes. The nobleman, who is clearly a Jew, in marked contrast to the Gentile Centurion, who sent his friends to Jesus on a similar errand later, came himself a journey of twenty miles, from Capernaum to Cana, to proffer his request in person. He asked Jesus to come down and heal his dying son. The answer is strange and startling: "Except ye see signs and wonders ye will not (or 'will ye not') believe."

We should not have anticipated any answer, except a ready compliance with so urgent a request. The trial of delay for a man in a state of nervous excitement was a severe one, and the next words shew that it was felt.

This particular answer seems as undeserved as it is unexpected. The nobleman had already done much, in leaving the bedside of his boy to go to Cana for help. Had he not given evidence of a power of believing without sight? Why does Jesus address him as a member of a class, when he seems to have given proof of having come out of it?

Here, however, as in the closely parallel case of the Syrophoenician woman (Mk. 7 : 24–30), we shall do well to notice the effect of the delay, and of enforced self-questioning on the petitioner, before we pass a final judgement. The nobleman was clearly in a hurry. His state of excitement was in itself inimical to faith, and, so far, an obstacle in the way of our Lord's working to grant his request. His feeling of stress and urgency sprang from a defective consciousness of God, from want of a rooted conviction of His all-sustaining, ever-present love and power. The first step in helping him must be to bring him into contact with a spirit of perfectly loving and trusting calm.

To put the same thought from another side. In the very sacrifice that the father had made in leaving his son to come to Jesus, there was an element of despair wrestling with the incipient faith. He was like a drowning man clutching at a straw. He needed help to recover his self-possession.

Granted, then, that a check of some kind was necessary, what, precisely, was the meaning of the remonstrance, or as the words may better be rendered, the wistful interrogation, "Except ye see signs and wonders will ye not believe?"

Is it the fruit of the experience at Jerusalem (2: 23 f.), which proved that faith based on signs did not provide a satisfactory foundation on which to build? Or is it a direct challenge, called for by the state of mind which our Lord saw in the nobleman?

Again, is the faith for which our Lord was looking, faith in Himself, or faith in His Father? In other words, does our Lord imply that the nobleman, instead of accepting the Baptist's witness frankly and wholeheartedly, had simply heard of what Jesus had been doing in Jerusalem, and came on the chance that there might be something in His claim? Or does He mean that a true faith in God would have saved him from all anxiety; just as, for instance, in the storm on the lake He takes the disciples to task for the alarm that they had shewn in the hour of danger? (Mk. 4: 40.)

It does not seem possible to give a dogmatic answer to these questions. All we can be sure of is that on His lips the words could have no meaning inconsistent with perfect love and tender thoughtfulness. And we can see that, disappointing as it was (cf. 2: 4), it somehow inspired hope.

The nobleman does not attempt to excuse himself, or indeed to inquire further into the exact meaning of the words he had heard. He knew what he wanted, and his need was urgent. His faith, he could not deny it, was weak. He did want the support of signs to enable him to believe in Jesus and in His Father. Surely Jesus would not let his son die for that. He would not quench the smoking flax or break the bruised reed.

In any case, Jesus had not refused to help. There was room for a repetition of the request, if he could bring himself to make it, with a deeper sense of his own helplessness and a growing trust in Jesus's power. So he re-states his need in the simplest form: "Sir, come down, ere my child die".

The answer, once more, is in form a refusal. Instead of

posting off at once with the nobleman to Capernaum, Jesus sends him away, with an assurance that the crisis had safely passed: "Go thy way, thy son liveth". In this form the answer presupposed and called into activity the power of believing without sight, which Jesus had just desiderated. The nobleman rises to the occasion. Helped, no doubt, by the presence and voice of the Speaker, he took Him at His word, and went his way believing, reaping an immediate harvest for the initial disappointment in a quiet, hopeful journey home, conscious that the strain of anxiety had been relaxed both for himself and those whom he had left behind to look after the lad.

What wonder that when the faith was crowned by sight, faith in the word that Jesus had spoken ripened into faith in Him and in His Father, both in the nobleman and in his whole household?

CHAPTER IX

JESUS AND THE PHARISEES

WE have seen that Jesus opened His public ministry by cleansing the Temple. He thereby challenged the High Priest, who was the official head of the nation, to acknowledge His authority and start a movement of national repentance at the house of God.

The High Priest and his family belonged to the sect of the Sadducees. The spiritual leadership of the people was in the hands of the rival party of the Pharisees. The Pharisees were not numerically a large party—about six thousand or seven thousand, we are told. But they exercised an influence out of all proportion to their numbers. They were the successors of the men who, in the hard times of Antiochus Epiphanes, had been ready to die rather than be disloyal to the faith of their fathers and the hope of Israel. They were, before all things, men of a book, zealots for the law. The one thing that mattered was to walk in all the statutes and ordinances of the Lord blameless. To this end they searched the Scriptures day and night. The one authority that counted was that of the Scribes, the men learned in the law, and that very soon came to be learned in what their predecessors had said about the law. So the authority of the law was merged in and subordinated to the authority of "The Tradition of the Elders".

Tradition formed a hedge about the law, and about the lives of all those whose highest ambition was to guard against the dangers of defilement that lurked in intercourse with those who were less strict than themselves. The common people followed them blindly. The Sadducees had no popular following. Nearly the whole of the religious education of the people in synagogues and schools was in the hands of the Pharisees. We can see, therefore, something of the difficulty of the problem with which Jesus was confronted in defining His relation to those who, as He Himself acknowledged, were sitting in Moses's seat.

S. Mark helps us to see what a close watch the Pharisees kept all through the Galilean ministry over all that Jesus said and did. They were shocked by the authority that He claimed to forgive sins; by the freedom with which He mingled with publicans and sinners; by His disregard of their rules of fasting, and of ceremonial washing. His attitude to the Sabbath aroused murderous hate.

Jesus justifies Himself partly by argument, partly by the evidence that God was with Him which came from miracles of healing. When they tried to evade this evidence by ascribing His power over evil spirits to demoniac possession, He unmasked the evasion, and uttered a solemn warning against the danger of consciously calling good evil. On one occasion He publicly denounced the evils into which they were betrayed by their idolatry of tradition.

At the end of His ministry, at what we have seen reason to regard as the second cleansing of the Temple, and in the parable of the Vineyard and the Husbandmen, He declares that they were bandits, ready to murder the heir that they might secure the divine inheritance for themselves.

In S. Matthew we have in the Sermon on the Mount the clearest statement of the fulfilment of the Law which Jesus had come to bring, and of the way to avoid the formalism of the Pharisees in drawing near to God. In chapter 23 we have in seven Woes a scathing indictment of their short-comings.

In Lk. 15, a different note is struck. In the parables of the Lost Sheep, and the Lost Coin, and the Lost Son, Jesus pleads with the Pharisees to share with Him in the joy of welcoming the returning penitent. In His sketch of the elder brother of the prodigal He expresses not unsympathetically the ground of the Pharisees' reluctance.

An even more direct and personal appeal was made to Simon the Pharisee, in the parable of the Two Debtors. But, as far as I can see, the Synoptists record no instance of any deliberate attempt on our Lord's part to explain the nature and ground of His claim to those who, when the decisive moment came, would be challenged to say whether it was or was not blasphemy for Him to claim to be "The Christ, the Son of the Blessed".

In S. John we have already studied the conversation with an individual inquirer. The immediate purpose in the mind of Jesus was, I think, to bring Nicodemus and his friends to the baptism which John preached, whether administered by the Baptist or by our Lord's disciples. Jesus does not come again into contact with the Pharisees until after the healing of the impotent man at the pool of Bethesda.

Here, as in all the cases of Sabbath healing, there can be no doubt that the challenge to Pharisaic prejudice was quite deliberate. The case was a chronic case, with no plea of urgency. A man carrying his pallet on the day of rest was sure to attract remark. Jesus seems, therefore, to have chosen the question of sabbath observance in order to raise, in its clearest form, the point at issue between Him and the teachers of Israel in regard to the whole meaning and purpose of the law.

THE DATE AND PLACE OF CHAPTER V IN S. JOHN'S GOSPEL

There is a preliminary question on which something must be said before we begin to examine the story of the impotent man in detail.

There is a strong consensus of opinion[1] in favour of transposing Chapter VI and V. At the end of Chapter V, Jesus is still in Jerusalem answering the questions raised by the healing at the pool of Bethesda. In Chapter VI we are, without any warning, transported to Galilee and taken across the Lake of Tiberias for the feeding of the five thousand. At the end of Chapter IV Jesus is in Galilee, and though He was still some distance from the Lake, we are led

[1] *The Fourth Gospel in recent Criticism and Interpretation.* By W. F. Howard, Appendix D.

to anticipate a ministry in Galilee and the incident in Chapter VI is in its place as part of it.

But S. John does not aim at giving more than detached scenes from the Life, e.g. in 21 : 1 we pass from Judæa to Galilee without any notice. So there is no difficulty in making 5 : 1 ff. an incidental visit to Judæa in the course of a ministry predominantly Galilean.

The Feeding of the Five Thousand came after the execution of S. John the Baptist—and the time was the Passover.

My own feeling is that the controversy on the sabbath began in Jerusalem and is presupposed in the Marcan account of the ministry in Galilee. There we have emissaries from Jerusalem almost from the beginning watching Jesus closely and keeping a keen eye especially on His relation to the sabbath. The notes in Jn. 5: 16, 18 "And for this cause did the Jews persecute Jesus, because he did these things on the sabbath" and "For this cause, therefore, the Jews sought the more to kill him, because he not only brake the sabbath, but also called God his own Father, making himself equal with God", ease the shock which we cannot help feeling when we are confronted in Mk. 3: 6 with "And the Pharisees went out, and straightway with the Herodians took counsel against him, how they might destroy him".

It is of course possible that the question, having been raised in Galilee, Jesus deliberately challenged examination in Jerusalem.

The parallelism of Mk. 2: 11 to Jn. 5: 8 is noteworthy. It is impossible to regard the two accounts as doublets. Apart from the fact that each relates the healing of a paralytic, they differ in every particular.

The command to take up the bedding may have in each case been part of the cure, as a test of the obedience of faith, and a sign both to the sick man and to the spectators of the restored vitality.

The feast in Jn. 5 : 1 is unnamed. The choice seems to be between that of Trumpets (Dr. Westcott) in September, and that of Pentecost (McLellan, p. 554) in May. The plucking of the ears of corn must have been between Passover and Pentecost. I should prefer September in the first year, unless indeed Jn. 4: 35 "Say not ye, there are yet four months, and *then* cometh the harvest. Behold, I say unto you, Lift up your eyes, and look on the fields, that they are white already unto harvest" fixes the date of the retirement to Galilee to December.

THE HEALING OF THE IMPOTENT MAN AT THE POOL OF BETHESDA

1 *After these things there was a feast of the Jews; and Jesus went up to Jerusalem.*

2 *Now there is in Jerusalem by the sheep* gate *a pool, which is* 3 *called in Hebrew Bethesda, having five porches. In these lay a* 5 *multitude of them that were sick, blind, halt, withered. And a certain man was there, which had been thirty and eight years in* 6 *his infirmity. When Jesus saw him lying, and knew that he had been now a long time* in that case, *he saith unto him, Wouldest* 7 *thou be made whole? The sick man answered him, Sir, I have no man when the water is troubled, to put me into the pool: but while I* 8 *am coming, another steppeth down before me. Jesus saith unto* 9 *him, Arise, take up thy bed, and walk. And straightway the man was made whole, and took up his bed and walked.*

10 *Now it was the sabbath on that day. So the Jews said unto him that was cured, It is the sabbath, and it is not lawful for thee* 11 *to take up thy bed. But he answered them, He that made me whole,* 12 *the same said unto me, Take up thy bed, and walk. They asked him, Who is the man that said unto thee, Take up* thy bed, *and* 13 *walk? But he that was healed wist not who it was: for Jesus had* 14 *conveyed himself away, a multitude being in that place. Afterward Jesus findeth him in the temple, and said unto him, Behold, thou art made whole: sin no more, lest a worse thing befall thee.* 15 *The man went away, and told the Jews that it was Jesus which* 16 *had made him whole. And for this cause did the Jews persecute* 17 *Jesus, because he did these things on the sabbath. But Jesus answered them, My Father worketh even until now, and I work.* 18 *For this cause therefore the Jews sought the more to kill him, because he not only brake the sabbath, but also called God his own Father, making himself equal with God.*

We can now pass on to see what Jesus did at the pool of Bethesda, and to examine the line that He took when He was challenged to explain His conduct.

The reference to the angel that used to trouble the waters was not part of the Gospel as S. John wrote it. It is clear, however, from the story, that the pool was credited with medicinal properties at recurrent intervals.

No hint is given here as to the reason which led Jesus to pick out this man from the rest for cure. In His defence (verse 19) Jesus implies that He had acted in obedience to a sign from His Father. He did not heal indiscriminately all the sick that came in His way. We are only told that the trouble was of long standing.

It is worth while to look carefully into the treatment that He adopted. We know from His own words on many occasions that cures can only be wrought in an atmosphere of faith.

The sick man in this case was a complete stranger, a chronic invalid, who had been so often disappointed that he might well have lost hope of ever being healed. Jesus has, therefore, first to get into human touch with him. So he fixes His eyes upon him, and realizing the situation, He puts a strange and challenging question to him: "Do you really want to be well?" It is only too easy for a chronic invalid to shrink from the responsibility of facing life again on his own account. But no one would willingly admit the fact. This sick man is anxious to avert the suspicion, and explains his ill-success in the past as due to his lack of friends. As he did so, faint flickerings of the hope, which in the first instance had brought him to the pool, may have begun to revive in his heart. And the very presence of Jesus would radiate confidence. It is not surprising, therefore, that the challenge to take up his bed and walk was met by a response in which the obedience gave practical expression to the faith.

The command to carry the bed home through the streets of Jerusalem on a sabbath day excited comments which Jesus must have anticipated. The man not unnaturally sheltered himself from the criticism by throwing the responsibility on his Healer, though he could not give His name.

Jesus, however, had not yet done with him. Whatever may be the case with other sufferers, in this case the sickness had really come on this man as a judgement. Jesus, therefore, seeks him out in the Temple and warns him to give up the sinful life that he was leading: "Sin no more—do not any longer continue in sin—lest a worse evil befall thee".

The man at once reports the name of Jesus to the Jewish authorities. There was nothing necessarily treacherous in the act. Jesus had no wish to shirk responsibility for what He had done. He courted inquiry, and He got it.

The line of defence that He adopts when put on His defence (clearly before an authoritative tribunal) shows at once that He was deliberately challenging not merely the details of their teaching on sabbath observance, but their whole attitude to the Law, of which they were the accredited expounders, because they had drifted out of touch with God who gave it. He does not, as in the Synoptists, defend His action on humanitarian grounds, or on scriptural analogy, but directly on the ground of His Sonship.

The Sabbath Law in Ex. 20: 11 is based directly on the divine example. It implies a kinship between the human nature and the divine—so close that the life of man, whether at work or resting, should reflect the life of God. Jesus claims that the relation in which God had declared that He, in His humanity, stood to Him, the relation of Son to Father, embodied that kinship; and that in what He had done He had simply been obeying the law that that kinship laid upon Him.

This claim raised at once the theological issue, which was the real source and spring of the difference between His moral standard and that of the Pharisees. The Pharisaic system was essentially deistic. It was based on a distinction between the divine nature and the human,—so deep that it could never be transcended. It pictured man as standing over against God in stark independence, receiving from Him a law, by obeying which he could, in his own strength, establish his right to his place in the Kingdom.

It was impossible, therefore, that they could avoid being

deeply shocked by the claim of Jesus that the title "Son" which had been given Him was no mere metaphor, but implied a real relationship, and carried with it practical consequences.

THE DIVINE SONSHIP

19 *Verily, verily, I say unto you, The Son can do nothing of himself, but what he seeth the Father doing: for what things soever he doeth* 20 *these the Son also doeth in like manner. For the Father loveth the Son, and sheweth him all things that himself doeth: and greater* 21 *works than these will he shew him, that ye may marvel. For as the Father raiseth the dead and quickeneth them, even so the Son* 22 *also quickeneth whom he will. For neither doth the Father judge* 23 *any man, but he hath given all judgement unto the Son; that all may honour the Son, even as they honour the Father. He that honoureth not the Son honoureth not the Father which sent him.* 24 *Verily, verily, I say unto you, He that heareth my word, and believeth him that sent me, hath eternal life, and cometh not into judgement,* 25 *but hath passed out of death into life. Verily, verily, I say unto you, The hour cometh, and now is, when the dead shall hear the* 26 *voice of the Son of God; and they that hear shall live. For as the Father hath life in himself, even so gave he to the Son also* 27 *to have life in himself: and he gave him authority to execute judge-* 28 *ment, because he is the Son*[1] *of man. Marvel not at this: for the hour cometh, in which all that are in the tombs shall hear his voice* 29 *and shall come forth; they that have done good, unto the resurrection of life: and they that have done ill, unto the resurrection of judgement.*

30 *I can of myself do nothing: as I hear, I judge: and my judgement is righteous; because I seek not mine own will, but the will of him that sent me.*

[1] *A son of man.*

The first statement of the content of the claim is found in this passage. It opens with a strong disclaimer of any power of self-originated action, "The Son can do nothing from Himself". Man was created in the image of God to attain and manifest His likeness in the world. To use a figure by which S. Paul illustrates the relation of the Christian to Christ, human nature is not called to create but only to mirror the divine likeness (2 Cor. 3: 18). To put the same thought from another side, the true Christian life is a response. The guiding, controlling, quickening power all through is the Spirit of Christ. Just so the guiding, controlling, quickening power at the back of every word that Jesus spoke, and of every act of His, was the Spirit which He received from His Father. He lived from moment to moment in conscious communion with Him. His words imply that He had had, for instance, a divine intimation that it was His Father's will that He should heal this impotent man as and when He did, and that in His act He was drawing on a boundless store of healing energy in God. These acts were meant to strike the popular imagination. They were also an assurance that God is mightier than all the powers by which man's life is assailed, up to and including death itself. The healing of the impotent man was, therefore, only an earnest of greater works, including the raising of the dead, that would follow.

The Jews were familiar enough with the thought of Divine Sonship as an attribute of the Messiah. It had been emphasized in the original promise given through Nathan to David. It had been reaffirmed by prophet and psalmist. But, somehow, they had never regarded it as more than an honorific title, familiar enough on the lips of the courtiers of an oriental despot, but never meant to be taken literally. They were, therefore, not a little startled when Jesus refused to regard it as a mere metaphor, and declared that His divine Sonship, so far from being a mere adjunct of His earthly sovereignty, was in fact the living root and ground of it. Men were ready to call Him Son, if it was God's good pleasure to make Him King. God made Him King because He was, and had shewn Himself worthy to be called His Son.

Unexpected consequences follow from this reversal of the popular conception of the relation between sovereignty and sonship. The divine Sonship attributed to an oriental despot was inevitably associated with thoughts of arbitrary irresponsible power. His will was law. No one could challenge his right to do what he liked.

The divine Sonship of which Jesus was conscious, was the

exact opposite of this. It made it impossible for Him to claim to be His own master in anything. At the heart of it lay a perfect communion of heart and mind with His heavenly Father, based on an absolute surrender of will. The Son could and would do nothing of Himself. He threw Himself into His Father's plan.

The Father loved and trusted His Son, sharing His secret counsels with Him and delighting in His intelligent co-operation (cf. 15 : 15). So far, therefore, from His losing Himself by the habitual surrender of His own will to His Father's, that surrender opened the gate by which all the resources of the divine wisdom, love and power could become available, through Him, for the blessing of men.

It gave Him his unique and incommunicable share in bringing in the Kingdom. It made every act of His a part of the revelation of the Father, which He had come to bring. It was the condition of the power that He wielded over the alien forces, by which the bodies and the spirits of men were kept in bondage. Even death itself would be shewn to be subject to Him. The wielding of this power would provide ample scope for the exercise of His will. The possession of it, even though (or, rather, because) there could be nothing arbitrary in His exercise of it, was the guarantee of the authority with which the Father had entrusted Him. His sovereignty over men was rooted in His self-abnegating Sonship.

Such are the implications of the teaching, which Jesus gave to the Pharisees to help them to see the significance of "the work that He had shewn them from the Father" in healing the impotent man, and the light that it threw on the title, "Son of God", which had been given to Him at His baptism.

The evidence would be incomplete until His power over death had been convincingly demonstrated. He, however, takes the fact for granted. The power to give life was already His, only waiting for its manifestation on His consenting will, because He was conscious that His Father was already raising the dead and quickening them.

What He meant by this power was something far deeper than the power on the physical plane by which, when the time came, He would summon Lazarus back to a fresh spell of life on earth. Jesus has a perplexing way of concentrating attention on the spiritual meaning of all the terms that He uses. He startles us, therefore, by linking the possession and exercise of this power of giving life with the power of judging. This, when we come to look into it, we see to be closely connected with the power to quicken. The refusal, in any particular case, to put out His power of giving life was, in effect, to confirm the hold of death.

He does not, therefore, shrink from asserting that this awful prerogative is included in the commission that has been given Him. In His Father's name He is called to be, not only the King, but also the Judge of all the world. But here again, His exercise of this prerogative takes an unexpected course. He takes great pains to help us to realize that in no sense can it be said that His coming brings death into the world. He comes into a world which is already in the grip of death. His message rings through the dark domain, and wherever it finds an open ear and a believing heart, it becomes a spring of eternal life. The soul, so far from being oppressed by the judgement which the message brings, finds itself delivered from the death, in which the message found it. His Gospel was, from the first, what S. Paul found it to be, the power of God unto salvation to everyone that believeth.

The hour had already come when dead souls could hear the voice of the Son of God, and those that hearkened awoke to newness of life. For, by the Father's gift, the Son was allowed to share with Him the power of becoming a well of life to His brethren.

This is not, however, a complete account of the matter. His coming as Light unto the world brought life to those who would open their hearts to receive Him; but to those who love the darkness rather than the light it brings judgement. It reveals, as nothing else can, the depth of their degradation. It brings them face to face with the naked horror of their sin. It is according to truth. It is inevitable. Indeed, we are bidden to see that it is no mere accident, applying only to one generation. We must all be made manifest before the judgement seat of Christ. The hour must come when all who are in their graves shall hear His voice, and come forth, they that have done good to a resurrection of life, and they that wrought evil to a resurrection of judgement.

There remains yet one more unexpected element in this revelation. We are prepared, I think, to believe that the power at the back of the judgement cannot be a vast abstraction, or a mechanical system. It must be intensely personal. But, for the most part, we regard it, as the Pharisees did, as an essentially divine prerogative. "Who can forgive, or judge, sins", we ask, "but God alone?" Jesus taught the Pharisees on one occasion that "the Son of Man had authority on earth to forgive sins". He tells us here that the Father gave Him authority to execute judgement because He was in all points like His brethren—a son of Man.

This fact, and this alone, can help us to apprehend the inexorable strictness of His sentence, and the love and hope that inspires it. There can be no appeal against the sentence. It comes, not from any alien, unintelligible source, but from the inmost heart of our common humanity. Our consciences cannot gainsay its justice. We refused to have "this Man" to reign over us. In a real sense we hated both Him and His Father. And yet, who can say what may not be the effect of tearing away the veils that have hidden from us the vision of the Son whom we were scorning? We cannot forecast the torment of those who must shrink in shame from His presence at His appearing; but even that shame has in it a seed of hope. It is rooted in His love. Is it impossible to believe that when no other way is left, He saves by judging? How else can He fulfil His promise that He will draw all men unto Himself?

HIS CREDENTIALS

31 *If I bear witness of myself, my witness is not true. It is another*
32 *that beareth witness of me; and I know that the witness which*
33 *he witnesseth of me is true. Ye have sent unto John, and he hath*

34 *borne witness unto the truth. But the witness which I receive is not from man: howbeit I say these things, that ye may be saved.*
35 *He was the lamp that burneth and shineth: and ye were willing*
36 *to rejoice for a season in his light. But the witness that I have is greater than* that of *John: for the works which the Father hath given me to accomplish, the very works that I do, bear witness*
37 *of me, that the Father hath sent me. And the Father which sent me, he hath borne witness of me. Ye have neither heard his voice*
38 *at any time, nor seen his form. And ye have not his word abiding*
39 *in you: for whom he sent, him ye believe not. Ye search the scriptures, because ye think that in them ye have eternal life; and these*
40 *are they which bear witness of me; and ye will not come to me*
41 *that ye may have life. I receive not glory from men.* 42 *But I*
43 *know you, that ye have not the love of God in yourselves. I am come in my Father's name, and ye receive me not: if another shall*
44 *come in his own name, him ye will receive. How can ye believe, which receive glory one of another, and the glory that* cometh
45 *from the only God ye seek not? Think not that I will accuse you to the Father: there is one that accuseth you,* even *Moses, on whom*
46 *ye have set your hope. For if ye believed Moses, ye would believe*
47 *me; for he wrote of me. But if ye believe not his writings, how shall ye believe my words?*

We come now to consider the analysis that Jesus gave in this passage, of the evidence on which He based His claim. He makes it clear that He did not ask them to accept Him on the ground of His own unsupported self-assertion. He came to them in the strength of a commission which had been given Him directly from His Father. His own consciousness of that commission was, no doubt, for Him the immediate basis of His claim. But He knew that it was not self-originated. It had come to Him from another, and His whole being responded to the reality of it. Nor was He left without objective support, both to maintain the strength of His own inner conviction, and to confirm His testimony to outsiders.

First and foremost there was, as we have seen, the testimony of His divinely appointed forerunner. The Jewish authorities had received the express witness of the Baptist. John had come to them, and they knew in their inmost hearts that he had come to them from God. He had been a burning lamp that shed what they recognized as rays of real light in the surrounding darkness.

But that was not all. That was, after all, only second-hand evidence mediated to them through another man's—albeit, a prophet's—consciousness. The cure of the impotent man opened up another source of more direct attestation. The work was one which it was clearly beyond the capacity of man to perform without divine assistance. Unless God had been with Him He could not have wrought that cure. God Himself was, therefore, bearing direct testimony to those who had ears to hear, through the works that He enabled His Son to do. But they, alas! as their rejection of His claim shewed, were deaf.

There remains yet a third witness to which He can appeal in confirmation of His claim. It is one which we should have thought might have had constraining force on such devoted students of the law: the witness of the Scriptures. But here again there was a fatal defect. The Scriptures were clearly a powerful force in moulding our Lord's life. They played a large part in feeding His faith and in guiding His steps. They bore a living witness to Him, throwing a searching light both on His origin and on the work that He had come to do. But, alas! the lawyers were blind to the connexion and would not come to receive the promised gift of life from Him.

The closing section (verses 41–47) links this appeal to the witness of the Scriptures to an analysis of the moral causes which lay behind this unbelief. It was due in the last resort to the fact that His life was God-centred, while they cared only for popularity and could understand no one but an egotist. Their failure was, therefore, serious; but they must not lay it at His door. It was due to their unfaithfulness to the teaching implicitly enshrined for them in the Law of Moses, an unfaithfulness which was revealed, but not created, by their attitude to Him. So He reasserts once more the fact that Moses had borne witness to Him, and declares that His living voice could have no chance with men who gave no heed to the written word.

Unfortunately, if that is the right word to use in such a case, the Evangelist does not tell us what passages our Lord appealed to in support of this claim. After the Resurrection, S. Luke—both in his Gospel and in the Acts—focuses attention on the prophecies of the Cross and of the Suffering Servant. He does also, in his account of the Sermon at Nazareth, shew that Jesus claimed to fulfil one of the Servant prophecies, not only by His Gospel to the poor, but by mighty works of deliverance. The same claim underlies the reply that Jesus sent to the Baptist in prison to confirm his faith. This, therefore, is no doubt part of the evidence to which Jesus may well have appealed on this occasion, if He was challenged to give an illustration of the kind of witness from the Scriptures that He had in mind. But there can be no doubt that the witness to Himself and the work that He had been sent to do, which Jesus found in the Scriptures, was not limited to a single section of Old Testament prophecy. As His words to Nicodemus shew, He found a Messianic significance even in the brazen serpent. In Chapter 6 He claims to fulfil the type of the gift of manna. We need not, therefore, be surprised to find that He found support for His claim in the Pentateuch, and states expressly in verse 46 that Moses had written of Him.

This, however, is only a subordinate point in relation to the main subject of the chapter. In this discourse our attention is concentrated on the significance of the work that Jesus had done. And there can be no doubt that here, and again and again later in the Gospel, Jesus does rest part of His claim expressly on what in the other Gospels are called His "miracles"; S. John calls them "signs".

The point craves close investigation for its own sake and also for its bearing on the relative value of S. Mark and S. John as historians of the life of Jesus. It has been confidently maintained that the Jesus of S. Mark could not have ascribed such a value to His miracles. He pointedly refused to substantiate His claim by working a miracle to order. He thoroughly distrusted the popular excitement that the miracles produced. Again and again He ordered those whom He healed to tell no man. How, then, we are asked, can we believe that He can have pointed to His possession of this power in confirmation of His personal claim?

As soon, however, as we come to look closely into the facts it becomes clear that this apparent contrast between the two historians is due simply to a difference of emphasis. There is no ground at all for the assertion that it amounts to a fundamental contradiction.

Jesus, in S. John, refuses point blank to work "a sign" to justify His claim to authority in the Temple Courts. He makes it as clear then as He did later in Mt. 12: 39, that no further sign could be given before His resurrection. He shews a consistent distrust of popular enthusiasm, which had no other support than the excitement caused by the miracles of healing (2: 24; 3: 2; 4: 48; 6: 14, 26; 7: 21).

At the same time we cannot help noticing that the healing and the preaching are closely united in the summaries that S. Mark gives of the different stages in the public ministry of Jesus. And when the Twelve are sent out in His Name they are bidden to continue the same two features in their witness to the advent of His Kingdom.

But we are not left even to this strong but indirect indication that healing was more than an accidental accompaniment of the preaching of the Gospel. Jesus Himself on one occasion, when He was accused of blasphemy because He had absolved the sick of the palsy, met the accusation by curing him of his sickness. And when His opponents asserted that He only cast out demons because He was Himself possessed by the prince of the demons, He claimed on the contrary that the power that He was exercising was proof positive that He was possessed by the Spirit of God. S. Mark is, therefore, fully alive to the evidential value of the miracles of Jesus.

We have no reason then to quarrel with S. John because he consistently describes them as "signs", and declares that Jesus Himself appealed to them directly as substantiating His claim. All, in fact, that S. John has done is to lay emphatic stress on an element that is undeniably present, though its significance is not so clearly marked in the earlier Gospels. It is not only that he blames the Jews for their blindness to this evidence (12: 37), He shews that Jesus Himself makes it a main feature of His indictment against them (15: 24) and challenges His disciples to realize the value of the signs as corroborating His personal testimony (14: 11).

At the same time, it is important to notice that the possession of the power to do these works belongs to the humanity which He shares with us. He declares that His disciples, after He had left the world, would be empowered to do even greater works in His name (14: 12).

We cannot, therefore, regard the miracles as in themselves direct evidence of our Lord's divinity, though they do prove that God was with Him.

Again, it is important to notice that there is nothing in S. John to countenance the popular description of miracles as violations of the laws of nature. It is true, of course, that S. John can have had no conception of what we mean by laws of nature. But though he is well aware that he could quote no precedent for the opening of the eyes of a man born blind, there is the clearest evidence to shew that he did not believe that lawlessness was any characteristic of the operation of the powers of the age to come. On the testimony of Jesus Himself he shews us that the exercise of this power depended on the strictest obedience to His Father's will. Jesus taught His disciples that they could only become channels for its manifestation, when they were acting as His representatives, in prayerful communion with Himself.

CHAPTER X

THE FEEDING OF THE FIVE THOUSAND

1 *After these things Jesus went away to the other side of the sea of*
2 *Galilee, which is* the sea *of Tiberias. And a great multitude followed him, because they beheld the signs which he did on them*
3 *that were sick. And Jesus went up into the mountain, and there*
4 *he sat with his disciples. Now the passover, the feast of the Jews,*
5 *was at hand. Jesus therefore lifting up his eyes, and seeing that a great multitude cometh unto him, saith unto Philip, Whence are*
6 *we to buy bread, that these may eat? And this he said to prove*
7 *him: for he himself knew what he would do. Philip answereth him, Two hundred pennyworth of bread is not sufficient for them, that*
8 *everyone may take a little. One of his disciples, Andrew, Simon*
9 *Peter's brother, saith unto him, There is a lad here, which hath five barley loaves, and two fishes: but what are these among so*
10 *many? Jesus said, Make the people sit down. Now there was much grass in the place. So the men sat down, in number about five*
11 *thousand. Jesus therefore took the loaves; and having given thanks, he distributed to them that were set down; likewise also of the*
12 *fishes as much as they would. And when they were filled, he saith unto his disciples, Gather up the broken pieces which remain over,*
13 *that nothing be lost. So they gathered them up, and filled twelve baskets with broken pieces from the five barley loaves, which re-*
14 *mained over unto them that had eaten. When therefore the people saw the sign which he did, they said, This is of a truth the prophet that cometh into the world.*

15 *Jesus therefore perceiving that they were about to come and take him by force, to make him king, withdrew again into the mountain himself alone.*

THE narrative in S. John is introduced abruptly, according to his wont. "After these things" (cf. 2: 12; 3: 22; 5: 1; 7: 1; 21: 1).

The incident must have come after the Galilean ministry

had been in progress some months. The apostles had just come back from their tour of witness. The Baptist must have been dead some time, because Herod, hearing of Jesus apparently as a result of their mission, was inclined to believe that John had come back to plague him. It seems as if this incident must be dated in the early spring, whether we read "Passover" in 6: 4 or not, because both S. Mark (6: 39) and S. John (6: 10) call attention to the grass, though this inference has been challenged.

The place was an uninhabited district on the further side of the sea of Galilee to which Jesus had retired in order to give His disciples rest after their labours. The reference to Bethsaida in Lk. 9: 10 must be to Bethsaida Julias on the north-eastern shore. S. Mark says that the multitudes saw that Jesus had embarked and followed Him by land round the head of the lake. He says also that "they outwent them". This can hardly mean more than that they arrived before the disciples had had the rest that Jesus had planned for them. When he says that Jesus "on coming out" saw a great multitude, he cannot mean "on disembarking from the boat". A great multitude with women and children cannot move much faster than a sailing boat. S. Mark may quite well mean (as Dr. Hort suggests) "coming out of His retirement". This is exactly what S. John says. Jesus and His disciples cross over, and go up into the high land above the lake, and from there see the multitude approaching, and prepare to welcome them.

According to S. John, Jesus foresaw the difficulty that must arise and set the problem to Philip at once. According to S. Mark, the problem did not become acute until after a long day of teaching and healing. And then the disciples suggest that He should send them away to fend for themselves. They have clearly been thinking over the situation. They had formed an estimate of the cost of providing bread. S. John tells us that Philip had made the estimate, and that Andrew had caught sight of the lad with his little store, and had kept him in reserve. Jesus told His disciples to marshal their guests, and taking the loaves He pronounced a blessing

(S. John calls it a thanksgiving) over them, and after they had all been filled, Jesus bade His disciples take up the "broken pieces"—the prepared portions—which He had in reserve—and there was enough for each of them to fill his basket.

Such is the story which comes to us from one who, as on other grounds we have reason to believe, was one of the actors in it. Substantially the same story is told by S. Mark, who also in other parts of his Gospel shews clear signs of dependence on another eyewitness. Various efforts have been made to supply a naturalistic explanation of the incident. But, as Dr. Bernard says (*I.C.C.*, p. clxxxi) "It is not easy to dispose of the available evidence, scanty as it is, by supposing this miracle story to rest on a mistaken tradition of what really happened".

It belongs to the class of nature miracles, and as such seems to contradict our normal physical experience more directly than the miracles of healing. It is an evidence that the divine power that at first called the material universe into existence can still on occasion shew itself in action. The mode of operation of this power is inconceivable. But if Jesus is what the Evangelist says that He was, He might on occasion have been able to call it into manifestation. Something of this kind is recorded in the Old Testament. The possibility of such action is presupposed in the account of the first temptation in the wilderness. And not only is the teaching which S. John records later in this chapter based on the sign, but also an utterance which has strong internal marks of genuineness (Mk. 8: 19) recalls the attention of the disciples to it. It is to be noted, however, that the lesson the disciples were expected to draw from it was trust in the ever-present helpfulness of God, without reference to anything out of the way in the manifestation of power. It is strange that neither the disciples nor the multitude seem to have been inquisitive with regard to the source of the supply.

This does not, however, mean that the incident, as a whole, had no effect. The feeding, we must remember, came at the end of a day of teaching and healing (Mt. 14 : 15; Lk. 9 : 12). S. Mark and S. Matthew tell us that at the end of it Jesus constrained His disciples to enter the boat and start on the return journey, while He Himself dismissed His guests, and retired into the mountain to pray. S. John drops a hint, which throws a flood of light on the situation. It clearly marked an important turning-point in the Galilean ministry. The common people had felt a strong attraction to Him, but what moved them was, according to S. John (2 : 23; 6 : 2), the signs that He wrought, rather than the teaching. This is not surprising, as in Galilee at least, He was consistently silent on the Messiahship, the one subject which had a direct popular appeal. Still they had flocked after Him in great numbers, and at the close of the day they acclaim Him as the Prophet whose advent was so eagerly expected; and if they could have had their way, they would have taken Him by violence and made Him a King, to lead them in throwing off the hated yoke of Rome.

It is not impossible that the disciples were in danger of being carried away by the enthusiasm of the multitude, and that they were sent off at once by themselves as a precaution.

JESUS COMES TO HIS DISCIPLES ON THE WATER

16 *And when evening came, his disciples went down into the sea; and*
17 *they entered into a boat, and were going over the sea unto Capernaum.*
18 *And it was now dark, and Jesus had not yet come to them. And*
19 *the sea was rising by reason of a great wind that blew. When therefore they had rowed about five and twenty or thirty furlongs, they behold Jesus walking on the sea, and drawing nigh unto the*
20 *boat: and they were afraid. But he saith unto them, It is I; be*
21 *not afraid. They were willing therefore to receive him into the boat; and straightway the boat was at the land whither they were going.*

The next incident is not recorded by S. Luke, who at this point omits a considerable section which is found both in S. Mark, and, with interesting traces of independent information, in S. Matthew. For instance, in this incident S.

Matthew tells how Peter got out of the boat to get to Jesus, but his faith was not strong enough to stand the test. Jesus had to support him back into the boat. The action of Peter, both in its strength and in its weakness, is characteristic. And the story is not likely to have been invented after the Church had begun to venerate the memory of the apostles. If this part of the story is true, it rules out the interpretation of S. John's narrative which regards it as consistent with an appearance, of Jesus, not on the water, but on the shore. And it implies that the power of walking on the water is not one which is peculiar to the Lord, but is within the reach of a disciple who fulfils the condition of faith.

S. John tells the story without comment, from the point of view of a member of the crew. He notes the gathering darkness, the sense of desolation in the absence of Jesus, the rising storm, the long strain of rowing two or three miles in a heavy sea, and then the welcome, but at first alarming, appearance of Jesus walking on the sea till He actually reached the boat. They welcomed Him in, and their troubles were at an end. They found themselves at their goal.

The story is no doubt full of lessons for disciples battling with adverse conditions in their work in the world, over and above the sovereignty over physical conditions revealed in it, but S. John does not pause to draw them out.

THE LIVING BREAD

22 *On the morrow the multitude which stood on the other side of the sea saw that there was none other boat there, save one, and that Jesus entered not with his disciples into the boat, but* that *his* 23 *disciples went away alone (howbeit there came boats from Tiberias nigh unto the place where they ate the bread after the Lord had* 24 *given thanks): when the multitude therefore saw that Jesus was not there, neither his disciples, they themselves got into the boats, and* 25 *came to Capernaum, seeking Jesus. And when they found him on the other side of the sea, they said unto him, Rabbi, when camest* 26 *thou hither? Jesus answered them and said, Verily, verily, I say unto you, Ye seek me, not because ye saw signs, but because ye*

27 *ate of the loaves, and were filled. Work not for the meat that perisheth, but for the meat which abideth unto eternal life, which the Son of man shall give unto you: for him the Father,* even
28 *God, hath sealed. They said therefore unto him, What must we do,*
29 *that we may work the works of God? Jesus answered and said unto them, This is the work of God, that ye believe on him whom he hath*
30 *sent. They said therefore unto him, What then doest thou for a*
31 *sign, that we may see, and believe thee? what workest thou? Our fathers ate the manna in the wilderness; as it is written, He gave*
32 *them bread out of heaven to eat. Jesus therefore said unto them, Verily, verily, I say unto you, It was not Moses that gave you the bread out of heaven; but my Father giveth you the true bread out*
33 *of heaven. For the bread of God is that which cometh down out of*
34 *heaven, and giveth life unto the world. They said therefore unto*
35 *him, Lord, evermore give us this bread. Jesus said unto them, I am the bread of life: he that cometh to me shall not hunger, and*
36 *he that believeth on me shall never thirst. But I said unto you,*
37 *that ye have seen me, and yet believe not. All that which the Father giveth me shall come unto me; and him that cometh to me I will in*
38 *no wise cast out. For I am come down from heaven, not to do*
39 *mine own will, but the will of him that sent me. And this is the will of him that sent me, that of all that which he hath given me*
40 *I should lose nothing, but should raise it up at the last day. For this is the will of my Father, that everyone that beholdeth the Son, and believeth on him, should have eternal life; and I will raise him up at the last day.*

We come now to the discussions that arose directly out of the feeding: first with the multitude (25–40), then in the synagogue at Capernaum (41–59), and finally with the disciples (60–65).

THE DISCUSSION WITH THE MULTITUDE

The discussion with the multitude is prefaced by a short account of the movement of some of the Master's guests who had not gone home with the others (22–24). They must have bivouacked for the night where they were, hoping to see Jesus in the morning. They knew that the disciples had gone off without Him in the only boat then available. In the course of the night other smaller boats had come to the shore. Dr. Westcott suggests that the adverse wind with which the disciples had contended forced them to land just here. As they had come from Tiberias, the scene of the feeding cannot have been, as some now suggest, in its neighbourhood. The searchers knew that Jesus had started on this excursion from Capernaum. So they make use of these boats to go there to continue their search for Him. This little note, which is curiously cumbrous in expression, must surely embody an historic reminiscence. When they find Jesus they naturally ask how He had got there. The sign, however, was not for them, so their inquiry was left unanswered. Jesus began instead to help them to probe the motives which were leading them to try to persuade Him to put Himself at their head. No doubt they were priding themselves on their spiritual insight. They had recognized the "Prophet" by the tokens that He was giving them that God was with Him. But the real source of the homage that they were prepared to pay Him, was not a willingness to accept His guidance, but a lively sense of the good things that they could get by being in His company.

He, however, would have them read the parable of physical hunger. There is a hunger of the spirit no less real than the hunger of the body. "If a man will not work, neither shall he eat" is a law in both departments. So our Lord presents Himself to them as the divinely accredited source of the supply of their spiritual need.

The victims brought to the Temple for sacrifice were, we are told, sealed when they had passed the test. Samples of food, according to Egyptian papyri, were sealed. Food which is, according to Jewish requirements, *Kosher* (i.e. fit for Jewish consumption), is, I believe, still marked with a seal. The claim that Jesus makes here to having been sealed by His Father must refer to the sign given him at His baptism and publicly attested by His forerunner.

Food, whether for the body or for the spirit, remains a divine gift to man even though he has to work for it. And, if they had eyes to see it, the witness which the Father had borne to Him, marked Him out as the source of the food appropriate to the life of the world to come.

The inquirers are interested enough in the offer to ask what they are to do to secure this supply, either as wages or as the direct result of their labour (verse 25). "The work of God" (meaning in this context primarily the task laid upon them by God, though it is at the same time in the deepest sense a work which they can only perform as God Himself works it in them) is a life of faith in His accredited representative (verse 29).

This demand for faith is met at once by a demand for credentials. One who claimed a divine commission, which implied a surrender on their part to His authority, was bound, they felt, to establish it by a sign which must compel belief. Had not the authority of Moses in the wilderness been sustained day by day by the gift of bread out of heaven? (verse 31).

They were still sense-bound, and manna was for them a sign from heaven, because it had come out of the sky. Jesus had only fed them with common bread, and they never seem to have thought of asking whence it came. Jesus, however, shews no concern about arousing their curiosity on that point. Such credentials as Israel had a right to expect had been given at His baptism. It would only have confused the issue to call their attention to the physical side of the sign that had just been given. He is interested only in helping His disciples to grasp its spiritual meaning. The reference to the manna had an important service to render in this connexion. It had (as we learn from Dt. 8: 3, Mt. 4: 4) a lesson for all time with regard to the source of the support of human life. So Jesus begins by correcting the popular misunderstanding which had ascribed the gift of manna to Moses. The Giver was Another than he. He may mean His Father. But it is possible that He saw in the gift of the manna, as S. Paul saw in the gift of the water (1 Cor. 10: 4), a sign that the Christ, the all-inclusive "Word" proceeding out of the mouth of God, had supplied the needs of His people, even in the wilderness.

In any case, the manna pointed forward to Him. He was the reality of which it was the shadow; and if they would receive it, the Father who had declared Jesus to be His Son was offering them in Him the true bread out of heaven, and life to the world.

They ask for it, as the Samaritan woman had asked for the living water, still thinking, no doubt, of natural bread. He, however, at once does what was possible to prepare the way for a spiritual answer to their prayer. He identifies Himself with the bread of life, and proceeds to reveal the forces which must lie at the back of any true coming to Him. This coming to Him He now introduces as the equivalent of the believing in Him which He had already told them was the contribution required of them by God towards the provision of their own spiritual food. This *coming* is clearly a personal self-surrender to the will of the Father as declared in His Son; but its source is deeper than the will of the would-be disciples.

Its real root is in a gift from the Father to the Son, and in the reception of that gift as a sacred trust by the Son (verses 37–40). In this connexion He lays remarkable emphasis on His own surrender in the matter to His Father's will, thereby reminding us indirectly what it must cost Him to lose nothing of His Father's gift and to raise up each in the last day.

THE DISCUSSION IN THE SYNAGOGUE

41 *The Jews therefore murmured concerning him, because he said, I am*
42 *the bread which came down out of heaven. And they said, Is not this Jesus, the son of Joseph, whose father and mother we know?*
43 *how doth he now say, I am come down out of heaven? Jesus answered*
44 *and said unto them, Murmur not among yourselves. No man can come to me, except the Father which sent me draw him: and I will*
45 *raise him up in the last day. It is written in the prophets, And they shall all be taught of God. Everyone that hath heard from*
46 *the Father, and hath learned, cometh unto me. Not that any man*

hath seen the Father, save he which is from God, he hath seen the
47 *Father. Verily, verily, I say unto you, He that believeth hath*
48 *eternal life. I am the bread of life.* 49 *Your fathers did eat*
50 *the manna in the wilderness, and they died. This is the bread which cometh down out of heaven, that a man may eat thereof,*
51 *and not die. I am the living bread which came down out of heaven: if any man eat of this bread, he shall live for ever: yea and the bread which I will give is my flesh, for the life of the world.*

52 *The Jews therefore strove one with another, saying, How can*
53 *this man give us his flesh to eat? Jesus therefore said unto them, Verily, verily, I say unto you, Except ye eat the flesh of the Son*
54 *of man and drink his blood, ye have not life in yourselves. He that eateth my flesh and drinketh my blood hath eternal life; and*
55 *I will raise him up at the last day. For my flesh is meat indeed,*
56 *and my blood is drink indeed. He that eateth my flesh and drinketh*
57 *my blood abideth in me, and I in him. As the living Father sent me, and I live because of the Father; so he that eateth me, he also*
58 *shall live because of me. This is the bread which came down out of heaven: not as the fathers did eat, and died: he that eateth*
59 *this bread shall live for ever. These things said he in the synagogue, as he taught in Capernaum.*

At this point the scene changes to the synagogue. When the Jews (verses 41 ff.) murmur at the report of His teaching, Jesus returns to the thought of the Father's drawing. Experience alone, not disputing, could vindicate His claim. Faith is the way of life. He is the bread of life, of a higher potency than the manna. Those who partake of this bread escape death.

The bread is then (verse 51) more closely defined as His flesh, the humanity which He took and developed on earth under our conditions. He held it in trust for the service of the world.

This is the only passage (except Lk. 24: 39) in which Jesus speaks of His flesh. It must have been startling to hear it spoken of as bread. The words were addressed to a mixed congregation, some friendly, some the reverse. The utterance, we are told (verse 52), roused a fierce contention among them. They were all puzzled, as Nicodemus had been when he was told that he must be born again. It seemed to them that Jesus was requiring a physical impossibility. For them both feeding and flesh had straightforward material significations, and they were not cannibals. Jesus treated their objection as He had treated the objection raised by Nicodemus. Refusing to give up the parable, He repeats and expands it. *Verily, verily, I say unto you, except ye eat the flesh of the Son of Man and drink His blood, ye have not life in yourselves.* Reiterating the word "flesh" which they found offensive, He connects it with His official title "Son of Man", and adds a reference to the life-blood which was coursing through His veins. The figure of drinking blood was, no doubt even more repellent than the figure of eating His flesh. For the Jew was forbidden to taste blood. But the reason for the prohibition, and for all the use of blood in Jewish ritual, was the fact that the blood was identified with the life of the victim. Might not this have helped a man who was trying to get at our Lord's meaning, though flesh had failed to suggest to him the thought of human personality? By the help of this clue, he might be prepared for the next sentence: "He that feedeth on my flesh and drinketh my blood hath eternal life, and I will raise him up at the last day: for my flesh is real food, and my blood is real drink". For power does go out from a man's personality. A strong character strengthens and transforms into its own likeness all who surrender themselves to its influence. And when the will to help has found expression in the sacrifice of life, it is not surprising that the issue should not stop short of mutual indwelling—"He that eateth my flesh and drinketh my blood, abideth in me and I in him". It is by no means a mere metaphor. It is in sober reality that Jesus claims that such a relation is possible between Himself and all who believe in Him. And He is emboldened to make this claim by His own experience in a deeper, and yet strictly analogous, relation. That which was unique in His personality, that which in the strictest sense constituted His individuality in the nature that He shares with us, lay in this: that He stood directly in a relation to the Father, which can only be ours in Him. *As the living Father sent me, and my life is quickened and sustained by the life of my*

Father, so he that feedeth on Me shall find in his turn that his life is quickened and sustained by Me.

It is no doubt strange that Jesus should bid us look for light on the nature of our dependence on Him to the support that He Himself derived from His Father. We assume that we must know more of our own relation to Him than we can know of His relation to His Father. Yet this is not the only place where Jesus speaks of Himself as standing between men and His Father with relations both ways that throw light on each other. In the revelation of Himself as the Good Shepherd, we shall find that the fact that He is our shepherd not only throws light on, but itself receives light from, the fact that He is the Lamb of God, and that God is His Shepherd. "I am the good shepherd, and I know mine own and my own know me, as the Father knoweth me and I know the Father" (Jn. 10: 14).

It is not difficult to believe that His own consciousness of His Father's relation to Himself, and of His own relation to the Father, was for our Lord a mirror in which He saw an image of the relation in which He was called to stand to His disciples, and of their dependence on Him (cf. Rev. 7: 17). If so, He may well have felt that the revelation of His eternal life, which was in communion with the Father, as S. John tells us in the opening words of his first epistle, and was manifested through His life in human flesh to His disciples, should have the same power to help them to understand their own position.

The thought that He is illustrating here is the thought of our spiritual dependence on Him as the bread of our life. When we have once grasped the thoughts condensed by Dr. Hort into a luminous aphorism "The spirit feeds on a person", we are prepared to accept an analogy between the strength and stay that came into His life from communion with the Father, and the strength and stay which may come to us from communion with Him. We should not, however, have known where to look for guidance in interpreting the analogy, but for the word which Jesus let fall on an earlier occasion, when after His conversation with the Samaritan woman (4: 34) He told His disciples that He had a food supply hidden from their ken, "My meat is to do the will of Him that sent me, and to finish His work". When will met will in obedient surrender a channel, as we saw, was opened through which the life of the Father could flow without let or hindrance into the life of the Son.

Following this analogy, the surrender of our wills to the will of our Lord in obedient service is the way by which we may in our turn feed on Him. If so, the necessity laid on us "to eat His flesh" must set us thinking how the flesh which He assumed at the Incarnation, and in and through which He developed a perfect human personality, gives us a revelation at once of the standard of life which union with Him must require of us, and of the power by which, when we surrender ourselves to its influence, we may hope in the end to attain to it.

At the same time the call "to drink His blood" must remind us that the life had to be given up to death in obedience to the Father's will before it could be offered to slake our spiritual thirst. Underlying, therefore, the whole thought of His human personality as the source of spiritual nourishment to the brethren, we can trace a clear consciousness in the mind of Jesus of the necessity for His death, as the way by which the Spirit, which was in Him, might find an entrance into them. The body broken and the blood outpoured, on which we feed in Holy Communion, are designed to keep the same thought ever fresh and clear in the spiritual imagination of His people. It was a sound instinct which led both S. Ignatius and S. Irenaeus to find in the Eucharist the most effective refutation of the error of Cerinthus.

Jesus sums up the whole matter once more in a final declaration of the contrast between what the Father was offering men through Him, and the gift of the manna to the children of Israel in the wilderness. That could only sustain a life that was on its way to death. The bread that came down from heaven was a pledge of immortality.

This concludes the account of the one specimen that S. John gives of our Lord's teaching in Galilee to the common people, first outside and then inside a synagogue. The only other account of a particular sermon that has come down to us is that given by S. Luke (4: 16 ff.) of His preaching in Nazareth. There, as here, He tells them that the resources of the age to come are at their disposal through Him. There as here, the people cannot believe that such power could be given to one who was so much one of themselves. S. Luke dwells more on the outward signs of deliverance from physical evil. In S. John the appeal is more directly to the sense of personal need; and the appeal for a personal surrender is more explicit. It is worth while to dwell upon it to remind ourselves how simply and universally human is this appeal, which so many nowadays are inclined to turn down off-hand as mystical and fantastic.

The root of the matter is simply this. Our souls can be hungry and thirsty as well as our bodies. We know this well enough. We have all known what it is to feel lonely and dejected. There may be ever so many people about but they do not understand. They positively misunderstand. What we want is someone who will understand and care. And, thank God, we also know what a difference it makes when someone shews that he can and does sympathize. It has meant a great deal to have had a mother to comfort us, a father to say "Well done", and a friend to believe in us. Think what that means. This sympathy or understanding is spiritual food. That is what our friends give us. We feed on one another. We give one another what we can. But there remains, as the Psalmist knew, a deeper need for nothing else than God Himself, the living God. And Jesus told us that it was a blessed thing to have an appetite like that. "Blessed are they that hunger and thirst after righteousness, for they shall be satisfied."

It was to satisfy that appetite that, as Jesus tells us in this chapter, He came into the world. At the back of everything He would have us see the Father seeking to meet our need, sending His Son, giving us to Him to keep and cherish, and drawing us to Him by our hunger and by His love.

There is, indeed, already a witness for God in every heart. S. John describes it as "the light that lighteth every man". We know it as a voice that says within us "you ought", or "you ought not" to do, or to have done, this or that. It witnesses to the will of God for us. It gives us again and again a chance of letting the light and power and love of God into our hearts by choosing His will by the surrender of ours.

We indeed are very dull of hearing in respect to that voice, partly because we have in the past so often disregarded it, and partly because of the low standard of the world in which we live. But Jesus came to let us know what we are missing by our neglect. He lived continually looking up to God. He always knew and chose and did His Father's will. It was food and life to Him. He came to make it possible for us to know and choose that blessed will, and find our food and life in doing it. We cannot, He warns us, get to God in our own strength. But we can through Him. As long as He was on earth, as long as we think of Him under the limitations of life in a material body, His words may well seem perplexing. But now that He has conquered death, and taken the fruit of His earthly experience, His perfectly developed human personality, to the right hand of His Father, we should not find it as hard, as His first hearers did, to understand that His personality is the food that our souls need, and that it is eternal life for us to make His will our law.

THE DISCUSSION WITH THE DISCIPLES

60 *Many therefore of his disciples, when they heard* this, *said, This*
61 *is a hard saying; who can hear it? But Jesus knowing in himself that his disciples murmured at this, said unto them, Doth this*
62 *cause you to stumble?* What *then if ye should behold the Son of*
63 *Man ascending where he was before? It is the spirit that quickeneth; the flesh profiteth nothing: the words that I have spoken unto you*
64 *are spirit, and are life. But there are some of you that believe not. For Jesus knew from the beginning who they were that believed*
65 *not, and who it was that should betray him. And he said, For this*

cause have I said unto you, that no man can come unto me, except it be given unto him of the Father.

This teaching produced a crisis even in the inner circle of those who had so far accepted the call of Jesus as to attach themselves to His company. The rest of the chapter (verses 60–71) deals with this crisis. Some of the disciples give voice to a protest: "This is a hard saying. Who can understand it (or Him)?" The hardness of the saying consisted, not so much in the obscurity of the language (the objection is not a simple repetition of verse 52), but in the character of the relationship between the Master and His disciples, which was involved in it. All the outward facts—His material presence, the very perfection of His humanity—seemed to make it impossible that He could be what He claimed and do what He promised. In fact, as Jesus goes on to hint, it was not until after His ascension that He could be fully manifested as the bread of life, and its Lord. Meanwhile, obedient discipleship was the only road to understanding between Him and them. This seems to come out from the two points that He stresses in His answer:

(1) "Does this disturb you? What if ye behold the Son of Man ascending to the home that he left to come here?" It has been disputed whether He expected that this would answer or increase the difficulty that they felt. There is, however, no necessity to decide that point. The Ascension would be the final justification of His claim to have come down out of heaven. It would at the same time bring the possibility of feeding on Him as the bread of life within the reach of all. But the evidence could not come home to any who would not take on themselves the yoke of obedient discipleship.

(2) He goes on, "It is the Spirit that gives life, the flesh cannot help at all". Outward following must remain barren as long as it was merely the expression of their own self-determination, of the will of the flesh. It could only bear fruit as a conscious surrender to the drawing of the Father. They must be born of the Spirit before they could

live indeed: and the Spirit could not be duly manifested till after the Resurrection. At the same time communications were continually passing over from Him to them, which, as they came out of His experience of the ultimate reality, were already capable of quickening and supporting faith. "The words that I have spoken unto you are Spirit and Life."

They could not, however, quicken those who still remained self-centred. So Jesus adds: "There are among you those who believe not" and "For this cause I have said unto you, that no man can come unto Me, except it be given unto Him of the Father".

As a result, many of those who had been following, including, no doubt, those who had been hoping to make Him king, departed from Him. They would have been prepared to leave all and follow Him, if in the end they could have their own way with Him. They cannot stand the test, when the demand of an absolute surrender is pressed home. The crisis, we may note in passing, is the counterpart in S. John of the crisis in the Synoptists, when Jesus warned His disciples that a man must take up his cross daily, if he would follow Him.

66 *Upon this many of his disciples went back, and walked no more*
67 *with him. Jesus said therefore unto the twelve, Would ye also go*
68 *away? Simon Peter answered him, Lord, to whom shall we go? thou*
69 *hast the words of eternal life. And we have believed and know*
70 *that thou art the Holy One of God. Jesus answered them, Did not*
71 *I choose you the twelve, and one of you is a devil? Now he spake*
of Judas the son *of Simon Iscariot, for he it was that should betray*
him, being *one of the twelve.*

We have still to learn the reaction of the inmost circle, the Twelve, whom S. John brings on the scene without introduction—a further proof, if any is needed, that he is writing for those already familiar with the general outline of the ministry. Jesus turns to them, and gives them an opportunity of retiring even then. Many illusions with which they had started on their discipleship had by this time vanished. They were only beginning to realize the stringency of His claim.

Surrender to it must not become the mechanical carrying out of a past decision. At the same time the putting of the question could not fail to draw them consciously nearer, if it helped them to realize, but for a moment, what the world would be for them wanting Him.

Simon Peter, as we might expect, answers the challenge on behalf of the body—"Lord, for whom shall we forsake thy guidance? We have at least learned our need of a leader. Thou hast a power of utterance strangely different from our accustomed teachers. Thy words are words of eternal life as thou hast said (verse 63). Casting our eyes back to the beginning of our discipleship, we are not disappointed. We believed then that God had set His seal on Thee as consecrated to His service, His Holy One. And experience has confirmed our early faith. What we believed then, now we know."

The answer of Jesus to this confession of loyalty is as aweful as it is unexpected. "Did not I choose you, the twelve? And one of you is a devil?"

The reference to His choice of them reasserts the principle of the Father's drawing, which has already been dwelt on repeatedly. His action in choosing was the outward expression of His Father's giving of them to Him. The re-assertion was necessary because Peter's words might seem to rest the relation in which they stood to Him on an act of theirs. And yet their individuality was not destroyed. They were not set free from responsibility. Nay, just in proportion as their position grew in importance did the issues for good or for evil deepen in intensity. They might rise higher or sink lower. They might render nobler service or inflict more fatal injury, in proportion to the trust reposed in them. Let none presume, *One of you is a devil. Now He was speaking of Judas, son of Simon Iscariot, one of the twelve.*

The mystery is impenetrable. He could not surround Himself with a group of intimate friends without exposing Himself to danger if any of them turned traitor. It was clear from the Scripture that that possibility would become actual. S. John is clear that Jesus was aware of the danger for Judas, and yet knew that it was His Father's will that He should choose Him. S. John has made us familiar with the last appeal that Jesus made to him before he went out from the Last Supper into the night (13 : 30). It is not impossible that S. John saw in this challenge to the Twelve, the deliberate opening of a door by which Judas might, if he chose, retire, now that Jesus had made it clear that He would not become the leader for whom the common people were looking.

This account of a challenge to the Twelve and of the confession that Simon Peter made in response to it, is in striking contrast, in spite of many points of similarity, with the account given in the Synoptists of a challenge made by Jesus somewhat later at Cæsarea Philippi. Here the challenge is addressed directly to their sense of personal loyalty, and the confession is a confession of a consciousness of personal indebtedness. There the challenge relates to the place that they were prepared to assign to their Master in the working out of the purpose of God for the nation and the world. Simon Peter declares that in spite of the evidence, by this time unmistakable, that the Jewish authorities had rejected His claim, and that He had not come to fulfil the popular anticipations of a national deliverer, they still believed Him to be the fulfilment of the promises of God, and the divinely appointed Head of the Kingdom that was at hand. Each account fits closely into its context, and it is impossible to regard them as divergent accounts of the same incident.

CHAPTER XI

THE SELF-REVELATION OF JESUS IN JERUSALEM

1 *And after these things Jesus walked in Galilee: for he would not*
2 *walk in Judæa, because the Jews sought to kill him. Now the*
3 *feast of the Jews, the feast of tabernacles, was at hand. His brethren therefore said unto him, Depart hence, and go into Judæa, that thy*
4 *disciples also may behold thy works which thou doest. For no man doeth anything in secret, and himself seeketh to be known openly.*
5 *If thou doest these things, manifest thyself to the world. For even*
6 *his brethren did not believe on him. Jesus therefore saith unto them,*
7 *My time is not yet come; but your time is always ready. The world cannot hate you; but me it hateth, because I testify of it, that its*
8 *works are evil. Go ye up unto the feast: I go not up yet unto this feast;*
9 *because my time is not yet fulfilled. And having said these things unto them, he abode* still *in Galilee.*

JESUS GOES UP TO JERUSALEM UNOFFICIALLY

THE period between the Passover and the Feast of Tabernacles is spent in Galilee. In this period fall the incidents recorded in S. Matthew and S. Mark between the feeding of the five thousand and the feeding of the four thousand, followed by the retirement to Cæsarea Philippi, the confession of Simon Peter and the Transfiguration, and a return to Capernaum, after which, according to S. Luke, Jesus set His face steadfastly to go up to Jerusalem. There is no further reference to Galilee in S. John till 21 : 1.

The centre of interest for S. John in the next five chapters is Jerusalem. He is recording a succession of efforts that Jesus made to help the common people in the capital and their leaders to understand who He was, and what He had been sent into the world to do. He had already dealt with the subject at length in the course of a judicial inquiry in ch. v. In these chapters He deals with criticisms and questionings that arose in various sections of the community. His main subject is His relation to God. The common people are again and again on the point of accepting Him as the promised Messiah. But the authorities refuse to recognize that He can be. And we learn, by the way, that they had decided to put out of the synagogue any who gave Him that name. When expressly challenged to declare Himself on that point He refuses to give a direct answer. The issue was complicated by His violation of their traditional rules of sabbath observance. But the real issue turns on the directness of relation between God and Man implied in His claim that God is in a real sense His Father.

It was a generally accepted rule that a Jew in Palestine should attend one of the three great feasts at Jerusalem every year. Jesus had apparently missed the Passover (6: 4) and Pentecost. It was to be expected, therefore, that He would go up for the Feast of Tabernacles. At this point S. John introduces his one reference to the brethren of the Lord, the chief of whom was James, afterwards the head of the Church in Jerusalem. There is nothing to shew whether they were younger brothers, or children of Joseph by an earlier marriage. It is, however, clear that they cannot have been in the number of the Twelve.

In the light of the fact that the Jews were seeking to kill Jesus, it is hard to account for the line that His brethren took. Evidently they did not anticipate that He would be in serious personal danger. They may have thought that in an actual crisis He would put out power to protect Himself. They do not question His personal authority. S. John's language only implies that they were not prepared to bide His time for manifesting it.

Their appeal is based on two grounds. First, there is the claim of the capital to be the scene of the works (clearly of an evidential value) that He was doing, that the followers He already had there (cf. 4: 1) might behold them. Were they aware of men of influence like Nicodemus and Joseph of Arimathæa (cf. 12: 42) who might come out on His side? They take no account of the Twelve.

Next, they plead for straightforwardness. They were clearly puzzled by His refusal to work a sign to order, coupled with the freedom with which He helped individuals privately. "No man who doeth anything in secret can retain his freedom". A secret of any kind is a check on speech and action. So they conclude "Since you have these things given you to do, do not shrink from letting the whole world know what you are".

Jesus in His answer rebukes the selfish, hurrying spirit that would choose its own path and time. To it all times are alike. The Son, here as at Cana (2: 4), waits for a sign from His Father.

Then He tells them that the manifestation which they thought must carry all before it, would rouse an opposition of which they did not dream. "The world cannot hate you: but me it hateth, because I testify of it that its works are evil."

His practical conclusion is that the time has not yet come for a public, so to speak official, entry into Jerusalem.

10 *But when his brethren were gone up unto the feast, then went he*
11 *also up, not publicly, but as it were in secret. The Jews therefore*
12 *sought him at the feast, and said, Where is he? And there was much murmuring among the multitudes concerning him: some said, He is a good man; others said, Not so, but he leadeth the multitude*
13 *astray. Howbeit no man spake openly of him for fear of the Jews.*

In the end He goes up as one of the crowd—with the result that any design that the leaders might have had of a deliberate attack on Him is postponed. There is, however, animated disputing about Him among the common people, who in their turn are forced into an attitude of reserve from fear of the authorities.

NONE BUT THE OBEDIENT CAN JUDGE OF HIS CLAIM

14 *But when it was now the midst of the feast Jesus went up into the*
15 *temple, and taught. The Jews therefore marvelled, saying, How*
16 *knoweth this man letters, having never learned? Jesus therefore*

answered them, and said, My teaching is not mine, but his that sent
17 *me. If any man willeth to do his will, he shall know of the teaching,*
18 *whether it be of God, or* whether *I speak from myself. He that speaketh from himself seeketh his own glory: but he that seeketh the glory of him that sent him, the same is true, and no unrighteous-*
19 *ness is in him. Did not Moses give you the law, and* yet *none*
20 *of you doeth the law? Why seek ye to kill me? The multitude*
21 *answered, Thou hast a devil: who seeketh to kill thee? Jesus answered and said unto them, I did one work and ye all marvel.*
22 *For this cause hath Moses given you circumcision (not that it is of Moses, but of the fathers); and on the sabbath ye circumcise a*
23 *man. If a man receiveth circumcision on the sabbath, that the law of Moses may not be broken; are ye wroth with me, because I made a*
24 *man every whit whole on the sabbath? Judge not according to appearance, but judge righteous judgement.*

He had Himself, however, no intention of seeking concealment. His message must be delivered. He is only anxious that attention should be concentrated not on Himself but on His message. We could have wished that S. John had dwelt a little more on the substance as well as the fact of His public teaching. It must have had, like the Sermon on the Mount as recorded in S. Matthew, a largely Scriptural basis, for His hearers are struck by His knowledge of the text of the Bible. That is what they meant by "letters". Such knowledge, they felt, would normally have only been acquired by a course of professional training. In the Synoptists the wonder is aroused even more by the manner than by the substance of the teaching. Jesus claimed an authority independent of tradition. In His answer He dealt with both points. The source of His illumination, and the authority that He claimed, were derived from His relation to Him that sent Him. Everything depended on the truth of that claim. And it was within the reach of any man who was sincerely desirous of knowing the will of God that he might do it, to verify the truth of that claim. The self-appointed teacher cannot fail to wish to draw attention to himself, and so to become indifferent to the interests both of the truth and of his hearers.

The hearers of Jesus, however, were, as He points out, in no state to apply this test. They were openly disobeying a law admittedly divine. He appeals in proof to the murderous hate that they are cherishing against Him. He is fully aware, and He does not shrink from letting them know it, of the opposition that His attitude to the sabbath has aroused, in Galilee (Mk. 3 : 6) as well as in Jerusalem (Jn. 5 : 18). As He is speaking in Jerusalem, it is not surprising that He should refer to the incident by which, as we have seen reason to believe, the attention of the Pharisees had first been called to His challenge to their whole attitude to the Law of which they were the guardians. The offence has not ceased, though eighteen months may have elapsed. And He indicates a fresh line of defence for His action, which recalls arguments which He used in Galilee (Mt. 12 : 5, 11).

The reference (verse 20) to plots against His life is resented by the multitude, who apparently do not know of the plots of the leaders. They think He must be mad, "You are possessed", they say, "Who is seeking to kill you?"

The charge is of a gratuitous type. A prophet is always liable to be taken for a mad fellow. It was one of the popular estimates of the Baptist (Mt. 11 : 18). It expressed one aspect of the popular verdict on Jesus at this time in Jerusalem (See S. John 8: 48, 10: 20). In Mk. 3: 22 we are told that the scribes from Jerusalem went so far as to assert that His power over the possessed was due to the superior power of the demon that was possessing Him. Jesus takes no notice of the charge here. He deals directly with the charge of sabbath-breaking which was the ground of the plotting.

"I did one work and you all marvel" not so much at the work itself, as at its violation of your conventions. And yet "for this cause" i.e. with the same end in view, the vindication for an Israelite of his true place in God's people, "you circumcize a man", sabbath or no sabbath, "on the eighth day". Clearly the restoration of an Israelite to the full exercise of all his powers is every whit as natural and right. *Do not be superficial in your judgements. Let your conscience guide your judgement.* This comes from the same mint as the warnings to the Pharisees in Lk. 11 : 39 f. and elsewhere.

JESUS MAKES A DIRECT APPEAL TO THEIR CONSCIENCE IN SUPPORT OF HIS CLAIM

25 *Some therefore of them of Jerusalem said, Is not this he whom they* 26 *seek to kill? And lo, he speaketh openly, and they say nothing unto him. Can it be that the rulers indeed know that this is the* 27 *Christ? Howbeit we know this man whence he is: but when the* 28 *Christ cometh, no man knoweth whence he is. Jesus therefore cried in the temple, teaching and saying, Ye both know me, and know whence I am; and I am not come of myself, but he that sent me is* 29 *true, whom ye know not. I know him; because I am from him, and* 30 *he sent me. They sought therefore to take him: and no man laid* 31 *his hand on him, because his hour was not yet come. But of the multitude many believed on him; and they said, When the Christ shall come, will he do more signs than those which this man hath done?*

S. John goes on with his notes on the discussions among different classes in the population of Jerusalem. "The multitude" in verse 20 seem to have been Galilean. This new group is aware of the plans of their leaders, and are puzzled by their inaction: "Can it be that the rulers really know that He is the Messiah?" That suspicion raised the whole question of the means of identifying the Messiah. The prophetic picture laid stress on the element of mystery that would attach to Him. "Surely we know too much about Jesus for him to fit the picture?"

Jesus makes an emphatic answer to this criticism: "He cries aloud" (as in 7 : 37; 12 : 44, cf. 1 : 15) as He is teaching in the Temple and states the problem for them: *Ye both know me, and ye know whence I am.* "I am indeed no stranger to any of you. You have all heard my voice in your hearts. And you are right in believing that everything depends on the source of my authority. That source is not in myself. My mission is from a Person who is no figment of my imagination. Though you know Him not—I know Him, for I left Him to come to you on a mission from Him."

This is no doubt an enigmatic utterance, and admits of divers interpretations. Jesus may accept their statement: "There is nothing mysterious about my earthly origin. The difficulty lies further back. You do not know the source of my mission". Or, the opening words may be an indignant repetition of their claim: "You declare that you know, and yet on the one point of vital importance you are ignorant". I have suggested a third interpretation, perhaps too boldly. S. John in his Prologue identifies "the Word" who became incarnate with "the light that lighteth every man", i.e. with the voice that speaks to every man's conscience. In the next chapter (8: 31, 37, 43) Jesus speaks of "abiding in His word", which is the counterpart on our side of His own "keeping of His Father's word" (verse 55). It may be, of course, that He is thinking of His Gospel as a seed, which when received will take possession of and transform a heart. I suggest that it is possible that in the opening words Jesus is alluding to their familiarity with this inner voice.

In any case Jesus affirmed with emphasis His consciousness of a mission from God. The issue on the one side was an abortive attempt to arrest Him, and on the other a response of faith on the part of many of the multitude.

HIS ANSWER TO THE FIRST EFFORT TO ARREST HIM

32 *The Pharisees heard the multitude murmuring these things concerning him: and the chief priests and the Pharisees sent officers to take*
33 *him. Jesus therefore said, Yet a little while am I with you, and I*
34 *go unto him that sent me. Ye shall seek me, and shall not find me:*
35 *and where I am, ye cannot come. The Jews therefore said among themselves, Whither will this man go that we shall not find him? will he go unto the Dispersion among the Greeks, and teach the*
36 *Greeks? What is this word that he said, Ye shall seek me, and shall not find me: and where I am, ye cannot come?*

The servants sent to arrest Him are the occasion of a solemn warning. Before very long He would be going back to Him who sent Him. Then they would feel their need of Him, but would not be able to find Him. And (even now) they cannot get where He is. This warning did not as yet suggest that He meant His death.

THE SPIRITUAL ROCK

37 *Now on the last day, the great* day *of the feast, Jesus stood and cried, saying, If any man thirst, let him come unto me, and drink.*
38 *He that believeth on me, as the scripture hath said, out of his belly*
39 *shall flow rivers of living water. But this spake he of the Spirit, which they that believed on him were to receive: for the Spirit was not yet* given*: because Jesus was not yet glorified.*

This is the first spontaneous utterance at the feast. All the earlier utterances were called out by opposition covert or express. It has direct reference to the ritual of the feast; which commemorated the experience of Israel in the wilderness. In contrast to the test (7: 17) the only condition is the sense of a need unsatisfied, as in the invitation in Mt. 11: 28 to the weary and heavy laden. It contains the promise of overflowing satisfaction.

This overflow for the refreshment of others is essential to the personal enjoyment of the gift, and the token of its presence. It is unforced, "The quality of mercy is not strained". Faith pierces down to a hidden eternal spring at the root of our being, and the water leaps up exulting, inexhaustible. The believer knows himself to be but the channel, and has simply to take care that the outflow does not get choked up. Self-surrender to Christ, as it is the source, so it is the abiding condition of our power to be a blessing.

It is not easy to identify "the scripture" that S. John had in mind, as foretelling that believers in the Christ should become sources of blessing. The nearest would seem to be Isaiah 58: 11: "Thou shalt be like a watered garden, and like a spring of water, whose waters fail not". But there is no necessity to change the punctuation as some of the Fathers did, in order that we may limit the prophecy to the work of the Christ. Each believer, as S. Paul makes clear, is called as "a member of Christ" to become an instrument in His hand for carrying on His work.

S. John's own comment connects the promise directly with the Holy Spirit (verse 39): *But this spake He of the Spirit which they that believed on Him were to receive, for as yet the Spirit was not given; because Jesus was not yet glorified.* S. John is writing, we must remember, for Christians who had grown up in the new world that sprang out of the outpouring of the Spirit on the day of Pentecost, and who had need to be reminded of the change that that had made in their privileges and responsibilities. The figure is repeated in the vision of the new Jerusalem (Rev. 22: 1) where "a river of the water of life" flows out of the throne of God and of the Lamb. S. Paul makes the same use of the symbolism of the gift of water to the thirsty in the wilderness, which the Jews were commemorating in the ritual of the Feast of Tabernacles, when he speaks of "the spiritual rock that followed them".

The most striking point in the picture as Jesus presents it, is that it makes us look for the advent of the Spirit, not from without and above, but from within and beneath, from the secret springs of our deepest being. In 6: 35, 55 Jesus had connected the quenching of spiritual thirst with faith in Himself, and with the drinking of His blood. It may well be that as we strive to enter into the Spirit of His perfect surrender, we open the flood-gates by which the living stream can well up from the hidden root of our being. S. John's comment is fairly paraphrased in our version "The Spirit was not yet *given*, for Jesus was not yet glorified."

40 Some *of the multitude therefore, when they heard these words,*
41 *said, This is of a truth the prophet. Others said, This is the Christ. But some said, What, doth the Christ come out of Galilee?*
42 *Hath not the scripture said that the Christ cometh of the seed of*
43 *David, and from Bethlehem, the village where David was? So*
44 *there arose a division in the multitude because of him. And some of them would have taken him; but no man laid hands on him.*

The immediate result of this appeal is popular confusion.

The natural instinct of the man in the street made it clear to him that there was genuine spiritual force here—He must be "the prophet" or "the Christ". This is confronted by the popular prejudice against Galilee, supported by an appeal to Scripture as asserting a Judæan origin of the Christ. This is a variation of the objection raised in verse 27 which had been based on another and apparently inconsistent element in the popular anticipation. In regard to the matter in dispute both sides were right, needing only, as S. Matthew shews (2: 23; 4: 12), a fuller knowledge of the life history of Jesus and of the teaching of the Scripture to justify the verdict of the popular instinct. But it was not God's will that faith in Jesus should in the first instance be built on the evidence of isolated texts.

45 *The officers therefore came to the chief priests and Pharisees; and*
46 *they said unto them, Why did ye not bring him? The officers*
47 *answered, Never man so spake. The Pharisees therefore answered*
48 *them, Are ye also led astray? Hath any of the rulers believed on*
49 *him, or of the Pharisees? But this multitude which knoweth not*
50 *the law are accursed. Nicodemus saith unto them (he that came*
51 *to him before, being one of them), Doth our law judge a man,*
52 *except it first hear from himself and know what he doeth? They*
answered and said unto him, Art thou also of Galilee? Search, and
see that out of Galilee ariseth no prophet.

At the same time the popular instinct had no power to assert itself either for or against Him. So S. John passes on to describe the reaction of the leaders. They are met first by the failure of their police to execute an arrest. The police were powerless against the personal ascendancy of Jesus. The leaders were driven in consequence to try by sheer weight of personal authority to overcome the impression He had made on them. "No one of weight or experience—only the rabble is moved by Him." It must have been disconcerting when one of their own body ventured to maintain that the accused had at least a legal right to be heard in His own defence. They find themselves driven to use in a less accurate form the argument from Scripture which had already been produced by the rabble: "His Galilean origin shows that He must be an impostor. Read your Bible and you will see". But there was a division of opinion even in the Sanhedrim. The visit of Nicodemus to Jesus by night had not been fruitless.

The story of the Lord's treatment of the woman taken in adultery, beautiful and no doubt true as it is, has no claim to be regarded as part of the Gospel according to S. John.

THE LIGHT OF THE WORLD

12 *Again therefore Jesus spake unto them, saying: I am the light of the world: he that followeth me shall not walk in darkness, but shall*
13 *have the light of life. The Pharisees therefore said unto him, Thou*
14 *bearest witness of thyself; thy witness is not true. Jesus answered and said unto them, Even if I bear witness of myself, my witness is true; for I know whence I came, and whither I go; but ye know*
15 *not whence I come, or whither I go. Ye judge after the flesh; I*
16 *judge no man. Yea, and if I judge, my judgement is true; for*
17 *I am not alone, but I and the Father that sent me. Yea and in*
18 *your law it is written, that the witness of two men is true. I am he that beareth witness of myself, and the Father that sent me*
19 *beareth witness of me. They said therefore unto him, Where is thy Father? Jesus answered, Ye know neither me, nor my Father:*
20 *if ye knew me, ye would know my Father also. These words spake he in the treasury, as he taught in the temple: and no man took him: because his hour was not yet come.*

In the midst of this confusion, when the blazing pyre in the Temple Courts on the last night of the feast was recalling the pillar of cloud and fire that had led Israel through the wilderness, came one clear unfaltering voice: *I am the light of the world. He that followeth me shall not walk in darkness, but shall have the light of life.* Here at least is a promise of guidance in all that we have to do, enabling us to see where we are, and to avoid the pitfalls by which our path is beset. Here is a source of power to act, for light is life-giving. And as the life deepens the light will grow for life is luminous.

This claim opens the way for a fresh cavil. It is the first "I am" of the Lord at Jerusalem. And according to His own canon (5: 31) a claim made by Him on His own behalf is unworthy of credit. Do not these words come under that category? "Thou bearest witness of thyself, thy witness is not true".

The objection is met directly on its own ground, without reference to His own use of the same words on an earlier occasion. As they put it, apart from its context, the canon is not true absolutely. The condition of true witness is accurate knowledge together with the will and the power to impart it. These conditions Jesus claims to fulfil—*I know whence I came and whither I go.* The tests which He had suggested before, had been *first* corroboration of His witness from without, and *next* the absence of self-seeking in His claim. Here the reference to His source and His goal proves (if that needed proving) the absence of self-seeking in His claim to possess the power to guide and help.

On the other hand only experts can test evidence. You must know before you can judge of the truth or falsehood of a statement. And the Jews did not fulfil this condition when judging of Christ's claim. For they did not know whence He came or whither He was going. And yet they were prepared to condemn Him as a liar on a suspicion of self-seeking.

It is important to remember this personal implication in their criticism. It will help us to understand the sudden reference to judgement in the middle of this discussion about the criterion of truth for a specific testimony.

Ye judge after the flesh, I judge no one. Yea and if I judge my judgement is true through and through, because I am not alone, but I and the Father who sent me.

All truth comes to us on personal testimony and requires examination and interpretation before we accept it. In accepting or rejecting it we pass judgement on the capacity and the honesty of the witness, and incidentally on ourselves. S. John has already pointed out (3: 19–21) how the coming of light into the world judged men. And Jesus Himself (in 5: 22–30) had dwelt at some length on the function of judgement which the Father had entrusted to Him as a son of man. Here Jesus points out the flaw in their exercise of this fundamental human faculty. He had warned them in 7: 14 against superficiality, here the warning goes deeper. They were allowing their judgement to be swayed by a false principle, by their lower nature, the flesh. This is the root of all Pharisaic censoriousness, which leads a man to despise his neighbours. That is why judgement is forbidden in the Sermon on the Mount. It is clearly in this sense that Jesus asserts that He judges no man. He goes on to explain here (cf. 5: 30) how His communion with His Father was His safeguard in the exercise of this fundamental human faculty, whether on Himself or on others. His judgement on Himself and others was the reflexion of His Father's, and so was in essence "witness".

This brings us back to the main subject: *It is written in your law that the witness of two men is true. I rely on the confirmation afforded by my Father to the testimony of my own consciousness of myself.*

This at once raised the question in a form that the lawyers could appreciate: "You speak of corroborative evidence. Produce your witness—Where is your Father?" (verse 19).

This reveals at once their incompetence and the hopelessness of the task on which Jesus was engaged as He strove to get His meaning home to them. Their ears were deaf to both His witnesses. They knew neither the Son, nor the Father. Only by the knowledge of the Son could they attain to knowledge of the Father.

With this hint of the goal towards which the light of the world is leading men, and the nature of the light of life which He promised, the section closes.

The treasury was close to the place where the Sanhedrim had their meetings. They were as impotent to arrest, as to comprehend, the witness. His hour was not yet.

THE LAST APPEAL TO THE PHARISEES

21 *He said therefore again unto them, I go away, and ye shall seek me, and shall die in your sin: whither I go, ye cannot come. The*
22 *Jews therefore said, Will he kill himself, that he saith, Whither*
23 *I go, ye cannot come? And he said unto them, Ye are from beneath;*

I am from above: ye are of this world; I am not of this world.
24 *I said therefore unto you, that ye shall die in your sins: for except*
25 *ye believe that I am* he, *ye shall die in your sins. They said therefore unto him, Who art thou? Jesus said unto them, Even that*
26 *which I have also spoken unto you from the beginning.*[1] *I have many things to speak and to judge concerning you: howbeit he that sent me is true; and the things which I heard from him, these*
27 *things speak I unto the world. They perceived not that he spake to*
28 *them of the Father. Jesus therefore said, When ye have lifted up the Son of man, then shall ye know that I am* he, *and* that *I do nothing of myself, but as the Father taught me, I speak these*
29 *things. And he that sent me is with me; he hath not left me alone;*
30 *for I do always the things that are pleasing to him. As he spake these things, many believed on him.*

Or *How is it that I even speak to you at all.*

S. John records one more effort made by Jesus to stir the authorities in Jerusalem to look seriously into His claim for recognition. He stresses (verses 21, 24) in the language of the Prophets the urgency of the situation. The loss of the light will rouse in them ineffectual longings to recover Him. Their rejection of Him would bring them into death. They would die in their sins. He would have passed out of their reach.

The Jews in response wonder whether He is contemplating suicide to get out of their reach. He has to remind them that there are other gulfs dividing men besides the gulf of death. Even now He and they are deriving their being, not by the fact of physical descent, but by their own choice, from fundamentally distinct sources: *You are from below, I am from above. You are of this world, I am not. That is why I told you that unless you believe that I am He* (or "that I am what I am"), *ye shall die in your sins*." But He still has hope that they may even at the eleventh hour grasp the salvation which He is offering them, so He adds *For unless you believe* "*that I am He*", (the promised deliverer) *ye shall die in your sins.*

This brings them at last to the question which lay deeper than the question of origin or goal. And they ask straight out "Who art Thou?"

There is a troublesome uncertainty (expressed in the alternative translations) about the precise nature of the challenge that He had made to them. The Greek is "that I am", and that may mean simply "that it's me" (cf. 6: 21, 9: 9), "that I am 'just myself'. My message is just my personality, and cannot be more closely defined in words". This is no doubt true in fact, but failure to discern that truth can scarcely have been visited with such a penalty. The alternative translation corresponds to a regular Septuagint usage in passages like Is. 43: 10, 12, 13, in which the Lord calls Israel to recognize His work in their salvation—"that I am He".

The whole evidence is before them, and He has nothing to add to it; though here again it is impossible to be quite sure of the meaning of S. John's Greek. S. Chrysostom certainly took the words to mean: "Why do I even speak to you at all?" This makes of the utterance a cry of suffering like "O faithless and perverse generation, how long shall I be with you, how long shall I suffer you?" Some, however, would translate it "From the beginning that which I am telling you". In any case He means that He has nothing to add to His revelation of Himself.

But it might still be possible to help them to an understanding of the causes of their failure. So He goes on: *I have many things to say about you and to judge. Howbeit He that sent me is true, and what I heard from Him, that I speak unto the world.*

The key to His meaning here is to be found in the words which sum up His final reflexions on the issue of His appeal to the nation in 12: 45 ff. There He says: "The word that I spake, that shall judge". Speaking and judging are inextricably combined (cf. 2. Cor. 2: 15), even as judgement is inseparable from the coming of the light into the world. The words here have reference to the solemn declaration "Ye shall die in your sins", which forces Him to turn for consolation to the truth of Him that sent Him, from whom came the utterances that were charged with this heart-searching power.

It is not surprising that, as S. John notes, His hearers should have failed to understand that it was really the Father whom He meant. Jesus has, however, still something to add which in the end might supply an answer to all their questions. *When ye have lifted up the Son of Man then shall ye know "that I am He", and do nothing of myself, but as the Father taught me I speak these things.*

Even their failure to respond, even their open rebellion, would not exhaust the divine resources. He would be lifted up by the Cross to His throne at the right hand of the Father, and His very humiliation would define and substantiate His claim.

For Himself He had not to wait for this outward vindication of His truth. He is here and now conscious of the presence of Him that sent Him. He knows that He is not alone. His Father's "Well done" is always ringing in His ears.

Some at least of the seed that He sowed at this time found hearts ready to receive it. *As He said these things many believed on Him*—outright and altogether. And even short of this, there were some who, if they did not make a complete surrender, yet felt that His words rang true. They were prepared to take Him seriously. They believed Him, though they did not believe on Him. The rest of the chapter describes the further appeal that Jesus made to them.

A FURTHER APPEAL TO THE WAVERERS

31 *Jesus therefore said to those Jews which had believed him, If ye*
32 *abide in my word,* then *are ye truly my disciples; and ye shall*
33 *know the truth, and the truth shall make you free. They answered unto him, We be Abraham's seed, and have never yet been in bondage*
34 *to any man: how sayest thou, Ye shall be made free? Jesus answered them, Verily, verily, I say unto you, Everyone that committeth sin*
35 *is the bondservant of sin. And the bondservant abideth not in*
36 *the house for ever: the son abideth for ever. If therefore the Son*
37 *shall make you free, ye shall be free indeed. I know that ye are Abraham's seed; yet ye seek to kill me, because my word hath*
38 *not free course in you. I speak the things which I have seen with*

my *Father: and ye also do the things which ye heard from* your
39 *Father. They answered and said unto him, Our father is Abraham.*
Jesus saith unto them, If ye were Abraham's children, ye would
40 *do the works of Abraham. But now ye seek to kill me, a man*
that hath told you the truth, which I heard from God: this did
41 *not Abraham. Ye do the works of your father. They said unto*
him, We were not born of fornication: we have one Father, even
42 *God. Jesus said unto them, If God were your Father, ye would love*
me: for I came forth and am come from God; for neither have I come
43 *of myself, but he sent me. Why do ye not understand my speech?*
44 Even *because ye cannot hear my word. Ye are of* your *father the*
devil, and the lusts of your father it is your will to do. He was
a murderer from the beginning, and stood not in the truth, because
there is no truth in him. When he speaketh a lie, he speaketh of
45 *his own: for he is a liar and the father thereof. But because I*
46 *say truth, ye believe me not. Which of you convicteth me*
47 *of sin? If I say truth, why do ye not believe me? He that is of*
God heareth the words of God: for this cause ye hear them *not,*
48 *because ye are not of God. The Jews answered and said unto him,*
Say we not well that thou art a Samaritan, and hast a devil?
49 *Jesus answered, I have not a devil; but I honour my Father, and*
50 *ye dishonour me. But I seek not mine own glory: there is one*
51 *that seeketh and judgeth. Verily, verily, I say unto you, If a man*
52 *keep my word, he shall never see death. The Jews said unto him,*
Now we know that thou hast a devil. Abraham is dead, and
the prophets; and thou sayest, If a man keep my word, he shall
53 *never taste of death. Art thou greater than our father Abraham,*
which is dead? and the prophets are dead: whom makest thou
54 *thyself? Jesus answered, If I glorify myself, my glory is nothing:*
it is my Father that glorifieth me; of whom ye say, that he is your
55 *God; and ye have not known him: but I know him; and if I should*
say, I know him not, I shall be like unto you, a liar: but I know
56 *him and keep his word. Your father Abraham rejoiced to see my*
57 *day; and he saw it, and was glad. The Jews therefore said unto*
him, Thou art not yet fifty years old, and hast thou seen Abraham?
58 *Jesus said unto them, Verily, verily, I say unto you, Before Abraham*
59 *was, I am. They took up stones therefore to cast at him: but Jesus*
hid himself, and went out of the temple.

In this section, as I understand it, Jesus proceeds to give utterance to some of the many things that, as He had just said (verse 26), He had yet to speak concerning them: utterances that would bring a judgement with them. It has certainly caused great searchings of heart among expositors. Some who are quite prepared to attach a high value to the Gospel as a historical document are sure that an alien element has at this point crept into the tradition. They find in it the record of an unseemly wrangle in which Jesus Himself could never have taken the part assigned to Him. This judgement seems to me hasty and ill-founded. We must not forget that the attitude towards Jesus of the section of the people with whom He is dealing was gradually hardening into a settled purpose to destroy Him. Their intent was murderous, under whatever cloak of religious zeal it might hide itself. There was surely no breach of charity involved in forcing them to realize exactly what it was that they were heading for, and what was the spiritual parentage of such a course of action. Both S. Matthew and S. Luke record denunciations of the Pharisees that are not less outspoken (Mt. 23, Lk. 11).

The section begins with a warning against the appearance of discipleship without the reality, and against a false assumption of knowledge and of personal freedom.

If ye abide in my word you are truly my disciples, and ye shall grow in the knowledge of the truth, and the truth shall set you free.

The danger is that they should be content with an intellectual appreciation of the claim that Jesus had set forth, without realizing that it made a personal demand upon them. It was no use believing that Jesus was the light of the world, if they were not prepared to follow His guidance. He had promised in verse 12 that those who followed Him should have the light of life. Here He substitutes "abiding in My word" for "following Me". His "word" is not any particular utterance. It may be His message as a whole, but it is more likely that "abiding in His word" means "staying within reach of the sound of His voice, and listening for it", as the guide of their steps, just as He tells us He Himself "kept His Father's word" (verse 55). His function as the food and the light of the life of all men involves, as we have already seen, an inner relationship with every man which makes itself known to us in the voice that speaks in conscience.

This teaching, when we come to look into it, is more full of promise than of warning. The fruit of abiding in the Word is intellectual and moral and, even more, spiritual, development. "Ye shall know the truth. Ye shall enter into living fellowship with the ultimate Reality, and shall find in that fellowship deliverance from all that hampers your freedom". Freedom can come only from the loyal acceptance of the true laws of our being. The knowledge of these laws is, therefore, a necessary first step to freedom. The priest's lips, if he would absolve, must keep knowledge. And again. Nothing but the truth can have either the power to control or the power to win our wayward wills. So from this point of view also, it is clear that the first step to freedom must come from the knowledge of the truth.

The response to this appeal shews that those to whom He was speaking were conscious of a note of judgement in it. They resent the implication of a present state of slavery from which they needed deliverance. *We are of the seed of Abraham, and have never been in bondage to any man, how sayest thou "ye shall be made free"?*

"Freeborn, of the noblest seed, heirs of the promises of God, who is free if we are not?"

Of course Israel had been in bondage in Egypt, and at the moment was in political subjection to Rome. But he was clearly thinking of personal slavery. His answer is meant to arouse the consciousness of spiritual fetters.

Verily, verily, I say unto you, Everyone that committeth sin is a slave [This is, I believe, the true reading, not "a slave of sin"]. *Now the slave abideth not in the house for ever. The son abideth for ever. Therefore if the Son shall set you free, ye shall be free indeed.* The man to whom sinning is still natural, for whom self-pleasing is still the ruling motive, or at least the ultimate object even of outwardly virtuous action, and who prides himself on being his own master, is a slave. Whether he is as the younger or as the elder brother in the parable, he is equally in bondage; most pathetically indeed, if, like the elder brother, he feels his Father's will to be a galling chain (Lk. 15: 29), even while living in his sight, and outwardly conforming to his lightest requirement.

In the household of God this condition cannot be permanent. The command, "Cast out the bond-woman and her son" is, as S. Paul saw, of universal application. Israel, when the time came for her to enter on her true vocation, must either accept it or be herself rejected, cut adrift from the whole range of outward ordinances which had been the tokens of God's favour and the instruments of her pride. Even so for each man who is called to enter on his sonship the moment is critical. If he shrinks from the sacrifice, and tries to bargain with God to be allowed to retain the ultimate control over his own actions at the price of any amount of burthensome religious practice, he is rejected. The very sacraments lose their power to bless and raise him. If he hears the call and longs to answer it, he becomes conscious as never before of the weight that drags him back, and he learns his need of the deliverer, even the Son, who by inspiring him with that which "by nature he cannot have"—the true Spirit of Sonship—can set him free.

In face of this fact, physical descent without spiritual resemblance goes for nothing. *I know that ye are Abraham's seed, but ye are untrue to your parentage. Ye seek to kill me, because my word has no room in you.*

The necessary condition for "abiding in the Word" is that the Word should be at home in us. It must find a welcome from a kindred spirit. Where it meets instead with murderous hatred, the spirit is not kin.

He gives them, therefore, this simple test—for character revealing itself in conduct is the real test of spiritual descent—*I am speaking what I have seen at the Father's side. Do ye then in your turn do what ye heard from the Father's lips.*

They seek to evade the test, falling back (in spite of the Baptist's warning [Mt. 3: 9]) on the indisputable fact of their physical descent. What need can there be for us to prove by any such test that "We have Abraham to our father"? The test, however, cannot be evaded. "If ye are children of

Abraham, do the works of Abraham. But instead of doing these, even while you speak, you belie your claim by your actions, and reveal a very different parentage".

Ye seek to kill me, a man who hath spoken to you the truth which I heard from the lips of God. This did not Abraham. You are doing the works of your father.

"The only other Father we are willing to admit is God."

Here then is the test for that claim also. And it is decisive against your claim: *I am here from God. If He were in fact your Father, you would love me. For indeed I have not come of my own will, but He commissioned me.*

He goes on to wrestle with the real cause of the difficulty which He is encountering in the effort to get His meaning across to them. It comes from the terrible possibility which, as He had already hinted, had become fact for them, that a man may be linking himself on to an evil stock.

Why cannot you understand my language? You cannot fulfil the first condition of discipleship, *Your ears are deaf to my word.* The cause of deafness is that very slavery from which only the knowledge of the truth can set a man free.

You are drawing your life from the devil. You are making him your father. Your wills are set on doing his desires. That is the proof of your kinship. He has two qualities that characterize him from his first appearance in history. He is out for the destruction of humanity; and is a rebel from the truth, because there is no truthfulness in him. When he gives utterance to the lie, he speaks that which he has originated in himself. For he is a liar and its father.

(This last sentence is capable of many different interpretations. The sense required seems to be "A liar by his very lie reveals his parentage.")

A further consequence of this spiritual kinship is incapacity to trust the truth.

As for me even though I speak the truth, you refuse to believe me (verse 45). Under normal conditions a man should surely believe the truth when he hears it. It is clear, therefore, that there must be a flaw somewhere. It is not in Jesus. *Which of you convicteth me of one moment's disloyalty to my Father?* (verse 46)

It must be in them. A man must draw his life from God before he can hear His words.

If I speak truth why do you fail to believe me? It must be because you are not of God. The Jews were clearly unprepared to consider the possibility of this solution. These must be the words of a frenzied Samaritan Magus (verse 48).

Argument is clearly impossible. If a man cannot distinguish between these opposites, no logic will help him. No answer is possible but a simple reassertion.

I am not possessed, but I claim the honour for my Father, which you refuse to me. I am careless of my own reputation. But you are not therefore free from responsibility for your judgement of me. There is one who cares and judges (verse 49). In S. John 12: 48 He tells us that it is "the word that He had spoken that shall judge". It wakes echoes in a man's conscience which he is powerless to still. We can see, therefore, how He can pass on from "abiding in my word" (verse 31), and "my word hath no room in you" (verse 37), and "One that seeketh and judgeth" (verse 50), to *Verily, verily, I say unto you, if any man keep my word he shall never see death* (verse 51).

As the word neglected and disobeyed reveals the condition of death into which we have sunk, so the word harboured and kept has power, not only to set free, but to give eternal life. The new revelation is proportioned to the depth of the need of which we have become conscious. To start with, men were regarded as slaves needing to be set free. As the discussion developed it became clear that men loved their chains. They regarded them as natural, revealing thereby signs of diabolic parentage, and of a state of spiritual death. If they become, however dimly, conscious of their true state, they need an assurance that the Word has power to bring men out of death into life. Interpreted in the language of moral life (1 Jn. 3: 14) this means that the new command "to love one another", if a man really embraces it, has power in every hour of trial to set him, and to keep him, free from the grip of the spiritual death of hate.

The claim is clear enough. The Jews have no doubt that

a man who could make it must be mad. *Now we know that you are possessed. You promise to give of your own resources more than fell to the lot of Abraham and the prophets. Who do you pretend to be?* (verse 52). Jesus takes occasion to reaffirm in unmistakable terms that He did claim to be the Son of God (verse 54). He says:

If my glory depends simply on my own assertion, it is nothing. But it does not. It is my Father's gift, even His whom you call your God, though indeed you do not really know Him. For my own part I know Him, and if I were to deny my knowledge of Him, I should be a liar after your stamp. For such a denial would really involve a claim that the wonderful words that I have spoken and the deeds that I have done were self-originated, and I should be claiming glory to myself on the strength of them. No—*I do indeed know Him and set myself to render to His Word the same obedient attention that I claim from you for mine.*

This claim does involve a claim to an unique position. But that position was not created by His appearance on earth. *Your father Abraham rejoiced in the prospect of my day. And he saw it and was glad.*

This suggests a physical impossibility (verse 57). *Thou art not yet fifty years old. And hast thou seen Abraham?* (or according to another reading, "has Abraham seen thee?"). It might have been possible in the light of the communion with Moses and Elijah to which the Transfiguration bears witness, to suppose that Jesus had also even in the flesh been in conscious touch with Abraham. In view of the stress laid on the exultation of Abraham at the birth of Isaac, which is commemorated in Isaac's name, it seems more likely that Jesus traced that rejoicing back to a recognition by Abraham of the promise of the coming Incarnation which was implicit in the birth of Isaac. There is, however, I think, no room to doubt that Jesus believed that as Messiah He had existed from all eternity. *Before Abraham came into being,* He says, *I am He.* He uses the same phrase that He had used with such emphasis in verses 24, 28. And here at least He brings it into sharp contrast with the word that connotes "birth into this world". It involves, therefore, a distinct claim to a personal substantial existence beyond time in communion with God, something more definite than a merely ideal pre-existence, such as we sometimes dream of, "in the mind of God".

This claim was more than the Jews were prepared to tolerate from the lips of a man. They were prepared to take the law into their own hands and stone Him at once for blasphemy. But somehow their eyes were holden and He escaped out of the Temple.

CHAPTER XII

THE MAN BORN BLIND

THE SIGN

1 *And as he passed by, he saw a man blind from his birth. And*
2 *his disciples asked him, saying, Rabbi, who did sin, this man, or*
3 *his parents, that he should be born blind? Jesus answered, Neither did this man sin, nor his parents: but that the works of God should*
4 *be made manifest in him. We must work the works of him that sent*
5 *me, while it is day: the night cometh, when no man can work. When*
6 *I am in the world, I am the light of the world. When he had thus spoken, he spat on the ground, and made clay of the spittle, and*
7 *anointed his eyes with the clay, and said unto him, Go, wash in the pool of Siloam (which is by interpretation, Sent). He went away therefore, and washed, and came seeing.*

"AND as Jesus passed along He saw a man blind from his birth." In the true text there is nothing to connect this chapter directly with the close of the last. The later text by introducing the word "passed along" into the concluding sentence in 8: 59, suggests that the incident followed directly on His escape from stoning. The day, we learn, was the sabbath, and it would seem unlikely that the minds of the disciples would have been sufficiently at rest after the excitement of the threatened stoning to raise an independent theological problem. The next notice of date is the reference to the feast of Dedication (10: 22). This implies an interval of a little more than two months after the close of the feast of Tabernacles. The sign may have been worked at any time during the interval. If *then* in 10: 22 (R.V. mg.) is to be taken strictly it would come at the very end of it.

And His disciples asked Him saying, Rabbi, who did sin, this man or his parents, that he was born blind? The case was one that raised very perplexing questions for minds that had been brought up to believe that sickness was always to be regarded as a judgement on sin. Was this man's suffering vicarious? The Jews were familiar with the thought that the sins of fathers may be visited on their children. There remained the possibility, accepted without question as the basis of the Hindu doctrine of Karma, that the man is expiating sins committed in a former state of existence. This implies, of course, the possibility of a transmigration of souls. The thought was familiar in Greece as well as India. It might quite naturally have arisen independently in Palestine.

Jesus answered, *Neither did this man sin, nor his parents, but* (*the suffering came*) *that the works of God may be manifested in him*, or "but let the works of God be manifested in Him"—the Greek may be translated in either way.

This is not of course a dogmatic assertion of the absolute freedom of this family from sin. It is simply a warning that we look in the wrong direction, if we think that it is our business to base any judgement of personal guilt in any individual on the ground of the presence of suffering. What we may find in suffering anywhere is a call for help. We know that we are working with God, when we are fighting to cast out sickness. So He calls His disciples to recognize the challenge as one addressed to them as a body. They had already been associated with Him in the feeding of the five thousand (6: 5, Mk. 6: 37). *We* [this is the true reading, not *I*] *must work the works of Him that sent me, while it is day. Night cometh when no man can work. As long as I am in the world, I am the light of the world.*

The fact that our days on earth are numbered is a stimulus to unwearied activity. He must do what He had bidden His disciples do. He must let His light shine that men may glorify the Father. So "having said this He spat on the ground (spittle had a recognized place in the pharmacopœia of those days) and made clay, with the spittle, and applied the clay to his eyes, and said to him, Go and wash in the pool of Siloam (which means 'Sent'). He went, therefore, and washed, and came seeing."

Sadly enough, but inevitably, even this shining of the light brought a judgement.

THE EFFECTS OF THE SIGN

8 *The neighbours therefore, and they which saw him aforetime, that* 9 *he was a beggar, said, Is not this he that sat and begged? Others said, It is he: others said, No, but he is like him. He said, I am* 10 he. *They said therefore unto him, How then were thine eyes opened?* 11 *He answered, The man that is called Jesus made clay, and anointed mine eyes, and said unto me, Go to Siloam, and wash: so I went* 12 *away and washed, and I received sight. And they said unto him, Where is he? He saith, I know not.*

13 *They bring to the Pharisees him that aforetime was blind.* 14 *Now it was the sabbath on the day when Jesus made the clay, and* 15 *opened his eyes. Again therefore the Pharisees also asked him how he received his sight. And he said unto them, He put clay upon* 16 *mine eyes, and I washed, and do see. Some therefore of the Pharisees said, This man is not from God, because he keepeth not the sabbath. But others said, How can a man that is a sinner do such signs?* 17 *And there was a division among them. They say therefore unto the blind man again, What sayest thou of him, in that he opened* 18 *thine eyes? And he said, He is a prophet. The Jews therefore did not believe concerning him, that he had been blind, and had received his sight, until they called the parents of him that had* 19 *received his sight, and asked them, saying, Is this your son, who ye* 20 *say was born blind? how then doth he now see? His parents answered and said, We know that this is our son, and that he* 21 *was born blind: but how he now seeth, we know not; or who opened his eyes, we know not: ask him; he is of age; he shall speak* 22 *for himself. These things said his parents, because they feared the Jews: for the Jews had agreed already, that* 23 *if any man should confess him* to be *Christ, he should be put out of the synagogue. Therefore said his parents, He is* 24 *of age; ask him. So they called a second time the man that was blind, and said unto him, Give glory to God: we know that* 25 *this man is a sinner. He therefore answered, Whether he be a sinner I know not: one thing I know, that, whereas I was blind,* 26 *now I see. They said therefore unto him, What did he to thee?* 27 *how opened he thine eyes? He answered them, I told you even now, and ye did not hear: wherefore would ye hear it again? would*

28 *ye also become his disciples? And they reviled him, and said,*
29 *Thou art his disciple; but we are disciples of Moses. We know that God hath spoken unto Moses: but as for this man, we know*
30 *not whence he is. The man answered and said unto them, Why, herein is the marvel, that ye know not whence he is, and* yet *he*
31 *opened mine eyes. We know that God heareth not sinners: but if any man be a worshipper of God, and do his will, him he heareth.*
32 *Since the world began it was never heard that any one opened the*
33 *eyes of a man born blind. If this man were not from God, he*
34 *could do nothing. They answered and said unto him, Thou wast altogether born in sins, and dost thou teach us? And they cast him out.*

The blind man's neighbours, and those who had known him before as a beggar, are at once interested. They bring the matter to the notice of the Pharisees. The case is complicated by the fact that the cure has been wrought on the sabbath. The man repeats his simple tale. The judges are divided. On the one side is the fact that it was the sabbath. On the other side is the fact of the cure. They appeal to the blind man for his verdict on his Healer, and he has no doubt that He is a prophet.

This conclusion seems inevitable, if the facts are true, so the parents are summoned to give evidence. They prove the identity of the man, but shirk the responsibility of passing any judgement on his Healer. We learn incidentally that anyone who confessed Jesus to be the Christ was liable to excommunication.

The Pharisees are anxious to close the mouth of this witness, so they send for him again, and try to make him recant his confession. "Give glory to God" they say, "We know that this man is a sinner". This does not apparently mean, "Give glory to God for your cure and not to Jesus". Giving glory to God has in the Old Testament the special connotation of "confess your sins". See Jos. 7: 19, 1 Sam. 6: 5 and 1 Es. 9: 8.

He refuses to be brow-beaten. *I for my part cannot say whether He is a sinner or not. The one thing I know is that I was blind and that now I see.* They challenge the validity of his inference from the facts of his cure. "All that Jesus did was to smear your eyes with clay. How could that have anything to do with the restoration of your sight?" The man is wise enough not to believe that the recovery of his sight by following the directions that Jesus had given him was only a coincidence. *It is no use telling the tale over again unless you are prepared to become His disciples.*

They scorn the suggestion in the pride of their unblemished orthodoxy, even though they are forced to admit that they could not say whence Jesus had come. The healed man feels that he can at least throw light on that question—*Why here is the marvel, that you do not know whence He is, and yet He opened my eyes. We know that God does not answer the prayers of sinners, but if a man worship Him and does His will, him He answers. Since the world began it was never heard that anyone opened the eyes of a man born blind. If this man were not from God, He could do nothing.*

The argument was unanswerable. The only way to avoid the conclusion was to discredit the speaker. And that way lay temptingly open on the current hypothesis with regard to sickness. A man born blind was clearly every inch of him conceived and born in sin. And had he the presumption to challenge the verdict of the accredited teachers?—So they excommunicate him.

JESUS AND THE PARTIES IN THIS DISPUTE

35 *Jesus heard that they had cast him out; and finding him, he said,*
36 *Dost thou believe on the Son of Man. He answered and said,*
37 *And who is he, Lord, that I may believe on him? Jesus said unto him, Thou hast both seen him, and he it is that speaketh with thee.*
38 *And he said, Lord, I believe. And he worshipped him. And Jesus*
39 *said, For judgement came I into this world, that they which see*
40 *not may see; and that they which see may become blind. Those of the Pharisees which were with him heard these things, and said*
41 *unto him, Are we also blind? Jesus said unto them, If ye were blind, ye would have no sin: but now ye say, We see: your sin remaineth.*

Jesus goes to look for the man in his new trouble, and

when He finds him, we are not told where, possibly in the Temple, He challenges him. It is His first express challenge for a specific confession of faith. He uses, according to the true text, His chosen title for Himself. *Believest thou on the Son of Man?* The man answers, *Why, who is He, Lord, that I should believe on Him?*

This was apparently his first meeting with Jesus after his cure. He had confessed Jesus to be a prophet. His excommunication suggests that that was regarded as equivalent to a confession of Messiahship. Jesus substitutes "Son of Man" for both titles. But the main stress of the question is on personal faith. The pronoun is emphatic, Do *you* wish to become a disciple? But the title Son of Man is strange to him, so the man asks for an explanation, and gets it in a singularly expressive form. Remember how few people comparatively the man had ever seen, and how his chief means of recognizing people hitherto had been by their voice, and then listen to the words: *Thou hast both seen Him, and He that speaketh to thee is He.* It is not surprising that the answer is simply, *I believe, Lord,* and that he worshipped Him.

Jesus passes on to draw out the moral of the whole incident. *For an act of judgement* (not to be myself the Judge, 3: 19; 12: 47) *have I come into this world, that they who see not may recover their sight, and they who see may become blind.* The characteristic of the blind man throughout has been his loyal acceptance of the simplest principles, humbly confessing his ignorance of everything else. The Pharisees had claimed complete knowledge, and so plunged deeper and deeper into denial. Thus the light they spurned blinded them, while it opened the eyes both physical and spiritual of the humble.

This comment of Jesus had been made in public. A mixed crowd including Pharisees were surrounding Him. They had an uneasy feeling that these words had a personal reference, so they speak: *Do you mean that even we are blind?* Not so long ago they had rejected the suggestion that they were in slavery. "If you mean that you have come to open our eyes, you may save yourself the trouble".

Jesus said to them, *If ye were blind you would not have had sin.* This means, I think: If you had been willing to confess your blindness, you would not have clung to your sin; but now that you say "we see", your sin remains. But it may mean, If you had really had no power of vision, you would have had no responsibility. What gives sin its hold over you, is the fact that you claim to have light, and sin against it. As long as that lasts you can find no deliverance (cf. 15: 24).

At this point there has been, I believe, a serious dislocation of the text. I would pass at once to 10: 19–21.

19 *There arose a division again among the Jews because of these*
20 *words. And many of them said, He hath a devil, and is mad; why*
21 *hear ye him? Others said, These are not the sayings of one possessed with a devil. Can a devil open the eyes of the blind?*

These words repeat the note of the divisions and discussions among the Jews which have marked each stage in our Lord's appeal to them during His visit to Jerusalem for the Feast of Tabernacles. They follow naturally on the discussion with which Chapter IX ends, and fitly close the episode of the man born blind.

CHAPTER XIII

THE GOOD SHEPHERD

X 22 *And it was the feast of the dedication at Jerusalem: it was* 23 *winter; and Jesus was walking in the temple in Solomon's porch.* 24 *The Jews therefore came round about him, and said unto him, How long dost thou hold us in suspense? If thou art the Christ, tell* 25 *us plainly. Jesus answered them, I told you, and ye believe not: the works that I do in my Father's name, these bear witness of me.* 26 *But ye believe not, because ye are not of my sheep.* 27 *My sheep* 28 *hear my voice, and I know them, and they follow me; and I give unto them eternal life; and they shall never perish, and no one* 29 *shall snatch them out of my hand. My Father, which hath given* them *unto me, is greater than all;*[1] *and no one is able to snatch* X 1 them *out of the Father's hand. Verily, verily, I say unto you, He that entereth not by the door into the fold of the sheep, but climbeth up some other way, the same is a thief and a robber.* 2 *But he that entereth in by the door is the shepherd of the sheep.* 3 *To him the porter openeth; and the sheep hear his voice: and he* 4 *calleth his own sheep by name, and leadeth them out. When he hath put forth all his own, he goeth before them, and the sheep* 5 *follow him: for they know his voice. And a stranger will they not follow, but will flee from him: for they know not the voice* 6 *of strangers. This parable spake Jesus unto them: but they understood not what things they were which he spake unto them.*

7 *Jesus therefore said unto them again, Verily, verily, I say unto* 8 *you, I am the door of the sheep. All that came before me are thieves* 9 *and robbers: but the sheep did not hear them. I am the door: by me if any man enter in, he shall be saved, and shall go in and go* 10 *out, and shall find pasture. The thief cometh not, but that he may steal, and kill, and destroy: I came that they may have life, and* 11 *may have* it *abundantly. I am the good shepherd: the good shepherd layeth down his life for the sheep. He that is a hireling, and not*

[1] Or *That which my Father hath given unto me is greater than all.*

12 *a shepherd, whose own the sheep are not, beholdeth the wolf coming, and leaveth the sheep, and fleeth, and the wolf snatcheth them,*
13 *and scattereth* them: he fleeth *because he is a hireling, and*
14 *careth not for the sheep. I am the good shepherd; and I know*
15 *mine own, and mine own know me, even as the Father knoweth me, and I know the Father; and I lay down my life for the sheep.*
16 *And other sheep I have, which are not of this fold: them also I must bring, and they shall hear my voice; and they shall become*
17 *one flock, one shepherd. Therefore doth the Father love me, because*
18 *I lay down my life, that I may take it again. No one taketh it away from me, but I lay it down of myself. I have power to lay it down, and I have power to take it again. This commandment*
X 30 *received I from my Father. I and the Father are one.*

"THEN[1] on the Feast of Dedication", in December, after an interval of uncertain duration, discussion breaks out afresh. This time it is started by the Jews who wish to throw on Jesus the responsibility for the state of suspense in which they find themselves. *How long art thou going to keep us in suspense? If thou art the Christ, tell us plainly.*

The difficulty of course was that while Jesus was indeed the Christ, He was not the kind of Christ that they expected. It was only by His life, and ultimately by His death, that He could make clear to them the kind of Christ He was. And their whole attitude to Him made it impossible for them to understand the evidence that He was even then bringing before them.

Jesus answered them, *I told you and ye believe not. I revealed myself even more appealingly in the works that I do in my Father's name, disclaiming all credit for myself in doing them. The real obstacle is not in me. It is in yourselves. If you would take your place among my sheep you would have the key that would solve your doubts. Faith is impossible to those who will not follow my guidance and take their place in my flock.*

In sharp contrast to the position of torturing uncertainty to which they were condemning themselves, He paints a picture of the blessedness of loyal discipleship. *My sheep hear my voice, and I acknowledge them as mine, and they follow me, and I*

[1] This is the true reading.

give them the life of the new age; and they shall never perish and no one shall pluck them out of my hand. Do you ask how I can hope to make good such a promise of sure protection? Here again it is not in me but in my Father. My relation as Shepherd to my sheep rests on the eternal foundation of my Father's will to give, and power to keep. That which my Father has given me is greater than all. He has given me an absolute supremacy over all the works of His hands, and no one can snatch anything out of the Father's hand.

At this point, I believe, and in the light of this introduction, Jesus introduces the teaching on His work as the Good Shepherd, which in the present text comes in so suddenly, and with apparently such slight relation to its context, after 9: 41.

It is true that when we look under the surface we can see that Jesus is contrasting His own work as Shepherd of God's sheep with that of the Pharisees. And they had just given a terrible example of the tyranny of which they were capable, in the treatment of the man born blind. But I cannot help feeling that if that were the connexion S. John would have given us some hint of it. Whereas on the arrangement I have adopted, Chapter IX finds a natural conclusion in 10: 19–21. The topic of the Shepherd and His sheep arises naturally out of the question raised by the Jews in 10: 24. And the similitudes that follow work out in detail the ground of the blessedness of belonging to Christ's flock, which has been stated so concisely and persuasively in 10: 26–29. This is given primarily in the form of a contrast between the true and the false embodiments of the ideal of leadership under the familiar Old Testament figure of shepherding. The characteristics of the true, or, as he is called here, the good (or beautiful) Shepherd, are contrasted first with those of a thief or bandit, and then with those of a stranger, and finally with those of a hireling. The sheep are pictured as constituting a single flock, but they are mixed with other sheep in a common fold. The sheep can only get in or out of the fold through the door, which is in the charge of a door-keeper. The wall of the fold is not too high for a man to scale.

The first point of difference is provided by the door. The true shepherd, the rightful owner of the sheep, uses the same means of access to the fold that they do. He has no need of force or guile to attain his object. The door-keeper opens to his knock. The sheep of his flock sort themselves out from the rest in answer to his call. He leads, He does not drive them, out to pasture. The voice of a stranger makes no appeal to them. They will not follow him.

This picture is, we are told, wonderfully true to the habits of shepherds in Palestine to this day. All the workings of consciousness in its rudimentary instinctive stages are wonderful. We cannot guess how each ewe distinguishes the bleat of its own lamb, calls to it, and is answered by it. We are ready to put a great deal to the credit of natural affinity. But a fresh line of thought opens out before us when we see an animal distinguish the voice of one man from another, and understand and obey a human word of command. Is not this a proof of a real—however remote—affinity between the shepherd and his sheep?

Our Lord, however, does not at this point press the human side of this analogy. He is content with indicating the contrast between Himself and the official leaders of Israel in their several relations to the baptism which John preached. That baptism of repentance unto remission of sins was the divinely appointed door into the Kingdom. Jesus had humbled Himself to enter in by it with the publicans and harlots. The Pharisees had not; and the consequences of that initial failure were working themselves out slowly but surely. They were lording it over God's heritage, as if they owed Him no allegiance. They had made the Temple into a bandits' cave. They were even then plotting the death of the heir, that they might seize on His inheritance.

Before He comes to the revelation of Himself as the Shepherd, even the inanimate door has a lesson of its own, which He will not let us overlook. For humble as the function of a door is—it can never be an end in itself, it can never be more than a means to an end—yet by virtue of this very humility, it is a true image of one aspect of the office that the Son came into the world to fulfil. He came not in

His own name, but in His Father's. He came that we might through Him have our access in the power of the Spirit to the Father. We may remember that He did on a later occasion reveal Himself as the Way. The door, however, has characteristics which are not conveyed under the image of the way. First, the door suggests, even more distinctly than the way, a certain exclusiveness of function. There may conceivably be more ways than one of getting to a goal. In the fold of which our Lord is speaking, He has already made it clear that there is but one door. This He emphasizes here by the words: "All that came before me are thieves and bandits," referring, of course, not to the Prophets, but (as Dr. E. A. Abbott paraphrases it) to "as many as have come to the flock, from the beginning, not waiting for the Good Shepherd's time, nor associating themselves with Him, but pressing forwards to rule mankind by the short methods of constraint" (*Johannine Grammar* 2362). "But", Jesus adds, "the sheep did not hear them". However cunningly they might disguise themselves as angels of light, they could establish no permanent hold over the hearts and minds of the elect. The Spirit of the Church in the end rejected them.

Again, the door, as distinct from the way, is part of a wider whole. All the blessed influences of the fold are exercised through it. In the security of its shelter the sheep can rest through the night. When the daylight comes, they are free to follow their Shepherd through it, wherever He may lead them. Thanks to the door, they enjoy rest and peace and freedom. This is the salvation that Christ came to bring. *By me*, He said, *if any man enter in, he shall be saved, and he shall go in and go out and find pasture.*

This blessed function of the door suggests yet another contrast with the false leader. *The thief cometh not, save to steal and slay and destroy; I came that they may have life, not for themselves alone, but enough and to spare.*

There remains yet another contrast which has to be worked out to bring out to the full the beauty and the depth of the similitude of the Good Shepherd. A man may be lawfully appointed to the care of sheep, and in quiet times be doing work which is outwardly indistinguishable from that of a shepherd; but in the hour of danger, when the wolf comes, the difference becomes manifest. The man who is no shepherd but only a hireling runs away; he is tending the sheep not from love of them, but simply as a convenient way of earning a living. Why should he risk his precious life for them? What matters it to him that individual sheep should be carried off, and the whole flock be scattered?

The good shepherd, on the other hand—the shepherd, that is, who, as we say, "makes good", who proves his worth in the eyes of God and man—stays to face the foe. The sheep entrusted to his care are in the deepest sense of the word *his own*. God, who has called him to be a shepherd and has put him in charge of them, has given them to him not to make money out of, but to tend and care for in his Father's name. The link that unites him to them is not formal or legal. In the eyes of men they may not be his at all but his master's. Still, as I have said, in the deepest sense they are his own. He and they belong to each other. Day in and day out he lives with them and for them in the closest intimacy. He has come to know them one by one in all their idiosyncrasies, and each of them knows him. What wonder that in the hour of danger he should be more concerned about their safety than about his own?

This is, we all feel, the truth about the human relationship. Jesus takes for granted in the parable of the Lost Sheep that no shepherd worthy of the name would be content to bring home ninety-nine out of a hundred sheep. We feel that the shepherd-lad who faced the lion and the bear in the name of the Lord was in training to become in due course the shepherd of his people, and was gathering the experience out of which the twenty-third Psalm might come.

The similitude builds on this foundation. Jesus Himself was pointed out by the Baptist as the Lamb of God. And whatever may be the sacrificial implications in the phrase, the author of *Ecce Homo* was clearly right in pointing out that it implied that the Lord was His Shepherd. It is a subtle but real link between the Revelation and the Gospel of S. John that we find in Rev. 7: 17 "the Lamb" who had been slain "shepherding" those who came out of the great tribulation. For Jesus Himself here calls attention to the fact that the relation between Him and His brethren had its antitype in the relation between His Father and Himself. *I am the Good Shepherd, and I know my own, and my own know Me, as the Father knows Me and I know the Father.* I learn my shepherding from Him. I am their Shepherd because He is mine.

Jesus goes on without a pause, as if this were the natural consequence of this intimate communion with the Father, *And I lay down My life for the sheep.* As Dr. Abbott points out in his *Johannine Grammar* (2126): "According to the Johannine doctrine the highest knowledge of all was that knowledge or understanding between the Father and the Son, which, in some mysterious way, implied self-sacrifice."

Only by such an utterness of self-concentration on behalf of those committed to Him could the Son express the completeness of His Father's devotion to "the Son of His love" (Col. 1: 13). And the extremity of human need was such as to give occasion and scope for such an expression.

This is how it comes to pass that the Cross (which had been implied in the revelation of the bread of life, for only by a violent death could the blood be separated from the flesh which He had assumed for the life of the world) comes full into view in the similitude of the Good Shepherd. It will be well to note summarily the different aspects under which it is presented.

It appears first as the final and supreme test of the love of the Shepherd for His sheep. We note next that its occasion is the extremity of the danger to which the sheep are exposed. Thirdly, His willingness to face that test, His self-consecration to death in fulfilment of the task committed to Him, which was, in fact, implied in His acceptance of baptism at the hands of John, had already called forth an assurance of the Father's loving approval. There is a clear echo of the voice heard on the banks of the Jordan in the words: "For this cause does My Father love Me, because I lay down My life".

We must notice, however, fourthly, that the death is not regarded for a moment as an end in itself. It is a means to an end. The gate into a fuller life. "I lay down My life that I may take it again," transfigured, glorified.

Fifthly, this fuller life would be manifested in a yet wider range of beneficent activity. He has "other sheep" who are not of the house of Israel. They too must learn to know the voice of their Shepherd and follow Him, and become "one flock" with their elder brothers, the firstborn in the family of God.

Sixthly, in the truest sense it was His own act. In it He rose to the full height of the responsibility committed to Him. He claimed and exercised to the full the right and power, which the Father gave Him, of His own free choice and will to lay down His life, to let death do its worst with Him, in the quiet confidence that He had the power to burst the bonds of death and rise again.

Yet, seventhly and lastly, in all this it was His continual strength and stay to know that He was simply, humbly, obediently walking along the path marked out for Him by His Father's will. He was only keeping the commandment which He had received from Him.

Then comes in, with overwhelming force, on this arrangement of the text, the assertion of the perfect unity in the strictest sense of the word, (moral or personal rather than metaphysical unity) by which His being as Son was knit into the being of His Father—*I and my Father are one*. The atonement which He came to make between His Father and His brethren was embodied in Himself before it found its final expression on the Cross.

REJECTION DELIBERATE AND FINAL

31 *The Jews took up stones again to stone him.* 32 *Jesus answered them, Many good works have I shewed you from my Father; for which*
33 *of those works do ye stone me? The Jews answered him, For a good work we stone thee not, but for blasphemy; and because that thou,*
34 *being a man, makest thyself God. Jesus answered them, Is it not*
35 *written in your law, I said, Ye are gods? If he called them gods,*

unto whom the word of God came (and the scripture cannot be broken),
36 *say ye of him, whom the Father sanctified and sent into the world,*
37 *Thou blasphemest; because I said, I am* the *Son of God? If I do*
38 *not the works of my Father, believe me not. But if I do them, though ye believe not me, believe the works: that ye may know*
39 *and understand that the Father is in me, and I in the Father. They sought again to take him: and he went forth out of their hand.*

This claim to be "one with the Father", even though it was only in respect of an absolute surrender of will to will, was too clear to be misunderstood, and once more provokes a murderous reaction. This time Jesus does not retire at once before it, but expostulates. His works were all, as He had told them, not His own but His Father's works in Him, and, as such, a proof of the reality and nature of the unity which He claimed.

He is told that such intimacy of communion with God could not be asserted by a man without blasphemy. *For a good work we stone thee not, but for blasphemy; that is, because thou, being a man, art making out thyself to be God.*

Jesus in reply shews that the Scripture used language which should have prepared them for the final revelation of the possibility of union between the human and the divine which He had come to bring. *Jesus answered, Is it not written in your law "I said, Ye are gods"* (Ps. 82: 6). This name is applied in the Law (Ex. 21: 6, etc.) to the Judges in Israel, who administered justice in God's name. As commissioned to declare His Will, they were recognized as of His kind. *If it calls them "gods" who had communion with the Word of God, and you cannot evade the pertinence of this reference,* (this scripture cannot be loosed or shewn not to be binding in this case), *do you say to one whom the Father consecrated and sent as His representative into the world*—a clear reference to the words at His baptism to which the Baptist had borne witness—*thou blasphemest because I said "I am God's Son"? If I do not the works of God*—once more the evidence of the signs that He had given is pressed home—*believe me not. But if I do them, even though you trust not me, trust the works, that you may recognize and apprehend the full intimacy of my union with my Father. They should assure you that in very truth He lives and works in me, and I live and work in Him.*

This is the final climax of His effort at self-revelation to the Pharisees. It was met by yet one more unsuccessful attempt to lay violent hands on Him.

RETIREMENT BEYOND JORDAN

40 *And he went away again beyond Jordan into the place where John*
41 *was at the first baptizing; and there he abode. And many came unto him; and they said, John indeed did no sign: but all things whatso-*
42 *ever John spake of this man were true. And many believed on him there.*

Jesus has said good-bye to Galilee. This time He returns to the scene of the Baptist's preaching and of His own baptism. It is interesting to notice that the memory of John lived on, and that men's minds were still busy with the question whether he had indeed been a prophet or not. The reference to the absence of miracles or signs in his ministry is connected with the discussion. The fact that he had borne specific testimony to Jesus also lived on. We should like to know more precisely in what points the people felt that Jesus had come up to the anticipations that John had led them to form.

CHAPTER XIV

JESUS FACE TO FACE WITH DEATH

THE revelation of Jesus as "the Resurrection and the Life" is intimately connected with the narrative of the raising of Lazarus, the third and most remarkable of the instances in which Jesus called back to life in this world a soul which, as far as human judgement went, had passed within the veil. It stands out from the rest, both by the deliberation which lay behind it, and by the supernatural foresight displayed in connexion with it. In the other two instances our Lord was brought, without warning, face to face with death, and we have what we may regard as the instinctive reaction of "the Life" to the shock of the sudden meeting. In this case the meeting and its issue were clearly foreseen and prepared for.

He reaches Bethany four days after the funeral, an interval which, while it does not preclude the hypothesis of a prolonged trance, yet seems designed to suggest the presence of a power which was able to hold in check or counteract the operation of the normal forces of corruption. Martha goes out to meet Him. She is overwhelmed by her sorrow. She has no hope of coming help. Both she and her sister had believed that if He had come at once in answer to their prayer, all would have been well—Lazarus would not have died. "And", Martha adds almost mechanically, for she does not seem to connect the words directly with her present need, "even now I know that, whatsoever thou shalt ask of God, God will give thee".

She did not connect our Lord's reply with this expression of faith on her part. "Thy brother shall rise again" seems only to have suggested the conventional consolations that she had left behind at home with Mary's friends. She did believe in a resurrection, but it was a long way off, "at the last day". Meanwhile, the dominion over man was in the hands of death. Her brother had passed as all men must pass, one by one in their turn, under his sway. In the midst of life we are in death.

This is the thought that Jesus met with an everlasting No when He said, *I am the Resurrection and the Life: he that believeth on me, though he die, yet shall he live; and whosoever liveth and believeth on me shall never die.*

It is surely a stupendous utterance, yet one which, in the light of the Lord's own resurrection we believe to be true, in spite of the apparently irresistible might of the forces of corruption and death in the world around us. Believing in Jesus as the Christ, the Son of God, "in the midst of death we are in life".

This being so, I must say that I do not find it as difficult, as do some of my friends who are at one with me in this fundamental conviction, to believe that the raising of Lazarus took place as S. John describes it, and that Jesus not only was and is the Resurrection and the Life, but was aware of the fact while He was on earth, and explicitly revealed Himself as such. If He be, indeed, the Resurrection and the Life, it does not seem to me incredible that, with a view to a more complete demonstration of the reality and extent of His power, He should have allowed His friends to taste in all its bitterness the cup of bereavement in circumstances which should make it clear that not only disease and death, but also the chemical forces of corruption are in His Father's hands. The height of the revelation is proportioned to the depth of the need to which it is a response.

One thing, however, we must not forget. If Jesus believed Himself to be the Resurrection and the Life, the evidence for the fact cannot depend on the accuracy of the report of an isolated utterance. His whole outlook on the world and on man must have been affected by it. Was this so? It is not surprising that, when we come to look for them, we find abundant traces of this conviction in the Gospel according to S. John. His words to the Jewish authorities in 2: 19, "Destroy this Temple, and in three days I will raise it up", have this conviction at the back of them. The account that He gives of the power manifested in the healing of the impotent man at the Pool of Bethesda, reaches its climax in the words (5: 21), "For as the Father raiseth the dead and quickeneth them, even so the Son quickeneth whom He will." In the following verses we hear a great deal of the passing from death into life; but the life and death that He speaks of are in a deeper region than the physical. If it were not for the phrase, "They that are in the tombs" (5: 28), we might have wondered whether the words had any direct relation to the departed. That verse, however, expressly connects the Son with a general resurrection, and directly prepares the way, as do 6: 40, 50 f., 54; 10: 17 f., for the revelation in our text.

The evidence of the Synoptic Gospels is not so direct, but it is not on that account less impressive. It is very difficult for us who have grown up in the faith that life and immortality have been brought to light by the Gospel to put ourselves back in thought into an age in which the power of death over the imagination and the heart of man was as yet unbroken; and so to feel the full wonder of the calm, assured confidence with which Jesus faced death. It is not merely that He set His face steadfastly to go to Jerusalem, though He knew what would befall Him there. It is that death itself had literally no terrors for Him. He knew and would have His disciples know precisely the limits of the power of the forces opposed to them.

Men can kill the body, but after that they have nothing that they can do. But, to the martyr, the laying down of the life is the road to an enriched personality. The death of the seed is the condition of fruitfulness. Death has no power to hurt the essential life of a man: "All live to God". The gates of the grave cannot check the growth of His Kingdom. Rightly seen, death is the gate into fuller life. So He does evince in all His words and deeds, in His unflinching courage in the present, and in the triumphant certainty with which He looked forward to the future, a complete mastery over death. It does not strike us that there is anything to be surprised at in the fact that Jairus's daughter, and the widow's son at Nain, should resume their life at His bidding. The raising of Lazarus only brings into clearer relief this significant feature in the whole ministry that had preceded it.

THE RAISING OF LAZARUS

1 *Now a certain man was sick, Lazarus of Bethany, of the village of* 2 *Mary and her sister Martha. And it was that Mary which anointed the Lord with ointment, and wiped his feet with her hair, whose* 3 *brother Lazarus was sick. The sisters therefore sent unto him,* 4 *saying, Lord, behold, he whom thou lovest is sick. But when Jesus heard it, he said, This sickness is not unto death, but for the glory of God, that the Son of God may be glorified thereby.* 5 *Now Jesus loved Martha, and her sister, and Lazarus.* 6 *When therefore he heard that he was sick, he abode at that time two* 7 *days in the place where he was. Then after this he saith to his* 8 *disciples, Let us go into Judæa again. The disciples say unto him, Rabbi, the Jews were but now seeking to stone thee; and goest* 9 *thou thither again? Jesus answered, Are there not twelve hours in the day? If a man walk in the day, he stumbleth not, because he* 10 *seeth the light of this world. But if a man walk in the night,* 11 *he stumbleth, because the light is not in him. These things spake he: and after this he saith unto them, Our friend Lazarus is fallen asleep; but I go, that I may awake him out of sleep.* 12 *The disciples therefore said unto him, Lord, if he is fallen asleep,* 13 *he will recover. Now Jesus had spoken of his death: but they* 14 *thought that he spake of taking rest in sleep. Then Jesus therefore* 15 *said unto them plainly, Lazarus is dead. And I am glad for your sakes that I was not there, to the intent that ye may believe; never-*16 *theless let us go unto him. Thomas therefore, who is called Didymus, said unto his fellow-disciples, Let us also go, that we may die with him.*

The scene opens with Jesus still in retirement beyond Jordan. A message arrives from two sisters whose brother

Lazarus was sick at Bethany. One of the sisters is identified as the woman who anointed the Lord's feet with ointment, and wiped them with her hair. This incident was still in the future. S. John records it at the beginning of his next chapter. But he assumes that it was well known to everyone, as Jesus had declared that it would be.

The message merely recorded the fact, "Your friend Lazarus is sick". No express petition accompanied it. But the hope that had prompted it is clear from verses 31 f. Jesus replied *This sickness is not unto death, but for the glory of God, that the Son of God may be glorified by it.* The words may have meant to the apostles and to the sisters, if the answer was sent to them, that Lazarus would recover: but in that case it is difficult to see how the glory of the Son of God would be established by it. The words in fact imply that the sickness would seem to end in a triumph of death, which should be overruled and become a triumph of enduring glory for the Son of God. In this sense, the issue includes not only the raising of Lazarus, but also the stimulus that that would give for the final attack of the Jews on Jesus Himself. This sickness would reveal Him as, in the fullest sense, the conqueror of death, and so redound to the glory of God (cf. verse 40).

The narrative proceeds: *Now Jesus loved Martha and her sister Mary and Lazarus. When therefore He heard that he was sick, then He abode in the place where He was two days.* After that, He says to His disciples, *Let us go into Judæa again.* S. John wishes us to see the love of Jesus in the delay no less than in the ultimate action.

The expostulation of the disciples brings out the risk involved in the journey. Perhaps by the thought of it they had been explaining to themselves their Master's lack of response to the appeal. Jesus in His answer strikes a different note from that which we heard when He was face to face with the man born blind. There He said, our life in this world has its appointed span which must be filled with the work we have to do. The night is coming which will make work impossible. Here He says, *are there not twelve hours in the day? If a man walk in the day, he avoids the obstacles in his path, but if he walk in the night, he stumbles because the light is not in him.*

He wants us to notice that in our earthly experience light and darkness alternate. Day passes into night. We have no "light in ourselves". We must use it while it is granted to us. If we do not, we may destroy our faculty of vision.

Jesus proceeds to give the reason for the move, but at first under a veil. *Our friend Lazarus has fallen asleep. I go that I may rouse him out of his sleep.* This really seems the natural language to describe the death of the body. Jesus seems to use it instinctively (cf. Mt. 9: 24). Nor was there any real room for misapprehension. The literal meaning was clearly, as the disciples saw, impossible. But they would not assume the deeper meaning, unless it was stated in terms more familiar to themselves, because the change of conception involved in substituting *sleep* for *death* did not of itself bring the hope of resurrection. This is not repeated in the open utterance. After *Lazarus is dead*, in place of "I will awaken him", He says *but I rejoice for your sakes that I was not there, that ye may believe—but let us go to him.* This joy is strange. It is called out by the prospect of the deepening of their faith, which would come out of the seemingly fatal consequences of His absence. The fact that He could rejoice might have a direct effect on them in keeping their faith alive. In any case "Let us go to him" would suggest that they were not going simply to visit a grave. It is not impossible that Thomas may have interpreted the words to mean "go to him by dying". There is a characteristic blending of utter loyalty with the deep despondency of one overwhelmed by the facts of life in his *Let us also go that we may die with Him.*

THE INTERVIEW WITH MARTHA

17 *So when Jesus came, he found that he had been in the tomb four*
18 *days already. Now Bethany was nigh unto Jerusalem, about fifteen*
19 *furlongs off; and many of the Jews had come to Martha and Mary,*
20 *to console them concerning their brother. Martha therefore, when*

she heard that Jesus was coming, went and met him: but Mary
21 *still sat in the house. Martha therefore said unto Jesus, Lord,*
22 *if thou hadst been here, my brother had not died. And even now I know that, whatsoever thou shalt ask of God, God will give thee.*
23 *Jesus saith unto her, Thy brother shall rise again.* 24 *Martha saith unto him, I know that he shall rise again in the resurrec-*
25 *tion at the last day. Jesus said unto her, I am the resurrection, and the life: he that believeth on me, though he die, yet shall he*
26 *live: and whosoever liveth and believeth on me shall never die.*
27 *Believest thou this? She saith unto him, Yea, Lord: I have believed that thou art the Christ, the Son of God,* even *he that cometh into the world.*

When His approach to Bethany is announced, Martha hurries to meet Him. Mary waits. When Martha meets Him, she pours out her grief, "Lord, if thou hadst been here, my brother had not died". There is in these words a strange blending of faith in His power and in His love, with a reproach that He had not come. The fact that Lazarus had been allowed to die seemed a clear proof of neglect. Yet her faith was deeper even than her despair: so she adds, *And even now I know that whatsoever thou shalt ask of God, God will give thee.*

It is worth notice that her faith rests on the power of Jesus with God, the power of His prayer. She knew that He did not work in His own name. She may even have heard His lesson on prayer to His disciples. Jesus in reply says simply, *Thy brother shall rise again.*

How hollow this consolation must have sounded! It was in form a mere repetition of the conventional words of comfort she had left behind at home. What help was there in the thought of this vague popular anticipation of a distant resurrection, when she was mourning over the loss of a brother in flesh and blood? How could she connect these words with her own amazing assurance that God would give Him whatsoever He should ask? And yet in using those words she must have had some vague expectation that He could bring her brother back to her. She need not have misunderstood. Perhaps she had expected Him to say, "I will raise him up", and so was more occupied with what He did not say, than with His actual words. Her answer simply restates her acceptance of the popular belief, to which she supposed that He had been alluding, *I know that my brother shall rise again at the last day.*

Jesus proceeds to unveil His whole relation to "the last enemy" of man (1 Cor. 15: 26). *I am the Resurrection and the Life. He that believeth in me, though he die shall live, and everyone that liveth and believeth in me shall never die.*

Martha had, no doubt, in some vague way connected the last day and the resurrection with the coming of the Christ. But she did not know the secret of the connexion, and had clearly never connected them with Jesus, even though in some sense she believed Him to be the Christ. He begins therefore with a revelation of Himself. On the lines of the earlier revelations of Himself as the Bread of Life, the Light of the World, and the Good Shepherd, He now adds the revelation of Himself as the Resurrection and the Life.

It is a strange order. Yet we become conscious of death and the triumph over it, before we are conscious of life in any true sense. Life of course must *be* first. Death is not, except by a temporary triumph over life. But it is by the reversal of this triumph of death that the true power of life is brought to light. We must know the resurrection before we can know the life.

This is true in every order, most clearly in the moral. "Dead in trespasses and sins" we cry aloud for deliverance from "the body of this death". We learn our need of one to be our Resurrection before we learn our eternal relation to Him as our Life. So here Jesus puts "though he be dead, yet shall he live" first. The wonder is that His voice can reach us even in our deadness, that even so we *can* believe and live. It shows how intimate our union with Him as Lord of the quick and the dead must be. In some ways the consciousness of our deadness is a condition of faith. That requires self-emptying. Faith can only come with self-despair.

Jesus goes on. *If any man liveth and believeth in me he shall never die.* This does not mean that the new life so derived can ever become self-dependent. Continuous attention to the quickening voice is a *sine qua non.* Nothing but our wilful disobedience can check the flow of life into every department of our being.

Yea, Lord, I have believed that thou art the Christ, the Son of God, even He that cometh into the world. The words seem to mark the dawning of the new revelation, not simply a recapitulation of an old formula. It is that, but it is that seen in the light of the words just uttered. She saw at least the possibility of a connexion between the old truth and the new. She begins to see why the thought of "the coming one" had always been connected with the resurrection. She begins her confession with "Yea".

THE SCENE AT THE TOMB

28 *And when she had said this, she went away, and called Mary her* 29 *sister secretly, saying, The Master is here, and calleth thee. And* 30 *she, when she heard it, arose quickly, and went unto him. (Now Jesus was not yet come into the village, but was still in the place* 31 *where Martha met him.) The Jews then which were with her in the house, and were comforting her, when they saw Mary, that she rose up quickly and went out, followed her, supposing that* 32 *she was going unto the tomb to weep there. Mary therefore, when she came where Jesus was, and saw him, fell down at his feet, saying unto him, Lord, if thou hadst been here, my brother had not* 33 *died. When Jesus therefore saw her weeping, and the Jews* also *weeping which came with her, he groaned*[1] *in the spirit, and was* 34 *troubled, and said, Where have ye laid him? They say unto him,* 35 *Lord, come and see. Jesus wept.* 36 *The Jews therefore said,* 37 *Behold how he loved him! But some of them said, Could not this man, which opened the eyes of him that was blind, have caused that* 38 *this man also should not die? Jesus therefore again groaning*[2] *in himself cometh to the tomb. Now it was a cave and a stone lay* 39 *against it. Jesus saith, Take ye away the stone. Martha, the sister of him that was dead, saith unto him, Lord, by this time* 40 *he stinketh: for he hath been* dead *four days. Jesus saith unto her, Said I not unto thee, that, if thou believedst, thou shouldest* 41 *see the glory of God? So they took away the stone.*

[1] Or *He was moved with indignation.* [2] *Being moved with indignation in himself.*

Practical as always, Martha hastens and tells her sister privately—a delicate touch—*The Master is come and calleth for thee.* We are not told that He had given this commission. But S. John is quite capable of leaving a fact like that to be inferred. Jesus would wish to remove the misunderstanding which Mary shared with her sister. And perhaps Mary had to help with her silent faith and prayer in the work that had yet to be done. In any case the old jealousy to which S. Luke testifies, which had been bred of the trouble of much serving, is gone altogether under the pressure of a common sorrow and a common hope.

S. John, after describing her movements and the action of the crowd of sympathetic friends, comes to her meeting with Jesus. She falls at His feet saying simply what Martha had said. It had been the burthen of their common sorrow, "Lord, if thou hadst been here my brother had not died". She has no words to match Martha's, "And even now I know", but she has fallen at His feet. The simple statement of her trouble is her prayer for help and light. The answer comes not in word but in act.

Jesus therefore when He saw her weeping and the Jews that came with her weeping, had indignation (*or groaned*) *in spirit and troubled Himself and said "Where have ye laid him?" They say unto Him, "Lord, come and see". Jesus wept. The Jews therefore said "Behold how He loved him!" But some said, "Could not this man that opened the eyes of the blind have prevented this man's death? Jesus therefore again having indignation* (*or groaning*) *in Himself cometh to the tomb. It was a cave and a stone lay against it.*

This little section, which cannot be attributed to creative imagination, is clearly of deep significance: but it is very hard to interpret. One important word which comes twice is diversely translated. In its literal meaning it describes the snorting of a horse. It is found on two other occasions in the Gospels, in Mk. 1 : 43 and Mt. 9 : 30. In each case it is translated "straitly charged", suggesting that there was sternness or strong emotion accompanying the injunction of silence that accompanied it. In each case we should notice that the injunction was disobeyed. It is at least possible that the word expresses the reaction of Jesus to a premonition of this disobedience. It seems here to describe a storm of passionate emotion that came over Him, though it did not find articulate expression. We are left, however, to discover for ourselves its precise nature and occasion. It does not seem to be merely a cry of pain. He is conscious of the presence of something evil which rouses His indignation. It has been suggested that the occasion of the first outburst is to be found in the conventional mourning of the friends, who were accompanying Mary, or in His prevision of their coming treachery (verse 46), and that the second outburst is accounted for by the approaching contest with this mortal foe of the race. George Macdonald in one of his *Unspoken Sermons* (Vol. III) suggests that it was caused by the dishonour that men do to God by refusing to trust Him with their dead. It seems to me, like the prelusive agony in the Temple Courts (12 : 27), to be a foretaste of Gethsemane, a reminder of the spiritual and emotional element in His conflict with death.

We should not overlook the faith involved in the command to take away the stone. As in the command to the servants at Cana and to the disciples at the feeding of the Five Thousand, His honour was pledged without reserve on the issue. There was faith also in the obedience of the attendants. There was a risk, put into words by Martha (who seems to have had many of the characteristics of S. Peter, as Mary had of S. John) of unsealing the evidence of loathsome corruption.

The reply of Jesus: *Said I not unto thee that if thou believedst, thou shouldest see the glory of God*, must refer to an unrecorded part of their conversation, unless it can be supposed to be implied in the answer returned through her original messenger.

When they had taken away the stone,

41 *Jesus lifted up His eyes to heaven and said, Father I thank thee that*
42 *thou heardest me. And I knew indeed that thou hearest me always: but because of the multitude which standeth around I said it, that they may believe that thou didst send me.*

This is a thanksgiving for answered prayer. It is natural to suppose that it was occasioned by the evidence, afforded by the sweetness of the air in the cave, that the forces of corruption had been kept in check. We can have no doubt that Jesus had been praying for Lazarus since He heard of his sickness. He gives public expression to His gratitude, in order that there should be no room for supposing that the work on which He was engaged was His and not His Father's. At the same time He is grasping, before it had actually been realized, the consummation of the answer in the return of Lazarus from the grave. And so far it is an illustration, from His own practice, of the fulfilment of the condition of prevailing prayer, which He laid down in Mk. 11: 24, where He bids His disciples grasp the answer to their prayer even while they were praying. This must be one of the reasons why in the New Testament thanksgiving is so constantly linked with petition in the apostolic exhortations to prayer.

43 *And when he had thus spoken, he cried with a loud voice, Lazarus,*
44 *come forth. He that was dead came forth, bound hand and foot with grave-clothes; and his face was bound about with a napkin. Jesus saith unto them, Loose him, and let him go.*

The only other occasion on which the Gospels say that our Lord spoke "with a loud voice" is on the Cross. There we find it in each of the Synoptists.

It is noteworthy that in all the three cases in which Jesus is reported to have raised the dead, He speaks out loud. This does not, I think, imply that the departed souls are to be regarded as, so to speak, within earshot, but that they were capable of responding to an expression of His will. Jesus speaks out loud that the bystanders might know what that will was. In the other two cases the word used suggested directly arousing from sleep. *Talitha kumi* would be what her mother might have said to Jairus's daughter on any morning when it was time to get up. S. Peter uses our Lord's word in Ac. 9: 40.

In picturing to ourselves the scene that followed, we do not know enough about the Jewish burial customs to arrive at any clear result. If the limbs were swathed separately motion, however impeded, would have been possible. The fact that Mary had an unused store of unguents (12 : 3) may be a sign that they had been used at her brother's funeral.

Jesus called on the bystanders to take their part in restoring Lazarus to freedom of action, just as after raising Jairus's daughter, He took care that something should be given her to eat.

THE CONSEQUENCES THAT FOLLOWED

45 *Many therefore of the Jews, which came to Mary and beheld that*
46 *which he did, believed on him. But some of them went away to the Pharisees, and told them the things which Jesus had done.*
47 *And the chief priests therefore and the Pharisees gathered a council, and said, What do we? for this man doeth many signs.*
48 *If we let him thus alone, all men will believe on him: and the Romans will come and take away both our place and our nation.*
49 *But a certain one of them, Caiaphas, being high priest that year,*
50 *said unto them, Ye know nothing at all, nor do ye take account that it is expedient for you that one man should die for the people,*
51 *and that the whole nation perish not. Now this he said not of himself: but being high priest that year, he prophesied that Jesus should*
52 *die for the nation; and not for the nation only, but that he might also gather together into one the children of God that are scattered*
53 *abroad. So from that day forth they took counsel that they might put him to death.*

Amongst the witnesses of the sign, many believed on Jesus on the strength of it. But some went and reported to the Pharisees what He had done.

The issue was a formal session of the Sanhedrim in which the High Priestly party, who were Sadducees, considered the situation side by side with the Pharisees. They were clear that if His ministry was not checked He would soon have all the people behind Him, and they took it for granted that He would then head a rising against Rome with disastrous results. The political, as contrasted with the religious leaders, thereupon took charge of the situation. Caiaphas, a Sadducee —who happened to be High Priest at that time, though there were four others still alive, including his father-in-law, who had at one time or another filled the office—openly declared that as a matter of expediency Jesus must be got out of the way. S. John records his words, *Ye know nothing and fail to realize that it is better that one man should die for the people to save the whole nation from destruction.* These words are susceptible of a meaning of which the speaker was absolutely unconscious. S. John delights in thinking that they may be regarded as having a prophetic character by virtue of his office, and points out that they received an overflowing fulfilment. This death delivered not the nation only, but the world, and gathered into one all the scattered children of God.

54 *Jesus therefore walked no more openly among the Jews, but departed thence into the country near to the wilderness, into a city called Ephraim; and there he tarried with the disciples.*

The situation that had developed necessitated one more retirement, the last before the end. There was an interval of about three months between the festival of the Dedication and the Passover. Part of this interval had already been spent beyond the Jordan. Now another part is spent near Ephraim, which may be the same as Ophrah, near Bethel, or Ephron which is beyond Jordan, and therefore would be safer. When Jesus returned to Bethany, wherever He had been, He joined the crowd of pilgrims from Galilee who crossed the Jordan to avoid Samaria and recrossed it at Jericho.

55 *Now the passover of the Jews was at hand: and many went up to Jerusalem out of the country before the passover, to purify them-*
56 *selves. They sought therefore for Jesus, and spake one with another, as they stood in the temple, What think ye? That he will not*
57 *come to the feast? Now the chief priests and the Pharisees had given commandment, that, if any man knew where he was, he should shew it, that they might take him.*

S. John gives another glimpse of the discussions in the Temple Courts among the pilgrims who had come from the country in preparation for the Feast, and also of the official notice from the authorities which shewed that they were on the watch. The Evangelist must have had friends in Jerusalem, who could let him know, either at the time or after (cf. 7: 11–13). We learn incidentally later that he had friends in the family of the High Priest.

CHAPTER XV

THE CLIMAX AT JERUSALEM

THE FEAST AT BETHANY

1 *Jesus therefore six days before the passover came to Bethany, where*
2 *Lazarus was, whom Jesus raised from the dead. So they made him a supper there: and Martha served; but Lazarus was one of them*
3 *that sat at meat with him. Mary therefore took a pound of ointment of spikenard, very precious, and anointed the feet of Jesus, and wiped his feet with her hair: and the house was filled with the odour of*
4 *the ointment. But Judas Iscariot, one of his disciples, which should*
5 *betray him, saith, Why was not this ointment sold for three hundred*
6 *pence, and given to the poor? Now this he said, not because he cared for the poor; but because he was a thief, and having the bag*
7 *took away what was put therein. Jesus therefore said, Suffer her*
8 *to keep it against the day of my burying. For the poor ye have always with you; but me ye have not always.*

THERE can be no doubt that this is the same feast as that described in Mt. 26 : 6 and Mk. 14 : 3, though they seem to date it three days and not six days before the Passover. S. John tells us that "they", apparently the people of Bethany, provided the feast. S. Matthew and S. Mark say it took place at the house of Simon the Leper. It clearly cannot have been at the house of the sisters, though they both were there, as well as their brother. Martha found relief in taking part in serving. It is not said that she superintended the servants. Mary's feelings had to find another outlet. The story, as S. John tells it, is full of difficulties, both in itself, and by reason of certain points in it in which it differs from S. Matthew and S. Mark, and agrees with the account given in S. Luke of a similar, but surely quite distinct anointing, which took place in Galilee at the house of Simon the Pharisee.

The woman in S. Luke's story is not named, but is commonly assumed to be Mary Magdalene. In view of S. John's introduction of Mary Magdalene in 19: 25 without any hint of her identity with the Mary who had already taken such a prominent part in his narrative, we surely must distinguish between Mary of Magdala and Mary of Bethany, whether the woman in the city that was a sinner was Mary Magdalene or not.

Mary's action, as S. John describes it, is to bring a costly offering of a pound of precious ointment. S. Mark and S. Matthew say that it was in a flask, and that she poured it on His head. S. Mark says "after breaking the flask". It would probably have been made of glass. S. John says simply that she anointed His feet and wiped them with her hair, the whole house being filled with the odour of the ointment.

The woman that had been a sinner first moistened the feet with her tears, and then wiped them with her hair, and then, after covering them with kisses, anointed them with ointment.

S. John lays special stress both in 12 : 3 and 11 : 2 on the fact that the ointment was applied to the feet. In 11 : 2 he says "she anointed the Lord with ointment and wiped His feet with her hair". So it seems probable that he takes the anointing of the head for granted, and only wishes to emphasize the anointing of the feet which was not recorded in the common tradition. Our Lord's words both in S. Mark and S. Matthew refer to an anointing of His body. He saw in the act a hint that Mary had a prevision of the end that was before Him, and chose this way of expressing her sympathy. An anointing of the head only would not have suggested preparation for burial. The words recorded by S. John according to the true text, "Suffer her to keep it for the day of my preparation for burial" suggest that she had not emptied the flask on His feet. The visit of the women to our Lord's tomb with unguents may be an echo of this utterance. We must, however, admit that Mary of Bethany is not mentioned by name as belonging to the company, unless she is to be identified with Mary of Magdala.

There remains the difficulty of understanding why she

wiped the feet with her hair. The ointment would not have needed to be wiped off. She was in a friend's house and, if necessary, could easily have borrowed a towel. In the other case, the woman that was a sinner was among strangers, and wiped her tears off the feet and not the ointment. As a symbolic gesture the violation of decorum involved in letting down her hair in public may, as Godet points out, indicate an overwhelming flood of emotion.

In the next chapter I have occasion to discuss the problems connected with the criticisms of Judas on her act, and with S. John's criticism of Judas.

9 *The common people therefore of the Jews learned that he was there: and they came, not for Jesus' sake only, but that they might see* 10 *Lazarus also, whom he had raised from the dead. But the chief priests took counsel that they might put Lazarus also to death;* 11 *because that by reason of him many of the Jews went away, and believed on Jesus.*

The feast, according to S. John, seems to have taken place the day before the triumphal entry. There is no reason to assume that it took place on the night of the arrival of Jesus from Jericho. This section seems to imply a stay of more than one day giving time for the crowd of pilgrims who had been accompanying Him to get into Jerusalem and spread the news of His arrival, and for the effect on the Judæan population to attract the attention of the authorities, bringing Lazarus also into danger.

THE TRIUMPHAL ENTRY

12 *On the morrow a great multitude that had come to the feast, when* 13 *they heard that Jesus was coming to Jerusalem, took the branches of the palm trees, and went forth to meet him, and cried out, Hosanna: Blessed* is *he that cometh in the name of the Lord, even the King of* 14 *Israel. And Jesus, having found a young ass, sat thereon; as it is* 15 *written, Fear not, daughter of Zion: behold, thy King cometh,* 16 *sitting on an ass's colt. These things understood not his disciples at the first: but when Jesus was glorified, then remembered they*

that these things were written of him, and that they had done these
17 *things unto him. The multitude therefore that was with him when he called Lazarus out of the tomb, and raised him from the*
18 *dead, bare witness. For this cause also the multitude went and met*
19 *him, for that they heard that he had done this sign. The Pharisees therefore said among themselves, Behold how ye prevail nothing: lo, the world is gone after him.*

The story of Palm Sunday is fully recorded in each of the Synoptists, both S. Matthew and S. Luke having additional features to contribute to the account as given by S. Mark. Jesus enters Jerusalem with a crowd ahead of Him and a crowd following. S. Mark tells us that it was already late when Jesus reached the Temple. S. John tells us of a crowd composed of the pilgrims who had come up for the Feast, who came out from Jerusalem to meet Him bearing palm branches—it is only S. John who mentions them. They were shouting Hosanna. We had already heard of their interest in Jesus in 11 : 56.

They must have heard of the approach of Jesus from the advanced guard of those who had come up with Him from Jericho. Their interest had been further specially stimulated by the testimony of the crowd who had been present at the raising of Lazarus. It was apparently in answer to this demonstration of popular enthusiasm that Jesus determined to make a formal, and so to speak state, entry into Jerusalem.

There can be no doubt, though His disciples were unaware of it at the time, that He Himself ordered His entry in such a way as to manifest His own understanding of the office and character of the Messiah, as He found it revealed in the Prophets. It was in sharp contrast to popular anticipation, and there was little chance that any even of His immediate disciples would see His meaning at the time. But the act would remain, and men in all ages would find in the inspired words of the Prophet a guiding clue to His mind and will. Mk. 14: 27 ff. gives proof that this is not the only passage in Zechariah that had a message for Him at this time.

The comment of the Pharisees marks their final surrender

to the opportunist policy of men whom in their hearts they despised for their worldly-mindedness.

INTERVIEW WITH THE GREEKS

20 *Now there were certain Greeks among those that went up to worship*
21 *at the feast: these therefore came to Philip, which was of Bethsaida*
22 *of Galilee, and asked him, saying, Sir, we would see Jesus. Philip cometh and telleth Andrew: Andrew cometh, and Philip, and*
23 *they tell Jesus. And Jesus answereth them, saying, The hour is*
24 *come, that the Son of man should be glorified. Verily, verily, I say unto you, Except a grain of wheat fall into the earth and die, it abideth by itself alone; but if it die, it beareth much fruit. He*
25 *that loveth his life loseth it; and he that hateth his life in this*
26 *world shall keep it unto life eternal. If any man serve me, let him follow me; and where I am, there shall also my servant be: if any*
27 *man serve me, him will the Father honour. Now is my soul troubled; and what shall I say? Father, save me from this hour. But for*
28 *this cause came I unto this hour. Father, glorify thy name. There came therefore a voice out of heaven,* saying, *I have both glorified*
29 *it, and will glorify it again. The multitude therefore, that stood by, and heard it, said that it had thundered: others said, An angel*
30 *hath spoken to him. Jesus answered and said, This voice hath*
31 *not come for my sake, but for your sakes. Now is the judgement*
32 *of this world: now shall the prince of this world be cast out. And I, if I be lifted up from the earth, will draw all men unto myself.*
33 *But this he said, signifying by what manner of death he should die.*

S. John has no need to go over the ground, fully covered in the common tradition, of the controversies with the Jews that took place in Holy Week, including the second cleansing of the Temple. But there was an incident, connected with a company of strangers, which was worth preserving. It led to a final direct appeal to His own people. Certain Greeks came to Philip and asked for an introduction to Jesus. Philip consults Andrew and they both tell Jesus.

S. John is too much engrossed in the resultant teaching to tell us expressly (what, surely, he leaves us to infer) that that teaching was uttered in the hearing of these new seekers after the truth. The words that he records shew that Jesus saw in their request a clear sign of the approaching passion. Their question was a foretaste of the ingathering of "sheep, not of this fold", which the Good Shepherd knew would follow His sacrifice of Himself. But the foretaste of triumph was a reminder of the suffering that must precede it.

The hour He said *has come* (and in S. John the hour is always the hour of the Cross). Then He goes on to characterize the hour, not as it must seem in the eyes of men, but in the light of the divine purpose. In the eyes of men it was an hour of shame and defeat, but, in reality, it would only bring into clear relief the true glory of the Son of Man. It would manifest to the world the completeness of His surrender to the redeeming love of His heavenly Father.

He goes on to expound the law of sacrifice, not now in terms of Jewish sacrificial ritual, but in terms of natural law. The sacrificial ritual dealt with the restoration of the right relations between God and man, which have been interrupted by sin. Jesus here shews from the conditions required for the germination of a seed, that the law of the Cross is laid upon all life. No seed can bear fruit except on the condition of the surrender of an isolated self-centred existence. *Except a grain of wheat fall into the ground and die, it abideth by itself alone. But, if it die, it beareth much fruit.*

S. Paul uses the same illustration in 1 Cor. 15: 36: "That which thou sowest is not quickened except it die". He is shewing that death in the vegetable world is the gate to new life for the surrendered individuality. Objection has indeed been taken to this illustration, because in our blindness we associate the thought of death with the extinction of personal existence—a contingency which, in the natural world, would be represented by the rotting of the seed under conditions unfavourable to reproduction. We fail to realize that on the lips of Jesus death is never a synonym for extinction. In His view, all human souls—both those who are still here, and those within the veil—are alive to God. In fact this illustration is clearly chosen, both by our Lord and by S. Paul, to transform our whole conception of death, and to help us to think of it as a necessary incident in the evolution of life—or, rather (to come nearer to the thought, as defined by our Lord in the next verse) to think of self-surrender as the condition of acquiring a true personality. *He that loveth himself* (our Lord goes on to say) *is destroying himself; and he that hateth self in this world shall bring himself safely into the life of the world to come.*

This is uncompromising teaching. If we are to act upon it, we need to be upheld by personal loyalty to our Lord and Master, by the inspiration of His example, and by the assurance of His continual support and sympathy. Jesus therefore goes on (in the consciousness that He has accepted this condition for Himself in its full stringency, and that His obedience would supply the supreme illustration of the fruitfulness of sacrifice) to add for the benefit of those who, on the strength of it, would devote themselves to His service: *If any man serve Me, let him follow Me.* There is only one way in which His disciples can enter into His purpose and carry on His work: and that is by walking in His steps, bearing each his own cross after Him.

This is not, however, a complete account of the matter. The death to which He was called would be no barrier between Master and servant. Step by step along the path of surrender and service, the servant would be sustained by conscious communion with his Lord. *Where I am, there shall also my servant be.* And as the Son was continually sustained by the consciousness of the Father's approval, He adds: *If any man serve Me, Him will the Father honour.*

This is the end and crown of the work of the Son, the perfected fruit of His passion. It was the "joy that was set before Him", the glory into which He was entering. But it could only be reached through suffering, the constant pressure of which finds expression on rare occasions in isolated phrases. It was "the baptism in which He was to be baptized", "the cup that He must drain". He was under sore constraint "until it was accomplished". The burthen seems to have grown more oppressive as the hour drew nigh. It was to come to a climax in Gethsemane.

S. John's plan did not include a repetition of the familiar story of the Agony in the Garden, but he records here an incident which shewed that the vision of the glory that should be revealed was accompanied by a sharp travail pang, not in the garden, but in the Temple Courts. Here, as in the garden, Jesus brings the burthen into His Father's presence, using—as later on, on the Cross—the words of a psalmist, who had in the past been upheld in the hour of his trial by communion with God, "Now is My soul troubled" (Ps. 42: 6).

It was not enough, however, merely to state the fact. He must consider, in the sight of God, the right method of dealing with it; that is, the prayer that He should offer to God as a result of it. The first that suggested itself is a prayer for deliverance. But this is not, we must notice, a prayer for deliverance *from* this hour, in the sense that He contemplates the possibility of asking to be spared the trial. The prayer, that He tests before He uses it, is a prayer to be saved *out of it*, that is to be brought safely through to the other side of it, like the prayer to be saved *out of* death in Heb. 5: 7. He felt, however, on reflection, that there was no need to ask for that. That deliverance was already sure. *For this cause*—that through it I might enter into My glory—*came I into the world.* So He turns to a prayer in which all thought of self is swallowed up. *Father, glorify Thy name.* This, after all, was the true fruit of the travail of His soul, for which He was looking forward. This was the glory that would transfigure the shame of the Cross.

This revelation of His inmost heart had been made aloud in public. The Jews were accustomed to pray out loud, even in their private devotions, as we have already had occasion to notice. On this occasion S. John heard not the prayer only, but its answer. The assurance came from heaven that the glory of the Father was in safe keeping. *I have both glorified it, and will glorify it again.* As in the past, so in the future, the Father would guard the glory of His name. This assurance of His Father's acceptance of His prayer came (He tells them) for the support not of His faith, but of theirs in the fiery trial that was before them. They, we must remember, would be confronted in less than a week with the

Cross in all its grim reality. So here, just as on the Mount of Transfiguration, a voice from heaven came to assure them that, even on Calvary, the Father was delighting in the Son.

From one point of view it was the hour and power of darkness. From another it was the hour of judgement on the "prince of this world". The spirit of selfishness by which men are enslaved would be cast out of their hearts by the very completeness of its apparent victory. *I, if I be lifted up out of the earth*, passing through the grave and gate of death to a mighty resurrection and a glorious ascension, shall become a centre of irresistible attraction: *I will draw all men unto myself.*

THE LAST APPEAL TO THE PEOPLE

There seems to be a dislocation in the text here. After Jesus has apparently taken a final leave of the people in verse 36, He is introduced again as making another final and emphatic public appeal. It is just possible to regard the section, verses 44–50, as a collection of the Evangelist's reminiscences of his Master's teaching, which he introduces here, after his own judgement on the terrible fact of the hardening of Israel, in order that we might know that Jesus had made a direct appeal to those of the leaders who were restrained by the fear of men from confessing their faith in Him, and that he might at the same time give his explanation of the hardening. But the record of a "loud cry" comes in very strangely after verse 36.

It seems as if it would be much more in place as a third emphatic public declaration of His claim to the people at Jerusalem. The first two are in 7: 28 and 7: 37. It would come in appropriately after the challenge from the crowd in verse 34 to explain what He meant by calling Himself the Son of Man—a challenge which on the present arrangement is left without any direct answer. And His reference to Himself as the light of the world in verse 46 leads up quite naturally to the closing appeal to

His hearers to use the light while they have it, in verse 36.

I therefore insert verses 44–50 between verses 34 and 35.

34 *The multitude therefore answered him, We have heard out of the law that the Christ abideth for ever: and how sayest thou, The*
44 *Son of man must be lifted up? who is this Son of man? And Jesus cried and said, He that believeth on me, believeth not on me, but*
45 *on him that sent me. And he that beholdeth me beholdeth him that*
46 *sent me. I am come a light into the world, that whosoever believeth*
47 *on me may not abide in the darkness. And if any man hear my sayings, and keep them not, I judge him not: for I came not to*
48 *judge the world, but to save the world. He that rejecteth me, and receiveth not my sayings, hath one that judgeth him: the word*
49 *that I spake, the same shall judge him in the last day. For I spake not from myself: but the Father which sent me, he hath given me a commandment, what I should say, and what I should speak. And*
50 *I know that his commandment is life eternal: the things therefore which I speak, even as the Father hath said unto me, so I speak.*
35 *Jesus therefore said unto them, Yet a little while is the light among you. Walk while ye have the light, that darkness overtake you not: and he that walketh in the darkness knoweth not whither he goeth.*
36 *While ye have the light, believe on the light, that ye may become sons of light.*

These things spake Jesus, and he departed and hid himself from
37 *them. But though he had done so many signs before them, yet they*
38 *believed not on him: that the word of Isaiah the prophet might be fulfilled, which he spake, Lord, who hath believed our report? And*
39 *to whom hath the arm of the Lord been revealed? For this cause*
40 *they could not believe, for that Isaiah said again, He hath blinded their eyes, and he hardened their hearts; Lest they should see with their eyes, and perceive with their heart, And should turn, And I*
41 *should heal them. These things said Isaiah, because he saw his*
42 *glory; and he spake of him. Nevertheless even of the rulers many believed on him; but because of the Pharisees they did not confess*
43 it, *lest they should be put out of the synagogue: for they loved the glory of men more than the glory of God.*

The multitude seems to have gathered, from the teaching that Jesus had given in answer to His Greek visitors, that He believed that He would before long have to lay down His life, and that the strange allusion to a lifting up of the Son of Man had some relation to His death. He had recently accepted public homage as the Son of David. They could not associate the thought of death with the Messiah, and the title "Son of Man" which He seemed to take to Himself in place of it, had no recognized meaning in this connexion.

So they ask, "Who is this Son of Man?". This was not a question which could be answered by a verbal definition. Only those who were prepared to enrol themselves as His disciples could find the clue to His meaning. But here as always His main object was to fix their attention, not on Himself, but on God who sent Him. "Faith in me is really faith in Him, and in all my words and deeds I am revealing Him". He had already in 10: 38 asked them to recognize, on the evidence of His works, the presence of His Father in Him. He will before long say in answer to S. Philip, "He that hath seen me hath seen the Father".

Here He comes back to the revelation that He had given of Himself in 8: 12 as the antitype of the Shekinah that guided Israel through the wilderness. This guidance He rendered chiefly through His words, and those words, because they were light, brought a sentence of judgement with them on those who heard and did not heed.

He is anxious to guard against a possible misconception of the whole purpose of His coming, into which men might fall, as they became aware of the judgement which His coming brought. His one all-inclusive purpose, implied in His name, was the salvation of the world. Nevertheless His presence did not act mechanically. Men were free to reject Him and to disregard His words. He would have them know that they did so at their peril, "The word that I have spoken, that shall reveal a man to himself when he comes into judgement—it may be by the memory of a revelation which has come from without, or by a still small voice making itself heard from within—for I have not been speaking in my own name but in loyal obedience to the Father who gave me commandment what to say and what to speak. I cannot help speaking, and the word must judge, and yet I know that my Father's commandment is life eternal. I, therefore, hand on to you without fear all that the Father gives me to speak".

The ground is now fully prepared for His final appeal. The spiritual light that shone from His personal presence would not be much longer available. Let them remember that the light was given as a guide to action. They would find themselves helpless when it was gone. And the reward of obedience was spiritual transformation. The disciples would in their turn become sources of light.

These last words are left to do their work, and Jesus as a teacher passes from their ken.

Then comes a short section in which the Evangelist draws the moral of the national rejection of the appeal which he has recorded. For a loyal-hearted Israelite, for John no less than for Paul, the issue was unspeakably tragic. He could only find relief in the recognition of the fact that all that had happened could be seen on the evidence of Holy Scripture to have been in accordance with the "determinate counsel and foreknowledge of God". He contents himself with two quotations. The first (Is. 53: 1) consists of the opening words of the central revelation of the Suffering Servant of the Lord. Those to whom the message is committed were from of old taught to expect its rejection.

The second comes from the chapter (6: 10) in which Isaiah describes his own call. Jesus Himself called attention to it when He was explaining His reasons for speaking in parables (Mt. 13: 14 f.). And so did S. Paul (Ac. 28: 26 ff.) after the rejection of his witness to the Jews at Rome. It is in close accordance with the teaching of Jesus in verses 47 f. It is meant as a permanent witness to our responsibility for the use of the light granted to us. We must never forget that it is by God's appointment that if His word does not quicken, it must deaden.

We cannot be too thankful for the assurance that Jesus Himself gives us in verse 47 that this judgement is not the final word of God to men

S. John takes occasion to declare that the vision that Isaiah had seen was a vision of the pre-incarnate Lord. He adds a note to shew that even among the authorities the appeal had met with some response, though the fear of man prevented them from confessing Him there and then.

CHAPTER XVI

INTRODUCTION TO THE PASSION

1 *Now before the feast of the passover, Jesus knowing that his hour was come that he should depart out of this world unto the Father, having loved his own which were in the world, he loved them unto*
2 *the end.*[1] *And during supper, the devil having already put into the*
3 *heart of Judas Iscariot, Simon's* son, *to betray him,* Jesus, *knowing that the Father had given all things into his hands, and that he came*
4 *forth from God, and goeth unto God, riseth from supper. . . .*

[1] Or : *To the uttermost.*

THE construction of verses 1–5 is awkward, but they constitute but a single sentence. The first three verses are really an introduction, not merely, as the ordinary punctuation suggests, to the single incident of the feet-washing, but to the whole of his account of the Passion. The passage on this hypothesis runs as follows:

Now, before the Feast of the Passover, Jesus knowing that his hour was come that he should depart out of the world unto the Father, —having loved his own which were in the world, he loved them to the uttermost—and, supper beginning, the devil having already put it into the heart of Judas Iscariot, the son of Simon, to betray him, knowing that the Father had given all things into his hands, and that he came forth from God and goeth unto God, riseth from supper. . . .

This punctuation avoids the suggestion, which is otherwise almost inevitable, that the words translated "to the end" or "to the uttermost" mean simply "to the end of his life on earth". If they mean, as they must mean, "perfectly", the completeness of His love for His own cannot be regarded as dependent on His knowledge that the end of His life on earth was at hand: and the only way to avoid suggesting that thought is to treat the whole sentence, "having loved His own whom He was to leave behind, He loved them perfectly", as a parenthesis, strictly parallel to all the other considerations which S. John wants us to take for granted as the key to the whole account that follows. A great part of our difficulty in understanding the next three chapters comes from the fact that we are so apt to forget that what was clear to Jesus all the time, and is clear to us because we know the sequel, was entirely out of sight of the disciples, to wit (1) that the hour of His departure had come; (2) that Judas had already betrayed Him; (3) that He was, by divine appointment, Lord of the universe, and on His way to the throne that He had left to come into the world.

JESUS WASHES HIS DISCIPLES' FEET

4 *Jesus riseth from supper, and layeth aside his garments; and he* 5 *took a towel, and girded himself. Then he poureth water into the bason, and began to wash the disciples' feet, and to wipe them* 6 *with the towel wherewith he was girded. So he cometh to Simon* 7 *Peter. He saith unto him, Lord, dost thou wash my feet? Jesus answered and said unto him, What I do thou knowest not now; but* 8 *thou shalt understand hereafter. Peter saith unto him, Thou shalt never wash my feet. Jesus answered him, If I wash thee not,* 9 *thou hast no part with me. Simon Peter saith unto him, Lord,* 10 *not my feet only, but also my hands and my head. Jesus saith unto him, He that is bathed needeth not save to wash his feet, but is* 11 *clean every whit: and ye are clean, but not all. For he knew him that should betray him; therefore said he, Ye are not all clean.*

12 *So when he had washed their feet, and taken his garments, and sat down again, he said unto them, Know ye what I have done to* 13 *you? Ye call me, Master, and, Lord: and ye say well; for so I am.* 14 *If I then, the Lord and the Master, have washed your feet, ye also* 15 *ought to wash one another's feet. For I have given you an example,* 16 *that ye also should do as I have done to you. Verily, verily, I say unto you, A servant is not greater than his lord: neither one* 17 *that is sent greater than he that sent him. If ye know these things,* 18 *blessed are ye if ye do them. I speak not of you all: I know whom I have chosen: but that the scripture may be fulfilled, He that eateth* 19 *my bread lifted up his heel against me. From henceforth I tell you before it come to pass, that, when it is come to pass, ye may* 20 *believe that I am* he. *Verily, verily, I say unto you, He that receiveth*

whomsoever I send receiveth me; and he that receiveth me receiveth him that sent me.

S. John has now set the scene for the story of the crowning revelation of His Master's love for His disciples. That revelation was given by His return to His Father, and by the door to abiding communion between Him and His which that return would open.

There is nothing in S. Mark's account to prepare us for the opening incident. S. Luke, however, drops a hint, which casts only too illuminating a light upon it. S. Mark has taught us (9: 34; 10: 40 ff.) that the harmony of the apostolic band was from time to time broken, after Jesus had accepted Simon Peter's confession of His Messiahship, by disputes as to precedence. S. Luke tells us that one such dispute took place in the Upper Room. It is natural to suppose that it was connected with the order in which they were to take their places at the supper table. The place of honour was, I believe, on the right of Jesus. The beloved disciple was on His left, with Simon Peter next to him. I suspect that Judas Iscariot was next to Jesus in the place of honour on the other side. There would be, in that case, nothing out of the way, if Jesus at the critical moment helped Judas first. However that may be, it was necessary that the broken harmony should be restored, and that the Lord should make one final effort to extirpate this terribly deep-seated root of bitterness. He had to bring home to them—at whatever cost of personal humiliation—the reality of the fact, to which He had called their attention on a similar occasion previously, "that the Son of Man had not come to be waited upon, but to wait upon others". He had actually undertaken, as S. Luke says, menial work for them. So He rises from supper and lays aside His outer garment, and girding Himself with a towel, He begins to wash His disciples' feet, one by one. When He comes to Simon Peter, He is met by a characteristic protest: "Lord are *you* going to wash *my* feet?" (Both the personal pronouns are emphatic.) He is met by a tender assurance that, though the meaning of His

Master's act was, for the moment, hidden from him—(both pronouns are again emphatic)—it would become plainer later. Peter, however, finds the humiliation unendurable, and Jesus has to warn him that he must submit or forfeit his discipleship. This touches Simon Peter on a tender spot, and with characteristic impetuosity he implores Jesus to wash his hands and his head as well. But to do this would be to destroy the symbolism of the act. Guests at a banquet, coming from a bath inevitably arrived with dusty feet, and so it was a matter of courtesy for a host to offer his guests an opportunity of washing them. There was no necessity, however, to bathe the whole body over again. Interpreted by this analogy the cleansing that Jesus was providing was for the removal of a surface defilement. It did not imply a deep-seated pollution that required a reconstruction of their whole system. Their acceptance of His call to discipleship had been whole-hearted. As He will assure them again later in 15: 3, "Already are ye clean, thanks to the word that I spoke to you". But there was an exception even to this. One of the Twelve had fallen from grace. So, as a hint of the coming denunciation, it may be as yet one more appeal to the conscience of the traitor, He adds, "But not all."

Then, after He has gone round the whole circle, He puts on His seamless coat again and, taking His seat at the table, He explains what He has done. He had, as their Lord and Teacher, claimed the privilege of serving His disciples in a menial office. He would extirpate the root of selfish ambition by leaving behind the memory of one outstanding example of the royalty of service. The brotherly spirit which was to be the hall-mark of their discipleship must be rooted in humility.

It is good, surely, to notice that the principle of the imitation of Christ, on which S. Peter, S. Paul, and S. John lay such stress, and which has at various times, notably in S. Francis of Assisi and S. Thomas à Kempis, left so deep a mark on the Christian life, is saved from the suspicion of presumption, because it can appeal to an express challenge from the Master Himself. And it is worth remembering that in the New Testament the feature in the divine example which we are challenged to reproduce is in every case His humility.

JUDAS AT THE LAST SUPPER

21 *When Jesus had thus said, he was troubled in the spirit, and testified, and said, Verily, verily, I say unto you, that one of you*
22 *shall betray me. The disciples looked one upon another, doubting*
23 *of whom he spake. There was at the table reclining in Jesus'*
24 *bosom one of his disciples whom Jesus loved. Simon Peter therefore beckoneth to him, and saith unto him, Tell* us *who it is*
25 *of whom he speaketh. He leaning back, as he was, on Jesus'*
26 *breast saith unto him, Lord, who is it? Jesus therefore answereth, He it is, for whom I shall dip the sop, and give it him. So when he had dipped the sop, he taketh and giveth it to Judas,* the son
27 *of Simon Iscariot. And after the sop, then entered Satan into him. Jesus therefore saith unto him, That thou doest, do quickly.*
28 *Now no man at the table knew for what intent he spake this unto*
29 *him. For some thought, because Judas had the bag, that Jesus said unto him, Buy what things we have need of for the feast; or, that he should give something to the poor. He then having received*
30 *the sop went out straightway: and it was night.*

The denunciation of the traitor is the first incident in the Upper Chamber recorded by S. Mark. He does not, however, mention Judas by name, He simply says that when the party had taken their places and the meal had begun, Jesus warned them, with an implicit reference to Ps. 41 : 9, that one of them would betray Him. The announcement caused consternation, and each of the disciples asked, "Is it I?" But Jesus only repeats that the traitor is one of His messmates.

In S. Matthew, Judas asks: "Is it I, Rabbi?" And Jesus answers: "Thou hast said". But we are not told who heard the answer.

In S. Luke the warning comes after the institution, and the disciples discuss the question among themselves. None of the three mentions the departure of Judas.

It is followed in S. Luke by the account of a wrangle on

precedence among the Twelve, and by our Lord's appeal to His own example of service, which seems to be reminiscent of the feet-washing, and of the teaching on discipleship that grew out of it.

In S. John the incident is described from within by one who claims to have played a leading part in it. (Compare Jn. 13: 23 and 21: 20.) He shews that the shock of the denunciation was carefully prepared for. First, at the time of the feet-washing Jesus gave a hint of the presence of deep defilement in one of the Twelve. Then, as He was pointing out the conditions of discipleship which His act had embodied, He quoted Ps. 41 : 9 in order that the treachery, when it came, might confirm their faith by its conformity with the prophecy. Then, just as in 12: 27 the prospect of the Passion, which had been brought very near to Him by the teaching that He was giving to the Greeks, troubled His soul, so here the thought of the betrayal troubled Him deeply and led to a solemn and personal denunciation: "One of you shall betray me".

The whole body were thrown into consternation. Simon Peter beckoned to the beloved disciple, who was reclining next to Jesus on His left, to ask who it was? Jesus, in answer, points out the traitor by giving him the next portion.

The devil (as S. John has already told us) had before this suggested the thought of treachery to Judas (cf. Lk. 22: 3), and we learn from S. Mark and S. Matthew that he was already in treaty with the Jewish authorities. But he had not completely surrendered to Satan until he had received "the sop". This "sop", given after Jesus had expressly emphasized the special strain to loyalty implied in sharing a common meal, must have come with an intense force of personal appeal. Judas deliberately closed his heart against it, and "then entered Satan into him".

It is an aweful mystery, whatever way we look at it. There is the mystery of the divine providence: "The Son of Man indeed goeth as it hath been determined; and woe to that man by whom he is betrayed". Here an abyss of treachery and shame, terrible to contemplate, is foreseen and taken up into the divine plan, and made to subserve the redemption of the world. I say, of shame—for the man after all, by his own will identified himself with the movement. It became, through his own act, a shameful thing for that man that he had ever been born. And yet eternal love, the everlasting mercy created him. He went to his own place, the place he had chosen for himself.

He must have had exceptional capacities. He was certainly chosen to enjoy exceptional privileges and opportunities. He had once left all to follow the Master whom he betrayed.

It is not surprising that efforts have been made to palliate his shame. It would in some measure shield the honour of our common human nature, if we could find some respectable motive to account for his action. Is it not possible that it was really over-zealous patriotism? May not Judas have believed that his Master was too shy to assert Himself, but that if the situation really became desperate He would have to produce His legions of angels?

S. John is the chief witness against any such hypothesis. He tells us in 12: 4–6 that the protest against the waste of the ointment in the house of Simon the Leper was voiced by Judas, adding that his real motive came from the fact that he was a thief and had used his position as treasurer for the company for his own advantage. If S. John had not good reason for believing this to be true, clearly his action in recording it is inexcusable. But, if he had, there is no more reason for charging him with lack of charity against Judas for relating the fact, than there is for saying that he must have had a grudge against Peter, because he tells the story of his denials. While we must guard carefully against the temptation to judge Judas or anyone else, yet, if we are to take warning from his fall, a real purpose is served by light on any possible predisposing causes. And this hint from S. John fits in with the fact that Judas made money for himself out of his treachery. The passion with which he flings it from him in the agony of his remorse is surely proof of the fatal attraction that the accursed thing had had for him. In this respect the account in Mt. 27: 3–10 is far preferable to the tradition, inserted by S. Luke in his report of S. Peter's speech (Ac. 1: 18, 19). Unless, indeed, the word "obtained", in verse 18, is to be taken ironically, as describing the net result of the transaction as the posthumous acquisition of a public cemetery. He had the grace to confess his fault, if not to Jesus, at least to His judges, and to cast away the fruit of his treachery. He then, by his own hand, executed the judgement on himself that he felt he had deserved, though his accomplices were precluded from passing sentence on him.

It is impossible, I think, to believe that the apostles could have had any suspicion of his honesty while he was in office. But the fact of his peculations may have been only too evident from the state of the fund as he left it. It must be salutary, though it is terrible, to contemplate what ruin a fault that in its beginning might seem insignificant may bring in its train.

CHAPTER XVII

INTRODUCTION TO THE DISCOURSES

AFTER Judas has departed, S. John gives us a priceless record of the most intimate self-revelation of Jesus to His disciples. In S. Mark and S. Matthew there is nothing to correspond, except a warning based on Zech. 13 : 7, to the whole body of a coming scattering, with the promise of a meeting again in Galilee, and the warning to Simon Peter of his denials.

In S. Luke there is a promise to the disciples of communion with Jesus, and of positions of authority in His Kingdom, coupled with a warning of a coming time of sifting for the whole body, and a hint to Simon Peter that he is in special need of his Lord's intercession. This culminates in the warning of his approaching denials. This is followed by an enigmatic instruction that the time was at hand when they would each need to have a sword, because Jesus Himself was soon to be "numbered with the transgressors". Each of the three records contains an account of the institution of Holy Communion. S. John does not repeat that account. He gives us instead what we may well regard as the Lord's sermon at the first Eucharist. Nor should we go very far wrong if we regarded the new commandment as its text. In form, however, it is an instruction rather than a homily.

The section to the end of Chapter 16, and indeed, to the end of Chapter 17, is a closely knit whole. But it falls into three clearly marked divisions. The first ends with the fourteenth chapter, the second with the sixteenth. In the seventeenth Jesus is speaking to His Father, but He means His disciples to hear what He is saying.

It has been supposed that the text here, as in some other

parts of the Gospel, has been dislocated. Dr. Bernard, for example, prints the second section before the first. He inserts chapters 15 and 16 after the opening words of 13: 31, and carries on with 13: 31b–14: 32 after 16: 33. This seems a violent remedy to avoid the verbal inconsistency between 13: 35 and 16: 5. When Jesus complained that none of His disciples were asking, "Whither goest Thou?" He meant, as His comment shewed, that they were so full of the effect of His departure on themselves that they failed to realize that there was another side to the question. It never occurred to them that their loss might be His gain. Peter certainly in 13: 36 is thinking only of the gulf that the departure would interpose between him and his Lord. I do not think that he could have asked this question after hearing our Lord say: "I came forth from the Father and have come into the world. Again I leave the world and go to the Father" (16: 28).

Assuming then, that the chapters are to be read in their traditional order, we notice that in the first division, while it is clear that Jesus has definite teaching which He is bent on imparting, He gives His hearers abundant opportunities to raise difficulties and ask questions. First, Simon Peter has something to say (13: 37). Then, after he has been answered, Jesus makes a fresh start, in 14: 1, and is interrupted first by Thomas (14: 5) and then by Philip (14: 8). A new stage in the teaching begins after the answer to Philip at 14: 15. This, again, is interrupted by Jude. Then Jesus returns, in verse 27 to the note He had struck in 14: 1. And the first stage in the teaching comes to an end as the party leaves the Upper Chamber.

The second division begins with the similitude of the True Vine, which may have been suggested by a tree that they passed on the way, or, as Dr. Westcott suggests, by the cluster of grapes, the emblem of Israel which Herod had affixed to the door that led from the outer court into the Temple precincts. If he is right, Jesus must have led His company to pay a last farewell to "His Father's house" by the light of the paschal moon, before going out to Gethsemane. This would not only give a special appropriateness to the new strain that appears in the teaching, it would also provide a very significant setting for the high-priestly prayer in chapter 17.

The fact that some change had come over the conditions under which the teaching was being given is, I think, apparent from the fact that we hear no more of interruptions from individual listeners. These are natural in a party sitting together in a room. They are not so easy under less formal conditions or in the open air. In 16: 17 the disciples when confronted with a difficulty, discuss it among themselves instead of bringing it straight to their Master. The teaching, in consequence, falls into more formal divisions, marked by the recurring formula: "These things have I spoken unto you". This comes only once (14: 25) in the first division. In the second it comes in 15: 11 (cf. 15: 17); 16: 1, 4, 6, 25.

It is, surely, noteworthy that the prominent word in chapter 14 is "Father"; Chapter 15 treats of the union of believers in the body of the Son; Chapter 16 brings to a focus the teaching on the Holy Ghost, the Comforter.

THE NEW COMMANDMENT

31 *When therefore he was gone out, Jesus saith, Now is the Son of man*
32 *glorified, and God is glorified in him; and God shall glorify him*
33 *in himself, and straightway shall he glorify him. Little children, yet a little while I am with you. Ye shall seek me: and as I said unto the Jews, Whither I go, ye cannot come; so now I say unto*
34 *you. A new commandment I give unto you, that ye love one another; even as I have loved you, that ye also love one another. By this*
35 *shall all men know that ye are my disciples, if ye have love one to another.*

The opening words: "Now is (or was) the Son of Man glorified", are certainly startling. But the difficulty is not removed by interposing chapters 15 and 16 between the two parts of 13: 31. The reference to "My commandment" in 15: 12 presupposes the giving of the "new commandment" in 13: 34. And, though the purging of the Vine by the Husbandman has, no doubt, a special point in relation to the "going out" of Judas, the disciples who thought that he had left the room on some special service could not have guessed at the connexion just then.

The best analysis of the situation that I know is that given by Dr. Abbott in his penetrating study of *The Son of Man*. In S. John's Gospel, we must remember that the Cross, so far from being a symbol of defeat and shame, is irradiated throughout by the victory that it won. It was the first step in the final manifestation of the true nature of the Son of Man; or, in other words, of His glorification. For the glory of the Son of Man, like the glory of God, is simply the manifestation of His true and essential nature. So S. John, writing in his own name, says: "The Spirit was not yet given because Jesus was not yet glorified". But, if we may trust his record, he did not invent that use of the term. Jesus Himself adopted it; He used it, for instance, in the Temple Courts when certain Greeks asked to see Him.

"The hour is come that the Son of Man should be glorified." Even so the prospect was disquieting, and Jesus found strength to face it by concentrating his attention on the ultimate issue. He prayed, "Father, glorify Thy name". When we come to chapter 17, we shall find the prayer repeated in the form, "Father, glorify Thy Son, that the Son may glorify Thee". Its occurrence here is deeply significant. It shews what it cost Jesus to let Judas go out into the aweful darkness of that night. It was the first act in the Passion. Jesus, therefore, for His own sake and for the sake of His disciples, describes it in its true nature, both as a present achievement, and as a pledge of what was to come. "Now, at this moment, is the Son of Man glorified". The Cross will be a perfect revelation of the true nature of His humanity. (This is the last occasion on which He uses the title "the Son of Man"). And it completes the work that He has come to do. "God is glorified in Him". What remains is altogether in God's hands. It is for God to vindicate the honour of His Son. "And God will glorify Him in Himself, and He will straightway glorify Him."

So understood, the words form a solemn and appropriate

introduction to the unreserved self-revelation which follows. He begins with a greeting of infinite tenderness: "Little children"—emphasizing at once their kinship to Him and their immaturity.

Then comes the first clear indication of the coming separation, which has the effect at the same time of marking the sacredness of this last opportunity for talking face to face and heart to heart. *Yet a little while I am with you: ye shall seek me, and, as I said to the Jews, "Where I am ye cannot come",* I say at this time to you also.

Then He passes on at once to the new commandment. It is, as we shall see, specially designed to bind them at once to one another and to Himself. *A new commandment give I unto you that ye love one another, as I loved you to the end, that you in your turn should love one another.*

These words, as they stand, may be construed in two ways. Dr. Abbott (*Johannine Grammar* 2116) translates: "A new commandment give I unto you, that ye love one another, even as I loved you, that ye also love one another."

He makes the second *that* simply a repetition of the first, amplified by the definition *even as.* In my translation I regard the second *that* as strictly independent of the first, and as defining one of the results that followed, and was meant to follow, from the Master's love for His disciples. His love was meant to weld them into a living brotherhood.

This thought, I am sure, is true, whether it is (as I think) directly contained in the Greek or not. By making His love for us the measure of the love which He would have us shew to our fellow-disciples, He supplies the motive which makes obedience possible. He makes us channels of His love by bidding us look with His eyes on all our brethren. So the effort to keep this commandment is meant to bind us closer to Him, though we can no longer see Him, at the same time that it binds us to one another. But even this does not exhaust its scope. The commandment was, to start with, intensely personal. It was addressed to a very narrow circle of men, who would before long find themselves face to face with a hostile world. Jesus has much to say later on with regard to the situation in which they would find themselves. He is content here with dropping a hint to shew that in His care for His chosen He had not forgotten the rest of mankind. "By this", He said, "shall all men know that ye are my disciples, if ye have love one for another". Such love is the hall-mark of true discipleship, and it is a mark which can be known and read by all men. Wherever two Christians love one another for Christ's sake, there is incontrovertible witness to the living power of Christ over the hearts of men. When the commandment is disobeyed, the witness is not marred only, it is falsified.

When at the long last the body of believers is perfected into one, in answer to our Lord's prevailing intercession, the world will believe. The closing verses of this section (17: 20–26) are a wonderful commentary on its opening sentences.

THE WARNING TO SIMON PETER

36 *Simon Peter saith unto him, Lord, whither goest thou? Jesus answered, Whither I go, thou canst not follow me now; but thou*
37 *shalt follow afterwards. Peter saith unto him, Lord, why cannot I follow thee even now? I will lay down my life for thee. Jesus*
38 *answereth, Wilt thou lay down thy life for me? Verily, verily, I say unto thee, The cock shall not crow, till thou hast denied me thrice.*

The giving of the new commandment was followed, we may imagine, by a short silence to give it time to sink in. The silence was broken characteristically by Simon Peter. "Impatient", as Dr. Hort suggests in his *Hulsean Lectures* (p. 8) "of the unexpected commandment which seemed to him to be a wandering from the engrossing theme of the discourse, he brought back the naked fact of departure. 'Lord, whither goest thou?' He received for answer the double assurance that he could not follow now, but that he should follow afterward. Again he flung aside the promise of the future, and demanded the reason of his inability to follow instantly, professing his readiness to suffer death for his Lord. His dream was still of an individual discipleship and an individual martyrdom, in the pride of which he was too willing to draw himself away from his fellow-disciples, and to forget altogether the world which he had to help to save. The personal testimony proffered after this fashion was itself fallacious—it argued a self-knowledge so slight and delusive that that *why* was of necessity asked in vain". Jesus answers: "Wilt thou lay down thy life for me? Verily, verily, I say unto thee, the cock shall not crow until thou deny me thrice".

This warning is found in each of the Synoptists. In S. Luke (as in S. John) it is given in the Upper Chamber. In S. Luke it follows the account of a dispute with regard to precedence, which, as we have seen, may have been the occasion of the feet-washing. The grateful acknowledgement of the faithfulness of the Twelve in the past, passes on into a promise of a share in His sovereignty in the time to come. Then Jesus turns to Peter: "Simon, Simon, lo! Satan has asked that he may have you [plural, the chosen Twelve], that he may sift you as wheat." It is implied that, as in the case of Job, God had granted his request. Then, in view of the special trial by which—owing to his impetuosity—he would be exposed, Jesus adds: "But I prayed for thee (singular) that thy faith fail not. And do thou, when thou hast turned again, strengthen thy brethren". It is difficult not to believe in the truth of this record of our Lord's individualizing intercession.

It is not, I think, impossible that Lk. 22: 31 f. was really part of our Lord's answer to one or other of Peter's questions. Certainly Lk. 22: 33, "I am ready to go with thee to prison and to death," comes in as unexpectedly and breathes the same spirit as "I will lay down my life for thee", in S. John.

In S. Mark and S. Matthew the warning to Peter comes after the party in the Upper Room had broken up. It follows a warning to the whole company, based on a prophecy in Zechariah. This is clearly parallel to Jn. 16: 32: "Lo, the hour is coming and hath come, that ye shall be scattered each to his own and shall leave me alone". Peter is represented as refusing to accept the possibility of this desertion. "Though all should be offended in thee, I shall never be offended." This draws out from Jesus what Dr. Westcott is prepared to regard as a solemn and more detailed repetition of the warning already given earlier in the evening: "Verily, I say unto thee that thou to-day, on this night, before the cock crow twice shalt thrice deny me". On that interpretation Peter must by this time have had a clearer understanding of the threatening danger. For he repudiates it with characteristic vehemence: "Though I must die with thee, I shall never deny thee".

It is, of course, possible that we have slightly varying accounts of a single warning. We must be content to leave the problem undecided. That Simon Peter fell in spite of repeated warnings should deepen our sense of the danger of trusting to our own emotion of loyalty. S. Mark tells us, indeed, that the cock would crow twice before the denials were consummated. Had Peter attended to this, the first cock-crow would have given yet one more danger signal.

The fact that Peter was silent for the rest of the evening, while others of the Twelve took up the talking, may be a sign that even the first warning subdued him for a time.

CHAPTER XVIII

CONDITIONS OF LIFE IN THE NEW ORDER

1 *Let not your heart be troubled: ye believe in God, believe also in me.*
2 *In my Father's house are many mansions; if it were not so, I would*
3 *have told you; for I go to prepare a place for you. And if I go and prepare a place for you, I come again, and will receive you unto*
4 *myself; that where I am,* there *ye may be also. And whither I go, ye know the way.*

THERE seems to have been a pause after the solemn warning to Simon Peter. He was silenced, and we may well believe that the hearts of the whole company were filled with fear. Then Jesus speaks. He is conscious of their distress, and sets Himself to allay it. Faith is the one cure for anxiety *Let not your heart be troubled. Believe in God and in me believe.* The last words are curiously ambiguous in grammatical construction. There is little doubt as to their general import. In any case it is to be noted that Jesus here links an appeal for faith in Himself to faith in God. The meaning as well as the construction of the words that follow is more uncertain. The word *mansion* quite strictly means a *resting place*; a station on a journey in which a traveller stays for a time before passing on. Of course it can be used as in 14: 23 of an abiding place, without any necessary implication of transitoriness.

So it is just possible that, when Jesus added: "In my Father's house are many mansions", He simply meant to assure His disciples that there was plenty of room in heaven. It is far more likely, however, that the word is to be taken strictly. Jesus believed that even here on earth we are in our Father's house (Lk. 2: 49). He wishes to assure them that by dying He would only be passing from one room to another in the same house. He even hints that there are many more stages ahead of us than just that one.

This is a very important thought. So much is said in the New Testament of the importance of this earthly stage in our existence, and of the strictness of the judgement that we all have to face, that we are apt to think of this life too exclusively as a probation. It is a great thing to have an assurance that that is not a complete account of the matter. It is much truer to think of this life as the first stage in our education. The lost opportunities can never return; but it is not beyond the bounds of hope that one who has been a failure in the kindergarten may do better in the preparatory school.

The primary intention of the words was, I believe, to prevent the disciples from thinking that Jesus Himself would pass through the gate of death into a shadowy world, and be cut away, as even some Psalmists feared, from the hand of God.

Even this does not bring us to the end of ambiguities. The words that follow are translated in our Bibles: *If it were not so, I would have told you; for I go to prepare a place for you.* The thought, I take it, is "If your gloomy forebodings are true, I could not have kept the truth from you, because the whole future of our relation to one another turns on a clear understanding of the purpose of my departure". I do not see any real objection in logic or grammar to this translation. Moffatt, however, and others translate "Were it not so, would I have told you that I go to prepare a place for you?" It is true, of course, that no such teaching is recorded. But references to unrecorded utterances are not unknown in S. John. See, for instance, Jn. 11: 40. Dr. Abbott, with even less probability, would read the reference to the "many mansions" as a parenthesis, and connect the words—"But if not"—with the appeal for faith. "Perhaps that demand is too great, I should have said: I go to prepare a place for you". He points out that in 14: 11, Jesus says: "Believe me that I am in the Father and the Father in me"; and after, "But if not" substitutes what might be a less exacting demand "to believe for the very works' sake".

Fortunately the main sequence of thought is not affected by the ambiguity. Dr. Hort (in his *Hulsean Lectures*, p. 9) traces it for us in these words: "As He had before taught love among themselves, so now He taught faith—faith resting on God and on Himself. Then He returned to the subject of His departure, shewing how its nature and purpose justified the twofold faith, and converted the seeming abandonment into a fresh token of attachment. The separation, He explained, was intended to lead to a future re-union on a higher stage; and meanwhile it was no disappearance into darkness—'Whither I go ye know the way'."

Even so, however, the gracious promise is liable to be misunderstood. When Jesus says: "And if I go and prepare a place for you, I come again and shall receive you to myself", we are far too apt to assume that He is speaking of coming again "at the last day", and that in consequence the restoration of communion between the disciples and their Lord to which He refers, is relegated to an uncertain date in the future, and has nothing to do with life here and now.

It is true that He does not give any note of time. But in 16: 16 His words are quite express: "A little while and ye no longer behold me, and again a little while and ye shall see me". The first "little while" was measured by hours. He cannot have meant that the second was to be measured by centuries. It is quite clear that the return to which He is referring began with the Resurrection. His words indicate the approach of the new conditions of discipleship that would be introduced by His conquest over death. He had come in flesh to be with us where we are. The time was at hand when men would be called to lift up their hearts to live in fellowship with Him where He is, at the right hand of His Father. The rest of the discourse is devoted to explaining the conditions under which such communion would be possible.

THE WAY TO THE FATHER

5 *Thomas saith unto him, Lord, we know not whither thou goest;*
6 *how know we the way? Jesus saith unto him, I am the way, and the truth, and the life: no one cometh unto the Father, but by me.*
7 *If ye had known me, ye would have known my Father also: from*
8 *henceforth ye know him, and have seen him. Philip saith unto*
9 *him, Lord, shew us the Father, and it sufficeth us. Jesus saith unto him, Have I been so long time with you, and dost thou not know me, Philip? he that hath seen me, hath seen the Father;*
10 *how sayest thou, Shew us the Father? Believest thou not that I am in the Father, and the Father in me? the words that I say unto you I speak not from myself: but the Father abiding in me doeth his*
11 *works. Believe me that I am in the Father, and the Father in me:*
12 *or else believe me for the very works' sake. Verily, verily, I say unto you, He that believeth on me, the works that I do shall he do also; and greater* works *than these shall he do; because I go unto the Father.*

Thomas is puzzled, and he at once voices his perplexity. *Lord, we know not whither thou goest. How can we know the way?*

Jesus answers with the deepest and most inclusive of all His revelations of the extent to which the whole life of every man is dependent on Him for guidance and light and inspiration. He had said that they knew the way, because that knowledge was implicit in their knowledge of Him. He had lived before them a life of complete surrender to the will of God. In so doing, He had marked out a track for us through what would otherwise be a pathless wilderness. It was not that He had given us an example that we should follow in His steps by any mechanical attempt to reproduce its outward form. He was not setting Himself before us as a pattern which we must set ourselves to reproduce in our own strength. He had revealed the possibilities that open out before a God-directed personality. He had shewn them that a man who lived from moment to moment in dependence on God did not walk in darkness, but had the light of life. And the disciple who strove to live in communion with his Lord would find that he too, was being led on a plain path, by the help of a compass, not a code. He need no longer feel paralysed in the presence of the darkest of life's riddles. His Master held the clue to them all. Nay, more, the very effort to follow Him was a perpetual inspiration, it was meat and drink to do His will. A man could run on this path and not be weary; he could walk and not faint.

Something like this is, as Dr. Hort in his *Hulsean Lectures* helps us to understand, the meaning of the wonderful self-revelation to Thomas, contained in the words, "I am the Way, and the Truth, and the Life". The conclusion of that revelation is only in form negative and exclusive. "No one cometh to the Father but by me". For the goal towards which this path leads is none other than the Father Himself, whose holiness is only the condition of the perfection of His love, and who seeing that there is but one way by which His children can be brought home to Him, has not shrunk from the cost of providing it. If, even so, we are troubled because the saying seems to shut out all who are not called by His name, we may remind ourselves that He is "the Light that lighteth every man", and that He Himself has told us that He has other sheep who are not of our fold.

The mention of the Father catches Philip's attention. The desire to bring others into touch with Jesus seems the characteristic note of his discipleship. Surely Jesus would hold back nothing which would enable a man to get into touch with His Father. So He breaks out with: *Lord, shew us the Father and we can want no more.*

This intensely natural petition opens the way for a much-needed and illuminating reply, *Have I been so long time with you and hast thou not known me, Philip?* It was of the utmost importance that His own disciples should not miss the significance of the fundamental fact of His ministry. He had taken very seriously the task committed to Him to appeal to men always and only in His Father's name. His life had been so closely knit into one with His Father's by the completeness of the surrender of His will, that it had throughout been a revelation not of Himself only, but of His Father. *He that hath seen me hath seen the Father.* Philip's need had been foreseen before he put it into words, and full provision had been made to satisfy it. Nothing more was necessary than to call attention to the open secret: *Believest thou not that I am in the Father and the Father in me?* All the memories of their discipleship would be transfigured when they realized all that was implied in this interpenetration of the personalities of the Father and the Son. Every word that He had spoken had been due to the prompting of His Father. The power that had found expression in His mighty works really came from Him. So He could appeal to His works in confirmation of His claim. Faith in the mutual indwelling of the Father and the Son must rest ultimately on the testimony of the consciousness of the Son. But if we ask, as we quite justifiably may, for external attestation, the works that He had done can meet that demand.

Jesus, as we can see, set great store on the evidence to the truth of His claim that an earnest inquirer could derive from the works, transcending normal human capacity, which He had been enabled to do. This evidence appealed most strongly to those who had been brought into direct contact with them. It would lose its power if it became a mere tradition, or if it were regarded as an unique prerogative of the human personality of Jesus. The disciples had themselves had experience in the exercise of this power, when they had been sent out on a preaching tour in the course of the ministry. So Jesus assures them that in the new order, the same power, even in an enhanced degree, would be at their service when they faced the world in His name.

PRAYING IN THE NAME OF JESUS CHRIST

13 *And whatsoever ye shall ask in my name, that will I do, that the*
14 *Father may be glorified in the Son. If ye shall ask me anything*
15 *in my name, that will I do. If ye love me, ye will keep my com-*
16 *mandments. And I will pray the Father, and he shall give you*
17 *another Comforter, that he may be with you for ever,* even *the*

Spirit of truth: whom the world cannot receive; for it beholdeth him not, neither knoweth him: ye know him; for he abideth with 18 *you, and shall be in you. I will not leave you desolate: I come* 19 *unto you. Yet a little while, and the world beholdeth me no more;* 20 *but ye behold me: because I live, ye shall live also. In that day ye shall know that I am in my Father, and ye in me, and I in you.*

The revelation of the conditions of life in the new order, which began after Judas Iscariot had been sent out into the night, makes steady progress by stages that become clear as we survey them.

The starting-point is the ultimate revelation of the inmost heart of the Father and of the Son, which was implicit in the Cross. In and through the Cross the glory of the Son of Man and the glory of God are manifested before the eyes of angels and men. Then, in the new commandment, the love of the Master for His disciples, consummated and consecrated by the Cross, becomes a living bond to unite them both to one another and to the Lord, when He has passed out of sight.

Then comes the revelation of the goal to which He was bound, and of the way to it, with an assurance that the communion, which for the time was to be broken, would be restored under new conditions. He was going to the Father, and His life in their midst had been at once a revelation of the way and of the goal. They had seen a life lived in human flesh in communion with God, based on a whole-hearted surrender to His will. That was "the Way". At the same time, that surrender had issued in such a perfect interpenetration of the personalities of the Father and the Son, that the heart of the Father was perfectly revealed by the Son, both in word and deed. In these words Jesus declares the full significance of the experience which the apostles had gathered from the years of their discipleship, and links our faith in Christ with our faith in God.

The works that He had done in their sight had, in certain specific instances, been of such a character that they provided a real confirmation of His claim to divine Sonship.

They had been due to the working of "the powers of the age to come", signs that the Kingdom of God had indeed drawn nigh.

Power would be given in answer to prayer in Christ's name, a condition which constitutes a fresh stage in the revelation of life in the new order. The disciples, linked to one another and their Lord by the new commandment, would be called to bear their Master's name before men. They would be His commissioned representatives. Men would judge of Him by what they saw of them. They would be instruments in His hands for the bringing in of His Kingdom.

This responsibility might well be overwhelming, if they were left to bear it alone. So He passes on at once to assure them that that was not a contingency which they had any reason to dread. While they, on their side, are responding to His love with loyal obedience, He in communion with His Father would be making full provision for their need. They would, indeed, be deprived of the support and guidance which had come to them from His visible presence, but they would find that His place would be taken by another Comforter. He does not explain the new word. But He uses it in such a way as to suggest its meaning. The Comforter would come to be to them for ever all that their Master had been. Their danger would come from the deceitfulness of the world in which they would have to live and witness. The Spirit would come from, and link them to, the truth. That Spirit, which the world, while it refused to abide in the Master's word, could not know, would be no stranger to them. He had been by their side, guiding and inspiring their Master throughout His ministry. Indeed, He was already at work in their hearts. [The true reading is not "shall be" but "is" in you.]

In these words He lifts the veil which shrouds His activity on our behalf in the presence of the Father, and lets us into the secret of His perpetual intercession. His mission from the beginning had been declared to be to baptize with the Holy Spirit. When He had been glorified, the way would be open for the fulfilment of that mission, and it would have the backing of His prayer.

THE TEST OF DISCIPLESHIP

21 *He that hath my commandments, and keepeth them, he it is that loveth me: and he that loveth me shall be loved of my Father, and*
22 *I will love him, and will manifest myself unto him. Judas (not Iscariot) saith unto him, Lord, what is come to pass that thou wilt*
23 *manifest thyself unto us, and not unto the world? Jesus answered and said unto him, If a man love me, he will keep my word: and my Father will love him, and we will come unto him, and make our abode*
24 *with him. He that loveth me not keepeth not my words: and the word which ye hear is not mine, but the Father's who sent me.*

The condition of discipleship is love of the Master, shewn in resolute and reverent obedience to His commandments. The privileges include a personal assurance of communion with the Father, and an unmistakable manifestation of their Master's presence.

This teaching implied a vital distinction, at least in regard to spiritual capacity, between the disciples and the world in the new order. Judas, not Iscariot, is perplexed by this implication, and asks for further light upon it. We have every reason to be grateful to him for doing so. Our Lord's answer helps us to understand that there is a spiritual law underlying the fact that the Lord shewed Himself alive after His resurrection, not to all the people, but only to specially chosen witnesses. No one can be qualified to give first-hand witness to the resurrection of Jesus, who does not give evidence of personal loyalty to the Master by listening with reverent attention to His word, and so becoming conscious of the moral approbation of the Father, and of the abiding presence with him both of the Father and of the Son. Attention to the words that Christ Himself is speaking in our hearts is possible only to one who loves Him. And the law to which our conscience witnesses is not His, but His Father's.

We must notice here first how, even in the new order, it remains true that Jesus refuses to come in His own name. His work remains incomplete, unless we pass through Him to the Father. The word that He heard at His baptism: "Thou art my Son, my beloved", which had been the inspiration of His own ministry, will ring on in the experience of all His disciples. Their lives would be filled, as His had been, with the sunshine of His Father's love. That which united them to Him would unite them to His Father. They would verify, in their own experience, the truth of His claim that He had come forth from, and was going back to, God.

We must notice next, that the motive to which He appeals is direct and personal loyalty to Himself. He was giving Himself without stint for them in love. The full price would soon be paid openly in the sight of all men on the Cross, but He does not here call express attention to it. He only claims, as of right, the response of their love, the surrender of their wills to His. The test of this surrender would be found in keeping, that is, in giving thoughtful heed to, what He calls first "His commandments", and then "His word".

He is, we must remember, not speaking to strangers, but to pupils who had been to school with Him for months, it may be for three years. His teaching had not been vague and indefinite; He had not shrunk from the clear enunciation of the spiritual principles by which life in the new order must be regulated. He had claimed, as we see from the Sermon on the Mount, authority not to supersede but to fulfil the law given on Mount Sinai. The new requirements were not less inexorable than the old, but they were directed to the regulation, in the first instance, not of outward action, but of motive. His aim had not been to substitute a new code of formal prescriptions, but to give them hints which would bring their whole lives under the government of the Spirit of Sonship, which was the law of His own life. He had been writing not on tables of stone, but on tables that were hearts of flesh.

These principles, embodied in pregnant word and significant act up to and including the washing of His disciples' feet and the new commandment, constitute the commandments to which, if we would shew our love to Him, we must give reverent attention.

We are not, however, dependent entirely for our knowledge of the will of God for us on precepts that come to us from without, whether in sacred writings or in the instructions of accredited teachers. The end of all moral education is to make men of quick understanding in the fear of the Lord, to open their ears to hear for themselves the voice that says: "This is the way, walk ye in it". This voice, which speaks in our consciences, is, as we saw in our study of the Prologue, the light which S. John tells us "lighteth every man". It is "the word for which we must find room in our hearts if we would know the truth and be made free". It is the word, to which, in the last resort, we must listen, if we would give the final proof of our love for our Lord.

THE INSPIRATION OF THE GOSPELS

25 *These things have I spoken unto you, while* yet *abiding with you.*
26 *But the Comforter*, even *the Holy Spirit, whom the Father will send in my name, he shall teach you all things, and bring to your remembrance all that I said unto you.*

The golden key to abiding communion with their risen and ascended Lord in the new order is obedience to His commandments, and reverent "listening in" to His voice as He speaks to us in our inner man. We cannot question the righteousness of the condition, however much our hearts may sink in the consciousness of our deep-seated incapacity for fulfilling it. We know ourselves to be wilful, unintelligent, and very forgetful. Our Lord knows our need better than we do. He proceeds at once to describe the provision that is at hand to meet it in the mission of the Comforter. At the back of all is the love of the Father seeking to save His lost children. He had already sent His Son to call them home in His name. Even while Jesus was still on earth the Holy Spirit had been coming forth from the Father, drawing the disciples to the Son. This drawing would be no less necessary when their Lord was taken from their sight. His mission under the new conditions would be even more effectual, because the one work of the Spirit would be to bear witness in their hearts to the ascended Lord. The years of their discipleship would not be fruitless. They had each been accumulating a rich store of experiences from the words that they had heard Him utter and the things that they had seen Him do. The love that found expression in the Cross would give the thought of Him an abiding claim upon them.

The work of the Spirit would be to keep alive their consciousness of that love. Death would be powerless to destroy, it would only consecrate and intensify, the Master's claim on their allegiance. So the Spirit, as witnessing in their hearts to the love of the Father and the Son, would be pre-eminently the Holy Spirit, working in them an ever-deepening surrender in heart and mind to the will of God. He would quicken their understanding of the treasures that were laid up for them and for their successors to the end of time in the experiences of their discipleship. In the days of His earthly ministry Jesus had been before all things their teacher. He had been striving to enable them to understand the inner secrets of life in the Kingdom of Heaven, and helping them to live in conformity with its laws. They would still need to have continual access to a spiritual "guide, philosopher and friend". The Spirit who kept them in touch with the love of their Lord would be just such a comforter for them.

As they followed His guidance from day to day, they would grow in spiritual understanding and, wonderful to relate, their new knowledge, so far from leading them to discard as childish and rudimentary the old lessons that Jesus had taught them, would only help them to realize the inexhaustible riches of the truth and the grace that came into the world through Him who had spoken them.

Surely we shall do well to ponder deeply on the mystery of this vital dependence of the life of the disciples, as they took their place in the new order, on the years of training that had preceded it. Jesus had come into a world strangely and terribly unwilling to receive Him. Yet there were some who, in spite of their manifold imperfections both in character and capacity, did answer to His call, and hang upon His lips. He was Himself the Gospel that He had come to bring. By a wonderful dispensation of providence His whole message was brought to the sharpest focus in one single act on the Cross for all the world to see. And He left His disciples behind Him to interpret that fact in the light of their experience, both before and after His death, in order that it might achieve its purpose and draw all men into His Kingdom.

It was an amazing trust to commit to a handful of unlearned and ignorant men. It must have been hard enough for them to revive their memories of the things that they had seen and heard, and to make them realize how much more those words and deeds had meant than they could perceive at the time. But they at least had the background of years of direct personal discipleship. This, however, is not all that was committed to them. They were called to be His witnesses to men who had not known Him after the flesh. And, wonderful to relate, they succeeded in leaving behind them a story of His life, which (as Erasmus says) brings Him nearer to us to-day than if we had gathered round Him with the crowds in Galilee.

Does not that fact give us solid ground for the conviction that the promise in our text was abundantly fulfilled? How could this result have come about unless that little band had, from step to step, been guided to recollect and master and shape their experiences for an end of which they can have had no comprehension? They have left behind materials by which the promise, which in the first instance had a specific bearing, and might seem to be limited to themselves alone, can be fulfilled for every believer to the end of time.

For us, also, it is abidingly true that the Holy Spirit, the

Comforter, can keep clear before our hearts and minds as a lamp to our path the words that in the first instance were addressed by Jesus to His disciples.

THE LEGACY OF PEACE

27 *Peace I leave with you; my peace I give unto you: not as the world giveth, give I unto you. Let not your heart be troubled, neither* 28 *let it be fearful. Ye heard how I said to you, I go away, and I come unto you. If ye loved me, ye would have rejoiced, because* 29 *I go unto the Father: for the Father is greater than I. And now I have told you before it come to pass, that, when it is come to pass, ye may believe.*

Jesus had completed the first stage in His revelation to His disciples of the conditions of the life in the new order which would begin with His resurrection. He comes back in 14: 27 to the present situation. The transition is a little abrupt. And, though I do not think there is much probability in the suggestion that chapters 15 and 16 follow directly after 13: 31, a case could, I think, be made out for delaying 14: 27–31 until after 16: 33.

There is a suggestion of finality about this section. The legacy of peace suggests a formal leave-taking. The Hebrew greeting (*Shalom*—Peace) was used not only at meeting, but also at parting. And the reference to peace in 16: 33 may prepare the way for a formal good-bye.

In itself the section certainly contains a formal leave-taking, and strikes again the soothing note with which chapter 14 had begun. The appeal: "Let not your heart be troubled" (in verse 1) is repeated and reinforced in verse 27. It was, in fact, implied in the parting word of blessing. This, like good-bye with us, easily becomes conventional, but was in effect a commendation to the care of God, and now contained the salve for all their woe. Peace is rooted in faith, and the sound of the familiar word must have stirred many associations. It was, in itself, a beautiful habit among the Jews that friends, on parting, should commend each other to the care of God. Jesus dwells upon the expression, and repeats it to make it clear that His use of it is not formal or mechanical. All the latent power of blessing that is stored in it stands revealed in this supreme instance of its use. The angels had greeted His birth as the advent of peace among men of good-will. All His life long He had been kept in perfect peace because His mind had been stayed on His Father. So, even though the immediate effect of His coming must be to bring, not peace into the corrupt society of the world, but rather division—and He had to warn His disciples of this—yet those that had followed with Him knew that the peace of God had had an abiding home in His heart, which no earthly storms could disturb. He would have them know therefore that His departure would only root that inner characteristic of His whole life deeper in their own being, because He was going back to that which had been its hidden source and stay.

The thought of His goal which is raised in this way, leads Him to make a final challenge to those who loved Him to forget their sense of present loss in the thought of His gain. In this connexion He adds, as the climax of His consolation, *My Father is greater than I.* These simple words have given rise to endless discussions, as if it were impossible for differences of greater and less to co-exist in the unity of the divine being. We find it very hard to realize that it is no less divine to obey than to command: that there must be Sonship in the Godhead as well as Fatherhood; a principle of subordination as well as a principle of authority. When you look into it you see that the one evidence of the truth of His claim to divine Sonship to which Jesus has appealed throughout is the completeness of His subjection to His Father's will. His claim to authority in the world rests entirely on His absolute dependence. Strength came into His own life (and I think this reference was meant to help His disciples to find strength in the hour of their need) from the recognition of the fact of the absolute sovereignty of Him who was at once His Father and our Father, His God and our God.

If so, the thought is closely connected with 10: 29. There, according to the reading of the text of the R.V., Jesus facing the prospect of the dangers that threaten His sheep, takes refuge in the thought that "My Father, which has given them to me, is greater than all."

THE LOVE OF THE CROSS

30 *I will no more speak much with you, for the prince of the world*
31 *cometh: and he hath nothing in me; but that the world may know that I love the Father, and as the Father gave me commandment, even so I do. Arise, let us go hence.*

Jesus cannot forget that the way on which His feet are set is the way of the Cross. His going on that way must carry with it, both at the time and after, a searching test of His disciples' faith. He therefore, here, as in 13: 19; 16: 4, calls express attention to His prevision. It would be a help to them to realize that, as He had told the Jews in 8: 14, He knew whence He had come and whither He was going. It should help them as much as the knowledge that His sufferings had been foretold in Holy Scripture.

He then warns them that the end of this period of His relation with them is close at hand. It would be rudely interrupted by "the prince of the world". The organized forces of human society, in a world that was estranged from God, would be left free to work their will, under the guidance of their head, on the unresisting Son of God. But in this, the prince of the world would only, as Jesus had already declared (12: 31), defeat himself (cf. Lk. 11: 51). For the armour in which Jesus was clad was proof against every attack. His faithfulness, when tried to the uttermost, would stand the strain. No inducement, and no terror, that the world could bring to bear on Him, could make Him falter in his allegiance. The Cross would be the final demonstration, before the eyes of the whole world, of the love of the Son for His Father, and of the perfection of His obedience.

These closing words are amongst the most wonderful, if not quite the most wonderful, ever uttered, and they are the key that the Saviour Himself has put into our hands to enable us to know what the Cross meant for Him. What Jesus says in this text, pointing to His Cross, is "Here, who will, may find the measure of my love". But He is thinking and speaking, we must notice, not now of His love for His friends, though He was laying down His life for them, but of His love for His Father. "Let the world take note that I love the Father and, as the Father gave me commandment, so I do".

We have, surely, (I can, at least, speak for myself) been singularly deaf to the message of these words. It is, if I mistake not, the one passage in which Jesus speaks of His own love to the Father. He speaks again and again of His Father's love for Him. Had not the voice at the Jordan given Him the right to do that?

"The Father loveth the Son and sheweth him all things that himself doeth". "For this cause doth the Father love me (here the reference to the voice is surely explicit), because I lay down my life, that I may take it again."

"If ye keep my commandments, ye shall abide in my love; even as I have kept my Father's commandments and abide in His love." And, lastly, "That the world may know that Thou lovedst them even as Thou lovedst Me"; and "I made known to them Thy name, and will make it known, that the love, wherewith Thou lovedst me, may be in them, and I in them".

He does not shrink from calling attention to His Father's love for Him. But, as I said, here only does He speak of His own love for the Father. If it were not for this, we might have been content to think of the Cross as the supreme test of obedience. It was that, of course. The garden of Gethsemane is the abiding witness of what it cost Him to take away sin by the offering of Himself, as He took up the rôle laid upon Him by the Psalmist and said "I come to do Thy will". The task was not a self-chosen one, and the sacrifice that was demanded of Him was a real sacrifice. His obedience, as He claims in this verse, was a proof of His love. But deeper than the dutiful devotion was the love that inspired it. This included, no doubt, unfathomable love for us in our misery and sin, whom He died to redeem. But deeper even than His love for His brethren was His love for the Father. The supreme attraction of the Cross—may we not say the joy that it set before Him—lay in the opportunity that it gave Him of shewing forth before the world all that there was in His heart towards His Father.

CHAPTER XIX

THE CHURCH AND ITS HEAD

1 *I am the true vine, and my Father is the husbandman. Every branch*
2 *in me that beareth not fruit, he taketh it away: and every* branch *that beareth fruit, he cleanseth it, that it may bear more fruit.*
3 *Already ye are clean because of the word which I have spoken unto*
4 *you. Abide in me, and I in you. As the branch cannot bear fruit of itself, except it abide in the vine; so neither can ye, except ye*
5 *abide in me. I am the vine, ye are the branches: He that abideth in me, and I in him, the same beareth much fruit: for apart from*
6 *me ye can do nothing. If a man abide not in me, he is cast forth as a branch, and is withered; and they gather them, and cast them*
7 *into the fire, and they are burned. If ye abide in me, and my words abide in you, ask whatsoever ye will, and it shall be done unto*
8 *you. Herein is my Father glorified, that ye bear much fruit; and*
9 *so shall ye be my disciples. Even as the Father hath loved me,*
10 *I also have loved you: abide ye in my love. If ye keep my commandments, ye shall abide in my love; even as I have kept my*
11 *Father's commandments, and abide in His love. These things have I spoken unto you, that my joy may be in you, and* that *your*
12 *joy may be fulfilled. This is my commandment, that ye love one*
13 *another, even as I have loved you. Greater love hath no man than*
14 *this, that a man lay down his life for his friends. Ye are my friends,*
15 *if ye do the things which I command you. No longer do I call you servants; for the servant knoweth not what his lord doeth: but I have called you friends; for all things that I heard from my*
16 *Father I have made known unto you. Ye did not choose me, but I chose you, and appointed you, that ye should go and bear fruit, and* that *your fruit should abide: that whatsoever ye shall ask of the*
17 *Father in my name, he may give it you. These things I command you, that ye may love one another.*

A BREAK of some sort is indicated in the closing words of Jn. 14: "Arise, let us go hence". The words suggest a change of scene and the discourse takes a new turn. If, as

I have already suggested, on leaving the Upper Chamber they paid a last visit to the Temple, the similitude of the Vine might have been suggested by the great golden vine that was figured on the gates. In any case the suggestion reminds us that in this similitude we find ourselves on Old Testament ground. The golden vine bore witness to the fact that both prophet (Is. 5) and psalmist (80: 8) had used the vine as a type of God's people. Earlier in the week Jesus Himself in the same Temple Courts had based the parable of the Vineyard and the Husbandmen upon it. Then, however, He appeared as the heir of the vineyard. Now He claims to be the eternal reality of which the prophet and the psalmist had had an intimation in their visions of Israel, and of which the vines in our vineyards and greenhouses are the material and transitory symbols.

The mind of Jesus is full of His disciples and the new stage in the relationship between Him and them which is at hand. When He was out of sight their eyes would be opened to the true nature of the tie by which He and they were bound into one, and it was important that they should be taught the conditions that they had to fulfil in order that the union might be fruitful. The similitude of the true vine expresses the deeply mysterious fact that the union between the disciples and their Lord was living and organic.

It is the same fact to which S. Paul calls attention when he speaks of the Church as "the body of Christ". His own experience on the road to Damascus must have opened his eyes to the fact that Jesus, even in His glory, was in living touch with His suffering members. Indeed, it taught him further that Jesus was not far even from His bitterest persecutor. He knew the inmost thoughts of his heart; He was only waiting for his consenting will to enter in and take up His abode in him. It was, perhaps easier for one who had not known Jesus in the days of His flesh to grasp in its fulness the fact of this personal indwelling. In any case he clearly verified in his own experience the truth of the relationship to which Jesus gave expression under the similitude of the True Vine, and shewed that this vital relationship was not to be the peculiar privilege of the first circle of disciples.

The relationship, as I have said, was vital and organic. Because it was intensely real, it could not take effect mechanically. It was, before all things, spiritual, and depended for its effectiveness on the co-operation of both the human and the divine elements embodied in it. Behind all is the Father. He is represented here, not as an absentee landlord, but as Himself watching continually over the growth of His vine, cleansing and pruning it.

Each believer is a branch, rooted directly in the stem of the vine, depending for power to bear fruit entirely on the sap supplied by the parent tree. The Lord Himself is the vine—His personality is the source of the life of the whole organism. And yet He is content to be dependent for fruitfulness, i.e. for the manifestation of His power in the world, on the loyal co-operation of His disciples.

This co-operation implies a mutual indwelling. The disciple who had heard His Master's call and followed Him must keep his ears continually open, listening for His voice. That is what "to abide in Him" meant to the disciples. At the same time the words of the Lord, both those which He had spoken in their hearing while He was upon earth, and those that would express His will in the heart and conscience of each individual disciple as he lived looking up to Him for guidance, would bring the Lord Himself into their hearts. That is His side of the abiding.

As a result, the disciple would be lifted up into conscious communion with the Father and the Son. He would possess the secret of prevailing prayer, for Father and Son alike have a direct interest in all that he does. The glory of the Father is made or marred by the faithfulness of the disciple. The wonder and the weight of this responsibility is saved from becoming intolerable by the thought that Jesus had borne it first in their sight, being sustained throughout in His life of unwavering obedience by the consciousness of His Father's love. What His Father's love had been to Him, that His love would be to them.

At this stage a fresh characteristic of the new life comes into sight. The work that they were to share with Him in bringing forth fruit to the glory of the Father would introduce them to His joy, filling them to the full with the joy for which they were created.

The road to this joy is through mutual love in obedience to the new commandment, even to the extent of the laying down of life by friend for friend. So we are brought back for the last time in our Lord's teaching to the fact of the Cross. He had declared earlier, when speaking of Himself as the Good Shepherd, that He would lay down His life for the sheep. Here there is no veil to hide the human relationship. He speaks as friend to friend. He does not, however, speak directly of His own sacrifice. He leaves that to be inferred. When it came, it would help His disciples to understand, as nothing else could, the full extent of the claim that the new commandment made on them, and at the same time give them the power to fulfil it (cf. 1 Jn. 3: 17 f.).

Meanwhile He would have them realize that He was using the great title "Friend" advisedly to express His relation to them. From one point of view, and for a limited period, the relation had been one of strict subordination. At the beginning of the supper He had had to require Simon Peter to accept a humbling service at His hands in blind obedience, though with a promise of fuller understanding hereafter. Here, however, He would have them know that as they responded obediently to the claims of His love, they would find that He was treating them with all the generous confidence of a friend, and had kept nothing back of His Father's message from them.

Even so, they might shrink from the apparent presumption of claiming so high and exacting a relationship to their Lord, so He reminds them that that relationship rested not on their choice, but on His. (Here again, notice that one of His own titles as "the servant of the Lord" was "the Chosen" (Lk. 23: 35).) He reminds them at the same time that the object of this distinction was not their personal aggrandisement. It gave them no ground for despising their less-fortunate neighbours. They had been chosen to bring forth fruit for the service of God and man.

As branches of the true vine, bearing fruit—not of themselves, but of their Lord—to the glory of God, they bore their Lord's name before the world; and so, for the third time, comes the revelation of the secret of prevailing prayer.

Let them face the responsibilities of their position, as in the sight of God, and the Father would give them all that they asked as the representatives of His Son.

Such in outline is the revelation that Jesus gave under the similitude of the True Vine of the organic relation in which He and His disciples stand to one another. It will not waste time to review the practical consequences that follow from that relationship.

The first is the vital importance of keeping open all the channels by which the sap from the tree flows into the branch. This is the ground of the command to the disciple to abide in, that is, to remain in conscious contact with, his Lord. The normal result of this abiding is fruit-bearing. The fruit is primarily a Christ-like life, which, manifesting the Spirit of Christ in word and deed, would lift men's hearts up to the Father, and thereby draw them into His Kingdom.

This abiding is, on the one hand, based on the divine action in constituting the relationship, and, on the other, on the depth and sincerity of our response to that action.

Jesus traces the root of the relationship back into the heart of His Father, whose love for Him He had passed on to His disciples by loving them. They had nothing to do to create that love. All they had to do was to respond to it by living their lives in obedience to His commandments, and guided by His example. For He had Himself shewn by His obedience His own response to His Father's love.

In verse 11, as we saw, a new note is struck. Jesus has again and again been speaking of His love. In 14: 27 He solemnly bequeathed to them His peace. There is a third element, lacking which our vision of life would be robbed of its most winning characteristic. This is joy. This is, no doubt, a strange context in which to begin to speak of His joy. His outward circumstances on the night of His betrayal were as far from joy as they were from peace. And yet, just as nothing could trouble the peace of the heart that trusted in God, so the malice and the bitterness of men could not dim the brightness that sprang from conscious communion with His Father. He therefore calls special attention to joy as a characteristic mark of the life of Christian discipleship.

He is content here with simply calling attention to this element in His experience, and suggesting that by obedience to His commandments they might become conscious of what He was feeling, and that their own beings might be filled to overflowing with joy from His. He goes on to speak of the sacrifice that love demands. But though, no doubt, there is an intimate connexion between joy and sacrifice, He does not call attention to it. He has not, however, exhausted the subject. He returns to it in the next chapter (16: 22 ff.) and once more in His high-priestly prayer (17: 13).

In so doing He was clearly looking far beyond the time then present. His words suggest that in letting us into the secret of His vision of the goal which He, while still with us, was praying that we might attain, He was helping us to understand what would be the subject of His perpetual intercession on our behalf, when He was seated as a priest on His throne at His Father's right hand. He is telling us what is the fruit of the travail of His soul for which He was looking forward. God had promised that He should see it and be satisfied. As His disciples entered into His purpose, and, supported by His prayers, took their part in working for its fulfilment, they too would share His satisfaction.

The experience through which He and they were soon to pass would give them a fresh vision of the measure of the love that the new commandment would require of them. His words imply, though they do not directly state, that on the Cross He would be laying down His life as the expression of His love for those He called His friends. We need not be afraid that by using this language He was narrowing the scope of the Atonement. While we were yet sinners, Christ died for all. He promised that when lifted up He would draw all men to Himself. What He declares is that there was that in every man to which His heart went out, and for the sake of which He was willing to die. Those to whom He was speaking would know what He meant, for they had already responded to His appeal. The time was at hand when they would realize that He was inviting them to a relation of closer intimacy than they had hitherto enjoyed.

They had been His disciples, even His bondsmen, calling Him Teacher and Lord, accepting His teaching and obeying His behests, because they were His, even though as yet they could not fully understand them. From henceforth they might enter into the inmost secrets of His mind and will.

As obedient disciples of a risen and ascended Lord they would become members of His privy council, stewards of His mysteries, as the Psalmist had realized (Ps. 25: 14, R.V. mg.). "The friendship of the Lord is with them that fear Him and His covenant to make them know it". So Jesus says here, *Ye are my friends, if ye do what I am from moment to moment commanding you. No longer do I call you bondsmen, for the bondsman knoweth not what his Lord is doing; but I have called you friends* (cf. 1 Macc. 10: 65, etc.), *for all that I hear from My Father I make known unto you.*

He had told His disciples earlier that the privilege of reading the riddle of the Kingdom (Mk. 4: 11) had been given them. On one occasion, in Lk. 12: 4, in close connexion with their responsibility for proclaiming secrets, He had called them friends. The use of the title here is meant to help them to realize that the door would be open in the days to come for an ever clearer apprehension of His mind and will.

He will have more to say about that later (16: 12 f.), when He is explaining the mission of the Comforter. Meanwhile the relationship itself, it was important for them to remember, was based on an individual and personal act of His. It was rooted in the act by which the Twelve had, at an earlier crisis in the ministry, been marked out from the rest of our Lord's followers for special training (Mk. 3: 13 f., Ac. 1: 2).

The Lord seems to have feared that the distinction might minister to spiritual pride. In any case, here (as in 6: 70 and 13: 18) He expressly claims responsibility for the appointment. It was due to an act of His sovereign will. This is not, of course, in the least inconsistent with His conviction that they had been given Him by His Father (Jn. 17: 6). What He wishes to exclude is the assumption that they could take credit to themselves for their response to His choosing, and forget that they had been set apart, not for self-glorification, but for service: "Ye did not choose me, but I chose you, that you should pursue your appointed and independent path through the world, and bear fruit; and that your fruit should abide, that whatsoever ye ask the Father in my name He may give it you".

In saying this He repeats and gives fresh definiteness to their original commission, bringing it into direct relation to the obligation of fruit-bearing which was rooted in their relation to Him as the vine. And He shews that the fruit would not be a merely temporary manifestation of His likeness in the world. It was meant to have abiding consequences, transforming the lives of those who witnessed it, and thereby extending His Kingdom over the hearts of men. It is not surprising, therefore, that the thought of their responsibility for bearing His name before men should bring with it a fresh sense of their dependence on the Father, and an assurance of an abundant answer to every prayer addressed to Him for the fulfilment of their work as the accredited representatives of His Son.

CHAPTER XX

THE CHURCH AND THE WORLD

18 *If the world hateth you, ye know that it hath hated me before* it
19 hated *you. If ye were of the world, the world would love its own: but because ye are not of the world, but I chose you out of the world,*
20 *therefore the world hateth you. Remember the word that I said unto you, A servant is not greater than his lord. If they persecuted me, they will also persecute you; if they kept my word, they will*
21 *keep yours also. But all these things will they do unto you for*
22 *my name's sake, because they know not him that sent me. If I had not come and spoken unto them, they had not had sin: but*
23 *now they have no excuse for their sin. He that hateth me hateth*
24 *my Father also. If I had not done among them the works which none other did, they had not had sin: but now have they both seen*
25 *and hated both me and my Father. But* this cometh to pass, *that the word may be fulfilled that is written in their law, They*
26 *hated me without a cause. But when the Comforter is come, whom I will send unto you from the Father,* even *the Spirit of truth, which proceedeth from the Father, he shall bear witness of me:*
27 *and ye also bear witness, because ye have been with me from the beginning.*

IT was strange, but it was true, that the world to which they were commissioned to bear the glad tidings of God's love, would meet them with bitter opposition. But that, He would have them remember, was the reception men had given Him. *If the world hates you, you know that it has hated me, your Chief. If ye had been of the world, drawing your inspiration from it, the world would be friends with its own. But because you are not of the world, but I chose you out of the world, for this cause the world hates you.*

This ought not, really, to come on them as a surprise. In the Sermon on the Mount (Mt. 5: 12 f.) He had warned them that they must be persecuted for His sake. When He had given instructions to the Twelve, He had expressly said "A disciple is not greater than his teacher, nor a servant than his lord. It is enough for the disciple to be as his teacher, and the servant as his lord. If they call the master of the house Beelzebul, how much more the members of his household". (Mt. 10: 25.)

So He recalls this former teaching to their remembrance, adding: *If they persecuted me, they will also persecute you.* And, that they might feel that the prospect was not altogether dark, *If they kept my word, they will keep yours also.*

He passes on to give the ground of this antagonism. It is not due to any imperfection in the disciple. It is the direct consequence of his faithfulness to his commission. *All these things will they do unto you for my name's sake, just because they see a likeness to me in you.* And this, in its turn, is due to their ignorance of the Father *because they know not Him that sent Me.*

This leads to a final judgement on the guilt of the world as measured by the light that He had brought into it, both by His words and His works. "If I had not come and spoken to them, they would not have had sin". It would not have been possible to assert beyond the possibility of contradiction that their rebellion against God was the result of their own act and choice, unless this clear revelation had been given them. But, as it is, the evidence of their guilt is irrefragable. *If I had not done among them the works that none other man did, they would not have had sin. But now they have both seen and hated both Me and my Father.*

This is a tremendous sentence. And when we stand face to face with the Cross, we admit its justice. There was no flaw in the presentation of the appeal of His love. Our rejection of that appeal was absolute and inexcusable. Granted that, in the fullest sense, none of those who slew Him were fully aware of what they were doing, yet they were themselves to blame for their ignorance. But the wonder is that on the Cross, Jesus Himself, in the perfection of His forgiveness, pleads their ignorance in extenuation: "Father, forgive them, for they know not what they do". Here, however, for the sake of those who had to suffer as He suffered, He stated the bare fact, that they might not reproach themselves for their failure, and shewed by a quotation from the Psalms that the experience of gratuitous hate was one through which the servants of God must expect to pass. While our hearts are set on going on our own way, we cannot but hate, and do what we can to extinguish, the light that condemns us.

There was, however, another side to the picture. He had already spoken to them of the mission of the Comforter, who, though invisible, would supply the support that companionship with Him in the days of His flesh had given them. His special function would be to keep alive the memory and to deepen the understanding of the lessons that their Master had taught them, and so keep His disciples and Him in living touch with one another.

The world, He had told them, could not directly apprehend the presence of this Comforter. He could find no resting place among men except in surrendered hearts. But Jesus promises that the Comforter would, in due course, Himself take up His abode in them, linking them both to their Lord and to the Father; and, in and through them, witness to Him before the world. With such a champion on their side they need not fear the opposition of the world. Their one care should be to be faithful to the witness for which their years of discipleship had been a preparation.

THE MISSION OF THE COMFORTER

1 *These things have I spoken unto you, that ye should not be made*
2 *to stumble. They shall put you out of the synagogues: yea, the hour cometh, that whosoever killeth you shall think that he offereth*
3 *service unto God. And these things will they do, because they*
4 *have not known the Father, nor me. But these things have I spoken unto you, that when their hour is come, ye may remember them, how that I told you. And these things I said not unto you*
5 *from the beginning, because I was with you. But now I go unto him that sent me; and none of you asketh me, Whither goest thou?*

6 *But because I have spoken these things unto you, sorrow hath*
7 *filled your heart. Nevertheless I tell you the truth; It is expedient for you that I go away: for if I go not away, the Comforter will*
8 *not come unto you; but if I go, I will send him unto you. And he, when he is come, will convict the world in respect of sin, and*
9 *of righteousness, and of judgement: of sin, because they believe*
10 *not on me; of righteousness, because I go to the Father, and ye*
11 *behold me no more; of judgement, because the prince of this world*
12 *hath been judged. I have yet many things to say unto you, but ye cannot bear them now.*

The thought of the opposition in store for them from the world gives occasion to further teaching with regard to this promised Comforter. Though the world could not directly apprehend His presence, He would have a very definite function to discharge in relation to it. His presence in the heart of any man, and *a fortiori* in a body of men, would bring every man within the reach of One who, whether men knew Him or not, was their true Lord and God and King. The members of the Church, therefore, which was commissioned to bear the name of Christ before the world, would not be left to bear their witness alone. The Comforter would be sent to them to keep them in living touch with their Head, and to enable them to manifest His presence.

This promise was no guarantee of immunity from suffering. In the Christian vocabulary *martyr* and *witness* would soon become convertible terms. Jesus, therefore, explains that the hatred which He had told them to expect would take the form of excommunication, and even death for blasphemy, at the hands of men who, in spite of their religious zeal, failed to recognize the Father as manifested in His Son. The memory of this warning would be a help to them when the supreme trial came, even though He was no longer in flesh by their side.

Thought has now come back to the crisis of His departure, which was immediately pressing. He has already (14: 28) tried to cheer them by the thought of what the approaching change would mean to Him, because He is going to the Father. He has now to assure them that His going away will be better not for Himself only, but for them. He prefaces the assurance with a criticism: *None of you asketh me, Whither goest Thou? But because I have said these things unto you, sorrow hath filled your heart.*

There is, no doubt, a verbal inconsistency between this verse and 13: 36. There Simon Peter had met the warning that Jesus was going out of the reach of His disciples with the question: "Whither goest Thou?" But in asking that question, as we have already seen, he was thinking not of the goal of his Lord's journeying, but of the distance that would separate him from His Lord. Since that first warning Jesus had, in various ways, been shewing that, even though out of sight, He would not be out of touch with His disciples. But it had not begun to dawn on them that the results of the departure, when it was seen to be simply the fulfilment of His commission, might include compensations which would more than counterbalance their immediate loss. They were not interested in the thought of what His departure would mean to Him. So He goes on: *Howbeit, I tell you the truth, it is better for you that I should go away, for if I go not away the Comforter will not come unto you, but when I have finished my journey I will send Him unto you.*

It is not easy to remember that the necessity for this departure did not lie simply in the general fact that the visible presence had to be withdrawn to make room for the invisible. There was a special ground. The Spirit could not be given till Jesus was glorified (7: 39). And He could only enter on His glory by the way of the Cross. The power to baptize with the Spirit was, no doubt, a great part of the joy that was set before Him, and gave Him strength to endure.

He passes on to make it clear that the object of the mission of the Comforter was not limited to the consolation and strengthening of the faithful, and increasing the condemnation of the unbelieving. When He comes He will convict the world of sin, and righteousness, and judgement. We must be careful not to miss the force of this promise. We are apt to think of the gift of the Spirit, which is the other side of the coming of the Kingdom, as a divine act in which nothing depends on our personal initiative. We forget that God's gifts never pauperize. We forget that we must put out all our strength in asking for and in appropriating the Spirit, which He is all the time freely bestowing. We fail to realize that it is only as we do that, that the Spirit can come and fulfil His mission in the world. Look, for instance, at His work in convicting the world of sin. This conviction springs from a vision of the claim of Christ on the life of every man. There is only one way by which men can be brought under the power of this vision. They must be confronted with the witness of men and women who have been born again of the Spirit, and who shew by their lives the transforming power of faith in Jesus Christ. That witness calls the attention of the man in the street to the presence in the world of a new power, and I do not think that in the last resort anything else can.

Again, the power to bear this witness provides an acid test by which the man in the pew or in the pulpit can try the completeness of his own surrender.

It is not, however, enough simply to convince a man that his life is on the wrong lines unless he is believing in Christ. He must be helped effectively to get on to the right lines, and to continue in them. So we are taught that the conviction of sin will pass on into an assurance of righteousness (that is, into a life of peace and power with God, in communion with the risen and ascended Lord) and of victory over all the forces of evil within us and without, because the prince of the world has been judged and cast out by the death of Jesus on the Cross.

THE GRADUAL APPREHENSION OF THE TRUTH

13 *Howbeit when he, the Spirit of truth, is come, he shall guide you into all truth: for he shall not speak from himself; but what things* 14 *soever he shall hear,* these *shall he speak: and he shall declare unto you the things that are to come. He shall glorify me: for* 15 *he shall take of mine, and shall declare* it *unto you. All things whatsoever the Father hath are mine: therefore said I, that he taketh of mine, and shall declare* it *unto you.*

Jesus had assured His disciples that the Comforter would be with them to enable them to bear effective witness to their Lord before the world by revealing to men the new quality of life that faith in Him was able to inspire. This, however, was only one side of the work of the Comforter. It was not only loyalty that the disciples would need as they went out to win the world for God. It is astounding, when we look back, to mark how utterly immature in mind, even more than in character, that little band of His disciples was when the visible presence of their Master was withdrawn from them. No wonder that He should shew that He was conscious both of their ignorance and of their present incapacity. But He does it to remind them that the Comforter, as the Spirit of the truth, would carry on the work of their education.

He had already told them that the Holy Spirit, when He came to enable them to realize that their Lord was Himself still in living touch with them, would work on the foundation of the lessons that they had already learnt from Him, quickening their memory and enlightening their understanding of what He had said. They must not, however, think that they had nothing to do but to brood over the treasures of the past. The Holy Spirit would carry on the work of their education from the point to which Jesus had brought them, until at length the whole truth had been unveiled.

It is an exceeding great and precious promise. We must be careful, however, not to overstress it. It is a promise of continual guidance by an infallible guide, with an assurance that in the end the whole Church shall grasp and embody the whole truth: but it gives no warrant for claiming that any particular conclusion at which the whole Church or any part of it may at any time have arrived is in itself infallible, or that the terms in which it was expressed must be held to be immune from criticism.

Our creed has to verify itself in every age by its power to meet the fresh problems by which, in the providence of God, we find ourselves confronted. The things in our heaven, no less than the things on earth, have sometimes to be shaken terribly, in order that the things that can stand the shaking may endure.

This does not, however, mean that there is nothing that we can take for granted. The Church was, from the first, built on faith in Jesus as the Christ, the Son of God. And "other foundation can no man lay than that which is laid". The Spirit of the truth does not come in His own name to bear witness of Himself. As the Son came not in His own name, but in His Father's, and did not speak "from Himself", even so the Spirit will only hand on the messages that He has Himself received. His task will be to enable us to see the hand and purpose of God in the circumstances in which we find ourselves. As all authority in heaven and on earth is committed to the Son, this will involve a progressive revelation of the unsearchable riches of Christ, a fuller and clearer understanding of all that was implied in the faith once delivered to the saints. So Jesus said: *He shall glorify me, for He shall take of mine and shall show it unto you. All that the Father hath is mine. Therefore I said that He shall take of mine and shall show it unto you.*

These words conclude our Lord's teaching with regard to that provision for the needs of His disciples to the end of time which would be included in the mission of the Comforter. He would constitute a living and personal link between them and their Lord, which would enable them to bring effective converting influence to bear on the world. This must always remain a primary part of their duty, though from time to time the immediate sense of its necessity may be dimmed, because the whole society in which the Church is set to work has been won over at least to an outward profession of loyalty to Christ. Such situations, when they arise, are full of danger; for our hold on the truth depends for its vitality on the efforts that we are making to share it with others. And a Church that is not missionary-hearted soon becomes formal and self-satisfied. In that case, as we see from the Letters to the Seven Churches, the Spirit has to make His voice heard in calling even Christian Churches to repent, with results that have from time to time proved fatal to the visible unity of Christendom.

There is, of course, always a danger in a spiritual movement. We can never escape the responsibility of testing the spirits. But as F. D. Maurice points out in his *Sermons on the Gospel of S. John*, our Lord here gives us a sure touchstone. The Holy Spirit does not speak of Himself. "He speaks whatsoever things He hears: He brings us the message of a Father from whom He comes. He will not make us impatient of a Lord and Ruler, but desirous of one, eager to give up ourselves to His guidance, eager to get rid of our own fancies and conceits, and to enter into fellowship with all men. He will not allow us to be satisfied with our advanced knowledge or great discoveries, but will always be shewing us things that *are coming*; giving us an apprehension of truths that we have not yet reached, though they be truths which are 'the same yesterday, and to-day and for ever'. That may not be the whole meaning of the words 'things to come'; the phrase may intimate that foresight which is given to those who study principles, meditating on the past, and believing in God. The Spirit which our Lord promises is assuredly the Spirit who spoke by the prophets of old and has spoken by all His servants who have humbled themselves, and sought light and wisdom from above. But these two senses do not contradict each other; and the first is, I think, more directly suggested by the context. It may also imply that the Spirit who does not speak of Himself, leads men away from that incessant poring over the operations and experiences of their inner life, which is unhealthy and morbid, to dwell upon the events which are continually unfolding themselves in God's world under His providence, and teaches them to expect the final issue of those events in the complete manifestation and triumph of the Son of God".

CHAPTER XXI

THE SORROW AND THE JOY OF THE DISCIPLES

16 *A little while, and ye behold me no more; and again a little while,*
17 *and ye shall see me.* Some *of his disciples therefore said one to another, What is this that he saith unto us, A little while, and ye behold me not; and again a little while, and ye shall see me: and,*
18 *Because I go to the Father? They said therefore, What is this*
19 *that he saith, A little while? We know not what he saith. Jesus perceived that they were desirous to ask him, and he said unto them, Do ye inquire among yourselves concerning this, that I said, A little while, and ye behold me not, and again a little while, and*
20 *ye shall see me? Verily, verily, I say unto you, that ye shall weep and lament, but the world shall rejoice: ye shall be sorrowful, but*
21 *your sorrow shall be turned to joy. A woman when she is in travail hath sorrow, because her hour is come: but when she is delivered of the child, she remembereth no more the anguish, for the joy*
22 *that a man is born into the world. And ye therefore now have sorrow: but I will see you again, and your heart shall rejoice, and your joy no one taketh away from you.*

JESUS has to come back from the prospect of the future to the hard fact of the present. *A little while*, He goes on, *and ye behold me no more; and again a little while and ye shall see me.* The change in this verse from *behold* to *see* is clearly significant. It seems, as Maurice says, to suggest that a time was at hand "when they would lose all perception of Him, even an intellectual perception"—when He should seem to have disappeared utterly and for ever. But this would be followed by a time when they should see Him with the eyes of the body as well as of the mind.

The disciples are growingly conscious of a terrible import in this repeated warning of a coming separation. And the accompanying assurance, which had recurred again and again since 14: 6, that the goal of His departing was the Father, only increased their perplexity. But they did not speak to Him of it. If the company had broken up from the supper table and were now clustered round the Lord, as He stood in the Temple Courts, it would be easier for them to share among themselves a trouble which they were too shy to refer directly to Him. Jesus, however, was aware of it, and sets Himself to deal with it.

The heart of the difficulty did not really lie in the length of the interval covered by "the little while". It lay in the nature of the experience that was ahead of them. The key to His meaning could in the last resort only be found in the event. Meanwhile He gave them yet one more parable by which they could interpret the experience when it came. "*Verily, verily I say unto you, that ye shall weep and lament, but the world shall rejoice; ye shall be sorrowful, but your sorrow shall be turned into joy. A woman when she is in travail hath sorrow because her hour is come: but when she is delivered of the child, she remembereth no more the anguish, for the joy that a man is born into the world. And ye therefore now have sorrow: but I will see you again, and your heart shall rejoice, and your joy no one taketh away from you*".

There is nothing here to indicate the date or the duration of the contrasted experiences. Attention is concentrated on their nature. The important thing was that those to whom they came should recognize their true character. In the first experience, the misery of the disciples at the loss of their Master would be in marked contrast with the exultation of the hostile world, because they had cast out their tormentor. But He gave them an assurance that their sufferings would be fruitful. They would be bearing their share in the travail pangs that, as was generally understood, were to introduce the Messianic age. The new order would spring out of those sufferings. The New Man should be born into the world.

We can, of course, appreciate the fact that to see their Master die must have caused untold anguish to all that loved

Him. It was not only through the heart of His blessed Mother that the sword passed on Calvary. What we generally overlook is our Lord's assurance that that suffering, because it was rooted in their love to Him, had something of its own to contribute to the ultimate triumph, even though at the moment it must have seemed utterly impotent and barren. S. Paul can hardly have been familiar with this tradition. But the truth to which it testifies may well have been the source of his conviction that there is something which we can all contribute towards "filling up that which is lacking in the sufferings of Christ" (Col. 1 : 24).

His thought in Rom. 8: 18–23, which implies a solidarity between our sufferings and the sufferings of all creation, and declares that all alike have the character of travail pangs, is closely akin. As James Hinton saw and expressed in a most suggestive essay on *The Mystery of Pain*, there is here an assurance of an ultimate solution of that terrible mystery. It is only the apparently meaningless and fruitless sufferings that are intolerable. The whole character of suffering is transformed when we can believe that none of it is forgotten before God.

This first experience was essentially transitory. As the psalmist said, "Sorrow may endure for a night, joy comes to abide with us in the morning". So Jesus goes on, after assuring them that their suffering had a meaning—"Ye *therefore* now have sorrow"—to promise that the broken communion between Him and them would be soon restored. In so doing He makes a significant change in the words that describe the restored relationship. He had said: "In a little while ye shall see me." They would have ocular evidence of His triumph over death. But in that form the experience would be transitory. The restored communion did not depend on the evidence of their bodily senses. It came from the conviction that He was alive for evermore, and that wherever they were His eye was still watching over them. So, instead of saying "ye shall see me", He says "I shall see you".

It is not surprising that a joy with this foundation should be proof against all the forces within or without that might endeavour to rob them of it.

OUR COMMUNION IS WITH THE FATHER AND HIS SON

23 *And in that day ye shall ask me nothing. Verily, verily, I say unto you, If ye shall ask anything of the Father, he will give it*
24 *you in my name. Hitherto have ye asked nothing in my name: ask, and ye shall receive, that your joy may be fulfilled.*
25 *These things have I spoken unto you in proverbs: the hour cometh, when I shall no more speak unto you in proverbs, but shall tell*
26 *you plainly of the Father. In that day ye shall ask in my name:*
27 *and I say not unto you, that I will pray the Father for you; for the Father himself loveth you, because ye have loved me, and have*
28 *believed that I came forth from the Father. I came out from the Father, and am come into the world: again, I leave the world,*
29 *and go unto the Father. His disciples say, Lo, now speakest*
30 *thou plainly, and speakest no proverb. Now know we that thou knowest all things, and needest not that any man shall ask thee:*
31 *by this we believe that thou camest forth from God. Jesus answered*
32 *them, Do ye now believe? Behold, the hour cometh, yea, is come, that ye shall be scattered, every man to his own, and shall leave me alone: and* yet *I am not alone, because the Father is with me.*
33 *These things have I spoken unto you, that in me ye may have peace. In the world ye have tribulation: but be of good cheer; I have overcome the world.*

The bliss of the new relationship has its roots in a yet deeper relationship, which had been the secret of His own joy all the time that He had been with them, and into which, indeed, He had come into the world to introduce them. He had told them that He was going to the Father to prepare a place for them. When He came again to take them to Himself that they might be with Him where He is, a door of communion would be opened, which would give them also direct access to the Father. Light on this new relationship is the culminating point in this "tender last farewell."

"In that day," He says, "when the new order has begun to dawn and you begin to enter on your heavenly citizenship, our relations to one another will be on a new footing.

Hitherto, and most notably during this last evening that we have spent together, you have consulted me in all your perplexities. But in that day ye shall ask me no questions". He does not tell them exactly what that implies. It must mean that in some way the period of doubt and perplexity would be over. And in any case they would know that He knew their necessities before they put them into words.

This did not mean that they would have outgrown the need of prayer. It meant that prayer itself would take on a new character. He had already, at two points in their talk, spoken of a new power which would come into their prayer-life from the realization of the relation in which they stood to Him as bearers of His name before the world. In 14: 13 f. He had promised to do anything for them that they felt to be necessary to enable them to bear their witness. In 15: 16 He had told them that one end of His choice of them was to give them confidence in drawing near to the Father in His name. Now He picks up that thought again. The name which they would bear had a repercussion, not only on their relation to men, but also on their relation to God. It was not only the honour of the Son that was at stake in the fruit that they were bearing. The Father Himself had an interest in it. And still more, Jesus would have them think that He would have an interest in them on account of the name they bore. So He goes on: *Verily, verily, I say unto you, if you ask the Father for anything He will give it you in My name. Hitherto you have asked for nothing in My name; ask and ye shall receive, that your cup of joy may be filled to the full.*

He had led them, little by little, to realize that the agony through which they were shortly to pass with Him, would, when it had issued in restored communion with Him on the further side of death, bring them into a new relation of intimacy with Himself. He now gives them to understand that as they found themselves drawn closer to Him in the bonds of loving obedience (15: 11), this experience would bring them into living touch with Him, who is their Father as well as His, and in whose presence they would find a fulness of joy which no trials through which they might have to pass could dim.

Here at last He had spoken out all His heart to them. His utterance was hampered by the imperfection that belongs to any attempt to convey spiritual truth in matter-moulded forms of speech. He had spoken in parables. But He gives them reason to hope that, in the new order, this limitation will be transcended. He and they will meet face to face, heart to heart, and they will grasp His meaning no longer "through a mirror in a riddle" (1 Cor. 13: 12). He will bring them messages straight from the Father.

In that day direct communion will be established between them and the Father, by virtue of the completeness of their identification with Himself as they draw near to make their petitions boldly in His name. The use of the name will remain, indeed, an abiding condition for effectual access, but it will be no real check on their freedom. They can only find themselves as they are content to lose themselves in Him. And He would have them realize that this condition, which is made necessary by our natural tendency to self-assertion, is not due to any reluctance on the part of the Father which could only be removed by His intervention. *I say not*, He says, *that I will make request to the Father for you* as if that were necessary to win His favour for you. *For the Father Himself loves you.* He has admitted you by His own choice into the intimate circle of His friends, *because you have been friends with Me, and have believed that I came forth from Him.*

This, of course, does not in any sense conflict with the truth of His perpetual intercession on our behalf. He has already said expressly that He will make request to the Father (14: 16), and that He will give us another Comforter. He is only guarding us against a misunderstanding with regard to the nature and ground of that intercession into which we are terribly prone to fall. When we ask a friend to intercede for us in our ordinary affairs, we do it because we think that he cares more for us than the man in power to whom we ask him to appeal. Christ is here assuring us that the Father needs no persuading to take an interest in us. The mission of the Son into the world had its source and spring in the love of the Father. The fact that the disciples had loved and trusted Him whom He had sent, was a direct link between them and the Father who had sent Him. So the whole message of the Incarnation is summed up in this final statement of its source and goal: *I came forth from the Father and have come into the world. Again I leave the world and am on my way to the Father.*

Something in this last appeal came home to the disciples. It may have been simply the sublime confidence of His tone. In any case they declare themselves at last convinced. They say—can it have been by the mouth of the beloved disciple? *—Lo! now speakest thou plainly and speakest no parable. By this we believe that thou didst come forth from God.* Alas! there is still self-confidence in this confession of faith. The crisis at hand will help to purge it out of them. But He acknowledges, as the next chapter will shew, genuine sincerity at the back of it. For the moment He is content with a loving warning: *Do ye now believe? Lo! an hour is coming, and has come, to scatter you each to his own and to leave Me alone. And yet I am not alone, for the Father is with me.*

Even though on the Cross He might lose the consciousness of the supporting presence, the everlasting arms would be under Him all the time. It was only in appearance that He would seem to be forsaken.

But He cannot end on a note of warning. He brings them back in His closing words to His parting legacy of peace. *These things have I said unto you, that in Me ye may have peace, In the world, both now and to the end of time, you must expect tribulation.* But as He had said before, *Let not your heart be troubled*, so He says now, *Never lose heart.* Your enemy is vanquished. *I have overcome the world.*

CHAPTER XXII

THE HIGH-PRIESTLY PRAYER

WE pass from the study of our Lord's farewell to His disciples to the prayer to His Father in which it found its perfect consummation. If the conversation recorded in Chapters XV and XVI took place in the Temple Courts, this wonderful intercession would, as we have seen, have had a most appropriate setting. In it He would be taking leave of His Father's house. He prayed, as seems to have been His custom, out loud; and, as we shall see, was conscious that His disciples were overhearing.

The prayer falls into three divisions. The first (verses 1–5) contains a prayer for Himself. The second (verses 6–19) contains a prayer for His disciples. In the third (verses 20–26) He intercedes for the Church and the world to the end of time.

The prayer as a whole takes the place in S. John's Gospel that is occupied in the Synoptists by the agony in the garden. There is a startling contrast between the two prayers, but no real contradiction. S. John has no desire to deny the reality of our Lord's sufferings. One main purpose of his Gospel was to shew in opposition to the false teaching of Cerinthus that Jesus came "not in the water only, but in the water and in the blood" (1 Jn. 5: 6). He has already recorded the foretaste of the agony which Jesus had experienced in the Temple Court (12: 27). But S. Mark's narrative, as it stood, seemed to suggest an agony so unrelieved that men found it hard to believe that one who was truly divine could have passed through it. That, I think, is the reason why S. John so consistently treats the Cross as the means of our Lord's exaltation, the radiating centre of His glory. He omits to record the cry of desertion on the Cross, but he has just recorded (in 16: 32) an utterance that can assure us that the Father had not really left His Son alone, even though the consciousness of His presence with Him had for the moment been overclouded.

At any rate he takes occasion here to shew us that, however bitter might be the struggle through which Jesus had to pass while He was seeking for strength to drink the cup which the Father was putting into His hands, "strong crying and tears" were not the only tones in which He could draw nigh acceptably to the throne of grace. The Cross, indeed, is in full view. He prays because the hour has come: and the prayer includes a definite act of self-consecration (verse 19). But His mind is fixed on the "joy that was set before Him." In the light of that joy the personal suffering that He has to face can for the time, at least, be left out of account.

THE PRAYER FOR HIMSELF

1 *These things spake Jesus; and lifting up his eyes to heaven, he said, Father, the hour is come; glorify thy Son, that the Son may glorify*
2 *thee: even as thou gavest him authority over all flesh, that whatsoever*
3 *thou hast given him, to them he should give eternal life. And this is life eternal, that they should know thee the only true God, and him whom thou didst send*, even *Jesus Christ.*

Let us come, then, to the actual words of the prayer. It is addressed to the Father. The name recurs at each crisis in the prayer, verses 1, 11, 21, 24, 25. Once He says "Holy Father" (verse 11), once "Righteous Father" (verse 24).

The hour is come. There was no need to define between them what the hour meant. Then comes the first petition, *Glorify thy Son, that the Son may glorify thee.* In two ways this is an unexpected, at first an unwelcome beginning. It is a prayer for Himself: and it is a prayer for glory. We must face this difficulty.

It is well to be reminded that Jesus was not a self-less being. He had a human heart that felt the shame of the Cross. He was not indifferent to the response that men made to the appeal of His love. The prayer in Gethsemane shewed that there was an element in that which lay before Him which, if it were possible, He would have wished away. He had to wrestle there in prayer for the power to choose and do His Father's will with His whole heart. But here He is concerned with events that were not dependent on Himself. They affected Him no doubt; but in what we may term His official capacity as Son, as the appointed representative of the Father in the world. He is asking for power to enable Him to fulfil the task committed to Him "to glorify the Father". There is clearly nothing in any evil sense selfish in the prayer.

Still it was a prayer for glory. And the associations of the thought of glory in our minds are unfortunate. That does not, however, mean that there is no such thing as true glory; or that it is an illegitimate object of aspiration. To understand the meaning of the term, it is important to think especially of the use of it in the Bible in relation to God. It is associated there, as we have seen, not so much with outward manifestations of kingly state or dignity, as with the tokens of His personal presence among men, and the revelation of His true being and character.

In praying the Father to glorify Him, Jesus was, in fact, only asking the Father to let men know who it was whom they had crucified and slain. Think what the difference would have been for our Lord, for the world, and for our whole thought of God, if Good Friday had not been followed by Easter Day. How should we have known that the Jews were not justified in condemning Him for blasphemy, for claiming to be the Son of God? How long should we be able to hold fast our own faith in God, if we had to believe that Jesus had trusted in Him, and been disappointed? S. Paul surely marks, I have no doubt unconsciously, the answer to this prayer, when he says in Ro. 6: 4 that Jesus was raised from the dead by the glory of the Father.

So closely is this prayer bound up with the work that had been committed to Him, that He proceeds at once to think out, in communion with His Father, the office to which He had been designated. "As thou gavest Him authority over all flesh, that whatsoever thou hast given Him, to them He should give eternal life".

It is well to ponder this revelation of His position in the world as He understood it, and the ground of it. It rested on the will of God. "Thou *gavest* thy Son authority". His position is securely founded on the boundless generosity of the great Giver. The Son is before all things, and all the time, a Receiver, and delights to have it so. Again and again in this prayer He recalls His Father's gifts to Him: His authority and the sphere over which it is to be exercised (verse 2), His work (verse 4), the inner circle of His disciples (verse 6), His words (verse 8), His Name (verse 11), and His glory (verse 22).

This characteristic of Sonship craves careful attention. It is just this, which, as we have seen, we find it hardest to reconcile with co-essential divinity. Yet it is just in this that the fundamental distinction between the Persons in the one Godhead lies.

We find it hard to realize that there is a divinity in receiving no less than in giving. Love is a reciprocal relation. God as Love must always have had an object to whom His Love could go forth, and from whom it could receive a response in kind, an answering self-surrender. The Fatherhood of God is an assurance to us of the eternal Godhead of the Son. For us, however, the revelation of primary importance here is the revelation of the loving heart of the Father, the great Giver, on whom the eternal Son was content to rest.

We must pass on now to consider the extent of His authority, and the work with which He had been entrusted: *Thou gavest him*, He says, *authority over all flesh, that as regards everything which thou hast given him, the Son shall give them eternal life.*

The sentence is grammatically irregular. It seems as if Jesus here (as in 6: 37) regards the sphere over which His authority is to be exercised as an organic impersonal whole, and then splits it up into its individual personal elements.

In any case it involves a clear consciousness of authority. As Son of God He claims to be *ex-officio* King of men. In a very few hours this position will be expressly challenged by the Roman Governor. And Jesus, in His answer, will declare that "the Truth", to which He has come to bear witness, is the fact of His Kingship. The peace and well-being of the world depends on the recognition of it. He would claim it, therefore, openly and fearlessly, though the claim was as dangerous in the political world as the claim to divine Sonship was in the religious. He gives Pilate to understand that it is none the less a real authority because He will use no violence to enforce it. His people must be willing in the day of His power. He will reign by serving. His throne will be a Cross.

We must notice before we pass on, the extent of His dominion. It is nothing short of world-wide. It includes "all flesh"—the whole race of man. Such a dominion was, we know, promised to the Messiah by prophets and psalmists. Jesus had, according to Mt. 11: 27, claimed it earlier in His ministry. He will repeat the claim after His resurrection (Mt. 28: 18). The stages by which this dominion is to spread until it reaches its consummation will come before us later. What confronts us immediately is the characteristic service which the Son is commissioned to render. *To all that the Father has given Him He shall give eternal life.*

The measure of man's need is the measure of the service of the Son—"Men", as S. Paul tells us, "are dead in trespasses and sins". Jesus Himself, as the Good Shepherd, had come, He said, that "we might have life in abundance, enough and to spare" (10: 10). And there is an implied promise that the blessing that He has come to bring shall not merely be offered, but bestowed effectually to its utmost limit. "All that the Father hath given me shall come unto me" (6: 37). The Son, therefore, finds not only a motive and a consecration, but also an abiding consolation in the thought of His commission.

His task is defined by the nature of the gift which He had

come to bring, and by the way by which men appropriate it. The words that follow are, if not a definition of eternal life, at least a clear statement of that which is both the source from which eternal life springs, and its characteristic fruit. *This is eternal life, that they should grow in the knowledge of Thee, the only true God, and of Him whom thou didst send, even Jesus Christ.*

A question has been raised in connexion with these words which is worth considering, even if we have to confess that we cannot decide between the alternative solutions. Dr. Westcott and others maintain that either the whole verse, or at least the descriptive titles, "the only true God" and "Jesus Christ", are an explanatory comment introduced by the Evangelist, and did not form part of the original prayer.

Godet pleads strongly on the other side. He points out that Jesus was distinctly contemplating the conversion of the Gentiles, and that so there would be a special point in the title which would mark the distinction beween the Father and the gods of the nations. The title "Jesus Christ" is no doubt the earliest Christian creed in its simplest form. It would be an anachronism if it were used as a proper name in addressing our Lord while on earth. Yet Godet finds an appropriateness in its use by Jesus of Himself in this supreme crisis, setting His seal beforehand to the use which would become habitual later.

In any case the statement itself is of fundamental importance, for it helps us to see that there is a true analogy between spiritual life and life as we know it in the physical realm. In the physical world, according to a familiar definition, life depends on, and is revealed by, correspondence with environment. A tree, for instance, lives by responding to the soil in which it is rooted, and to sunshine, air and water. Similarly, when we look into human life we see how much it depends for its fulness and variety on the development of the intellectual, æsthetic and emotional faculties, each of which has the power to give us access to a new world when we have got the key. There is nothing, therefore, to surprise us in the thought that eternal life consists in being alive to God; in knowing

Him and getting to be ever more and more at home with Him.

If this be so, it surely helps us to see the nature of the commission entrusted to Jesus, and the way in which He fulfilled it. He came to open the kingdom of heaven to us, to give us the key by which we may correspond to this part of our environment. He did it by living the eternal life in constant conscious communion with His Father, in human flesh by our side. By so doing He shewed us what human life at its highest is meant to be, and made it possible for us to attain to it. For not only did He reveal the Father by all that He said and did, but He has just been teaching His disciples how, by His death and resurrection, and by the gift of the Holy Spirit, it would be possible for them, to the end of time, to have access in and through Him to His Father and our Father, to His God and our God. This comes out, as we shall see, in His survey of the life that was now drawing to its close.

THE PERFECT WORK: ITS SOURCE AND GOAL

4 *I glorified thee on the earth, having accomplished the work which*
5 *thou hast given me to do. And now, O Father, glorify thou me with thine own self with the glory which I had with thee before the world was.*

In these words Jesus declares the inner meaning of the work already done under the old conditions in the body of His humiliation. Even in the flesh He has already glorified the Father.

Let us face this amazing fact. Here, on this earth, under all the limitations that belong to it, in a nature in all points one with ours—except in His refusal to yield to the tendency to self-assertion, which is in all men, though it is no true part of them, but has to be overcome and cast out before they can attain to a complete and unified personality—He had lived a life of perfect obedience, trust and love in relation to His Father in heaven. He had loved to the uttermost those whom He is not ashamed to call His brethren.

Some men had seen at the time, or at least had acquired

the experience which, in due course, would enable them to see shining forth from that life, "the glory of an only begotten from a father". The glory of God does, indeed, as S. Paul tells the Corinthians, shine out with power to transform after its likeness the heart of any man who can catch a glimpse of it in the face of Christ. In the fullest sense He has for us the value of God. That is what I have called an "amazing fact".

Logical difficulties with regard to the possibility of any revelation of the infinite to finite minds vanish when they are confronted with the facts. We cannot define, but we can apprehend and worship perfection when we see it. We can rest assured that the revelation of love on the Cross can never be transcended. In these words Jesus shews that He knew that His work had attained its end. As He reviews it in His Father's sight, before He finally commends it to His Father's keeping, He says: *I glorified Thee on the earth, having flawlessly fulfilled the work which Thou gavest me to do.* The effectiveness of the work depended on the perfection of the workmanship. It was the positive side of what we call His sinlessness. It is the outward expression of His holiness, i.e. of the completeness of His inner devotion to His Father, a fact surely incredible, inconceivable, if it had not appeared. And this devotion is the image after which we were created. Have we not infinite need to pray that the darkness and blindness by which "the god of this world" shuts out the light from our hearts, and from the hearts of other men, may be done away, so that "the knowledge of the glory of God in the face of Jesus Christ" may penetrate and transform us through and through after His likeness?

We must pass on now to consider the last clause in this opening section of the High-Priestly prayer, in which Jesus defines what the glory for which He prays must involve. *And now, O Father, glorify thou me at thine own side with the glory which I had at thy side, before the world was.* He is asking, in fact, that the world may know that He had gone back to the life of unbroken communion with His Father in heaven, which He had left to come into the world. So this opening section of

His prayer issues in a climax of self-revelation. He helps us to realize that what was required of Him at the moment was an act of absolute self-surrender—"Glorify thou me". It must be the direct act of the Father Himself. The work of the Son had its fixed limits. The time was at hand when even He must lie still and wait for the salvation of God. His death would give the opportunity for the Father to reveal Himself by a crowning act of deliverance. It must be what we call a miracle, a revelation of the hidden power by which all life is being guided and urged forward to its goal. It was necessary as a final demonstration of the truth of His claim that the Father had sent Him. That is the ground on which He prays His Father to put forth His power.

Man's necessity, as the great Greek tragedians shew again and again, is God's opportunity. Here in the climax of the eternal tragedy of human life is the knot which nothing but direct divine intervention could untie.

Again, the glory for which Christ prays is a freshly realized and revealed communion with the Father. Men must recognize that He, as man, has been raised to the right hand of the Majesty on high. The mystery that lies behind is unfathomable, but not unsubstantial. We cannot even dimly conjecture what it meant for the Son, in the ineffable unity of the Godhead, "to come forth out of the Father, and to come into the world". But the experience that we have to contemplate is expressed in the terms of His humanity. His words imply that for His human consciousness, presence in human flesh in this world involved the surrender, for the time, of the joy of full uninterrupted communion, an absence from the Father, even the possibility of that hiding of His face which makes the darkest of all human utterances a true expression of His experience as man: "My God, my God, why didst Thou forsake me?"

Once more, the thought which again and again lit up the darkness of the coming agony, as He had looked forward to it in His converse with His friends, had been just this: "I am going to my Father". So here the prayer, "Set me once more in my old place at Thy right hand" is simply "Let me pass on from this state of trial and discipline to the new state in which I shall no longer see Thee by a mirror in a riddle, but face to face." And the fact that nothing less than this was the goal of His earthly career helps us to believe that nothing less can have been its source and spring. Looked at from this side, how natural it is! "Grant me the perfect fruition of the relation which was my birthright before the world was."

And yet what depths are involved in it! What light it throws on the words in which S. John, in the opening of his first Epistle, declares the inmost meaning of his experience of what Jesus had said and done in his sight! The life he had seen had been the manifestation of an eternal life, which had not had its first beginning when it was manifested to men to be perceived and tested by their physical senses. "It *was* from the beginning". As the human birth of Jesus had not created it, there was nothing unnatural in the fact that the death of His body could not destroy it. That eternal life is the ultimate reality of the universe. It lies behind the earliest beginning of creation. It contains the assurance of a power in God able to redeem the world from its uttermost rebellion. For it is the communion of the Father and of the Son, of the Word and God. The blood of the Lamb, by which we are redeemed, was shed from the foundation of the world. He was manifested to bring us back to God. And He calls us to share the fruits of His victory. "To him that overcometh will I give to sit with me on my throne, as I also overcame and sat down with my Father on His throne".

WHAT HIS DISCIPLES WERE TO JESUS

6 *I manifested thy name unto the men whom thou gavest me out of the world: thine they were, and thou gavest them to me; and they have*
7 *kept thy word. Now they know that all things whatsoever thou hast*
8 *given me are from thee: for the words which thou gavest me I have given unto them; and they received* them, *and knew of a truth that I came forth from thee, and they believed that thou didst send me.*
9 *I pray for them: I pray not for the world, but for those whom thou*

10 *hast given me; for they are thine: and all things that are mine are thine, and thine are mine: and I am glorified in them.*

We come now to the second division of the prayer (17: 6–10). It is all strictly intercessory, though Jesus does not frame a specific petition till verse 11. For intercession, as George Macdonald helps us to realize, is, at the heart of it, simply "thinking of God and our friends together, and of ourselves in relation to both". We ought not, of course, to bring their needs to God, as if He did not know them: we bring them because He knows (Mt. 6: 8). We learn in prayer to think God's thought after Him, and so to enter more fully into His plan.

Our Lord's intercession is for a limited group, which at the same time is representative. So it has its lessons for all who are called in any way to share their ministry. He is asking for us now, what He asked for His disciples then.

It is worth while to dwell for a moment on the individualizing aspect of intercession. What Jesus is doing for the apostles, as a body, He had already done for Simon Peter. "Satan", He had said earlier in the evening, "has asked to have you as a body for sifting, and I have prayed for *thee* that thy faith fail not" (Lk. 22: 32). It is a help to know that we are being upheld by the intercessions of faithful friends. S. John's record is an assurance that our great High Priest is not unmindful of any one of us. There was an abiding meaning in the fact that under the old covenant the High Priest bore on his breast plate the names of each of the twelve tribes of Israel when He entered into the Holy of Holies.

The first point that craves expression, when Jesus begins to think of the Twelve and His Father together, is that the Twelve had been given to Him out of the world. It was on their faithfulness to the seed of the word that He had sown in their hearts that the permanence of His work in the world would depend.

I manifested Thy name unto the men whom Thou gavest me out of the world. Thine they were, and Thou gavest them to me, and they have kept thy word.

He had, indeed, as He had just been reminding them (13: 18; 15: 16), Himself chosen them. But He had spent a whole night in prayer first. We can see, therefore, how it was that the Twelve became a constant link between Him and His Father. When any men came to Him it was in response to the Father's drawing. (6: 44, 65). It was not flesh and blood, it was the Father Himself that inspired Simon Peter's great confession (Mt. 16: 16).

He goes on to point out that their tie with the Father was at the same time a tie with Himself. He had manifested the Father's name to them. Their response had shewn that they had the root of the matter in them. They had loved the light, and come to the light. Their wills were set on doing the will of God; so they had kept His word. They reverenced, listened for, and obeyed His voice speaking in their hearts. So they recognized and followed it when it spoke to them in His Son.

He passes on to describe the effect of this manifestation of the Father's name on those who kept His word. The vital element in it was what we call in technical language faith in the Incarnation: but He expresses it in terms of a living personal experience.

They know that all things whatsoever Thou hast given me, are from Thee. For the words which Thou hast given me I have given unto them: and they have received them, and know of a truth that I came forth from Thee, and they believe that Thou didst send me.

The main content of this faith is the conviction that the whole life of Jesus had been rooted in God. It had come into clear expression in the closing words of the conversation that they had just had together. They had realized that in Him God had come directly and personally into living touch with our human race. They had grasped what He meant when He had told them that the power manifested in His works and the wisdom of His speech, was not self-originated, but strictly God-given. This faith was throughout quickened and enlightened by His words. These include His claim to be Son of God and King of men. But the words that He bade them watch over in their hearts were primarily revelations of life and duty. In view of this fact and of the consequent importance of accurate transmission of His teaching, it is startling, as I have noticed more than once, that He should have trusted entirely to their memories to hand on what they had learned (Mt. 28: 20).

Such, as He saw them, were the qualifications of this little immature group, who were to be His witnesses to the end of the earth. He has set Himself to pray specifically for them. Yet, even so, He lingers to deepen His sense of His own unity with them, and with the Father, all through the testing time of separation from His visible presence that He sees approaching. He recapitulates the points of distinction between them and the world for which He is not, at this time, setting Himself to pray directly.

I pray for them. I pray not for the world, but for those whom Thou hast given me, for they are Thine: and all things that are mine are Thine, and Thine are mine: and I have been glorified in them.

He goes back, we see, to the wonder of the direct touch with the Father, which was constituted by the fact that they were a gift to Him of that which was and still remained the Father's. He had said: "Thine they were". Now He changes the tense: "Thine they are". The Father did not resign His interest in them—they became His by a yet closer tie, as the disciples of His Son.

This thought leads on to a further reflection on the fellowship in possession which the Son enjoyed with His Father. The Father has nothing which He keeps back from the Son. Nothing is the Son's that is not first His Father's, and held by Him in trust for the Father. But on that condition He is Lord of all. Here, in this little group of disciples is His most cherished possession. He has been *glorified* in them. He has found in them human hearts, on whom His love can pour itself out freely, and to whom He can speak freely of His Father, and so bring into clear expression the inmost secrets of His own being.

KEEPING IN THE NAME

11 *And I am no more in the world, and these are in the world, and I come to thee. Holy Father, keep them in thy name which thou hast*
12 *given me, that they may be one, even as we* are. *While I was with them, I kept them in thy name which thou hast given me: and I guarded them, and not one of them perished, but the son of perdition;*
13 *that the scripture might be fulfilled. But now I come to thee; and these things I speak in the world, that they may have my joy fulfilled in themselves.*

By the picture that Jesus put before Himself of His disciples, when He set Himself to intercede with His Father for them, He was helping them to understand what they and their successors to the end of time (that is what each one of us, so far as we are true to our calling) mean to Him. He was counting up His jewels, His Father's gifts to Him.

Their faith, the fact that they had heard and been able to respond, however imperfectly, to the call of His love, was the result of the drawing of the Father through the Spirit. The link, therefore, that bound them to Him, bound Him and them at the same time to the Father. This is the foundation on which His intercession for them rests.

He proceeds to outline the approaching crisis in the fewest possible words: *And I am no longer in the world, and they are in the world, and I am coming to Thee.* "Whither I go", He had told them, "ye cannot follow Me now". There was no need to tell the Father what that would involve. He was obeying His Father's call to come home. That meant that they would, to all appearance, be left alone to face their responsibilities in difficult and hostile surroundings. Then at last, with the actual situation for Him and them clearly defined, the yearning of His heart for them takes shape in definite petition.

Holy Father, keep them in thy name, which thou hast given me, that they may be one as we are.

We notice first the title under which He addresses God.

It is unique. As a rule He is content with "Father". Here alone He begins *Holy Father.*

Holiness is the fundamental characteristic of the divine nature. It is the ground of the *mysterium tremendum*, the sentiment of awe, which is our instinctive response, when we become conscious of God's presence. It is the inspiration of worship, as we see from the vision of Isaiah in the Temple in Jerusalem (Is. 6: 3); and from the vision of S. John when a door was opened for him into heaven (Rev. 4: 8).

In itself holiness connotes perfect purity. This involves, negatively, a fiery rejection of sin and selfishness, but still more a longing to impart itself as holy spirit to those who will receive it. The will of God is our sanctification (1 Thess. 4: 3). It is not law only, but impulse. Its command is an inspiration. So the use of the title prepares the way for the prayer for the sanctification of His disciples, which is to be the climax of this part of the intercession.

Then comes the petition: *Keep them in thy name, which thou hast given me.*

Jesus is referring to the name that had been given to Him. (Notice the reading). He is not thinking of His Father's gift of the disciples. The disciples would be exposed to serious risks. They would have no choice but to live dangerously. What they would have to guard against will be defined later. Here He calls attention to that which would be their defence. It is the Name of God either, as we shall see, His own, or His Father's. The thought, as Canon Bernard shews in his beautiful book on *The Central Teaching of Jesus Christ*, is condensed and not easy to interpret. He takes the Name to be "the revelation of God committed to the Son" to be realized and revealed in His person. If so, the Name is the name Father. He believes that Jesus prayed that His disciples should be kept in heart and mind true to the faith enshrined in the Name.

It may be, however, that the Name is the name Son, given to Jesus at His baptism, and that Jesus is praying that the disciples may be kept true to the Sonship, which is theirs in Him.

There is a third interpretation possible. Jesus may be appealing to the Father to be true to His own name, to shew Himself Father by His watchful care over His children. This is, I think, more in harmony with the next verse, in which He claims to have done on earth what He asks His Father to do from heaven. *When I was with them, I kept them in Thy name which Thou hast given me.* This seems to mean, "I kept them as Thy representative, as the instrument of Thy Fatherhood". And this suggests that He is appealing to His Father, if we may say so, to carry on on His own account when He has no longer a visible representative in the world.

In any case, the fruit of that keeping, the sign that would prove that it was effectual, would be the unity of the believers.

That they may be one as we are.

We cannot help noticing that He attaches the utmost importance to the relations of the disciples to one another. They must be drawn closer to one another as they are drawn closer to God. In giving them the New Commandment He told them that their unity among themselves, which was to spring from His love, would be the hall-mark of their discipleship in the sight of men. Here in a single startling phrase the unity within the Godhead is revealed as the source and pledge of unity among men. "Make them one as we are".

He passes on to work out what is implied in this keeping, and to give His request fresh urgency, by emphasizing the fact that what He is asking is simply the carrying on of the work that He has been doing while on earth, and which His ascension will compel Him to relinquish. Here are His words: *While I was with them, I kept them in thy name, which thou hast given me: and I guarded them, and not one of them perished, but the son of perdition, that the Scripture might be fulfilled. But now I come to thee, and these things I speak in the world, that they may have my joy fufilled in themselves.*

The Jews, as we have had to notice from time to time, were

in the habit of praying even their private prayers out loud. And we can see that, if this prayer was to have its full effect, those for whom He was praying must understand what He was asking the Father to do for them (i) that they might see the Father's hand in the answer when it came, and (ii) that they might supply the co-operation which was required of them.

In the prayer itself His claim is that throughout His ministry He had been keeping them in the Name that had been given Him. He had been commissioned to act as His Father's representative, and to reveal Him to men, and His likeness to His Father had come out in His care for them. He had been their Shepherd, as the Father was His. When the Father Himself took on the work, the disciples in their turn would enter on the commission that had been His. The mission of the Comforter in the Son's name would help them to realize in their turn the responsibility of witness that was resting on them.

He enforces His claim by what He says of the cost and of the success of His efforts. First the cost. He had not only watched over their training, He had, as their Good Shepherd, stood between them and their foes; He had risked His life; He was soon to lay it down in their defence.

Next—the success. He claims that it was complete, but for one inevitable exception. The exception is recorded here, we cannot doubt, as a warning against presumption for all on whom spiritual privileges are showered abundantly. Even divine protection cannot avail for an unsurrendered will.

One last point. Faithful co-operation would open the way into the fulness of joy. His joy came from being true to His Sonship, keeping His Father's commandments and abiding in His love (15: 11). It was the exultant response of His whole being to His Father's approval. This joy He would have us share with Him. We, too, may hear the Father say: "Thou art my Son, my beloved; in thee I am well pleased." "Servant of God, well done."

THE COST OF OUR SANCTIFICATION

14 *I have given them thy word; and the world hated them, because they*
15 *are not of the world, even as I am not of the world. I pray not that thou shouldest take them from the world, but that thou shouldest*
16 *keep them from the evil* one. *They are not of the world, even as*
17 *I am not of the world. Sanctify them in the truth: thy word is*
18 *truth. As thou didst send me into the world, even so sent I them*
19 *into the world. And for their sakes I sanctify myself, that they themselves also may be sanctified in truth.*

Verses 14 and 15 describe the nature and the source of the danger from which Jesus is praying His Father to protect His disciples. The danger is inherent in their discipleship. He had opened the way for them into the fulness of His own joy in the consciousness of His Father's approval. He had done this by giving them His Father's word. That is, He had opened their ears to hear His Father's voice claiming them as His sons. He has already (verse 6) testified that they have kept that word, as a result of His manifestation of the Father's Name. Receiving the word had given them the right to take up their position as children of God. They had been born of Him. This marked their distinctness from the world. The unbelieving Jews shewed that they had not the word of the Father abiding in them, because they refused to believe Him whom He had sent (Jn. 5: 38). But this spiritual kinship of the disciples with their Lord (Mk. 3: 35) exposed them to the hatred—the murderous hatred—of the Jews (Jn. 15: 18, 23 ff).

In view of this fact He might have prayed for their removal from the world at once without suffering. But this possibility He rejects. They must witness as He had done. The death of the body was not in itself anything to be afraid of. The real danger was the danger of the spiritual death into which they might fall, if they yielded to the terrors or the enticements of the evil one, the prince of this world.

So Jesus prays the last clause of the *Pater Noster* on their behalf, as He had already prayed it on behalf of Simon Peter (Lk. 22: 32).

This close contemplation of the danger leads to a renewal of the prayer with increasing definiteness: *They are not of this world, even as I am not of this world. Sanctify them in the truth. Thy word is truth.*

The danger is inevitable as long as they are in the world. For, as the *Pater Noster* implies, and as S. John says expressly (1 Jn. 5: 19), "The whole world lieth in the evil one". It is in the sphere of his influence. It is exposed to the craft of him who was the liar, the manslayer, from the beginning (8: 44).

There is only one way by which a man can be brought safely through the trials that beset him from the "wiles of error" (Eph. 4: 14), and that is by being inwardly transformed after the image of the Son, and by being filled with His Holy Spirit. So the prayer to "keep" becomes a prayer to "sanctify". Nothing but the Holy Spirit, the Spirit of the Truth, can win the full response of a man, and guard him against the wiles of the devil, when he comes, as he always essays to do, under the guise of an angel of light. For God alone is the ultimate reality: His Spirit is "The Spirit of the Truth". He alone can make and keep a man true, by enabling him to lay hold and to keep hold of Jesus Christ as the Truth, the perfect revelation of the glory of the Father.

This power was already at work in the hearts of the disciples. It is the life inherent in the seed of the word, already sown in their hearts, even the word of the Father, which Jesus had given them, and which they had received and kept. Abiding in that word, as He had told the Jews, brings a growing apprehension of the truth; and the truth would make and keep them free (8: 32).

The last sentence in this section is the deepest and most constraining: *As thou didst send me into the world, I also send them into the world, and for their sakes I sanctify myself, that they also may be sanctified in the Truth.*

The consecration of His disciples, for which He is praying, has a wider aim than their individual perfecting. And Jesus, as Son, has throughout a part of His own to play in regard to it. The consecration was to an office. It implied a specific commission, which is entrusted indeed to the Church as a body, but which was laid with special emphasis on the apostles, as its leaders and representatives.

This commission had in the first instance been entrusted to the Son. The Father had consecrated and sent Him into the world at His baptism (10: 36). The sign of that commission and the power to fulfil it came from the gift of the Holy Spirit. His work, as the Baptist defined it (1: 33), was to baptize others with the Spirit that He had received.

The fulfilment of that part of His commission had, however, to wait until He himself had been glorified, and that involved the removal of His visible presence. He had, therefore, all through His public ministry, been preparing those whom the Father had given Him to receive the Holy Spirit from Him after His ascension. He is helping them here to realize that the gift, when it came, would bring with it the responsibility of carrying on His work, and baptizing others in His name. He is shewing them that they would share His commission, if they shared His consecration.

In such a consecration a man cannot be merely passive. Although the consecration must originate with God, men must respond to it. But even this power of response must be provided for them, and quickened in them by the Son. How that could be, His disciples, in spite of pregnant hints thrown out from time to time in the course of His ministry, could not as yet have guessed. Now, however, at this supreme crisis, in their hearing and in the presence of the Father, He takes the whole burthen and cost of that provision on Himself when He says: *And for their sakes I sanctify myself that they also may be sanctified in very truth.*

This is the last occasion, before the final crisis in Gethsemane, on which Jesus takes up His Cross. It implies a deliberate choosing of His Father's will for the service of His brethren, knowing that the choice meant death. The Good Shepherd is deliberately facing death for His sheep. He had come—He knew that He had come—"to give His life a ransom for many."

Before we pass on, it will be worth while to look closely into the spiritual forces that spring from this self-consecration.

First, and most obvious, is the thought of the constraining power of the cost of our redemption. The Cross is a magnet. Our only adequate response is self-surrender.

This, however, is not all. The self-consecration that lay at the heart of the sacrifice was the element in it which gave it power with God. The Epistle to the Hebrews (10: 5–10) leaves us in no doubt about this:

"Wherefore when he cometh into the World, he saith,
Sacrifice and offering thou wouldest not,
But a body didst thou prepare for me;
In whole burnt offerings and sacrifices for sin thou
hadst no pleasure:
Then said I, Lo I am come
(In the roll of the book it is written of me)
To do Thy will, O God.

Saying above, Sacrifices and offerings and whole burnt offerings and sacrifices for sin thou wouldst not, neither hadst thou pleasure there-in (the which are offered according to the law), then hath he said, Lo, I am come to do thy will. He taketh away the first, that he may establish the second. By which will we have been sanctified through the offering of the body of Jesus Christ once for all".

There are mysteries in the Atonement, which we cannot expect to fathom. But I make bold to say that this is not one of them. The problem to be solved in setting a man free from his sin is just to find a means by which his will, which has become perverted and is out of line with God's will, can be set right. There is nothing to be surprised at, though it is infinitely wonderful, that the act of Jesus in choosing God's will, at the cost of Calvary, in loyal and loving obedience to His Father, and in self-sacrificing service to His brother men, should have just that power over any man who can be brought within reach of its influence. The outward sign and symbol of that perfectly surrendered will was the shedding of His blood. As a man faces that fact, as he accepts his Lord's invitation to drink that blood, he opens his own heart to let that perfectly surrendered will flood his being. Must it not, as he does that, in Tennyson's beautiful phrase, "flow through his will and make it pure"? That, surely, is the reason why "As we walk in the light, as He is in the light, the blood of Jesus His Son, little by little, cleanses us from all sin" (1 Jn. 1 : 7). As we find grace in the power of that communion to offer ourselves, our souls and bodies, to be a reasonable, holy and living sacrifice to God, we shall have no difficulty in understanding why, when Jesus had prayed to His Father for the sanctification of His chosen, He passed on at once to consecrate Himself to death on their behalf. So only could He help them to take their own share in the work of their consecration.

THE UNITY OF THE CHURCH

20 *Neither for these only do I pray, but for them also that believe*
21 *on me through their word; that they may all be one; even as thou, Father,* art *in me, and I in thee, that they also may be in us: that*
22 *the world may believe that thou didst send me. And the glory which thou hast given me I have given unto them; that they may be one,*
23 *even as we* are *one; I in them, and thou in me, that they may be perfected into one; that the world may know that thou didst send me, and lovedst them, even as thou lovedst me.*

In the closing section of the prayer the horizon expands to include the whole Church to the end of time, and to declare the effect of the witness of their unity on all the world:

Not for them only do I make request, but for those also that believe on me through their word, that they may be one, as thou, Father, art in me and I in thee; that they may in their turn be in us, that the world may believe that thou didst send me.

The prayer is for us. We and the whole Church are built on the foundation of the apostles. All our knowledge of Jesus rests on the Gospels, the Acts, the Epistles, and the Apocalypse, in which their witness to what He proved Himself to be to them, before and after His resurrection, is enshrined.

The substance of His prayer for us is the same as for them. It includes keeping and sanctifying, with the same goal of unity, and the whole is irradiated with the hope of a coming conversion of the world. It is clearly important, therefore, to look closely into this prayer for unity. In the case of the Twelve, the obstacles came, as the candid revelation of their short-comings in the Gospel shews, from their individual rivalries and ambitions. In the case of the Church at large, there are wider and deeper gulfs of colour and sex, of race and training, to be bridged, before all the sheep from different folds can be brought together. The unifying power in the two cases, as the prayer defines it, is the same. It is the unity of the Father and the Son, revealed by the life of the Incarnate Word before the eyes of the original disciples.

Into this unity disciples enter, as He had just been teaching them (14: 20 ff.) by keeping the word and the commandment of the Son in the power of the love which He had shewn them in His life, and of which His death would be the consummation. Here are the words:

"In that day ye shall know that I am in my Father, and ye in me, and I in you. He that hath my commandments and keepeth them, he it is that loveth me; and he that loveth me shall be loved of my Father, and I will love him and will manifest myself to him" (14: 20 f.).

"If any man love me he will keep my word, and my Father will love him; and we will come to him and make our abode with him" (23).

We can see, therefore, why the prayer for the unity of the disciples after the pattern of the unity of the Father and the Son, leads on to the prayer that they may be each and all in living union with the Father in His Son, *that they may be in us*.

Even this, however, is not the end. He is not praying directly for the men of the world, whose sin He was bearing, and whom He would die to save, but they were not forgotten. He had already given the apostles a commission to carry on His work among them. He had, at an earlier stage (16: 8 ff.), promised that the Spirit, when He came, working in and through them, would convict the world of sin, of righteousness, and of judgement. Here he prays that the sight of the unity of the Church might convert the world.

That the world may believe that thou didst send me.

The witness to the presence and the power of the Spirit in the Church, which unity would bring, would be the final (His words imply an effectual) witness to the world of the mission of the Son.

The faith "that thou didst send me", as His words in verse 8 shew, is the characteristic of true discipleship.

This declaration of the goal is repeated and expanded in the words that follow: *And, as for me, the glory which thou has given me, I have given them, that they may be one, even as we are one; I in them and thou in me, that they may be perfected into one: that the world may know* (not only believe, but directly perceive), *that thou didst send me, and lovedst them, even as thou lovedst me.*

These words follow naturally on those that preceded them. For before praying for their fulfilment He had already been working for that end. He has committed to His disciples the glory that He had Himself received from the Father.

This brings us back to the thought with which the whole prayer had opened. His glory, as we saw, consisted in the fact that the task of manifesting the presence of God in the world as He really is, had been committed to Him. He had already declared that the apostles had had their share in glorifying Him by letting all that was in His heart towards them come out into free expression. He now declares that He has called His disciples to share His glory in the task of revealing the presence and character of God to men. He had done this by calling them, and enabling them to share His Sonship. Baptism with His Spirit would throw on them the responsibility of bearing His name, and so of revealing the Father.

The thought, if we try to take it home to ourselves, is overwhelming. It will be well, therefore, to remind ourselves that S. Paul has given independent expression to it. In 2 Cor.

3: 18 he tells us that in the new dispensation we are called to gaze directly on the glory of the Lord, as it radiates from the face of Jesus Christ. As we do so we mirror it. We take it down into ourselves, and reflect it as a mirror does the image presented to it.

But the process is a vital, not a mechanical one. The likeness can only be shewn in life. We are transformed ourselves by that on which we gaze "from glory to glory as from a sovereign Spirit".

Jesus here works out the ultimate consequences of the gift of His glory and their response to it. The interpenetration of personalities implied in it would, little by little, perfect the unity along the lines laid down already: *That they may be one, as we are one.* "I in them" but not I alone, for my whole being is fulfilled in Thee; so "I in them" brings with it at the same time, "Thou in me"—*That they may be perfected into one.*

This is, surely, a reassuring expansion of the original thought. Jesus seems to take our unity so much for granted, though, as we think of our actual condition, we are conscious chiefly of interminable and desperate divisions. Here, however, He holds unity before us, not as our starting point, but as our goal. At the same time, we must not forget that there is an inner reality of unity, even now, however imperfect may be its external manifestation.

Here again S. Paul helps us. In Eph. 4: 13 he speaks of the building up of the body of the Christ, "until we all attain unto the unity of the faith and of the knowledge of the Son of of God, unto the full-grown man, unto the measure of the stature of the fulness of Christ". He, too, tells us that the perfecting of the unity must be a slow process. The unity of the whole body remains incomplete until the perfecting of each several member is attained.

The perfecting of the unity brings with it, as our Lord's words suggest, an intensification of its effect on the world: *That the world may know that thou didst send me, and lovedst them as thou lovest me.* Knowing is more than believing.

"The synagogue of Satan", our Lord promised to the

Church in Philadelphia, "will come and worship at thy feet, and *know* that I have loved thee."

A general conviction of the divine mission of the Son will pass on into an open acknowledgement of the fact that a mission has been committed to the Church, and that they are living and working, as He has done, in the sunshine of the Father's love.

THE BEGINNING AND THE END IS LOVE

24 *Father, that which thou hast given me, I will that, where I am, they also may be with me; that they may behold my glory, which thou hast given me: for thou lovedst me before the foundation of the world.*

We now come to the final stage in the intercession of our great High Priest. It takes the form, not of an imperative, or what it would be more fitting to call a precative "glorify", "keep", "sanctify"—but of a simple expression of His will.

As He had told His disciples (15: 7): "If ye abide in me, and my words abide in you, ask whatsoever ye will, and it shall be done unto you"; so here He says simply: *Father, I will.* There is no sign of strain or struggle in choosing the will of the Father. The time for that will come before long in the garden. Here there is nothing but the quiet confidence of a perfect harmony of heart and mind and will. *I will that where I am, they may also be with me.*

It is a prayer for a perfect restoration of communion between Him and His disciples within the veil. He had already promised them this restoration. "Where I am, there shall also my servant be" (12: 26). "Thou canst not follow me now: but thou shalt follow later" (13: 36). And especially in 14: 2, 3: "I go to prepare a place for you: and if I go and prepare a place for you, I come again and will take you to myself, that where I am you may be also."

In its perfection, of course, this restoration of communion must wait till the end for its consummation. But this must not blind our eyes to the fact that all through His farewell discourse Jesus had been explaining to His disciples the conditions of life in the new order which would begin with His resurrection. He had come down to earth to be with us for a time where we were. But in the new order our lives would be hid with Christ in God. We are bidden to lift up our hearts that we may, in the spirit of the collect for Ascensiontide, and of the *Prayer of Humble Access*, abide with Him continually where He is.

As the prayer goes on, it brings us back to the petition with which it had started. He had begun, as the shadow of the Cross fell upon Him, by praying that the Father would vindicate His honour in the sight of men. We saw how the Father's honour, no less than the Son's, was concerned in that vindication. The truth of His claim could not be established unless He was reinstated in the dignity which He left when He became man. But the men of the world could not directly appreciate that vindication. They could have no direct experience of the power of His resurrection unless they believed. None but loving and obedient disciples could see the risen Lord, or bear witness to His ascension. Those, however, whose hearts God had touched, and who were ready to receive His Holy Spirit, would be brought into effective touch with Him in His essential glory. They would see down into the love of the Father for the Son, which was its living heart. They knew that that love had found expression in the voice at His baptism. His consciousness of that love had come into clear expression at the renewal of His self-consecration to death for His sheep as the Good Shepherd (10: 11). He had spoken (15: 9f.) of His love for them as an outcome of it. Here He teaches them that it did not begin with His appearance in the world. It was coeval with His Sonship.

The prayer closes with a concise summary of the whole situation, leading up to a re-statement of the deliverance that He had come to bring by the revelation of the Father in the terms of love.

25 *O righteous Father, the world knew thee not, but I know thee;*
26 *and these knew that thou didst send me; and I made known unto them thy name, and will make it known; that the love wherewith thou lovedst me may be in them, and I in them.*

This statement is prefaced by a fresh invocation of the Name of the Father. Once more with an epithet. This time it is not "Holy", but "Righteous". Holiness is an attribute of the being of God, on the side of His aweful purity. His righteousness characterizes His relation to men. It is connected, no doubt, with His office as Judge (Rev. 16: 7). But in S. Paul and in S. John the underlying thought is not the execution of judgement, but the passion for righteousness, and the longing to impart it—"He is faithful and righteous that He may forgive" (1 Jn. 1: 9). "Our advocate with the Father is Jesus Christ the Righteous" (1 Jn. 2: 1).

The fundamental difficulty in the way of the satisfaction of Christ's passion for imparting righteousness came from the blindness of those whom He would help. He does not close His eyes to the facts. But the tragic situation is summed up in the fewest words: *The world knew Thee not.* He had Himself come to His own home, and His own people had refused to receive Him. They could not recognize either Him or His Father.

There was, however, another side to the picture. The Son Himself had come, and in human flesh, under human conditions, He had succeeded where the world failed. He had known the Father. And, further, His disciples had at least recognized the fact of His mission from God; and so it had been possible for Him to shew them the Father. He had manifested His name to them, if not completely, at least in germ, and that work it would be in His power to carry on to the end. Provision had thereby been made for a perfect restoration of communion between earth and heaven. The recognition of the love of the Father for the Son was the starting-point: and He had lived on earth, and would die and rise again, to shew that mankind is included in the outgoing of that love, and that men are called to open their hearts to receive it. The recognition and reception of that love, which Jesus, by His love for them, had brought within reach of His disciples, and which is indeed indistinguishable from His Holy Spirit, would bring His presence with it, and establish Him in His rightful place on His throne in the heart of each and all.

In the midst of all our doubts and perplexities His witness rings out clear and unfaltering down the ages: *Righteous Father, the world knew Thee not, but I knew Thee.* What though all the rest, in spite of their groping, failed to respond to Thy tender pleading, yet I set my seal to this that Thou art true. And this little flock has at least acknowledged that my mission was not self-originated. Knowing Thee but dimly, they yet could make a beginning in the apprehension of Thy name, and I can, and will, lead them into fuller knowledge. Out of this revelation the love wherewith Thou lovedst me—even the Holy Spirit that Thou bestowest upon me—shall take up His abode in them: and with Him, I myself shall find a home in the hearts of each and all."

In these words this wonderful section of the self-revelation of the Word Incarnate to His disciples comes to an end. Before we pass on it will be well to pause a little on it to let the wonder of it sink in.

In the section that preceded it (Chapters 7–12) S. John gave us what stood out in his memory as salient points in the effort that Jesus made to help the nation as a whole to understand the nature of His claim on their allegiance. In this effort He followed the plan, which as we see from 2 Cor. 4: 2, is marked out for the missionaries of His Gospel to the end of time. He strove by the manifestation of the truth to commend Himself to every man's conscience in the sight of God.

He claimed that anyone whose heart was set on doing the

will of God would have in himself the means of testing the divine origin of His teaching (7: 17).

He declared that all men could tell intuitively who He was and whence He came (7: 28).

He promised that those who would commit themselves in faith to Him should become well-springs of the water of life (7: 38), and that those who followed Him as the light of the world should have the light of life (8: 12).

At the same time, He warned them that the time was short in which they had to make up their minds as to the attitude they were to adopt towards Him (7: 36; 8: 21).

He warned them that they were failing to use the intuitive power of which He had spoken (7: 17) and that that failure to recognize Him would bring them into judgement (8: 24), though even out of their rebellion would come the final justification of His claim (8: 31).

When their pride rebelled at this declaration of their powerlessness to help themselves, He had to unmask the true source of the murderous hate that His claim was arousing. So He points out that those who would follow Him in His obedience to the word of His Father would triumph over death. Those who would not, were choosing the devil, not God, to be their father.

The intimacy of the relationship to God that this claim implies issued in a first attempt to stone Him (8: 31–59).

Then, after the failure of the sign that He gave of His power as the Light of the World to restore sight even to those who were congenitally blind, He was challenged afresh to accept or disown Messiahship (10: 24). He avoids the word, but under the figures of the Door of the fold and the Good Shepherd, He reasserts His claim; and, especially in His faithfulness, even unto death, to the care of the flock committed to Him, He asserts His oneness with His Father in heaven.

This involves an explicit claim to kinship with God, even to an interpenetration of personalities, a conscious and vital unity of will with God, which inevitably leads to a second attempt to stone Him.

These attempts represent the reaction of Pharisaic opinion. The popular reaction to the raising of Lazarus rouses at last the settled and deliberate determination of the Sadducean hierarchy to put Him to death. Jesus goes up to Jerusalem to meet His doom. He makes one final appeal to the people to follow the light they had while it was still with them, basing this on a final declaration (12: 44 ff.) that He had by His words and works given those who would use their eyes a true revelation of Him who had commissioned Him.

There is a deeply significant change in atmosphere when we come to the record of the conversation in the Upper Chamber after the retirement of Judas. Jesus is alone with His friends, and He can speak out all that is in His heart to them as they are able to bear it.

This is no doubt an important limitation. It goes, indeed, so deep that it might seem to make all effective communication between them impossible. And yet love, meeting a response of love, however blind and deaf, finds a way to transcend the barrier. He had, we must remember, for some months been speaking to them of His coming crucifixion and resurrection, in spite of the fact that His meaning was hid from them, and that they dared not ask Him to explain, because He knew that the event when it came would open their eyes. So now He sets Himself to live in thought with them under the new conditions that His return from the grave would introduce, putting into words teaching which their experience would make luminous when it came, in quiet confidence that death could only consecrate, it could not destroy, the link of love that was already binding them to Him.

The new commandment made this love which is to follow the foundation of the revelations.

Then, in answer to the questions, which first one and then another was emboldened to put to Him, He helped them to realize that in the knowledge of Him, which was already an assured fruit of their discipleship, there was guidance, illumination and inspiration sufficient to enable them to keep in touch with Him, even when He had moved on to another room in His Father's house. In answer to Philip He declared, in words of inexhaustible significance, the open secret of His whole life in the flesh as a revelation of the Father, and coupled the declaration with a promise of the power that His disciples would share with Him, when they found that His mantle had fallen upon them, and that they in their turn were to appeal to men in His name, as He had appealed to them in His Father's name.

Then came the unveiling in three stages of a new quality of prayer when uttered "in His name"; and a revelation, also in three stages, of the other Comforter, the Holy Spirit, the Spirit of the truth, whom the Father would send into their hearts in His Son's name in answer to His prayer, that they might know that they were not deserted. He promised that as they strove to live in loving obedience to the commandments of their Lord in watchful submission to His word, they should enjoy unclouded communion with Him and with His Father.

Then He passes on to the mystery of the corporate union of all His people with one another in Him, as figured under the similitude of the Vine. He forewarns them of the path of suffering which their witness to Him before an unbelieving world would involve, and points to the power at the back of their corporate witness that would spring from the presence with them of the Comforter, who would at the same time be their guide into truth as yet beyond their comprehension.

After a short section referring to the sharp trial through which they would have immediately to pass, and the consolation in restored communion both with Himself and with His Father that would follow, something, perhaps the final proof that He had just given of His power to read the unexpressed questionings that were rising in their hearts, drew aside a veil, and the disciples awoke to the consciousness that they had indeed been in touch with the living God in Him.

Jesus found in their confession an assurance that the contact that He had come to establish between God and man had indeed been made, and after a brief warning of the trial still in store for Him and for them, He gave them a final revelation of all that was in His heart for them and for His Church to the end of time, as He pleaded with His Father for the consummation of His glory in the conversion of the world.

We read these chapters in the light of the experience of the Church in the first, and in all the ages that have followed the first, with ever deepening conviction of the truth and power of the teaching they contain.

From very different points of view the conviction finds expression that in them Jesus is speaking to each of us heart to heart as "a man speaketh to his friend", and is laying bare the secret of the new order in which He would have us live, so vividly that the words seem to come to us directly from Him as He is now in His glory.

There are indeed some who, finding such words in the work of an Evangelist whom on other grounds they are unwilling to acknowledge as a first-hand witness to the events that he describes, can only account for their presence on the hypothesis of a direct revelation. This is certainly a bold suggestion to come from those who as a rule require very strict demonstration before they will accept any deviation from the normal, and such a hypothesis seems entirely unprecedented. It is perhaps possible that the Letters to the Seven Churches in the Apocalypse were dictated directly to the seer when he was "in the spirit on the Lord's day". But that is a very different thing from inspiring an imaginative creation of a conversation that never took place.

At the same time, it is well to be reminded that this teaching, with its clear understanding of what would be the conditions of life for men in the new order, came before the Cross. It is certainly difficult to account for such prevision without some previous experience of those conditions. We saw, however, in considering a sentence in our Lord's conversation with Nicodemus, that He claimed to have already in a real sense ascended into heaven at His baptism. While He had been living as Man a life of unbroken communion with His Father, His true home had been in the new order. That being so, even before the Cross, His own experience would have supplied the materials for forecasting the conditions that His brethren would have to fulfil.

If, in fact, He knew indeed that He had come from God and was going back to God, it is not surprising that He should know the conditions under which His disciples could retain touch with Him, though the Spirit could not be given to them until He had been glorified. Since His own baptism the other Comforter had been with Him.

We can see, therefore, how Jesus, even before His resurrection, must have learnt the conditions of life in the new order from His own experience of communion with His Father in the power of the Holy Spirit, and so could declare them to His disciples on the lines recorded here.

If we wonder, as we well may, that the memory of these words remained so vividly in the mind of the Evangelist, a suggestion made by Canon Anthony Deane cannot be ruled out as merely fanciful. If the beloved disciple spent the first Easter Eve in obedience to His dying Master's bequest in dutiful attendance on the bereaved Mother, he may well have had occasion to go over with her the precious memories of what he could now see had been meant to prepare those that loved Him for the terrible trial that had come upon them.

CHAPTER XXIII

GETHSEMANE IN S. JOHN

1 *When Jesus had spoken these words, he went forth with his disciples over the brook Kidron,*[1] *where was a garden, into the which he* 2 *entered, himself and his disciples. Now Judas also, which betrayed him, knew the place: for Jesus oft-times resorted thither* 3 *with his disciples. Judas then, having received the band* of soldiers, *and officers from the chief priests and Pharisees, cometh thither* 4 *with lanterns and torches and weapons. Jesus therefore, knowing all the things that were coming upon him, went forth, and saith* 5 *unto them, Whom seek ye? They answered him, Jesus of Nazareth. Jesus saith unto them, I am* he. *And Judas also, which betrayed* 6 *him, was standing with them. When therefore he said unto them,* 7 *I am* he, *they went backward, and fell to the ground. Again therefore he asked them, Whom seek ye? And they said, Jesus* 8 *of Nazareth. Jesus answered, I told you that I am* he*: if there-* 9 *fore ye seek me, let these go their way: that the word might be fulfilled which he spake, Of those whom thou hast given me I* 10 *lost not one. Simon Peter therefore having a sword drew it, and struck the high priest's servant, and cut off his right ear. Now the* 11 *servant's name was Malchus. Jesus therefore said unto Peter, Put up the sword into the sheath: the cup which the Father hath given me, shall I not drink it?*

[1] Or: *The brook of the Cedars.*

S. JOHN passes from the High-Priestly prayer to Gethsemane and the arrest. He is writing, we must remember, for Christians already familiar with the Synoptic account, at least in S. Mark's form of it, and quite possibly in S. Luke's. He is writing also for those who felt with Cerinthus the difficulty of associating the suffering and shame and defeat of the Cross with the human experience of the Son of God. One main object of his Gospel is no doubt to insist on the reality of the human experience. He was the witness of a true Incarnation. And the earthly life had been closed by a real death. Jesus Christ came, not in the water only, but in the water and in the blood. To this he bears express testimony. We might have expected, therefore, that he would have welcomed the opportunity, even at the cost of repeating an oft-told tale, of recording the suffering side of his Lord's experience in the garden.

This, however, is just what he does not do. He has no wish to conceal or deny the reality of the deep waters through which the soul of Jesus had to pass. He has already recorded (12: 27) an agony in the Temple Courts. But he seems to have felt, as he looked back over the whole story, that there was another side even to the human experience than that which met the eye. We have already seen that to him the Cross, so far from connoting humiliation and defeat, was the symbol of uplifting, of glory, and of victory. So here, he is content to recall the spiritual struggle by a single phrase (verse 11). He records exclusively words and deeds which shewed that Jesus remained throughout absolute master of the situation. He is so, of course, even in the Synoptic account: but there is so much else in the picture that the fact may easily be overlooked.

S. Mark tells us that the scene was a private property called Gethsemane (14: 32) on the Mount of Olives (14: 26). S. Luke tells us (22: 39) that he had been in the habit of going there. Throughout Holy Week according to S. Mark (11: 11) Jesus and His disciples had gone back to Bethany. S. Luke says that they had bivouacked on the Mount of Olives (21: 37).

It will be remembered that S. Luke apparently describes the scene of the Ascension in Ac. 1: 12 as "the Mount of Olives". In the Gospel (Lk. 24: 50) apparently the same event took place "over against Bethany". So that there is no necessary contradiction between his tradition and S. Mark's. Dr. Armitage Robinson has pointed out that S. Luke describes Gethsemane (22: 40) simply as "the place", and notices that in 11: 1, just after a reference to Martha and Mary, he describes Jesus as "praying in a certain place". Gethsemane must in any case have been close to Bethany. As Dr. Robinson points out, the story of the agony in Gethsemane is full of echoes of the Lord's prayer, which, according to Lu. 11: 2–4, Jesus had taught His disciples in "a certain place", presumably not far from Bethany.

S. John in 18: 1 tells us that Jesus and His disciples crossed "the brook Cedron". In the R.V. margin, following another text, we read "The brook of the Cedars". Then He entered a garden. He adds that Judas knew the place, because Jesus often went there with His disciples. It must clearly have been in friendly hands, and Jesus must have availed Himself of the hospitality that it offered on more than one of His visits to Jerusalem. It looks as if the earlier nights in Holy Week had been spent there. If so, it would be the first place in which Judas would look, when he found that Jesus had left the Upper Chamber.

According to S. Mark, Judas is accompanied by a crowd with swords and staves from the chief priests and the scribes and elders (14: 43). In S. Luke (22: 52) Jesus remonstrates with the chief priests and captains of the Temple and elders. S. John's language suggests that the Roman soldiers were called out in full force with their commander, as well as servants both of the high priests and of the Pharisees. He also remembers the lanterns and torches.

According to S. Mark, Jesus, when He roused His disciples for the last time warned them that the hour of His betrayal had come. S. John puts into words what this implies when he says that Jesus "knowing all that was coming" went to meet those who had come to seek Him outside the garden.

In the Synoptic account Judas comes at the head of the crowd, guiding them, having given them a sign by which they might know whom to arrest. According to S. Mark and S. Matthew he went up to Jesus and kissed Him effusively.

S. Matthew records a curt command "Comrade, do what you have come to do", in the same spirit as the "What thou doest, do quickly", of Jn. 13: 27. S. Luke does not say that he actually kissed Him; but he records a loving remonstrance, "Judas, betrayest thou the Son of Man with a kiss?"

S. John tells us nothing of this. It is not unnatural to suppose that Judas fell back abashed into the crowd when Jesus went forward to face His pursuers. The recoil which followed His challenge and His confession is not necessarily miraculous. On other occasions (e.g. at Nazareth, Lk. 4: 30, cf. Jn. 8: 59) murderous hate had cowered before His purity, and His quiet confidence in God. Here the recoil emphasizes what is implied in the Synoptic account, the voluntary character of His surrender. He could, had He chosen, even without calling for the heavenly legions, have passed through the midst of them. The only use that He made of His ascendancy was to secure the safety of His disciples. The impetuosity of Simon Peter almost frustrated this loving purpose. The Synoptists tell us that when the Jewish officials came near to arrest Jesus, one of His followers drew his sword (one of the two which were all they had, Lk. 22; 38), and without waiting for a signal from Him, struck blindly at the head of one of the servants of the High Priest, cutting off his right ear (Lk. 22: 50; Jn. 18: 10). S. Luke tells us that Jesus immediately healed the wound, and prevented reprisals. S. Matthew records a general warning against the use of the sword. S. John couples with the command to return the sword to its sheath, the words, "The cup that My Father hath given me, shall I not drink it," echoing, as we have seen, the prayer in the agony recorded by the Synoptists.

These words, he tells us, were addressed to Peter, who as he has already told us, struck the blow. It is not difficult to understand why this identification should have been suppressed in the primitive Jerusalem tradition. The identification of the High Priest's servant as Malchus may be due to the fact that in gratitude for the healing he became a disciple; but it suggests the intimate knowledge of the other disciple, who was known to the High Priest (18: 15 f.), and who secured admission for Peter into the courtyard of his house.

The reason which led S. John to reveal Peter's name in this connexion is no doubt the light that it throws on the tragedy of Peter's denials. His loyalty led him to seek to be as near Jesus in His trial as possible, but the guilty consciousness of his rash act made a coward of him. He dared not face identification as the disciple who had struck the blow. So to save himself he denied his Lord.

THE EXAMINATION OF JESUS BEFORE ANNAS

12 *So the band and the chief captain, and the officers of the Jews,*
13 *seized Jesus and bound him, and led him to Annas first; for he was*
14 *father in law to Caiaphas, which was high priest that year. Now Caiaphas was he which gave counsel to the Jews, that it was expedient that one man should die for the people.*

15 *And Simon Peter followed Jesus, and* so did *another disciple. Now that disciple was known unto the high priest, and entered in*
16 *with Jesus into the court of the high priest; but Peter was standing at the door without. So the other disciple, which was known unto the high priest, went out and spake unto her that kept the*
17 *door, and brought in Peter. The maid therefore that kept the door saith unto Peter, Art thou also* one *of this man's disciples? He*
18 *saith, I am not. Now the servants and the officers were standing* there, *having made a fire of coals; for it was cold; and they were warming themselves: and Peter also was with them, standing and warming himself.*

19 *The high priest therefore asked Jesus of his disciples, and of*
20 *his teaching. Jesus answered him, I have spoken openly to the world; I ever taught in synagogues, and in the temple, where all*
21 *the Jews come together; and in secret spake I nothing. Why askest thou me? ask them that have heard* me, *what I spake unto them:*
22 *behold, these know the things which I said. And when he had said this, one of the officers standing by struck Jesus with his hand,*
23 *saying, Answerest thou the high priest so? Jesus answered him, If I have spoken evil, bear witness of the evil: but if well, why*
24 *smitest thou me? Annas therefore sent him bound unto Caiaphas the high priest.*

25 *Now Simon Peter was standing and warming himself. They said therefore unto him, Art thou also* one *of his disciples? He denied,* 26 *and said, I am not. One of the servants of the high priest, being a kinsman of him whose ear Peter cut off, saith, Did not I see* 27 *thee in the garden with him? Peter therefore denied again: and straightway the cock crew.*

The detachment of Roman soldiers and the Jewish police bound their prisoner, and carried Him off for trial by the Jewish authorities. Time was pressing. The Sanhedrim could not pass a sentence of death before daybreak. But it was possible to expedite matters by collecting evidence against the prisoner. S. Mark and S. Matthew make a clear distinction between the examination before Caiaphas by night, and the formal meeting of the Sanhedrim in the morning to ratify the sentence. They describe the examination at some length, and take the conviction by the Sanhedrim for granted. S. Luke records only proceedings before the Sanhedrim. These seem to have followed, with slight but significant variations, the proceedings before Caiaphas.

S. John concentrates attention on a yet earlier stage, which had been passed over in the common tradition: an examination before Annas, father-in-law of Caiaphas, the head of the high-priestly family, and the real director of its policy. This examination seems to have been short and comparatively private. Annas may have been curious to see Jesus, and make up his mind about Him. In any case it would save trouble if he could make the prisoner commit Himself to some actionable statement. Jesus gave him no help, and the task of collecting evidence against Him, including, in the last resort, an official challenge to declare Himself, had to be taken on by Caiaphas.

It may seem strange that S. John should have thought it worth while to record this apparently fruitless stage in the proceedings. But no doubt the memories of the night were unspeakably precious to him: and the love which urged him to follow, even into the examination room, enabled him to preserve two words of the Lord, the first of which helps to explain His subsequent silence before His persecutors, while the second shews how, on occasion, He met official insult with dignified remonstrance.

I take for granted that "the other disciple, known to the high priest", who followed Jesus into the courtyard, and spoke to the damsel to let in Peter, was none other than S. John. The indirect method of alluding to himself is characteristic of the Evangelist.

It ought not to surprise us to learn in this way that another disciple, and one who did not shrink from owning his allegiance, was in the courtyard that night. No doubt S. Mark tells us that "all (S. Matthew says 'all the disciples') left Him and fled", and S. John has shewn us that Jesus by asking for a free passage for His disciples had made it clear that it was His will that they should leave Him. But if, in spite of this, Peter plucked up courage to "follow afar off", we need not be surprised if another of the disciples, who had not Peter's need for concealment, followed even more closely. And the Synoptists, when we read them attentively, make it clear that it was even so.

The maid-servant, according to S. Mark, challenged Peter with the words, "You *also* were with Jesus the Nazarene?" This significant *also* is repeated by S. Matthew on the occasion of the second challenge. It occurs in the form "This man *also*" three times in S. Luke.

It need not, therefore, surprise us to learn from S. John that the question was asked by the maid-servant who kept the door, and who at the other disciple's request had let in Peter. Her question may not at first have meant more than "Are not you like your friend one of the disciples of Jesus"?

The rash blow struck in the garden, as S. John hints in verse 26, made it dangerous for Peter to risk recognition. So he missed this golden opportunity of appearing in his true colours. The maid clearly did not believe him, and his denial only served to rouse her suspicions. She seems to have communicated them to others, and so challenge after challenge led to denial after denial, and in the end to perjury.

There is one further link between the Fourth Gospel and S. Mark, to which it is worth while calling attention. S. Mark tells us twice over (14: 54, 67) that Peter was drawn into the tell-tale light of the fire to warm himself. This is recorded besides only by S. John, who, as having also been out that night, had special reason to remember how cold it had been (verse 18).

THE TRIAL BEFORE PILATE

28 *They lead Jesus therefore from Caiaphas into the palace: and it was early; and they themselves entered not into the palace, that* 29 *they might not be defiled, but might eat the passover. Pilate therefore went out unto them, and saith, What accusation bring ye* 30 *against this man? They answered and said unto him, If this man were not an evil-doer, we should not have delivered him up unto* 31 *thee. Pilate therefore said unto them, Take him yourselves, and judge him according to your law. The Jews said unto him, It is* 32 *not lawful for us to put any man to death: that the words of Jesus might be fulfilled, which he spake, signifying by what manner of death he should die.*

33 *Pilate therefore entered again into the palace, and called Jesus,* 34 *and said unto him, Art thou the King of the Jews? Jesus answered, Sayest thou this of thyself, or did others tell it thee concerning me?* 35 *Pilate answered, Am I a Jew? Thine own nation and the chief* 36 *priests delivered thee unto me: what hast thou done? Jesus answered, My kingdom is not of this world: if my kingdom were of this world, then would my servants fight, that I should not be delivered* 37 *to the Jews: but now is my kingdom not from hence. Pilate therefore said unto him, Art thou a king then? Jesus answered, Thou sayest that I am a king. To this end have I been born, and to this end am I come into the world, that I should bear witness unto* 38 *the truth. Everyone that is of the truth heareth my voice. Pilate saith unto him, What is truth?*

And when he had said this, he went out again unto the Jews, and 39 *saith unto them, I find no crime in him. But ye have a custom, that I should release unto you one at the passover: will ye therefore* 40 *that I release unto you the King of the Jews? They cried out therefore again, saying, Not this man, but Barabbas. Now Barabbas was a robber.*

In S. Mark, Jesus, having been condemned to death by the Jews for blasphemy, is brought before Pilate. Pilate for no apparent reason asks Him, "Art thou the King of the Jews?" Jesus answers, "Thou sayest", which seems to mean "Yes", or "Sayest thou that?" Then follows an arraignment by the chief priests, to which Jesus makes no reply, even when Pilate presses Him. Then, when the crowd asks for the release of a prisoner, Pilate seizes the opportunity to play the people against their rulers, because he sees that the charge of sedition has no foundation.

The supporters of Barabbas were, however, too strong for him. No doubt his partisans were already hoping to use the privilege of the feast in his favour, and the chief priests had little difficulty in securing a popular vote for him. Then Pilate asks what he is to do with Jesus; and though convinced of His innocence, he yields to the popular demand for His crucifixion.

S. Matthew adds the appeal of Pilate's wife in favour of Jesus, and the attempt of the Governor to evade responsibility by washing his hands.

S. Luke explains Pilate's question by shewing that the Jewish authorities brought a charge of political disaffection against Jesus. Pilate, after hearing the answer of Jesus, acquits Him. In answer to continued pressure he sends Him to Herod. Herod acquits Him mockingly as a King *pour rire*. Pilate then once more acquits Him, offering to scourge and release Him. This leads to the demand for the release of Barabbas, and for the crucifixion of Jesus. Pilate yields to popular clamour.

According to S. John the trial took place in the Roman Court House, the Jews remaining outside for fear of defilement. They try first to secure judgement off-hand. This Pilate refuses. They are forced, therefore, to produce a charge of which the Roman Law could take cognisance. This accounts for the sudden appearance of the political count. Jesus, who is in the Praetorium, naturally asks where this new count comes from? When Pilate indicates it had been made by the chief priests, Jesus, to Pilate's evident surprise, does not deny the charge; though He makes it clear that the sovereignty that He claimed differed fundamentally in origin, and in the force that lay behind it, from that which it was Pilate's duty to exert as the representative of Cæsar. To avoid the possibility of mistake, Pilate repeats his question: *Art thou a king then?* and Jesus answers, *Thou sayest that I am a king. For this have I been born and for this I came into the world, that I may bear witness to the truth. Everyone that is of the truth heareth my voice.*

These are clearly words of inexhaustible significance. As Dr. Westcott points out, they are "the good confession" which He witnessed before Pontius Pilate (1 Tim. 6: 13), corresponding to the confession before the High Priest.

They reveal the purpose of the Incarnation, not now as the fulfilment of the promises of God to His chosen people through the prophets, but in terms which make it the answer to the age-long searching of the human spirit.

It is, however, by no means easy to determine how far Pilate was in a position to grasp their meaning, especially in relation to the subject immediately under discussion.

We may assume that he was an educated Roman gentleman, familiar with the points at issue between the rival schools of philosophy that flourished in his day. If so, a claim to kingship based on a witness to the truth would have suggested the well-known Stoic doctrine that the wise man was the true king. Plato had declared that his ideal state must await realization until a king appeared who was also a philosopher. The Stoic went further and maintained that the ideal wise man, with or without a crown, had the essential characteristics of a king. He, and he alone, had the vision of truth, the intelligent apprehension of reality, which made him master of his circumstances and gave him the capacity to guide and rule his fellows.

Jesus, therefore, in basing His claim to kingship on His witness to the truth, at least gave Pilate a reminder of the existence of a kingdom, in this world though not of it, in which Cæsar's writs did not run, and which his legions could not help him to annex. Pilate's reply, "What is truth?"—in spite of Bacon's epigram—was no jest, though he did not wait for a reply. It was the natural answer of a Sceptic, when asked to give his assent to any positive proposition. It suggests that he had caught at least something of the Lord's meaning. A deeper understanding of the words, as they themselves declared, depended on a spiritual condition which Pilate failed to fulfil. As his subsequent conduct shewed, he believed in the innocence of his prisoner, but dared not face the consequences of acting up to his convictions. He was not of the truth, and so failed to hear the voice of the King.

We must not, of course, limit the words to the meaning which Pilate was capable of apprehending. There is no reason to suppose that they were addressed exclusively to him. The truth expressed in them concerns the whole world. The examination was held in open court, though religious scruples prevented the prosecution from setting foot in it. So there may well have been among those who heard "the good confession" some who were better qualified than the Roman Governor to appreciate it. If, for instance—and it is by no means an extravagant supposition—"the other disciple" who had followed His Master into the house of the High Priest, followed Him on into the Governor's palace, and himself heard the cross-examination which he reports, the reference to the truth would have recalled at once the revelation to Thomas—"I am the Truth"—which he had heard but a few hours before. And the two utterances would have begun at once to receive light each from the other, as they cannot fail to do as soon as we take them together.

This private examination before Pilate was followed by a formal acquittal.

CHAPTER XXIV

THE CRUCIFIXION

1 *Then Pilate therefore took Jesus, and scourged him. And the*
2 *soldiers plaited a crown of thorns, and put it on his head, and arrayed*
3 *him in a purple garment; and they came unto him, and said, Hail,*
4 *King of the Jews! and they struck him with their hands. And*
Pilate went out again, and saith unto them, Behold, I bring him
5 *out to you, that ye may know that I find no crime in him. Jesus*
therefore came out, wearing the crown of thorns and the purple
6 *garment. And* Pilate *saith unto them, Behold, the man! When*
therefore the chief priests and the officers saw him, they cried out,
saying, Crucify him, *crucify* him. *Pilate saith unto them, Take*
7 *him yourselves, and crucify him: for I find no crime in him. The*
Jews answered him, We have a law, and by that law he ought to
8 *die, because he made himself the Son of God. When Pilate there-*
9 *fore heard this saying, he was the more afraid; and he entered*
into the palace again, and saith unto Jesus, Whence art thou?
10 *But Jesus gave him no answer. Pilate therefore saith unto him,*
Speakest thou not unto me? knowest thou not that I have power
11 *to release thee, and have power to crucify thee? Jesus answered*
him, Thou wouldest have no power at all against me, except it
were given thee from above: therefore he that delivered me unto
12 *thee hath greater sin. Upon this Pilate sought to release him: but*
the Jews cried out, saying, If thou release this man, thou art not
Caesar's friend: everyone that maketh himself a king speaketh
13 *against Caesar. When Pilate therefore heard these words, he*
brought Jesus out, and sat down on the judgement-seat at a place
14 *called The Pavement, but in Hebrew, Gabbatha. Now it was*
the Preparation of the passover: it was about the sixth hour. And
15 *he saith unto the Jews, Behold, your King! They therefore cried out,*
Away with him, *Away with* him, *crucify him. Pilate saith unto*
them, Shall I crucify your king? The chief priests answered, We
16 *have no king but Caesar. Then therefore he delivered him unto*
them to be crucified.

APPARENTLY after the trial and mockery by Herod, and the infliction of the scourging, which Pilate offered, according to S. Luke, as a preliminary to release, Jesus is mocked by the Roman soldiers, and displayed in a general's cloak, and crown of thorns, Pilate once more pronouncing a formal acquittal. The chief priests, however, refuse to be satisfied and demand crucifixion. Pilate once more refuses, and they are forced to reveal the real ground of their sentence. He claimed to be a Son of God. This leads to a fresh interview between Pilate and Jesus, in which, though he gets no direct answer to his question, Pilate is solemnly warned that the authority that he is wielding is a trust from God.

S. John clearly regards Pilate as, in consequence, genuinely desirous of securing the release of Jesus. Pilate is warned, however, that this would expose him to a charge of disloyalty before the Emperor.

Pilate, however, makes one more effort. He presents Jesus to them as their King. If, as S. John's language suggests, he was still trying to release Jesus, he cannot have done this in mockery. That could only infuriate. If, as we generally assume, the threat of prosecution had been too much for him, and he had already yielded to the pressure, he must have done it in order to make his surrender in as insulting a form as possible. But it is just conceivable that he meant the words seriously—that he was prepared to recommend Tiberius to give Judæa a king once more in the person of Jesus. It gives tremendous significance to the act of national apostasy, if they deliberately preferred Cæsar to Jesus. Their protest against the title on the Cross, suggests that there was real ground for thinking that Pilate meant it to be taken literally.

16b *They took Jesus therefore:* 17 *and he went out, bearing the cross for himself, unto the place called The place of a skull, which*
18 *is called in Hebrew Golgotha: where they crucified him, and with*
19 *him two others, on either side one, and Jesus in the midst. And*

Pilate wrote a title also, and put it on the cross. And there was
20 *written,* JESUS OF NAZARETH, THE KING OF THE JEWS. *This title therefore read many of the Jews: for the place where Jesus was crucified was nigh to the city: and it was written in Hebrew,*
21 and *in Latin,* and *in Greek. The chief priests of the Jews therefore said to Pilate, Write not, The King of the Jews; but, that*
22 *he said, I am King of the Jews. Pilate answered, What I have written I have written.*

23 *The soldiers therefore, when they had crucified Jesus, took his garments, and made four parts, to every soldier a part; and also the coat: now the coat was without seam, woven from the top*
24 *throughout. They said therefore one to another, Let us not rend it, but cast lots for it, whose it shall be: that the scripture might be fulfilled, which saith, They parted my garments among them, And upon my vesture did they cast lots. These things therefore*
25 *the soldiers did. But there were standing by the cross of Jesus his mother, and his mother's sister, Mary the* wife *of Clopas,*
26 *and Mary Magdalene. When Jesus therefore saw his mother, and the disciple standing by, whom he loved, he saith unto his*
27 *mother, Woman, behold, thy son! Then saith he to the disciple, Behold, thy mother: And from that hour the disciple took her unto his own* home.

We pass from the story of the trial of Jesus to the story of His crucifixion. I write on the hypothesis that S. John is addressing Christians who were already familiar with the Synoptic narrative. He is therefore under no obligation to tell the whole story. He is free to select such details as may bring out the bearing of each incident on the development of the main theme of his Gospel. His object throughout (as he tells us in 20 : 31) is to shew that "Jesus is the Christ, the Son of God". He seems for the most part to confine himself to the things that had come under his own observation. We have no right to assume that he denies anything that he does not choose to record.

At times, no doubt, there seems to be a direct conflict between his testimony and that of the Synoptists. And for the most part, we are left to find our own solution to any apparent discrepancy, with very various results. A notable instance comes before us in connexion with both parts of the chronological note which S. John gives (19: 14) to fix the day and the hour of the condemnation of Jesus. *It was the preparation for the passover. It was six o'clock.* There is no doubt that S. John means us to understand that the crucifixion took place on the first day of unleavened bread, the day on which the passover was killed. This day, according to Jewish reckoning, began at sunset on the evening before and included the night of the Last Supper.

The paschal lamb would not be eaten till after sunset, when, according to Jewish reckoning, a new day would have begun. S. John, therefore, and S. Luke (22: 7) are at one in regard to the day of the month. When we remember that the day which followed the night on which the passover was eaten was always kept as a strict sabbath, on whatever day of the week it fell, we can see that S. Matthew and S. Mark imply the same thing, though their language, and perhaps S. Luke's, gives the impression that the Last Supper was the Passover, i.e. a feast on the paschal victim. We cannot suppose that Jesus and His disciples killed and ate their lamb a day too soon. It was then the custom of the Jews to usher in every sabbath with a family meal, held the night before, at which bread and wine were solemnly blessed, and on the eve of the Passover that blessing would have included an express reference to the approaching feast. This may account for the Synoptic use of the term Passover in relation to the Last Supper.

The difficulty with regard to the hour of our Lord's condemnation is no less serious. S. Mark tells us (15: 25) that Jesus was crucified at the third hour, i.e. 9 a.m.; and that there was darkness over all the land from the sixth to the ninth hour (verse 33), i.e. from noon to 3 p.m. Crucifixion was a lingering death, and as the bodies had to be taken down at sunset, 9 a.m. is none too early for the execution of the sentence. S. John, however, gives the sixth hour as the time of the condemnation. If he meant by that twelve noon he must surely have made a mistake.

There were, however, different ways of reckoning time in the Roman Empire. S. Mark, no doubt, follows the ordinary usage, which held both in Europe and in Palestine. But J. B. McClellan in a remarkable book on the Gospels (*The New Testament*, *Vol.* I Macmillan 1875) has shewn that the Romans reckoned what they called "the civil day" as we do, from midnight. He points out also that there is evidence from the accounts of the martyrdoms of Polycarp and Pionius, who both suffered at Smyrna in the second century A.D., that that method of reckoning was in vogue in the Roman Province of Asia, of which Ephesus, where S. John's Gospel was written, was the capital. There is, therefore, no inherent impossibility in the supposition that S. John gives 6 a.m. as the hour of condemnation. Dr. Westcott examines carefully the other notes of time in S. John (1 : 39; 4 : 6, 52), and shews that they fit in best with the system of reckoning by "the civil day". McClellan also claims—I think with justice—that S. John by dating the appearance of our Lord to the disciples (20 : 19) on the day of the resurrection, shews that he followed what is to us the natural method of reckoning days.

In regard to specific incidents we may notice that the national apostasy consummated, according to S. John, by the chief priests when they declared that they had no king but Cæsar, has its parallel in the terrible words of the people recorded by S. Matthew (27 : 25) : "His blood be on us and on our children."

The scourging of Jesus is recorded by S. Matthew and S. Mark as being a preliminary to crucifixion after the sentence had been finally passed. S. John, and by implication, S. Luke, place it earlier. We need not suppose that He was scourged a second time.

When the procession started for Calvary, Jesus—as S. John tells us—was bearing His own Cross. This was, of course, the regular custom. Simon of Cyrene, would not have been impressed into the service, if Jesus had not sunk beneath the burthen. We cannot lay any stress on the fact that S. John does not mention Simon. He may have seen the procession start for Calvary, and then have gone to fetch the Blessed Mother.

S. John's account of the title on the Cross lays stress on the fact that Pilate himself was directly responsible for the form that it took, and saw to it that it should be intelligible to all beholders by causing it to be put up in Hebrew, Latin and Greek.

S. John records, as the Synoptists also do, the division of our Lord's clothes among the soldiers. The language in which the incident is recorded is in each case reminiscent of Ps. 22: 18. S. John alone quotes the passage expressly, and explains how it came about that they had to cast lots. He clearly was struck by the exactness of the correspondence between the historic event and the prophetic picture. If the fact was as he related it, the coincidence is certainly remarkable. There is no justification for supposing that he invented the fact to emphasize the resemblance to the prophecy.

S. John passes on to call our attention to a group near the Cross, of whose presence at this time and place the other evangelists give no sign. S. Mark and S. Matthew record the reviling crowd of passers-by, and the bitter mockery by the chief priests and scribes. They tell us that even the crucified robbers at His side joined in the reviling. S. Luke has another account of the behaviour of the robbers, and adds that the soldiers, repeating the challenge to Jesus to save Himself, mocked Him by offering Him vinegar. He does not say that they took it away before He could taste it; but, as they stand, his words suggest it. We may note, however, that he says nothing of the offer of drugged wine, which Jesus refused before He was nailed to the Cross, or of that gift which S. John will bring before us later, a hint of which is found in S. Matthew and S. Mark.

Reference to the presence of friends, especially of women, including—according to S. Matthew and S. Mark—Mary Magdalene, and Mary, the mother of James the little and of Joses (or Joseph), and Salome, the mother of Zebedee's children, is found in all three, but not till after the death, and then they are standing "afar off".

S. John makes no mention of the presence of the hostile or of the indifferent. He concentrates attention on a little group of loyal friends, four women and one man, standing some time before the death close to the Cross. They are the mother of Jesus, and His mother's sister, Mary the wife of Clopas, and Mary Magdalene. The presence of the man in the group is only revealed because Jesus has something to say to him—a hint which shews that the narrative comes from one of the group and enables us to identify him. The similarity of the names to those in S. Mark's list (15:40) is remarkable, and suggests interesting identifications. If "James the little" is the same as James the son of Alphaeus, whose name is found in all the lists of the apostles, Clopas would seem to be an alternative transliteration for "Halphaeus". "His mother's sister" in S. John corresponds to Salome, the mother of Zebedee's children, and it is natural to identify them. It would be quite in the manner of the Fourth Evangelist to keep back his mother's name. This relationship would, as Dr. Westcott points out, help to explain the passing over of "the brethren of the Lord" in the bequest that follows: *When Jesus therefore saw his mother, and the disciple standing by, whom he loved, he saith unto his mother, Woman behold thy son! Then saith he to the disciple, Behold, thy mother!* The ground of this bequest, however, lies deeper than any tie of blood-relationship, and we can be content without absolute certainty in regard to the tempting identification. For this, the first of the three utterances from the Cross recorded by S. John, has a self-attesting depth and beauty, the wonder of which is inexhaustible.

Think of the situation. The dying Lord is taking His leave of the two who were His dearest upon earth, His mother and the disciple, to whom, beyond all the rest, His heart had gone out, and who had responded to His love.

They were the two who would feel most keenly the pang of separation, and the loss of the visible presence which had meant so much for them. He, therefore, gives them to each other in such a way that each might be to the other a living link with Him, and supply from the first an object for the service that it had been their joy to render to Him while He had been with them in the flesh.

28 *After this Jesus, knowing that all things are now finished, that the*
29 *scripture might be accomplished, saith, I thirst. There was set*
there a vessel full of vinegar: so they put a sponge full of the vinegar
30 *upon hyssop, and brought it to his mouth. When Jesus therefore*
had received the vinegar, he said, It is finished: and he bowed his
head, and gave up his spirit.

After this sacred commission had been conferred on him, we read that from that hour the disciple took his Lord's mother "to his own home". That does not imply that he had at that time a separate establishment of his own, independent of his family. The phrase is simply "into his own things". She became in a special sense his own. He assumed the charge of her. He may have taken her back at this time to the place, in Jerusalem, or in Bethany, where she was living. Her name is not mentioned with the other three, who were standing afar off, when Jesus breathed His last, after the three hours' darkness (Mk. 15: 40). S. John, however, says nothing about the darkness. In any case before its end he must have been back again at his station near the Cross. His complete silence with regard to the darkness, and to the cry, "My God, My God, why didst Thou forsake Me?" is remarkable. He cannot, I think, have meant to deny that they took place. The absence of any reference to them, like his silence with regard to the agony in the garden, concentrates our attention on the completeness of the victory. It is only if we read his story without reference to the Synoptic background, that he seems to minimize the cost at which the victory was won. His narrative, as it stands, contains, as we shall see, fresh indications of intense personal suffering.

The first of these is supplied by what is commonly, and I think rightly, regarded as the fifth word from the Cross—"I thirst". S. John introduces it in such a way as to shew that he regarded it as a deliberate reference to Ps. 69: 21. *After this Jesus knowing that all things are now finished, that the scripture might be accomplished saith, I thirst.*

The construction is, as Dr. Abbott shews (*Johannine Grammar*, 2115), ambiguous. His conclusion is worth quoting.

"The writer indicates (1) that all things were accomplished that the Scripture might be fulfilled; (2) that Jesus knew this when He uttered the words 'I thirst'. He leads us to infer that Jesus uttered the words as the crown of that accomplishment and with a view to that fulfilment." Of course the comment is due to the Evangelist. Here, as in 13: 1, 3; 18: 4, he read the mind of Jesus from what He said and did. In this case the word of Jesus shewed that He was passing through an experience corresponding to that described by the psalmist.

And the utterance called out a response from the bystanders similar to that which the psalmist had either himself experienced or anticipated. The literal correspondence between the anticipation and the fulfilment is striking, as in the case of the casting of lots for the seamless robe: but we must for the present refrain from commenting on it.

The Evangelist calls attention to the presence of a vessel full of vinegar or sour wine ready at hand. It was probably there for the refreshment of the soldiers. *They, therefore,* (S. John does not tell us who they were) *put a sponge full of the vinegar on hyssop and brought it to His mouth.*

This is clearly the same incident as that described in Mk. 15: 36; Mt. 27: 48, directly after the cry, "My God, my God", which the bystanders regarded as a cry for Elijah to come and save Him. One of them, they say, ran and filled a sponge with vinegar and put it on a reed, and gave Him to drink. His object apparently was to help to keep Jesus alive in case Elijah came in answer to the cry. The "let be" may have been addressed to the soldiers, apologizing for making free with their drink.

The reference to hyssop in S. John is puzzling. One thing is certain, it cannot be the same as the reed, by the help of which, according to S. Matthew and S. Mark, the sponge was raised to our Lord's lips.[1]

[1] Unless there is an error in the text in S. John, the sponge must have been fastened to the hyssop, and that in turn to the end of the reed. This is the solution suggested in the article "Hyssop" in Hastings's *Bible Dictionary*. "S. John mentions both the articles used to mitigate the thirst of our Saviour, but omits telling how they 'put it to His mouth.' It is clear that this could not

There is a further problem of a different kind which craves consideration. The sufferer in Ps. 69, so far from being grateful for the gall and vinegar, imprecates a curse on those who offered them. "Let their table before them become a snare", i.e. "Let it be to them what they made mine to me". It is difficult to believe that S. John, in calling special attention to the fulfilment of this scripture, thought only of the evidence given by our Lord's words for the fact of the thirst, and overlooked the complete difference in spirit in the response that it evoked. It is, therefore, interesting to notice that in the apocryphal *Gospel according to Peter* (§ 5) we read, "And it was noon, and darkness covered all Judæa, and they were troubled and distressed, but the sun was going down, since He yet lived: [for] it is written for them, that the sun go not down on him that is put to death. And one of them said, 'Give Him to drink gall with vinegar'. And they mixed and gave Him to drink, and fulfilled all things, and accomplished their sins against their own head". The writer here clearly regards the drink as poisonous in intention.

---

have been done by the hand alone. Matthew and Mark omit the hyssop, but mention the reed by which the sponge, vinegar and hyssop were 'put to His mouth'. . . . Like the peppermint it (hyssop) tastes at first hot, but this is followed by a cooling, refreshing feeling, and a flow of saliva which quenches thirst. The addition of this substance to the vinegar or sour wine on the sponge would be eminently suited to the purpose of moistening and cooling the mouth of the parched sufferer on the Cross."

This is, no doubt, a complicated proceeding, not easy to understand in detail. It is, however, worth notice that an Alexandrian writer of the fifth century, Nonnus, in his paraphrase assumes that this is what took place. He is probably at this point dependent on Origen. And both Origen and S. Cyril of Jerusalem (13 : 39) expressly distinguish the hyssop from the reed. If the hyssop had a recognized effect in mitigating the sufferings of the crucified from thirst, it is possible that a store of it was provided from the same source as the drugged wine offered to the condemned at the time of their crucifixion.

Another solution is, however, possible. The Greek word for a javelin, *hyssos* differs from *hyssopos* only by a single syllable. It has been very ingeniously suggested that S. John really wrote, "They put a sponge full of vinegar on a javelin". The javelins were three and a half feet long. Each Roman soldier carried two. So the only difference between S. John and the Synoptists would be that S. John gives a more precise description of the rod, on which the sponge was brought to our Lord's lips.

The word for javelin is not a very common one, and the temptation to substitute the familiar hyssop would be very great. There is, however, a real difficulty in accounting for the complete disappearance of the true reading from all our excellent authorities for the text.

Origen in his notes on S. Matthew § 137, implies that our Lord's enemies offered Him a baneful drink with intent to do Him hurt. Origen was familiar with the *Gospel according to Peter*, but he speaks in the same context of those who put the sponge full of vinegar with gall and hyssop on a reed and brought it to the mouth of Christ, so there can be no doubt that he believes that he has the authority of S. John for what he says. Nonnus is clearly of the same opinion. For he says in his paraphrase that a "certain quick-witted man when he heard, filled a sponge . . . and reached up to him vinegar of destruction mingled with hyssop".

There is some authority besides that of Origen for reading "vinegar with gall", in Jn. 19: 29 f., and Mt. 27: 34, clearly influenced by Ps. 69: 21, substitutes wine mingled with gall for the "myrrhed wine", which we find in S. Mark, at the time of the crucifixion. Some authorities complete the assimilation to this psalm by reading "vinegar" instead of "wine". Neither S. Matthew nor S. Mark shew any trace of "gall" on this later occasion.

At the same time, some of us will, I feel sure, be reluctant to surrender the relief which this incident, if we regard it as an act of pity, provides in the midst of the terrible revelation of human malignity on Calvary. S. Luke's story of the penitent robber and the story of the confession of the centurion after our Lord's death, suggest how good might be mingled with evil even in the crowd. The weight to be attached to the original meaning of the prophecy must be considered later. I cannot help feeling that Origen's interpretation introduces an element alien to the context in S. John, and was really derived from the Gospel of Peter, which aims throughout at emphasizing the guilt of the Jews.

The words from the Cross, after the three hours' darkness, must have followed one another quickly. The offering of the vinegar followed so closely on the cry of desertion that in S. Mark and S. Matthew it is treated as a response to it. The word "It is finished", followed directly after the taking of the vinegar. Then, as S. John tells us, Jesus "reclined" His head and gave up His Spirit, a gesture and an act which, as we shall see, are interpreted for us by the last word recorded only by S. Luke. We are now concerned with the last word recorded by S. John, *It is finished*.

S. John's comment (19: 28): "seeing that all things were now finished", suggests that the words refer to the purpose of God in the things which were appointed for Him to do and suffer. Jesus Himself had said in the Upper Chamber (Lk. 22: 37): "This that is written must be fulfilled (finished) in Me, and he was reckoned with transgressors: for that which concerneth me hath fulfilment" (an end). From the same point of view, S. Paul, in the Pisidian Antioch (Ac. 13: 27) said: "They that dwell at Jerusalem and their rulers, because they knew Him not, nor the voices of the prophets, which are read every sabbath, *fulfilled* them by condemning Him".

The word in S. John and in S. Luke means "to finish", or "bring to an end".

It is different from the word which our Lord used when He said: "I came not to destroy the law or the prophets; but to fulfil", i.e. to bring to perfection; and which S. Paul used at Antioch. S. Matthew uses it in speaking of a prophecy being "fulfilled" when an incident in our Lord's life brought out the full meaning of the inspired anticipation.

At the same time we cannot doubt that the words have another and a more personal bearing. If the scriptures were finished, it was because He had run the race that was set before Him: He had "finished His course" (2 Tim. 4: 7; Ac. 20: 24). The time had come when His work on earth was finished and He could go home.

S. John has already given us foregleams of this. In 4: 34 he records a word of Jesus to His disciples: "My meat is to do the will of Him that sent me, and to finish His work". In Lk. 13: 32 we have a closely related utterance: "Lo! I cast out devils, and perform cures to-day and to-morrow, and the third day I am perfected".

The great intercession (Jn. 17) just before the agony in the garden, begins with the surrender of the work of His earthly ministry into His Father's hands. The only thing left for Him to do was to die. And now that act also, which began with His willing acceptance of the cup from His Father's hand in the garden, had reached its goal. He might with a clear conscience give up His spirit.

This is all done so simply, and in S. John's narrative with such a complete absence of effort, that we may easily miss the wonder of it. It is hard for us to realize that Jesus, according to S. Luke's reckoning, was under thirty-five. In the eyes of men he had achieved nothing. He was being crushed out in the fulness of physical life and vigour. The forces arrayed against Him were still unbroken. They were allowed to work their will to the uttermost. They had power to kill the body, and they were allowed to exercise it.

We have already considered the completeness of our Lord's mastery over the fear of death. But by the grave of Lazarus, He claimed further to be Himself the Resurrection and the Life. He had claimed the power to destroy death and to bring life and immortality to light. The mastery shewn in this utterance on the Cross is closely connected with this claim, but it had to wait till the third day for its triumphant vindication in the sight of men.

Meanwhile there is another element in the situation which craves attention. Judged by human standards, the earthly life of Jesus, as we have seen, was strangely incomplete and unsuccessful. Jesus Himself, however, shews a sublime unconsciousness of this. He worked on "without haste and without rest", while it was called to-day. His Father set Him His work and determined His hours of labour. He did the work of each day in its day, leaving His Father to fit the details into the whole that He had planned. So when the last call came He knew that His work here was done.

We, too, if we are wise, are at least, as General Gordon was, "predestinarians after the event". If no sparrow can fall to the ground without our Father, much more must this be true of His own children. So, after the event, after the call has come, we realize that the dead man's work was done, however hard it may be to believe it. It is not strange, therefore, that to Jesus the call and the conviction that His work was done came together. The wonder lies further back. It is hard for us to understand how, when everything to outward appearance looked so unfinished, Jesus could have believed that it was really His Father's voice calling Him home. We must not, however, forget that His human spirit indwelt by the Spirit of God had an insight into the will of His Father which may well transcend our experience. And besides, the Gospels bear constant witness, not least in this immediate context, that He found clear corroboration of the correctness of His spiritual intuition in the Scriptures.

S. John goes on to describe the act of dying. He tells us that Jesus "reclined His head and gave up His spirit". The words, as Dr. Abbott shews (*Johannine Vocabulary*, 1541–8) repay careful examination.

In S. Mark we read simply "breathed His last", expired. In S. Matthew we have "let go" (or "dismissed") "His spirit". S. Luke records the last of the seven words: "Father, into thy hands I commend my spirit", and then using S. Mark's word, says: "He expired". S. John's phrase, "He gave up His spirit", seems to echo the word recorded by S. Luke. The act was accompanied by a gesture, bending or laying down His head. The exact movement of the head indicated here is not easy to determine. Under normal conditions the phrase suggests going to bed, as in our Lord's word (Mt. 8: 20; Lk. 9: 58): "The Son of Man hath not where to lay His head". In any case, as Dr. Abbott points out, the thought is not of submission or resignation, but of simple trust. He quotes (*Johannine Grammar* 2644 i) a beautiful comment from Origen. "If we have understood the meaning of bending the head . . . let us be urgent so to keep our own lives that in our departure we too may be able . . . to deliver up our spirit even as Jesus who *bent the head and took His departure in the act of resting it, as it were, on the lap of the Father, who could cherish it and strengthen it in His bosom*" (in Matt. 138).

31 *The Jews therefore, because it was the Preparation, that the bodies should not remain on the cross upon the sabbath (for the day of that sabbath was a high* day), *asked of Pilate that their*
32 *legs might be broken, and* that *they might be taken away. The soldiers therefore came, and brake the legs of the first, and of the*
33 *other which was crucified with him: but when they came to Jesus, and saw that he was dead already, they brake not his legs: howbeit*
34 *one of the soldiers with a spear pierced his side, and straightway*
35 *there came out blood and water. And he that hath seen hath borne witness, and his witness is true: and he knoweth that he saith truth, that ye also may believe.*

S. John tells us nothing of the rending of the veil of the Temple, nor of the comment of the centurion, both of which are recorded by all the three Synoptists; nor does he mention the earthquake and the appearances of the dead, which we find only in S. Matthew. The only topic which he has in common with the earlier narrative is the burial of the body of Jesus by Joseph of Arimathæa.

Before he comes to that, S. John has another incident to record, which came under his own eye and to which he clearly attaches deep significance. It arose out of a request made by the Jews to Pilate that the bodies might be taken down before sunset, and that death might be accelerated to secure this end. The Jewish custom in obedience to the Law of Moses (Dt. 21: 23) required this removal in all cases: but as S. John notes, the situation was the more urgent because that sunset was the beginning of a sabbath of special solemnity. The regular weekly sabbath coincided that year with the opening day of the paschal festival, which in any case was kept as a sabbath.

The soldiers, when they came to expedite death by breaking the legs of the crucified, found Jesus already dead. One of them, however, to make assurance doubly sure, pierced His side with a spear. The body was dead, but had not been dead long. And when the spear head was withdrawn, S. John saw a strange sight. There came out of the side of

Jesus what looked like a stream of blood, followed by a stream of water. There is strong scientific evidence to shew that this is what might be expected if Jesus died quite literally of a broken heart. Rupture of the heart with escape of blood into the heart-sac is a known cause of sudden death. The effused blood naturally separates in its new receptacle into two portions, the more solid red clot sinking and the paler watery-looking serum rising to the surface. If the spear head pierced the heart-sac, the red blood, if it had not had time to coagulate, would pour out first, and be followed by the serum.

Attention was first called to this fact by Dr. Stroud, in a book on *The Physical Cause of the Death of Christ.* His opinion was confirmed by high medical authority. Dr. Charles Creighton, however, in a note contributed to Professor Cheyne, and included in his article on *The Cross* in the *Encyclopaedia Biblica,* challenged Dr. Stroud's statement. But Sir Alexander Simpson in an article in *The Expositor* (October 1911), subjects Dr. Creighton to very trenchant criticism, and gives an illustration from a *post-mortem* examination, which he had himself made, which exactly confirmed Dr. Stroud's hypothesis. He points out also in a footnote that there is no ground for the further objection, which is sometimes urged, that the separation of the red corpuscles from the serum would imply that corruption had already set in. I am sorry to see that Archbishop Bernard in his illuminating commentary on S. John's Gospel, overlooked Sir Alexander Simpson's refutation, and has given Dr. Creighton's unfounded assertions a new lease of life.

Assuming then that Jesus died literally of a broken blood-vessel in the neighbourhood of the heart, we must remember that this hypothesis only proposes to give us the proximate physical cause of our Lord's death. It is strictly irrelevant to our faith that in the spiritual sense Jesus "died of a broken heart", whether the words are true in the literal sense or not. All that it does is to provide a simple, natural explanation of the phenomenon, which made so deep an impression on the beloved disciple. The importance that he attached to it is indicated by the solemn asseveration with which he attests his record. "He that hath seen hath borne witness and his witness is true through and through, and He knoweth that he is saying true things, that ye in your turn may believe".

On the right understanding of this verse (see p. 22. f.) depends the solution of the problem of the authorship and purpose of the Gospel. It is unfortunate that at one important point the words are ambiguous. The question is, to whom does the emphatic pronoun "He" (literally "that one") in the phrase "He knoweth" refer? Does it refer directly to the main subject of the sentence? Does "he" mean "he who hath seen and hath borne witness"? If so, the author of the Gospel would seem to be distinguishing himself from the beloved disciple. We must postulate, as Archbishop Bernard does, an elder John, other than the apostle, recording the experience of his master. He must have heard his master say, "I have seen and I have borne witness and I do know that I am speaking the truth". In reporting this he would naturally turn the first person into the third. But then he ought to have turned the second person into the first. He was himself one of those with whom the apostle wished to share his faith. It is important also to notice that the tense employed, the perfect, not the aorist, brings the witness before us as still alive. A disciple recording his master's teaching after his death, would say, "he that saw" not "he that hath seen". The perfect expresses a past experience, the power of which is still living in the present. The same tense, we may remember, recurs in 1 Jn. 1 : 1–3, side by side with the aorist.

I am quite prepared to believe that the Gospel was taken down by dictation. Bishop Lightfoot pointed out, as we have seen, significant hints of the reaction of a circle of disciples on the teacher in the course of the narrative. But a scribe is not an editor. And the whole story of the Cross as recorded here bears the stamp of direct personal testimony, though the narrator speaks of himself in the third person.

But if so, what are we to understand by the emphatic "he"? I quite agree that it cannot refer to the author. In the first place, the form of the sentence is against it. The form recurs more than once in S. John's writings. In Jn. 21 : 24 we read "This is the disciple that testifieth these things, and that wrote these things, and we know that his testimony is true". Again in 3 Jn. 12, "We also bear witness, and thou knowest that our witness is true". In each case the clause introduces an external attestation. Nothing really is gained by saying, "My testimony is true, and I know it". But if not, what other interpretation of the words is possible? If we are familiar with S. John's writings, I do not think we need have any hesitation as to our answer. No doubt in the course of the Gospel narrative this emphatic pronoun occurs normally without any special *nuance*. But this is not narrative. It is a comment on his narrative, by the narrator. And when the author speaks in his own name, as he does throughout his first Epistle, he has a remarkable way of using the emphatic "he" in reference to His Master, which no one who knew him and His Master could fail to understand, even though the name Jesus does not occur anywhere in the context. See 1 Jn. 2: 6; 3: 3, 5, 7, 16; 4: 17. I believe, therefore, and I have great names on my side (Zahn, Sanday, and Abbott), that the Evangelist, having made an emphatic assertion of the essential truth of his testimony, lifts his heart to heaven and claims confirmation from his living Lord.

The Evangelist sees a connexion between this incident as a whole, and the anticipation of Scripture, but he gives us no hint as to the special significance of the two-fold stream. The stress that he lays on the truth of his testimony is sufficiently accounted for by the fact that men had begun to question the reality of the Passion. What he had seen was at least a demonstration of the reality of the death. Whether he attached any special significance to the stream, that he not unnaturally called water, that followed the blood must remain uncertain. He calls attention in 1 Jn. 5: 6–8, to "the water" and "the blood", but then he is referring directly, and perhaps exclusively to the two stages in our Lord's coming, which were marked by His Baptism and by His Cross.

36 *For these things came to pass, that the scripture might be fulfilled,*
37 *A bone of him shall not be broken. And again another scripture saith, They shall look on him whom they pierced.*

S. John concludes his account of the crucifixion by calling attention to the remarkable way in which our Lord's death corresponded in what we should regard as insignificant detail to Old Testament types and prophecies; or, to use his own words, "fulfilled the Scripture".

In the first place, the fact that He was dead when the soldiers came saved Him from having His legs broken, and so preserved His correspondence with the type of the paschal victim (Ex. 12 : 46), to which S. John attached great importance. In calling attention to this fact, S. John uses the words of Ps. 34: 20, in which the psalmist seems to have seen a fulfilment of this type in God's care of one of His servants.

In the second place, the piercing of the side brought the death of Jesus into relation with the picture of the rejected prophet in Zechariah. There seems to be some dislocation in the text of Zechariah which blurs the picture. It seems, however, clear on any arrangement of the text, that Zechariah foretold the murder of a divinely accredited prophet by the nation, and their repentance when their guilt was brought home to them. The echoes of this section of prophecy in the account of the Passion are recurrent and striking. On some occasions Jesus Himself calls attention to it. The method that He chose for His triumphal entry into Jerusalem (Jn. 12: 15) was clearly meant to suggest Zech. 9: 9, though the disciples did not realize it at the time. He quoted Zech. 13 : 7 on the way to Gethsemane (Mk. 14: 27). In other cases the Evangelists discovered parallels: S. Matthew (27 : 9) quotes Zech. 11 : 13 in connexion with the treachery and remorse of Judas. It is not surprising therefore that S. John should think of Zech. 12: 10 as foreshadowing the piercing of our Lord's side.[1]

We have already had occasion to call attention in passing to S. John's references to "the fulfilment of Scripture" in his account of the Passion. The fact is important in itself, and has besides a present interest in view of current controversies with regard to the authority and the interpretation of the Bible. It will be well, therefore, to look closely into the questions raised by these references before we pass on. Dr. Bernard's section on *The Authority of the Old Testament* (pp. cxlvii ff.) in the International Critical Commentary on S. John is particularly helpful. He points out that for the Evangelist, as for the Jews of his time, the Old Testament was "the fount of authority". He shews how Jesus appealed to it as containing illuminating principles and binding laws, both in controversy (8: 17; 10: 34), and in popular teaching (6: 45; 7: 38). The book, however, was not only authoritative, it was predictive in the judgement both of the common people (6: 14, 30; 7: 42; 12: 34), and of the disciples (2: 17, 22; 12: 16, 41; 20: 9). This characteristic was implied in the title "Christ", which the disciples gave to Jesus (1: 41, 45), and which Jesus accepted (1: 50; 4: 26; cf. Mk. 14: 62).

Most illuminating in this connexion is the claim that Jesus makes in discussion with the Jews (5: 39) to be Himself the main subject of the Old Testament witness. Dr. Bernard, by

[1] It is interesting to notice that if he had been dependent for his knowledge of Zechariah on the LXX version, the resemblance would not have occurred to him. The fact that the same text caught the attention of the author of *The Revelation of S. John* will be interpreted by different minds in different ways, in accordance with their judgement on the relation in respect to date and authorship between the Gospel and the Revelation which tradition attributes to the same author. It is possible to postulate a common source, such as a Greek version of an early collection of proof texts, to which the two writers, supposing that they were two, had access independently. But the two books in spite of marked differences, are in origin closely connected with Ephesus at the end of the first century A.D. They are under the surface closely connected in thought. They are products of the same school. There is no difficulty in supposing that the later writer, whichever it was, had had his attention called to this text by the earlier. In Rev. 1: 7 the seeing referred to belongs, as in Mk. 14: 62, to "the coming in clouds". There is nothing to exclude that reference in Jn. 19: 37; cf. Mt. 24: 30. In any case the reference is to an incident recorded only in the Fourth Gospel.

a rearrangement of the text, brings 5: 46 into close and suggestive connexion with 7: 15. He thinks that it was our Lord's mastery of Scripture—as shewn in support of this claim—that made His opponents wonder who had taught Him. It is disappointing that no details of this teaching are recorded in that connexion. S. Luke tells us expressly that Jesus after His resurrection, "beginning from Moses and all the prophets, interpreted in all the Scriptures the things concerning Himself" (24: 27, 45). But he also gives no illustrations. The only passages to which Jesus called public attention in relation to Himself in the course of His public ministry are Is. 61: 1, 2, the text of His first sermon at Nazareth (Lk. 4: 18); Ps. 118: 22, after the parable of the Vineyard and the Husbandmen (Mt. 21: 42); and Ps. 110: 1, at the close of the day of questions in Holy Week (Mk. 12: 36).

Dr. Bernard calls special attention to the phrase, "the fulfilment of Scripture". It suggests the presence of a prophetic, predictive element in all God's earlier revelation of Himself, which was waiting its consummation in the coming of the Christ, and which, when that consummation was worked out before the eyes of men in the life, death and resurrection of Jesus, produced in enlightened minds, an irresistible conviction that the whole had been worked out in accordance with a divinely predetermined plan (Ac. 2: 22).

It is noteworthy that neither S. Mark nor S. Luke introduce the thought of their own accord into their narratives. The phrase: "Then was fulfilled the Scripture", is found only in S. Matthew. The phrase: "In order that the Scripture might be fulfilled", is found nine times in S. Matthew on the writer's authority, and three times in S. John. All the evangelists, however, agree that Jesus Himself spoke again and again of the fulfilment of Scripture in the events of His life, and especially of His passion.

The conception is no doubt characteristically Jewish. Gentile Christian writers in the second and third centuries, as Dr. Bernard points out, fight shy of it. It is one into which we find it peculiarly difficult to enter with any sympathy to-day. Our modern advance in the understanding of the Bible has come from a resolute determination to recover, as far as possible, the original meaning of each inspired utterance, and from the refusal to consider any meaning of the words which could not have been consciously present to the mind either of the speaker or hearers when the words were first spoken or written. We therefore rule out for the time being the consideration of anything beyond the vaguest element of prediction in a prophetic utterance, and in effect deny the possibility of its presence.

And yet, however hard we may find it to account for the fact, and whatever confusion, foreshortening and even positive misunderstanding in the minds of the prophets may introduce, both into the record and into its interpretation, an element of prediction is there, and cannot be explained away. The Jews in our Lord's day were expecting the advent of a Messiah on the strength of what they believed to be the promises of God recorded in their sacred writings. Jesus shared in their expectation and claimed to be its fulfilment.

THE LORD'S ENTOMBMENT

38 *And after these things Joseph of Arimathæa, being a disciple of Jesus, but secretly for fear of the Jews, asked of Pilate that he might take away the body of Jesus: and Pilate gave* him *leave.*
39 *He came therefore, and took away his body. And there came also Nicodemus, he who at the first came to him by night, bringing a*
40 *mixture of myrrh and aloes, about a hundred pound* weight. *So they took the body of Jesus, and bound it in linen cloths with*
41 *the spices, as the custom of the Jews is to bury. Now in the place where he was crucified there was a garden; and in the garden a*
42 *new tomb wherein was never man yet laid. There then because of the Jews' Preparation (for the tomb was nigh at hand) they laid Jesus.*

S. Mark tells us that Joseph of Arimathæa, a distinguished member of the Sanhedrim, who was at heart a disciple, plucked up courage and applied to Pilate for permission to bury the body. This permission was granted, after the fact of the death had been confirmed. Then Joseph, after wrapping the body in a winding sheet which he had bought, laid it in a grave hewn out of a rock, and rolled a stone to the door of the tomb. S. Matthew tells us that the tomb was his own, and he and S. Luke tell us that no one had as yet been buried in it.

S. John adds that Joseph had kept his discipleship a secret for fear of the Jews. He also associates with him another member of the Sanhedrim, Nicodemus, who had not as yet had the courage to confess his faith in Jesus openly, though he has already been mentioned twice in the Gospel (3: 1 ff., 7: 50 f.). Nicodemus contributes nearly a hundred pounds' weight of myrrh and aloes (the pound contained twelve ounces). S. John says that they bound the body in linen cloths with spices. He does not tell us that the tomb belonged to Joseph, but simply that it was situated in a garden conveniently near. Dr. Westcott suggests that the body was swathed in the linen bandages, smeared with the ointment and then wrapped in the shroud. S. John also speaks, in 20: 7, of "the napkin that was upon His head" as distinct from the linen cloths.

There are facts which suggest a special and unsuspected importance in the details of S. John's account of the state in which the wrappings were found after the Resurrection.

Special interest in the evidential value of the grave cloths was roused in England by Henry Latham's *The Risen Master*. He saw a dead man being carried out to burial in Constantinople with a napkin wound into a turban round his head. His thought went back to the singular fact to which S. John calls attention, that the napkin that had been upon the head was lying by itself still retaining the shape into which it had been wound. From this he inferred that our Lord's body must have passed out of the grave cloths without disturbing them, just as it passed through the closed doors of the room where the disciples were assembled on the evening of the first Easter day. This cannot, as Dr. Bernard says, be regarded as certain. But if we accept the witness of S. John to the presence of the grave cloths in the tomb, it is very difficult indeed to account for the phenomena on any other hypothesis. The evidence of the empty grave cloths is more difficult to explain away than the evidence of the empty tomb. It negatives even the suggestion that has been put forward with all seriousness, that the body was swallowed up by the earthquake that burst open the door of the tomb.

Still more recently attention has been called to certain very remarkable facts with regard to what purports to be the very shroud itself in which the body was wrapped. There is to-day at Turin a linen cloth about fourteen feet long, on which there are a number of dark stains, which somehow suggest, rather than represent, the front and back of a human body. There is more than the suggestion of a human face, but with a perplexing inversion of light and shadow which it is difficult if not impossible to ascribe to artistic ingenuity.

This relic is preserved in the Cathedral at Turin, and the opportunity was taken when it was publicly exposed in 1898 to photograph it. This led to an entirely unexpected result. When the lights and shadows were reversed on the photographic plate, there appeared a positive picture of singular grace and dignity. It represents the front and back view of a full-length human figure. Both front and back are scored with the weal marks left by a Roman scourge, the lashes of which had been reinforced by leaden pellets. The left wrist, which covers the right, has a nail print, and so have the feet. The side has been pierced. There are blood stains on the forehead. It looks as if even the majestic face had been disfigured by a savage blow.

This discovery has led to careful and minute scientific investigation, with the result that we are assured that the stains on the shroud might have been due to the action of gases given off by febrile sweat on linen impregnated with alum. We are told further that if corruption had set in, the whole plate, to speak in photographic language, would have been completely fogged.

This suggestion was put forward by a French scientist, M. Vignon, in a book on *The Shroud of Christ* published in French and English in 1903. The conclusion was challenged by a French ecclesiastic, Canon Chevalier, on the ground that the genuineness of the relic had been discussed in the time of Clement VII, and that an artist had confessed that he had forged it.

The evidence of the photographs cannot be so easily upset. The stains on the linen were due to chemical action and not to paint. And it is incredible that an artist in the fourteenth or any other century painted a picture which could only become intelligible after it had been photographed.

The whole question has been re-investigated with great care by Mgr. Barnes in *The Holy Shroud of Turin*, published by Burns, Oates & Washbourne in 1934 (7s. 6d.). It clearly deserves far closer attention than has yet been paid to it by students of the Gospels. It does not seem possible as yet to reconstruct the whole story of the entombment in the light of the fresh evidence. The stains that represent the back and the front of the body may well have been caused by direct contact. Mgr. Barnes contends, however, that the image of the face could not have been formed in the same way without considerable distortion. The ears would in that case have been a foot apart when the cloth was spaced out. This, no doubt, is true. But he omits to notice that the ears are entirely covered by the hair, or as he seems to think, by a bandage. The impression of the forehead could have come from direct contact. We need not suppose, therefore, that the shroud was pressed tightly over the face.

Mgr. Barnes suggests, as at least a possible hypothesis, that the time during which the shroud was in direct contact with the body was limited to the time during which it was being conveyed from the Cross to the grave, and the period after that, while preparations were being made to swathe it in the linen cloths, with the spices contributed by Nicodemus. He thinks also that the body, when swathed, was covered with the shroud, and the *sudarium* which, according to S. John had been over the head, is just the shroud. He points out that the shroud was known as *sudarium* in Constantinople.

This is not quite satisfactory because the shroud would have covered the whole body and not simply the head, and the face of Lazarus had been bound in a *sudarium*. The residual difficulties, however, may well be left over for further discussion. They leave the positive evidence for the genuineness of this most precious relic, as far as I can judge, irrefragable.

CHAPTER XXV

THE FIRST EASTER DAY

1 *Now on the first day of the week cometh Mary Magdalene early, while it was yet dark, unto the tomb, and seeth the stone taken* 2 *away from the tomb. She runneth therefore, and cometh to Simon Peter, and to the other disciple, whom Jesus loved, and saith unto them, They have taken away the Lord out of the tomb, and* 3 *we know not where they have laid him. Peter therefore went forth,* 4 *and the other disciple, and they went toward the tomb. And they ran both together: and the other disciple outran Peter, and came* 5 *first to the tomb; and stooping and looking in, he seeth the linen* 6 *cloths lying; yet entered he not in. Simon Peter therefore also cometh, following him, and entered into the tomb; and he beholdeth* 7 *the linen cloths lying, and the napkin, that was upon his head, not lying with the linen cloths, but rolled up in a place by itself.* 8 *Then entered in therefore the other disciple also, which came first* 9 *to the tomb, and he saw, and believed. For as yet they knew not* 10 *the scripture, that he must rise again from the dead. So the disciples went away again unto their own home.*

WE come now to the events of the first Easter Day. Here, as elsewhere, S. John draws directly on his own reminiscences. He is not engaged in writing a complete account of everything that took place. He aims simply at telling what he had himself heard and seen. It is not quite clear whether he and Peter were lodging in the same house. In any case it looks as if they were in different rooms.

The preposition is repeated before the second name, and that suggests that they had to be summoned separately. They cannot, I think, have been very far apart; for they start together on what S. John describes as if it had been a race to the tomb. He was, no doubt, the younger man, and he notes, as Lord Charnwood suggests, with a little touch of self-congratulation, that he got there first. He does not directly name himself. He appears throughout this scene simply as "the other disciple", defined as the one who was Jesus's friend. He is clearly the same as the disciple whom Jesus loved, who leaned on His breast at the Last Supper (13: 23; 21: 20), and who stood by the Cross (19: 26). A different Greek word is used to describe our Lord's feeling for him. It is the word used in 11: 3 of His feeling for Lazarus. But the variation does not seem to be significant.

If he takes credit to himself for being the first to reach the tomb, he gives the credit to Peter for having been the first to venture to go right in.

The cloths in which the body had been bound were visible from outside. Apparently they were lying on the slab on which the body had been laid, the body having simply passed out of them. The *sudarium* which had been on the head was lying folded (or, perhaps, rolled into a turban) in a place apart. If the *sudarium* is to be identified with the shroud, it must have been specially folded up and tidied away. John had not seen it until he followed Peter into the tomb. The empty grave cloths were enough to convince him that Jesus had risen. The comment that he adds: "For as yet they knew not the Scripture that He must rise from the dead", has caused much perplexity. It is, I believe, put forward apologetically. He had believed on the evidence of his bodily senses. He could not claim a share in the blessing, which Jesus pronounced on those who "had not seen and yet had believed" (20: 31) without the help of ocular demonstration.

The disciples returned to their own homes. According to one text of S. Luke (24: 12), Peter went home alone pondering. John's faith had, apparently not yet taken a shape in which he could share it with anyone else.

MARY MAGDALENE

11 *But Mary was standing without at the tomb weeping: so, as she*
12 *wept, she stooped and looked into the tomb; and she beholdeth*

two angels in white sitting, one at the head, and one at the feet,
13 *where the body of Jesus had lain. And they say unto her, Woman, why weepest thou? She saith unto them, Because they have taken*
14 *away my Lord, and I know not where they have laid him. When she had thus said, she turned herself back, and beholdeth Jesus*
15 *standing, and knew not that it was Jesus. Jesus saith unto her, Woman, why weepest thou? whom seekest thou? She, supposing, him to be the gardener, saith unto him, Sir, if thou hast borne him hence, tell me where thou hast laid him, and I will take him*
16 *away. Jesus saith unto her, Mary. She turneth herself, and saith unto him in Hebrew, Rabboni; which is to say, Master.*
17 *Jesus saith to her, Touch me not; for I am not yet ascended unto the Father: but go unto my brethren, and say to them, I ascend unto my Father and your Father, and my God and your God.*
18 *Mary Magdalene cometh and telleth the disciples, I have seen the Lord; and* how that *he had said these things unto her.*

Meanwhile, Mary Magdalene herself returned, though not at a run, to the tomb. S. John's interest in her hitherto was confined to the fact that she had come by herself to bring him word that the body was missing from the tomb. Her words imply that she had gone with others to visit it. She must also have gone up to it and learnt that the body was gone, for she said: "They have taken away the Lord out of the tomb, and *we* know not where they have laid Him". If she had heard the message of "the young man" (Mk. 16: 6 f.), she does not seem to have gathered from it more than the fact that she should get into touch with Peter.

Now, after the apostles had gone, she was alone by the tomb, and we may well believe that what follows is based on what S. John heard from her own lips that same morning.

She was standing outside the tomb weeping. Then she, too, peered into the tomb and became aware of the presence within it of two angels in white, sitting, one at the head and the other at the feet where the body of Jesus had lain. And they said: "Woman, why weepest thou?" She simply repeats the story of her loss: "It is because they have taken away my Lord, and I know not where they have laid Him".

Then, when she had said this, something made her turn her head and look behind her. And she saw Jesus. She did not know that it was Jesus. He, in His turn, asks her why she is weeping? But He adds: "Whom seekest thou?" partly, no doubt, as Dr. Westcott suggests, because such sorrow could only come from a bitter personal loss; but partly, I think, as in the case of the travellers to Emmaus, to revive the memory of all that He had been to her. She, thinking Him to be the gardener, says: "Sir, if you have borne Him hence, tell me where you have laid Him, and I will take Him away". Jesus shews that He knows her, though as yet she does not know Him. He calls her by name. She turns and addresses Him by His old familiar title "Rabboni", and clasps His feet. S. John does not tell us this. But it is, I think, implied in the Lord's words: "Relax your grasp". "Do not cling to me". It is not, as some have thought from the familiar rendering, "Touch me not", as if He shrank from being handled. His object was to wean her from her dependence on sense-impressions, which could only interfere with the abiding communion which was in store for her. *Do not cling to this manifestation of me, for I have not yet ascended to the Father.* "The time has not yet come, though it is close at hand, when you will find in lifting your heart to your Father in heaven that you are in touch with me. But go to those whom I can now call to a fuller apprehension of their relationship to me, go to my brethren, and tell them I am ascending to my Father and your Father, to my God and your God".

The dark night of sorrow, of which He had forewarned them, was over. The goal of His journeying would be made clear, that they might in heart and mind thither ascend, and with Him continually dwell.

The story ends with a brief record of Mary Magdalene's fulfilment of her commission. The time had not yet come when the news of His resurrection was to be broadcast to the world. But there was work that she could do in preparing the hearts of those that loved Him to realize His triumph over death.

THE EVENING OF THE FIRST EASTER DAY

19 *When therefore it was evening, on that day, the first* day *of the week, and when the doors were shut where the disciples were, for fear of the Jews, Jesus came and stood in the midst, and saith*
20 *unto them, Peace* be *unto you. And when he had said this, he showed unto them his hands and his side. The disciples there-*
21 *fore were glad, when they saw the Lord. Jesus therefore said to them again, Peace* be *unto you: as the Father hath sent me,*
22 *even so send I you. And when he had said this, he breathed on*
23 *them, and saith unto them, Receive ye the Holy Ghost: whose soever sins ye forgive, they are forgiven unto them; whose soever* sins *ye retain, they are retained.*

The account that S. John gives of the evening of the first Easter Day is illuminated throughout by the account in S. Luke. The day had been full of incident from early morning, when the faithful women found the tomb empty. S. John has told us of his own running to the tomb, and what he saw there, of an appearance of Jesus to Mary Magdalene, and of the message sent to His brethren through her.

The story of the disciples on the way to Emmaus shews how quickly the rumour had spread. On their return they find "the eleven and those with them gathered together", presumably in the upper chamber, and they are greeted with the news that He had appeared to Simon.

S. John tells us only that the doors were shut for fear of the Jews. The news of the tomb being empty must have come to the ears of the authorities who, S. Matthew tells us, had set a guard upon it. The disciples had no means of telling what the rulers' reaction to that news would be. Apparently the Jews seem to have thought that it would be unwise to call public attention to the fact. They left the disciples alone.

S. John, however, at once leaves behind all anxiety on that score. For Jesus Himself appeared, standing in the midst of them and bringing them the familiar greeting of "Peace". He assured them of His identity by calling their attention to the wounds in His hands and His side. This is further developed in S. Luke by an invitation from Him to come and prove for themselves that His body was solid to the touch, and by His taking and eating fish before them. It is not good, I think, to spend time on enquiring what this implies in regard to the nature of His resurrection body. It clearly belongs to another order of existence than that which we know. It could pass through closed doors, and yet could be handled, and could break bread and eat. But we have not yet the faculties for understanding what this means. The one point that really matters, is the assurance that He gave them that He had passed unscathed through death, and was still the same Jesus whom they had known on earth, and that He had carried the fruits of His earthly experience into a new order.

The result of that assurance was, as He had told them it would be, joy (16: 20). He takes, however, pains to make them realize that to possess this joy for themselves is not enough. It was a treasure that they held in trust for the whole of mankind. Every appearance of the risen Lord carries with it a commission—"Go and tell". But this, in a special sense, is an appearance to the Church as His body, and defines the work it would have to do for Him to the end of time. It is prefaced by a fresh greeting of Peace, which would come to them with fresh power now that they knew who was speaking. It would also act as a reminder that a messenger of Peace must first be filled with peace.

He goes on to authorize them to act in His name as they carried on the work that He had begun while He was with them on earth. *As the Father has commissioned me, I in my turn send you.* There is a variation, you will see, in the words which our versions translate "send". The first word implies an embassy with a commission to act as a representative. The other is a simpler word "to send on a message"; now and then it means to "escort". As we share His commission, we shall be supported by His presence.

Then followed a symbolic afflation: and an assurance that power is given them both to forgive and retain sins. *He breathed on them and said, " Take Holy Spirit. Whose soever sins ye remit they are remitted to them. Whose soever sins ye retain they are retained*".

These words stand out as amongst the most important ever uttered. They define what in our Lord's mind was to be the characteristic work that His disciples were to do among men as His representatives.

When on an earlier occasion He had sent them out, two by two, they were bidden to preach the Kingdom, to heal, and to give a greeting of peace. There was no special mention of the promise, implied in the baptism of John, of remission of sins.

Again on the way to the Ascension, their work is briefly summed up (Ac. 1: 8) as personal witness ("ye shall be my witnesses"), without any direct reference to sin. We all of us, I imagine, are inclined at times to prefer this later charge. We shrink from facing in all its nakedness the fact of sin.

Yet we cannot face the fact of Christ without being brought up at once directly against the fact of sin. His name Jesus was given Him because He was to save His people from their sins. He came to the waters of Jordan to share with them in the acknowledgement of guilt, and to pledge Himself to death that it might be done away. So the Baptist saw and testified that He was indeed the Lamb of God, and that the burthen of the sin of the whole world was on His conscience. He had told His disciples at the Last Supper that His blood was being shed for the remission of sins. It is not surprising, therefore, that after He had died for our sins (Rom. 4: 25) and risen again as a token from God that His sacrifice had been accepted, He should declare (Lu. 24: 47) that the time had come when repentance unto remission of sins should be preached in His name to all nations, and here solemnly lay on the conscience of every one of His disciples the responsibility of sharing with others the redemption, which their Lord had won for them.

There are, no doubt, many different ways of fulfilling this ministry. In the Anglican communion the authority to pronounce an absolution in God's name in the public services in Church, or to penitents in private, is specially committed to priests at their ordination. There are those who believe that these words were in the first instance addressed only to the apostles and that they have no message for laymen. But Dr. Westcott (*Revelation of the Risen Lord*, pp. 79 ff.) shews that, according to S. Luke, others beside the ten apostles were present, and Dr. Hort points out that even if we believe that the words were directly and principally spoken to the eleven, there are good reasons for supposing that this charge was given them, not as members of an exclusive order, but as representatives of the whole Ecclesia of the future (*Christian Ecclesia*, p. 35).

It is an integral part of faith in the universal prophethood and priesthood of the laity, as I see it, that every believer should realize that he has his own specific and inalienable part in that commission. It is a heart-searching question to be brought up against, whether you are in holy orders or not, "What have I learnt of Christ that it is life or death to me to share with my brothers?" "If my own heart condemns me for my lukewarmness, is it because I do not think that *He* cares enough for me or for my brother, for it to make any difference to Him, whether we believe in Him or not? or Is it because *I* do not really care enough for Him, even though I say that I believe that He gave His life for me?"

Remember it is "Heart on heart Christ rules". Here is a striking verse from George Macdonald's *Diary of an Old Soul*, of which it always does one good to be reminded:

> From Thine, as then, the healing virtue goes
> Into our hearts—that is the Father's plan.
> From heart to heart it sinks, it steals, it flows,
> From these that know Thee still infecting those.

It is well, surely, if we can conclude with George Macdonald:

> Here is my heart—from thine, Lord, fill it up,
> That I may offer it as the holy cup
> Of thy communion to my every man.

We must not omit to notice that Jesus, before He gave this commission, "breathed" on those to whom He gave it, saying, "Receive a Holy Spirit". The action was clearly connected with the promise that He gave in S. Luke. "And lo! I send forth the promise of my Father upon you", or, as it stands in the Acts of the Apostles, "Ye shall receive power after that the Holy Spirit is come upon you, and so shall ye be my witnesses to the end of the earth".

But here again there is an uncertainty about the precise interpretation of the word of the Lord. He does not use the article before Holy Spirit. It was a preparation for and not a foretaste of the day of Pentecost.

It is, I think, a definite command, meant to be acted upon by the disciples then and there "Breathe the air that I am breathing. Keep yourselves in heart and mind and will near enough to be with me where I am." There was, He assures them, power coming from Him even then which they could assimilate, even though the time for the full baptism with the Holy Spirit had not come.

We can, I believe, see something of the effect of their response to this command in the spirit of joy and fellowship and prayer, which were the marks, as S. Luke tells us, of the waiting Church in the first rogationtide. One effect, I cannot doubt, was the renewing in each one of them of a right spirit, for which the psalmist prays (Ps. 51: 10), so that the Holy Spirit found in them "a mansion prepared for Himself", a spirit in them ready to take Him in.

THE DOUBTER CONVINCED

24 *But Thomas, one of the twelve, called Didymus, was not with them*
25 *when Jesus came. The other disciples therefore said unto him, We have seen the Lord. But he said unto them, Except I shall see in his hands the print of the nails, and put my finger into the print of the nails, and put my hand into his side, I will not believe.*

26 *And after eight days again his disciples were within, and Thomas with them. Jesus cometh, the doors being shut, and stood in*
27 *the midst, and said, Peace* be *unto you. Then saith he to Thomas, Reach hither thy finger, and see my hands; and reach* hither *thy*

hand, and put it into my side: and be not faithless, but believing.
28 *Thomas answered and said unto him, My Lord and my God.*
29 *Jesus saith unto him, Because thou hast seen me, thou hast believed: blessed* are *they that have not seen, and* yet *have believed.*
30 *Many other signs therefore did Jesus in the presence of the*
31 *disciples, which are not written in this book: but these are written, that ye may believe that Jesus is the Christ, the Son of God; and that believing ye may have life in his name.*

The feast of the Passover lasted a week, and S. John makes it clear that the disciples did not leave Jerusalem until it was over.

It is clear from S. Mark and from S. Matthew that they knew that it was their Lord's will that they should go back to Galilee. But they would, not unnaturally, wait till they could go back with their friends at the conclusion of the festival.

Meanwhile, even among the eleven, there was one loyal soul who remained inconsolable. S. John has already introduced Thomas to us, first, as the spokesman of a desperate resolve, when it had seemed as if Jesus was facing certain death in going to Bethany; and then as putting into words the difficulty of an inquiring mind when the consolation that Jesus offered in prospect of His approaching withdrawal seemed to bring darkness rather than light. "Lord, we know not whither thou goest. How can we know the way?" (14: 5).

For some unexplained reason Thomas had not been with the rest on the first Easter night, and he resolutely refused to believe in the truth of the Lord's resurrection on anything short of the direct evidence of his own senses. Jesus, according to S. Luke, had not only called attention to His wound prints, He had invited the disciples to add the evidence of touch to the evidence of sight. S. Luke does not tell us whether any of those present accepted the invitation. Thomas's test may mean either "Why did not you take the confirmation that He offered?" or "I can be satisfied with nothing less than what convinced you".

In any case his scepticism did not exclude him from the communion of his fellow disciples. And a week later, ready it may be to start for home on the morrow, the feast being over, the whole company were once more gathered in the upper chamber. And once more Jesus stood in the midst. This time He addresses Himself directly to Thomas, and offers him, of His own accord, exactly the confirmation that he had demanded.

We may note in passing that, for Palestinian Greek, "thrust" is really an over-translation of the word used in verse 25 and verse 27.

We are not told whether Thomas applied the test. Dr. Westcott assumes, from the fact that Jesus in verse 29 only says "seen" that he did not. The really demonstrative evidence came from the fact that Jesus could read the inmost thoughts of his heart. No physical sign by itself could have brought him that assurance.

His experience is closely akin to that recorded of Nathanael in 1: 48 f. The difference in the resultant confession is a measure of the development of spiritual insight that had come to the disciples in the interval, though in each case the truth confessed represented a piercing intuition, rather than a clearly thought out and established conviction. In each case Jesus gave a warm welcome to the faith expressed in the confession. Nathanael's confession shewed that he felt himself to be in the presence of One who stood so close to God that He could not be less than the promised King of Israel. Thomas, who had gone down with his Lord into the valley of the shadow of death, seems as soon as he is convinced that He has come back alive, to have realized in a flash the truth that Jesus had been trying to unfold to His disciples in that last night before He suffered. He had, indeed, as He had said, come forth from God and had gone back to God. From henceforth loyalty to One whom he had known and followed as his Lord on earth must rise into adoration of One who could not be in essence less than Divine.

S. John in his prologue has shewn that the meditation of a lifetime has verified the truth of this intuition. So the record of it is naturally the climax of his Gospel. It is enough simply to record the words in which Jesus had greeted the confession: *Is it because thou hast seen me that thou hast believed?* You demanded a confirmation of the truth that must be mediated through the senses. That confirmation has been brought within your reach. But your conviction does not really rest on that. *A special beatitude is theirs who have believed without direct physical attestation.*

This last beatitude in the Gospel is very difficult to interpret. Origen felt that it was unreasonable to suppose that those who had accepted the testimony of the apostles who had seen, were more blessed than the apostles.

I cannot, however, help feeling that the key is to be found in the comment that S. John makes on his own reaction to the evidence of the empty grave cloths. He had needed, and responded to, the evidence of sight, for as yet he knew not the Scripture that He must rise from the dead. Had he known that, no further evidence would have been necessary.

It is not certain, but our Lord's words suggest that there were even then some, Mary of Bethany, perhaps, and His blessed mother, who had fulfilled the condition.

The purpose which the Evangelist had in mind when he began his Gospel is now fully worked out. He recalls that purpose in the fewest possible words. He had made no attempt to record all that he had seen and heard. His one object had been to make a representative selection of the significant events. This he had done that he might enable his readers to grasp in its fulness the Christian faith in the person of their Lord, who is "the Christ", the fulfilment of all the promises made by God to the Fathers, and in Himself "the eternal Son of God". That faith accepted and lived in is the spring of the life which is life indeed.

CHAPTER XXVI

THE APPEARANCE BY THE LAKE

1 *After these things Jesus manifested himself again to the disciples at the sea of Tiberias; and he manifested* himself *on this wise.* 2 *There were together Simon Peter, and Thomas called Didymus, and Nathanael of Cana in Galilee, and the* sons *of Zebedee, and two other of his disciples.* 3 *Simon Peter saith unto them, I go a fishing. They say unto him, We also come with thee. They went forth, and entered into the boat; and that night they took nothing.* 4 *But when day was now breaking, Jesus stood on the beach: howbeit the disciples knew not that it was Jesus.* 5 *Jesus therefore saith unto them, Children, have ye aught to eat? They answered him, No.* 6 *And he said unto them, Cast the net on the right side of the boat, and ye shall find. They cast therefore, and now they were not able to draw it for the multitude of fishes.* 7 *That disciple therefore whom Jesus loved saith unto Peter, It is the Lord. So when Simon Peter heard that it was the Lord, he girt his coat about him (for he was naked), and cast himself into the sea.* 8 *But the other disciples came in the little boat (for they were not far from the land, but about two hundred cubits off), dragging the net* full *of fishes.* 9 *So when they got out upon the land, they see a fire of coals there, and fish laid thereon, and bread.* 10 *Jesus saith unto them, Bring of the fish which ye have now taken.* 11 *Simon Peter therefore went up, and drew the net to land, full of great fishes, a hundred and fifty and three: and for all there were so many, the net was not rent.* 12 *Jesus saith unto them, Come* and *break your fast. And none of the disciples durst inquire of him, Who art thou? knowing that it was the Lord.* 13 *Jesus cometh, and taketh the bread, and giveth them, and the fish likewise.* 14 *This is now the third time that Jesus was manifested to the disciples, after that he was risen from the dead.*

THIS chapter is clearly an appendix. But it must have been added before the Gospel was put into circulation. It is in style indistinguishable from the rest, though it contains a note at the end which is probably by a different hand. It is, perhaps, idle to guess at the motive which led the Evangelist to add this postscript. But it is clear that the thoughts of his friends about him were being distorted by a misunderstood tradition of a word of the Lord. The best way to correct the misunderstanding would be to give the saying in its original context, which in other ways was worth recording.

The narrative helps us to correct a possible misapprehension of the story of the forty days as given by S. Luke. S. Luke carries on his record of the teaching of Jesus on the evening of the first Easter with no clear break, until he gives us what must surely be an account of the Ascension. He is in the habit of letting his narrative run on without giving specific notes of time. But when he starts on his second volume, he makes it clear that an interval of forty days separated the Resurrection from the Ascension; and that the prohibition against leaving Jerusalem affected only the ten days before Pentecost. At the same time his tradition of the period shews no trace of a knowledge of any appearances in Galilee. The command to go into Galilee is explicit in Mt. 26: 32; 28: 7, 10, 16, and Mk. 14: 28; 16: 7. The variation in Lk. 24: 6 is puzzling. But in itself the return to Galilee was inevitable. And whether S. Luke was aware of it or not, there is no reason to challenge the account that S. Matthew gives of an appearance there.

Dr. Hort (*Christian Ecclesia*, p. 237) suggests that the incident recorded by S. John took place on the night of the return from Jerusalem. The apostles had, indeed, been called away from their business as fishermen to follow Jesus, but that did not mean that Zebedee went out of business. And Simon and Andrew were partners with James and John. The disciples seem never at a loss for a boat when they want to cross the lake. It was, therefore, quite natural that when they found themselves once more in familiar surroundings—the same and yet so strangely different, because Jesus was no longer visibly at their head—they should have gone back to their fishing. The suggestion characteristically emanates from Simon Peter. His comrades that night included his partners, the sons of Zebedee, with Thomas and Nathanael, and two unnamed disciples. That night, we are told, they took nothing. It was a not unprecedented experience in a fisherman's life. Three of those on board may well have remembered another night on the same lake just before a supreme crisis in their own relation to Jesus, when they had toiled all through the night without success.

But on this occasion the approach of dawn made a difference. A figure is dimly discernible on the shore, about a hundred yards off. And a voice is heard: "Lads, have you anything to eat?" The word used is not the word for bread, but for that which is eaten with bread. So the question meant "Have you caught anything?" But it suggested "Have you anything for me?" When they say "No", the voice comes again: "Cast on the right side of the boat and ye shall find". A spectator from the shore might quite easily (as the author of *In the Steps of the Master* points out) have noticed the approach of a large shoal. The fishermen take the hint and are immediately rewarded. And there the matter might have ended, but one of the seven was becoming "of quick understanding in the fear of the Lord". He felt that there was more than a coincidence in this catch. So he turned to Peter and said, "It is the Lord".

Peter incontinently leaped into the water in his eagerness, leaving the rest to bring the boat to land. The writer goes on to complete the story from the point of view of one of those who stayed in the boat. They came to land and found a fire kindled, and fish being cooked and a loaf of bread. Jesus bade them supplement this provision from their haul. So Peter goes to drag the net to shore. They had not been able to get it up into the boat. As fishermen they were interested in counting their catch. They noted, perhaps with reference to their contrary experience on the earlier occasion, that this time the net did not break.

The words attributed to Jesus are very few. He simply said: "Come and break your fast", and then, in the old familiar way, presided at the meal giving to each his portion of bread and fish. An awe fell on the company which prevented them from asking for a verbal confirmation of the conviction in their own hearts as to His identity. The Evangelist simply catalogues this, as the third appearance of Jesus to a company of His disciples, before he passes on to relate the special teaching to Simon Peter which followed the meal. He gives us no hint of any special significance of this appearance for the education of the disciples as a body. His language, however, suggests that it had such a significance.

The lesson of the first appearance was, as we saw, fundamental to the whole commission of the Church in the world. The Church is here to help all men everywhere to attain to the deliverance from the bondage to sin which Christ has won for them. At the same time it was clearly indicated that the message would make the sense of slavery more galling for those who scorned it.

The second appearance was related to the removal of the difficulties in the way of faith in the fact of the Resurrection. The doubter refused to believe at second-hand. He claimed that the same direct evidence should be brought within his reach which had been offered to others. His doubt was not allowed to separate him from the fellowship built up during months and years of common discipleship. And then the Lord Himself appeared, to satisfy the test he had proposed. The result of this condescension, and the conviction that it brought to Thomas that he was in direct spiritual touch with One who could read the inmost thoughts of his heart, issued in an adoring confession that He whom he had followed while He was on earth as his Master, was in very truth his Lord and his God.

This confession was clearly rooted in something deeper than the evidence of sight and sound and touch for which Thomas had craved. And the lesson for all time from this appearance is to be found not only in the fact that Jesus satisfied this true-hearted inquirer and accepted his adoration, but also in the indication that Jesus set a higher value on the faith which trusts to the intuition of a pure heart, than on that which requires the evidence of the senses. It encourages us to believe that if we love Him and keep His word, we can dispense with physical demonstration. The Lord manifests Himself directly to those who follow the light that is in them.

When we come to the third appearance we have to be on our guard against a tendency to take shelter in premature allegorizing. It is tempting to say at once that the boat is the Church—the apostles are fishers of men afloat in the world. They work under guidance from the Lord and they harvest their toil on the shore of heaven, when at last they get to land. True as, no doubt, in great measure this picture is, we shall miss the primary message of the event, and dissipate its real force, if we give our fancy such freedom too soon. The value of the event as a parable springs from the fact that it was first of all a vital human incident in the lives of a tired company of fishermen at work in their own, what we call secular, business. It assured them, first of all, that their Lord from heaven was watching over, guiding and blessing that work, and was Himself the source of their daily bread by which their tired energies were refreshed and fed. The conquest over death which Jesus won for us by His resurrection, has a direct message to brighten our daily work and to prevent its falling a prey to the pessimism which is deeply rooted in the apparently irresistible tyranny of death. As we grasp that, and encourage ourselves and our brethren to labour on unceasingly, "because we know that none of our labour can be in vain in the Lord", we shall be able to pass on to its application to the other departments of our life, and especially to that in which we are bending the energies of soul and spirit to win our brother men to His service. Our earthly labour must, to a large extent, be a matter of routine and done mechanically. But the winning of souls can only be done under guidance.

I cannot myself doubt the reality of the guidance given to those who listen for it and act upon it with complete self-surrender, and with constant watchfulness against the danger of self-deception. But the evidence of that reality is meant to encourage the recipient, and can never be of such a kind as to convince a gainsayer. And we must beware of presuming that we can ourselves declare for anyone else what God's guidance is for him, in defiance of the verdict of his own conscience.

This then, seems to me the abiding lesson of the first part of this narrative of the third appearance—that which deals with the fishing. The second part, which describes the communion between the workmen and their Lord after their toil is over has, I believe, no less direct significance for the members of the Church Militant.

Our lives, if we are to be true to our calling, have need of guidance. They have at the same time constant need of food. And this experience teaches us that we may look to our Lord Himself to supply this food, this living bread, which as S. John has taught us, is none other than Himself—His flesh and His blood. It is wonderful enough when we think of it in the terms of the human nature which He wore in the days of His life on earth. But it is well to be reminded that our communion is with Him, not simply as He was in the body of His humiliation, but as He is in the body of His glory, at His Father's right hand. He would have us absorb into our inmost being His perfected humanity in all the glory of His triumph over sin and death, so that we may share, even now, in the power of His resurrection, and unite ourselves with Him in His availing intercession.

15 *So when they had broken their fast, Jesus saith to Simon Peter, Simon,* son *of John, lovest thou me more than these? He saith unto him, Yea, Lord; thou knowest that I love thee. He saith*
16 *unto him, Feed my lambs. He saith to him again a second time, Simon,* son *of John, lovest thou me? He saith unto him, Yea, Lord; thou knowest that I love thee. He saith unto him, Tend*
17 *my sheep. He saith unto him the third time, Simon,* son *of John, lovest thou me? Peter was grieved because he said unto him the third time, Lovest thou me? And he said unto him, Lord, thou knowest all things; thou knowest that I love thee. Jesus saith*
18 *unto him, Feed my sheep. Verily, verily, I say unto thee, When thou wast young, thou girdedst thyself, and walkedst whither*

thou wouldest: but when thou shalt be old, thou shalt stretch forth thy hands, and another shall gird thee, and carry thee whither
19 *thou wouldest not. Now this he spake, signifying by what manner of death he should glorify God. And when he had spoken this, he saith unto him, Follow me.*

We must pass on to the second part of this story. The appearance to a group of disciples leads to a special interview with one of them. As often in S. John, we are left to re-create the setting of the scene for ourselves. Apparently Jesus led Simon Peter away by himself. But the only hint that we get of this comes when in verse 20 Peter, turning about, sees John following.

The disciple whom Jesus loved could not keep away from his Lord. The others, no doubt, would be busy lading the boat with the fish. Jesus, however, is not directly concerned with him. He has an intensely personal communication for Simon. John may have been within earshot, and have overheard it. His neighbourhood would not have been felt to be intrusive. Simon may, of course, have told him afterwards what the Lord had said.

The lesson began with a threefold challenge, which became more searching, step by step. First: "Simon, son of John, lovest thou me more than these?" This clearly meant *not* "more than you love these", *but* "more than these your fellow-disciples love me?"

"Do you still wish to assert the proud pre-eminence of your loyalty as you did on the way to Gethsemane?"

In reply, Simon leaving all thought of others out of sight, simply claims to be His Master's friend.

The challenge on the second occasion leaves out all reference to others. It turns simply on the question of his personal affection. Once more Simon appeals to His Lord to vouch for the sincerity of his friendship.

He uses, we must notice, on each occasion a weaker word for love than that which Jesus used. But the challenge, when it comes the third time, turns on this weaker word: "Simon, do you claim to be my friend?" It was the use of this word on the third occasion (not, I think, the mere fact of the threefold repetition of the challenge) that struck home.

Simon, in reply, can only flee for refuge to the heart that knew him better than he could know himself. He says: "Lord, thou knowest all things; thou knowest that I am thy friend."

No wonder that when the beloved disciple, in his First Epistle, had to find consolation for those whose own hearts condemned them when they sought to draw near to God, he bade them, following Simon's example, take courage from the fact that "God is greater than our hearts, and knows all things" (1 Jn. 3: 20).

The answer to each challenge was followed by a special commission. Simon is taught in each that he is henceforth to regard himself, not merely as a fisher of men, drawing men into the Kingdom out of a perishing world, but as a shepherd, trained by apprenticeship to the Good Shepherd to care for the souls committed to his charge, giving them their meat in due season, and guarding them from all dangers from within and from without.

There is a subtle gradation in the commissions, as in the challenges that preceded them. *First:* "Feed my lambs". Provide the pure milk of the word for the babes in Christ. *Then:* "Shepherd my sheep"—guide and guard and discipline them as they grow to maturity. *Lastly:* "Feed them from your own resources with the solid food required by grown men".

Then comes the closing word, the promise that in outward form looks like a warning: "Verily, verily, I say unto thee, when thou wast young, thou girdedst thyself and walkedst whither thou wouldest. When thou shalt be old, another shall gird thee, and carry thee whither thou wouldest not".

That which was most characteristic in Simon Peter was his power of initiative. He expresses the hopes and aspirations, the doubts and difficulties of the body of disciples without hesitation or reserve. If anything is to be done he will do it. There is a strange mixture of strength and weakness in this impetuosity. The one thing necessary to make this capacity for complete self-devotion fruitful was that it should shed its self-confidence. He must learn the necessity of absolute dependence on God, both for guidance and for strength. The bitter humiliation of his fall would not be wasted if it taught him that. And the willing acceptance of that guidance, wherever it might lead, would be the cross, which he must school himself to take up day by day, until he, too, sealed his testimony with his blood.

This, S. John notes, was, after the event, seen to be prophetic of his martyrdom. Jesus Himself adds nothing but the old call to discipleship: "Follow thou me".

20 *Peter, turning about, seeth the disciple whom Jesus loved following; which also leaned back on his breast at the supper, and said, Lord,*
21 *who is he that betrayeth thee? Peter therefore seeing him saith*
22 *to Jesus, Lord, and what shall this man do? Jesus saith unto him, If I will that he tarry till I come, what* is that *to thee? follow thou me.*

Then follows a parallel, but strangely contrasted, declaration of the future in store for his fellow-disciple. Peter, turning, sees the beloved disciple following, and asks: "Lord, what shall this man do?" Jesus does not leave the question unanswered, though He seems to suggest that there was an element of danger in this inquisitiveness. *If I will that he abide, while I am coming, what is that to thee? Follow thou me.*

The reply is clearly meant for John as well as for Peter. It seems deliberately to avoid giving any satisfaction to the instinct of curiosity, very much as on the way to the Mount of the Ascension, Jesus said expressly: "It is not for you to know the times and seasons". And yet, here as there, He gives an assurance which should have the power to preclude anxious foreboding. Then the apostles were expressly bidden to remember that "the times and seasons" were at the absolute disposal of the Father. It was their wisdom to rest on that assurance. So here Peter and John are reminded that all our times are in our Saviour's hands. It is His will in the last resort that decides whether we stay here or are called to work elsewhere in His vineyard.

And further, all the time (this is what the actual words suggest) "The Lord is drawing nearer," whether the eyes of men can see Him or not. A true disciple must learn to recognize for himself and to teach others to recognize the signs of His appearing.

The lessons of this stage in the third appearing are thus addressed not to the disciples as a body, but to two temperamentally contrasted leaders among them—one, before all things, energetic and practical; the other, with whatever latent capacity for impetuous loyalty, predominantly self-restrained and contemplative. They had each their special cross to bear, testing most searchingly the completeness of their personal surrender to the will of God. The active soul is perfected by passive suffering. The contemplative is tested by a protracted discipline of waiting and watching. Each in his own way is led on until all self-will is purged out, and his will becomes, in fact, what it has been in intention all the while, one with the will of God.

23 *This saying therefore went forth among the brethren, that that disciple should not die: yet Jesus said not unto him, that he should not die; but, If I will that he tarry till I come, what* is that *to thee?*

The story is told, but there was a misunderstanding current arising out of it, which the Evangelist feels that he must correct. In spite of our Lord's express warning, we cannot, apparently, cease from the effort to determine precisely the date and time and place of the appearing of the Lord, which is to mark for us the consummation of the present age—what Jesus calls "the regeneration" (Mt. 19: 25), and S. Paul "the end" (1 Cor. 15: 24). Jesus had given His disciples signs by which they could recognize one crisis in His appearing, which would come in the lifetime of some of them. The judgement on Jerusalem and the destruction of the Temple were included in these signs (Mk. 13: 4, 14 ff.). But the date of "that day" (verse 32), the day presumably of "the end", we must be content not to know.

I believe that it was the same beloved disciple who saw the vision of the Apocalypse, and tried to help the Church to recognize a real coming of the Lord in the fall of Jerusalem. But Jesus was, for him, still "coming in the flesh" (2 Jn. 7). The Church was still living in "a last hour" (1 Jn. 2: 18). The thought of His appearing was still a challenge to Christian loyalty, and a transfiguring hope (1 Jn. 2: 28; 3: 5). The apostle is, therefore, still anxious to guard his flock against thinking that his death, if and when it came, would mark a failure in the divine promise. So he calls attention to the precise form of the Lord's answer to Simon. He is content to end on that.

24 *This is the disciple which beareth witness of these things, and wrote these things: and we know that his witness is true.*

25 *And there are also many other things which Jesus did, the which if they should be written every one, I suppose that even the world itself would not contain the books that should be written.*

Nothing remains now but that the witnessing body, in whose name he has been speaking since 1: 14 (cf. 1 Jn. 1: 1–5), should differentiate themselves from him and add their attestation (verse 24).

They do not give their names. They were clearly well known in the circle to whom the Gospel and the First Epistle of John were in the first instance addressed. The tradition preserved in the Muratorian Fragment, which, as we have seen, Bishop Lightfoot thought might be derived ultimately from Papias, gives a simple account of a situation which is, in many ways, unique. The words themselves expressly identify the author of the Gospel with the beloved disciple. If the tradition in the Fragment is correct they would have been added in his lifetime. The final comment, in the first person singular, may come from the amanuensis who had written the attestation, and perhaps the whole Gospel. In form it is hyperbolic, but in sentiment it is closely akin to 20: 21.

EPILOGUE

SO the Gospel is as it were signed, sealed and delivered to the Churches that had asked for S. John's help. The postscript did not seem to require a more formal conclusion from the author. He is, we may well imagine, content to let the last recorded word of his Master be "If I will that he tarry while I am coming". There was in that an assurance that the will that he had learned to know and love was the sovereign power ruling his life to the end, as it rules all life. And there was the promise that He is all the time drawing nearer to make His presence manifest in the ordering of the world.

The whole purpose of his Gospel, as we have seen, had been to hand on the revelation of the inner life of God which had come to him through the things that he had seen and heard in the course of his discipleship. Faith in Jesus as the Christ, the Son of God, is, as he can testify from his own experience, a spring of eternal life to the believer. And his Gospel records words and deeds of Jesus by which He had helped His chosen to understand who and what He was and is.

We have gone steadily chapter by chapter through his record. We have read it as embodying genuine reminiscences for the instruction of Christians who had been brought up on the Synoptic tradition and who needed help in understanding the divine background of the familiar story. They do not, except in the opening chapter, take the form of a diary. But they do seem to be arranged in chronological order; and enable us to trace a coherent plan in the development of our Lord's appeal to His people.

It was based from the first on the witness of the Baptist. It began with a direct challenge to the High Priest and his party, who were in control of the Temple, and were the political leaders of the nation. Their response to the cleansing of the Temple shewed that they were not prepared to acknowledge His authority. And Jesus goes forward on the path which from the first He knew was leading to the Cross.

The family of Annas and Caiaphas were Sadducees, the religious leadership was in the hands of the Pharisees. S. John helps us to trace the course of the appeal that Jesus made to them, both by answer to individual inquiry like that of Nicodemus, and by a public challenge deliberately made through an act of mercy on the sabbath. The response to this challenge revealed the depth of the Pharisaic antagonism to the revelation of the Fatherhood of God which it was the special function of Jesus as the Son of God to bring to men. It was proof against all the efforts that Jesus made to explain the nature of His Sonship, and to point out to them the causes of their unbelief. This antagonism also could issue only in the Cross.

Meanwhile He was steadily at work revealing to those who were prepared to listen, the inner secrets of His own relation to God, and of the life in the Kingdom of Heaven which He was bringing within their reach.

We come to the study of S. John's record of this teaching after nineteen centuries of Christian experience. And there is abundant confirmation, both in the story of the past and in the events of our own time, to justify us in believing that the Jesus to whom S. Paul and S. John testify is indeed the spiritual power-centre of the universe. We can read the wonderful declarations that S. John records as from His lips, defining His own relation to the Father, and the nature and extent of our personal dependence on Him as the Bread of Life, the Light of the World, the Good Shepherd, and the Resurrection and the Life. Such are the revelations of Himself that He gave in the course of His public ministry. We can read the even more intimate revelations of Himself that He gave to the inner circle of His disciples as the

"Way and the Truth and the Life", and as the True Vine. We feel that they throw light on hidden secrets of our own private, personal relation to Him. Our whole hearts go out to greet the truth of these wonderful self-revelations. We are ready to receive with devout adoration the light that comes from them, as long as we may regard them as coming from the right hand of God. But we cannot ignore the fact that courage seems to fail many of our leaders when they find themselves challenged by S. John to believe that Jesus gave these revelations while living in human flesh among His brethren, because He was even then directly conscious of the place that is His and His alone in relation at once to His Father and to His brethren.

And yet—here is the Gospel, and these are the words that the beloved disciple says that he had heard Jesus say. Unless, therefore, we are prepared to believe that he was under some strange delusion, must we not accept his evidence and believe that the Word who was in communion with God, and was Himself a partaker of the divine nature, had in very truth become flesh and tabernacled among us?

PRINTED BY WESTERN PRINTING SERVICES LTD., BRISTOL

CANTERBURY CHRIST CHURCH UNIVERSITY